LEEDS UNITED,
MISSION:
IMPOSSIBLE

**Following Leeds United through the
2015/2016 season**

By the same author:

All books available from Amazon.co.uk

**LEEDS UNITED,
IN PURSUIT OF
THE PREMIERSHIP**
The 2010/2011 season

**LEEDS UNITED,
LIGHT AT THE END OF
THE TUNNEL**
The 2011/2012 season

**LEEDS UNITED,
Déjà vu**
The 2012/2013 season

**LEEDS UNITED,
FIASCO**
The 2013/2014 season

**LEEDS UNITED,
The Kids Are Alright!
**
The 2014/2015 season

Click link to view books on Amazon: **www.amazon.co.uk**

LEEDS UNITED,
MISSION:
IMPOSSIBLE

Following Leeds United through the 2015/2016 season.

The author recounts his story of following Leeds United home and away.

David Watkins

First published in the UK in 2016
This paperback edition published 2016

ISBN 9781849149655
ISBN10 1849149658

Self-Published using
CompletelyNovel.Com

Websites: _http://dlw10.wix.com/leedsunited_

http://www.completelynovel.com/search?query=david+watkins+leeds+united&commit=Go

ACKNOWLEDGEMENTS

This is the sixth book about my travels following Leeds and these days the famous rollercoaster has become more of a creaking carousel; going around in stuttering circles. The more things change at Leeds, the more things remain the same. The ultimate objective of a return to the Premier League seems more than ever a, 'Mission: Impossible'.

My original intention was to write just one book, based on the belief I had back in 2010/2011 that it would only take Leeds one more season to return to the Premier League. Consequently, I only expected to put my proof readers, friends and family through this chore once! I'm thus indebted to all who've played a part in bringing this sixth tome to life and all those who allowed me to selfishly devote myself to the task. In particular, I'm once again indebted to my good friend Brian for his dedication to duty in proof reading and to his wife Sheila and his mother Joyce I apologise once more for dragging him away from the far more important duties of husband and son.

Following Leeds is time consuming and if you add in the hours I've spent researching and writing the books, fitting a few extra games in to 'do the 92' and watching my 'other' team, Worcester City, you'll understand there isn't much left for the family. Hence to my wife Karen and sons Mark and Adam I beg forgiveness and plead for the opportunity to do it all again next season!

Finally, to all Leeds fans, especially those I've spent time with at games this season, many of whom will be mentioned in the following pages, thank you for your comradeship and for making every game a trip into the unknown! Keep the faith folks; we'll get there!

David Watkins

A note on the Author

David Watkins worked as an accountant and Finance Director in the engineering industry for more than 33 years before he 'retired' in March, 2011. He promised himself he would then spend time (and money) indulging his passion for Leeds United, a passion he'd never been able to fully pursue in the past due to work, family and financial constraints. He's followed Leeds since the 1960s, although he readily confesses that most seasons he would only get to see a handful of games. He has now missed just seven in the past six seasons and by his own admission is completely 'addicted'. The original intention was to write just one book, the one documenting the return of Leeds United to the Premier League; this is book six and he says he will now have just one more go... next season!

Calm before the storm?

For the majority of the summer break there was something very strange going on in Leeds; for the first time in most fans' memories, Elland Road became a place of calm where the decisions being made were, well, logical, sensible even. It started as early as May 11th, before the play-off games had even been completed; not that we were involved in those of course. It was announced on the Leeds United official website (OS) that Adam Pearson had been appointed an executive director of the club. In his first interview, he explained he'd been brought in by Massimo Cellino as the Italian's 'right hand man'. Pearson is well known to Leeds fans; he was commercial director at the club 15 years earlier, before leaving to buy Hull City and then, after a successful period there, he took over Hull FC, the Super League rugby outfit. Pearson's appointment was cautiously welcomed by most Leeds fans who regarded him as 'a safe pair of hands'. The caution concerned the inevitable question as to why Pearson, a sensible and successful businessman in his own right, would suddenly join the manic and unpredictable world of Massimo Cellino. After all, Pearson had only recently taken up an advisory role at Sheffield Wednesday, and his good mate Mike Farnan, with whom Pearson was involved in the Together Leeds outfit, initially scoffed at rumours AP was joining Leeds at all, tweeting:

"Adam Pearson going to Leeds is not true; if ever he goes we go together". Pearson joining Leeds looked to have more to it than first met the eye; some concluded it was the first move of an imminent takeover, with Pearson installed on behalf of the new owners. Only a few thought it might just be Cellino seeing sense at long last, bringing in someone to organise what was still a pretty dysfunctional club. Time would tell.

May 11th also saw news on the OS that Lewis Cook had signed a new contract; another piece of news that had most of us nodding like the proverbial Churchill dog... *"Oh Yes"*. Next, the Football League (FL) announced they'd lifted our transfer embargo on the basis of an initial look at the club accounts for 2014/15. More nodding and rubbing of hands at the prospect of some exciting new signings in the summer... *"Oh yes!"*

The announcement of the list of released players was pretty much universally accepted as reasonable and logical too. Some, including me, were disappointed that Rudy Austin's name was on it but even I reasoned there must be better and younger 'enforcers' out there somewhere. Of those in last season's squad, the list also included goalkeepers Stuart Taylor and Alex Cairns, midfielder Michael Tonge and, perhaps more surprisingly, Zac Thompson and Aidy White. None of the names could be described as a shock though.

In fact, the only thing that wasn't looking quite right and proper at the club during those halcyon days in mid-May was that Neil Redfearn appeared to have had no say in that list. It was rumoured Cellino had not even spoken with Redfearn since the previous season ended and everyone was convinced that meant Cellino was about to appoint another new head coach. It was oh so reminiscent of the way Cellino ignored Brian McDermott twelve months earlier when we were all left asking: *"Where's Brian?"*

There was just one moment when all the madness returned. I was heading for Adams Park, Wycombe, for their League 2 Play-Off semi-final against Plymouth Argyle, the latest conquest in my 'doing the 92' challenge, while at Elland Road, a press conference was being given by Pearson and Cellino. Whilst sat in the pouring rain in Wycombe, I tweeted to ask how the conference went. The first response I got was from @MOTForever, the Twitter account behind the excellent 'Travels of a Leeds Fan' blog. It read simply: *"You spelt conference wrong. It's C.i.r.c.u.s".*

The following day, I watched a video of the whole thing and I was gobsmacked. Pearson shifted uncomfortably in his seat and looked everywhere but at Cellino, while the Italian proceeded to ramble on about everything and nothing in a totally unintelligible slur. We learned very little and it was hard to understand why the conference was even arranged. In short, it once again put the club in the category of laughing stock. Cellino did appear to discount any form of takeover happening any time soon, as he claimed he'd not sell the club for at least two years and then only if he failed to get Leeds back into the Premier League by then. He also claimed he'd made no decision on the future of Neil Redfearn but then told the assembled press corps that he would not bow to pressure from the fans on that subject. *"I have to find the right coach and not because I want to please the fans for 15 days. Not because I don't want them saying, "Cellino, it's time to go", like they did* [at the last few games]. *I'm used to that."* He confirmed he'd not spoken with Redfearn and then criticised his coach for failing to show up at the party held to welcome the Italian back to the club after his ban. I'm sure the Leeds fan base was collectively holding its head in its hands again thinking the recent spell of sense had come to an end. The circus act continued for a few days more.

An online article by Anthony Clavane for 'The Mirror' did its best to stir up the fans with the headline: *"Leeds to sack Neil Redfearn because owner Massimo Cellino says 'weak' manager turned the fans against HIM".*[1] In typically colourful language Cellino was quoted as saying:

"He thinks that he's so strong that he can put me in the s**t because I'm worrying about the fans.
"F*** me, what kind of chairman have you got?

---

[1] *http://www.mirror.co.uk/sport/football/news/leeds-sack-neil-redfearn-because-5709088*

"He tried to play the fans against me to keep his place.

"Do you think that Neil Redfearn loves Leeds more than me?

"Tell me why I am in Leeds, why am I so involved with the club? Why am I putting in a lot of money, killing myself? Because I fell in love with this club. But to love this club is to do something for this club.

"Neil Redfearn does the [Leeds United fans'] *salute. He challenged me. If you are good I can accept the challenge. But not if you are a bad coach.*

"He has to respect the chairman. He has to respect the club. He's like a baby. He's been badly advised and used by someone. He is not a bad person but he has a weak personality."

After reading all that, and assuming it was accurately quoting Cellino, I could see no way on God's earth that Redfearn would be head coach come August or even back at the academy as we all believed his contract terms allowed. Could you work for anyone who spoke about you like that? I'm no employment law expert but is that not akin to constructive dismissal or harassment?

Within days, rumours were doing the rounds suggesting the new head coach was to be Uwe Rösler, who was most recently with Wigan and on May 20th, at a press conference hosted by Pearson, Rösler was unveiled. Anyone involved in writing on the subject of Leeds United was madly trying to learn how to type, 'ö', on a windows based keyboard. (Alt, 0 2 4 6 with the numbers lock on…since you ask!). The good news, apart from Rösler being acknowledged as a decent enough coach, was that Pearson ran the press conference with a degree of authority and in a reassuringly business-like manner not seen at Elland Road for donkeys' years. He stated that further appointments would be made in the coming days to fill the gaps in the club management structure including a head of recruitment, a football secretary and an assistant for Rösler.

Rob Kelly, former short term manager of Leicester City was eventually announced as Assistant Coach while Martin Glover became Head of Recruitment and Stuart Hayton, recruited from Liverpool no less, took the post of Football Secretary.

We were finally putting in place all the resources a football club needs…these were all top people who were well regarded in the game and presumably none of them was cheap. Once again, the obvious thought was that Adam Pearson was getting his own way in structuring the club like a well-run business.

Cellino was very quiet, almost invisible… but not quite. Every now and again his influence could be seen, like over the appointment of Glover. Initially, the job of Head of Recruitment was reported to have been given to Norwich City Chief Scout, Steve Head. But when Cellino heard that Head had a two week holiday booked in the close season, the Italian withdrew the job offer saying he needed his Head of Recruitment *"NOW"*, not in two weeks' time![1] Glover had most recently worked with Sam Allardyce at West Ham, before Big Sam was sacked at the end of last season and was another recruit who was professionally acclaimed in the game.

Two players had already been signed; goalkeeper Charlie Horton, a USA Under-23 international signed from Cardiff City on a two-year deal and Motherwell's young striker, 21 year-old Lee Erwin, on a three year deal. I didn't know much about either but was nervous that yet more youngsters were being signed when I felt it was vital to get some experience in to guide the kids we already had. It was early days though and Erwin was cheap, brought in on a free transfer. Hopefully he was better than Doukara, Antenucci, Sharp, Morison, Walters and the rest of the seemingly endless list of bang average strikers we already had on the books!

The new home strip was officially unveiled on July 10th but a few weeks earlier, at yet another press conference, Adam Pearson broke the news that Kappa had replaced Macron as the team's kit supplier. It was a move said to be good for both parties with Kappa effectively re-launching themselves in the UK and Leeds needing a new supplier having fallen out with Macron. There was still some pain to come with this change

---

[1]   *http://www.yorkshireeveningpost.co.uk/sport/leeds-united/latest-whites-news/leeds-united-hunt-for-head-of-recruitment-takes-a-new-twist-1-7281655*

though, as Macron were apparently suing the club for breach of contract to the tune of five million quid. The Macron deal had one more season to run but we all guessed they were on the way out when the club put all their remaining Macron stock up for sale at a fiver a shirt! Mums all over the country were ecstatic at the news of the demise of Macron as it meant the end of delicately hand washing the kids' replica kits for fear of all the badges falling off.

There was no let-up in the queue of folk waiting to sue the club; legal firm Mishcon de Reya was suing for fees they were allegedly owed from 2014 while Cameron Stewart had already won his case for something like £500,000 or £750,000 depending on who you believed. That was triggered when Cellino refused to sign the winger at the end of his loan spell despite his loan contract specifying it was a done deal.[1] As seems to be Cellino's standard practise, the money was still not paid by the start of July and the Professional Footballers' Association (PFA) lobbied the FL to impose a new transfer embargo on the club. The man just doesn't seem to learn does he? Perhaps it was all the legal stuff that was keeping Cellino quiet and away from football matters…not a bad thing you may say. Cellino also had a couple more tax evasion cases to face in Italy in the summer. The Steve Thompson affair wasn't over yet either; he was likely to be bringing a case over his dismissal at the end of last season as was McDermott's assistant Nigel Gibbs. The legal boys were going to have a good season.

Mrs W and I were away on holiday for a couple of weeks at the end of May; a fabulous trip of a lifetime to the Rocky Mountains, Vancouver and then to the Canadian Grand Prix in Montreal. It was a stunning trip in every way. I was keeping up to speed with the goings on at Elland Road via Twitter whenever I could get a Wi-Fi link and was posting photos from the trip most days. It was in response to one such tweet that @LewisRamsey spotted we were due in Montreal. He's a

---

[1] *http://the72.co.uk/27552/stewart-wins-compensation-claim-against-leeds/*

Leeds fan, originally from Harrogate but now living out there with his Canadian girlfriend. He offered to meet up and give us a few sightseeing tips. Mrs W and I spent a fabulous couple of hours in his company over a lunch of Poutine[1] and a couple of local beers and as well as swapping notes on our very different life stories we talked Leeds United; lots of Leeds United. It's amazing how far and wide the Leeds family is spread but no less amazing how we can quickly feel comfortable with anyone who shares our passion. Lewis has an enviable lifestyle in Canada but I know that not getting to Elland Road on a Saturday afternoon is one of very few downsides for him.

And Lewis was not the only Leeds fan we came across on the trip. Whilst enjoying a couple of days on the fabulous Rocky Mountaineer train journeying from Lake Louise to Vancouver, we met a couple from York. The wife was now in her eighties but told us she'd been a regular at Elland Road in the Revie days. Their son is a huge Leeds fan albeit now living in Hong Kong. There really are Leeds fans everywhere!

Once we got home, I researched the possibility of getting out to one or both of the pre-season games Leeds had arranged in Europe. The team was going to Austria for a week's training camp and was playing one game there before going on to Norway for the second. I've wanted to do an overseas game with Leeds ever since this odyssey of mine began, five years ago. Initially, the cost of flights from anywhere in the North of England put me off; I just couldn't justify it on top of doing another full season home and away and fitting in the remaining 18 football league grounds I still needed in order to complete my '92'. I'm well and truly into the 'ski-set' now, (that's 'Spending the Kids Inheritance') but a degree of sense has to prevail and Mrs W wouldn't be too happy if the cash ran out completely! But then my good buddy Kentley came to the rescue. He came up with a cunning plan to drive down to Gatwick to get a cheaper flight from there. Coincidentally,

---

[1] *Poutine is served almost everywhere in Canada and is basically chips, cheese and gravy. I know it sounds weird, but it works!*

@Flanagan1963 tweeted how he was flying to Munich to then get a train to Salzburg and that's precisely the plan Kentley came up with. We'd get a £100 return flight out to Munich; a train to Salzburg; another train to the game in a place called Eugendorf; and then spend one night in a cheap hotel back in Salzburg. We'd get one day's sightseeing in too, before flying back to Gatwick on the Wednesday night. I guessed there wouldn't be much sleep to be had for three consecutive days... but what the heck! If you think Kentley and I were mad with our plan, @Flanagan1963 was going to take in the Oslo game in Norway as well; spending 39 hours on a train between the two venues!

The fixtures proper came out on 16th June, the day after the Capital One Cup (COC) First Round draw. In the cup, we were handed a visit to Doncaster which I was frankly disappointed with. It's not a bad trip but it's one I've done several times now and I was hoping for another new ground to help out with my '92'. I was hoping for Carlisle or maybe Hartlepool. I wasn't as excited as usual to see the league fixtures the following day either. In fact I forgot they were out until Mrs W mentioned it. The first game was a juicy pick mind; Burnley, fresh from their one season in the Premier League, at Elland Road, That would be a great marker for the rest of the season. The Doncaster game was soon moved to the Thursday, to allow it to be featured live on Sky TV and that of course would free me up on the Tuesday or Wednesday to pick off another ground in the COC! Four of our first six games were to be shown live on Sky, pandering once again to the 400,000 plus TV fans that regularly tune in for any Leeds game. The constant date and time changes would become a major issue for the club and its fans as the season wore on.

Still the calm around Elland Road continued, and the next soothing news was that Sol Bamba had finally put pen to paper, accepting a two-year deal. Sol is not the best centre back in the world but he's the best we've seen at Elland Road for quite some time and once again most of us saw this as a positive move. Adam Pearson was still promising three or four more players and he as good as said they'd be experienced ones. Even the announcement from Italy that Cellino had been fined another 40,000 euros in the latest of his tax evasion cases didn't seem to cause any great panic. The FL was waiting for the written report of the judge but a vague statement that Italian Customs were not pursuing criminal charges had us thinking that maybe, just maybe, the Italian would get through this one without a ban. This was the Range Rover VAT case and the ramifications would rumble on all season.

The Leeds OS then announced that Nicola Salerno had officially parted company with Leeds *"by mutual agreement"*. It had been former Head of Recruitment Salerno who supposedly fell out with and effectively sacked Steve Thompson a few months earlier, getting rid of Neil Redfearn's second in command apparently without discussing it at all with Neil himself. Now, the club posted a very conciliatory note saying that Salerno, *"...will always be welcomed back to Elland Road in the future"*. What the hell was going on? Where had all the angst and intrigue gone? Once again, most fans assumed the soothing, calming influence of Adam Pearson was at work here. Sadly, the calm at Elland Road was not reflected around the world generally as we all took in the events of 'Bloody Friday'; 26th June, 2015...

On a beach, in the popular resort of Sousse in Tunisia, 38 holiday-makers, most of them British, were gunned down by a terrorist in the name of the so-called Islamic State group. In France, another terrorist beheaded a man and hung the severed head on the gates of a gas production facility where it was believed a plot to blow up the factory was thwarted. And in Kuwait City, a suicide bomber attacked a Shia mosque, killing 27 worshippers. It was another day that left ordinary folk around the world fearing for the future of mankind.[1]

As so often when appalling events occur, it was no surprise that the football community was caught up in this one, such is the widespread involvement of people in the game in our country. As the names of the victims were gradually released to the media, three Walsall fans were amongst the first to be

---

[1] *http://www.theguardian.com/world/2015/jun/26/tourists-relive-horror-of-gunmans-attack-on-tunisian-hotel-killing-37*

identified; three generations, father, son and nephew. The BBC reported: *"Adrian Evans, 44, from Tipton, West Midlands, died along with his father, 78-year-old Patrick Evans and nephew Joel Richards, 19, from Wednesbury."*[1] Then came news that former Birmingham City player, Denis Thwaites, was killed in the Tunisia massacre, along with his partner, Elaine[2]. We learned that Marc Albrighton, the Leicester City winger had lost his partner's mother, Sue Davey and her partner, Scott Chalkley.[3] It was reported that a couple from Perthshire, Billy and Lisa Graham had been killed and St Johnstone FC paid tribute to Billy who worked on the turnstiles at McDiarmid Park.[4] Philip Heathcote, the brother of Graham, a former non–league football club manager was also among the dead. The world of football would once again come together to remember them all at matches during the new season, as has become the custom and rightly so.

On July 1st, the opening day of the new transfer window, Leeds announced the signing of 23 year-old Chris Wood from Leicester City for an undisclosed fee. The six foot three inch striker was given a four year deal. Once again, this transfer was almost universally acclaimed by Leeds fans as just what we needed. Now, if we could just bring in a winger to give Wood some ammunition. Although undisclosed, it was widely reported that the fee could end up in the region of £3 million if various trigger points were reached. Even Uwe Rösler expressed his surprise that Leeds had managed to nail Wood. The Yorkshire Evening Post (YEP) quoted him as saying:

"I didn't realise this [Wood signing] *was possible – when I compare our wage budget to others. And our wage budget is what I was told last week. But with the help of Mr Cellino, it has happened. It is a clear sign of our intent that we want to*

---

[1] http://www.bbc.co.uk/news/uk-england-33303204
[2] http://www.bbc.co.uk/news/uk-england-lancashire-33319011
[3] http://www.theguardian.com/football/2015/jun/28/leicester-marc-albrighton-partner-mother-tunisia-massacre
[4] http://www.thecourier.co.uk/news/local/perth-kinross/st-johnstone-chief-leads-tributes-after-bankfoot-couple-die-in-tunisia-terror-attack-1.887349

build something. That was the message when I started and it is still the same now."[1] Wolves were said to have been keen on Wood too but pulled out when the figure of £3 million was muted. There were plenty of 'Wood' jokes doing the rounds on Twitter, most of them concerning the delight at getting Wood first thing that morning…ahem.

Incredibly, Neil Redfearn came out and told reporters that he *did* intend to return to his old job as manager of the academy, despite everything that had gone on and all those hurtful words from Cellino. On 11th June, he'd told the YEP; *"My contract had said that if I wasn't offered the* (head) *coaching job, then I will go back to being the academy manager. That is what will be happening and I will go back on the first of July, as it stands at the moment."*[2]

It came as little surprise when on July 1st it was reported there was no sign of Redfearn at Thorp Arch and even less surprise when we were told the club was negotiating a severance package.

Meanwhile, there was yet another new member of staff unveiled at Elland Road. Julian Darby was appointed First Team Coach. Darby had previously worked at Preston, Derby, and Bolton and worked with Rob Kelly at Forest. It was another sign of the intent to ensure that all the pieces were in place to have a real go at the Championship this season. Our first clue as to whether or not we had the *right* pieces would come at Wetherby Road; home of Conference North side, Harrogate Town.

---

[1] *http://www.yorkshireeveningpost.co.uk/sport/leeds-united/latest-whites-news/leeds-united-big-money-deal-for-wood-takes-rosler-by-surprise-1-7337597?utm_medium=twitter&utm_source=twitterfeed*

[2] *http://www.yorkshireeveningpost.co.uk/sport/leeds-united/latest-whites-news/leeds-united-redfearn-confirms-return-to-former-academy-role-1-7303257*

Slow beginnings

I was driving for the July 10th opening pre-season friendly at Harrogate; it was a Friday evening. Excited as I was about getting the season underway, my regular passenger Kentley and I were soon tearing our hair out as we battled with the M6 traffic, no doubt not for the last time this season. We thought we were setting out in good time; I picked Kentley up at 2pm but it was already 5:30pm when we arrived. We found a roadside parking spot within sight of Bettys Café Tea Rooms, the iconic establishment that's been serving afternoon teas for almost 100 years in fashionable Harrogate. The plan was to meet up with Nigel and an old school-pal of mine who I hadn't seen for 40 of those 100 years.

The day after the Harrogate game, I was due at a reunion at my old school in Worcestershire; it was almost 40 years to the day since I and the rest of my 'class of 75' left to go our various ways. In the days leading up to the event, I learned that one chap would not be at the reunion but found out he now lived in Harrogate and in our exchange of e-mails I established that Rob was not only going to this game but was also a season ticket holder at Elland Road, along with his lad Pete. I'd completely forgotten that Rob, along with several other lads in our class, followed the mighty Whites. Eventually we established that Rob's seat in the Revie Stand was no more than thirty yards from mine! We hadn't spoken in 40 years, yet we'd probably brushed past each other in the North Stand concourse countless times without realising.

Kentley and I were having trouble spotting Nigel as we slowly worked our way round the massive Winter Gardens Wetherspoon on Parliament Street. To be fair, Kentley was way more interested in the Andy Murray v Roger Federer Wimbledon semi-final being shown on the TV screens. We were also distracted by the bizarre sight of a Leeds fan ordering at the bar wearing a full rubber face mask in the image of Ali G. Eventually we spotted Nigel wearing his trademark gold away top and we settled down with him and waited for Rob. Within a few minutes of *his* arrival we were all chatting away like we see each other every week; just four members of the Leeds United family enjoying a common passion for the club and a few pints.

When we arrived at The CNG Stadium, it was pretty full, with around 3,500 crammed in on all sides. The capacity, according to www.footballgroundguide.com is 3,800.

Rösler picked two different elevens to play each half, exactly as Dave Hockaday did this time last season. The first side, which we could now see lining up was:

Silvestri
Wootton Bellusci Cooper
Byram Phillips Mowatt Antenucci Ajose
Wood Erwin

I'd forgotten all about Nicky Ajose; he'd now returned to the club after his loan spell with Crewe last season. Wood and Erwin were making their debuts of course, while the rest were all regulars in the starting line-up last season. I reckoned this eleven might well contain many of the players who'd start the all-important first league game against Burnley, in a month's time. The missing names I thought were Sol Bamba and Lewis Cook, both of whom would feature in the second-half. The problem was, if this first-half side did indeed represent the majority of our best players...then it would need to play a hell of a lot better than this.

In the opening minutes, Harrogate ran us ragged! Yes, there were a few probing runs from the polished Wood (!) and Erwin, and Ajose had a couple of forays down the left wing but Harrogate were regularly finding their way through our defence. Indeed, the best player on the pitch was Marco Silvestri. He pulled off a string of tremendous blocks to keep us in the game, while Liam Cooper in particular looked very rusty. Marco was, of course, one of the 'sick-note six', the half dozen players who cried off injured before the Charlton game at the end of last season and that episode was clearly not forgotten by many Leeds fans; some of them could be heard booing Bellusci throughout the first-half. After the game, Peppe tweeted: *"For those who did not understand. I said: '(You) don't like me ok. But the first game you should support the team, not me."*[1] Much as the incident upset me at the time, I had to agree it should now be forgotten and we should all get behind any players wearing the white shirt. It's what we do.

In the 32nd minute, the home side were ahead. Marco brilliantly beat out a wildly deflected free kick but it fell perfectly for Cecil Nyoni who was first to react to touch the ball home from close range. That wasn't in the script!

We'd learn after the game from interviews with Rösler, that the '3 – 5 – 2' formation had only been worked on for two training sessions and it certainly looked that way. The best thing that happened in that first-half was the appearance of the lovely Jo E with a supply of her fabulous peanut brownies that Kentley, Nigel and I eagerly tucked into.

At half-time, Kentley and I wandered round to the other side of the ground and on the back row of a little stand over there we spotted Massimo Cellino, Adam Pearson and other members of the club hierarchy. Cellino appeared to be teaching our new Football Secretary, Stuart Hayton, how to tie

---

[1]   *http://www.yorkshireeveningpost.co.uk/sport/leeds-united/latest-whites-news/leeds-united-bamba-ready-to-step-up-to-captaincy-if-required-1-7355057*

- 14 -

the perfect tie knot! At that stage I was hopeful we might get a 'tie' out of the game; a defeat to lowly Harrogate in our first outing would not set the right tone at all.

The side we put out for the second-half had ten changes; Silvestri stopped in goal and I did wonder if that was a late change of plan due to the pressure the home side had put us under. The full second-half side was:

Silvestri
Berardi Bamba Killock Taylor
Sloth Cook Bianchi
Doukara Morison Sharp

They set up in a '4 – 3 – 3' formation and whether it was that, the fact our legs were now fresher than the home side's on a warm Yorkshire evening, or whether this group were better players on the day, it did the trick. Suddenly we upped the tempo, bossed the possession and started to create chances. Just four minutes into the new half we were level; and what a goal it was!

Sol Bamba had a long look before launching the ball diagonally out to the right wing where Souleymane Doukara controlled it perfectly and went past a defender. He touched the ball back to the supporting Casper Sloth and his wicked first time cross was met just a couple of yards from goal by the head of Steve Morison. It rocketed into the net. He scored our final goal of last season to beat Wednesday up at Hillsborough and now he had the first this season. Something for Uwe to ponder in the coming weeks! Good chances came and went begging for Leeds throughout the half, something else we'd have to get used to as the season wore on but somehow the home goal remained intact and it ended all square, 1 – 1.

Kentley and I were still fiercely debating who made the brilliant cross for the Leeds goal as we negotiated the streets of Harrogate after the game. I was convinced at the time that Doukara crossed it but Kentley correctly spotted that Douk actually touched it back to Casper Sloth and it was Sloth's great cross. I was still arguing the toss as I realised I'd gone past a no entry sign into the bus station! An angry looking bus driver shook his fist at us and pointed the way back out onto the road…

As I drove down to Hanley Castle in Worcestershire, to my school reunion on Saturday morning, I had time to think about the Harrogate game again. My over-riding feeling was one of disappointment. I knew it was far too early to use the game as any sort of a pointer for the coming season but I did think we were way too easily undone in that first-half. Second-half, we looked much better and yet all logic told me that the second-half team had fewer players in it that would be in the team for that Burnley game on August 8th. Surely Chris Wood would start? But it was Steve Morison who came up with the goal. Surely Doukara and Sloth would not start ahead of the likes of Antenucci, Cook, Mowatt, Murphy when he's fit again and several more? Yet it was the Douk and Casper who combined so well to set the goal up. Uwe had some serious thinking to do ahead of our next friendly; a trip to York City's Bootham Crescent, on Wednesday.

The day after the Harrogate game, the Leeds Fans United (LFU) outfit held a meeting to give an update on their progress in raising funds to support the buying of shares in the club. When they launched the initiative last season, they'd spoken of raising £5 million or even £10 million and they were targeting the shares of GFH. Massimo Cellino was still adamant he was selling none of his holding though and he had first call on the GFH shares even supposing they *did* wish to sell. Reports from folk at the meeting suggested only £400,000 had thus far been raised, and that came from around 1,250 fans, most of whom had invested the minimum £100 each. It was starting to look an unlikely proposition.

York City

Good news was still coming thick and fast. On Monday 13th July, we learned the club had struck a deal to sponsor the South Stand and had also repurchased the catering and beverage rights that were sold off to raise cash under Ken Bates. The partner now branding the South Stand was Global Autocare, a fleet management company and they immediately announced free MOTs for Leeds fans. Very appropriate I thought!

A fifth signing of the summer was also announced on this marvellous Monday; Tom Adeyemi, a 23 year-old midfielder was signed on a season long loan from Cardiff. A strong tackling, six foot plus midfielder, he was seen as a natural replacement for Rodolph Austin. The day was then rounded off with the news that Luke Murphy had signed a new four year deal although that news was tempered by the fact he'd injured a knee in training and was now likely to miss the start of the season. It was widely rumoured that Murphy took a pay cut to seal the long term deal.

In a late change to the pre-season schedule, it was announced that a strong Leeds United XI would travel to play a friendly game at Tadcaster Albion at the same time as another squad did the York City trip. The idea, according to Uwe Rösler, was to ensure he could get more minutes of match time into all his first team squad. The players who started at Tadcaster were: **Silvestri, Coyle, Killock, Cooper, Denton, Phillips, Sloth, Doukara, Walters, Antenucci and Sharp.** The subs were Grimes, Skelton, McDaid, Lyman, Parkin, Mulhern, Stokes and an unnamed trialist. We'd learn later that this squad came away with a well-deserved 3 – 0 victory with goals from Antenucci, Sharp and Doukara. But Kentley and I had already committed to the York trip.

We'd arranged to drive up to York early with every intention of doing some sightseeing but in the event it turned into a bit of a pub crawl! Thankfully, it was Kentley's turn behind the wheel. After an uneventful journey, we went straight to the ground and pulled onto the little carpark at the front of Bootham Crescent. Kentley slotted the BMW into space number '17' as we reckoned if Massimo was turning up at all he wouldn't want that one. We then went into the club shop and got chatting with the guy behind the counter. He told us we could leave the BMW in the car park where it was. In hindsight, we realise now he probably meant we could leave it there *while we went into town* and he probably expected us to move it before kick-off...

We'd already taken a call from our old mate Nigel, who informed us he was waiting at the Duke of York and despite the fact he told us the beer was £3.95 a pint; we reluctantly agreed to meet him there. Kentley soon pulled up the directions to the Duke of York on his iPhone and we set off. We arrived at the pub in Kings Square around 1:30pm and found it to be a very pleasant Leeds Brewery establishment with numerous real ales and a decent menu. I ordered a pint of Leeds Best and a large Coke for Kentley and remarked that Nigel must have been over-charged. We couldn't see him anywhere at this point so assumed he was in the bogs upstairs but as time passed and he didn't appear we pondered where he might be. Eventually, something crossed my mind and I asked the bartender, *"There isn't another Duke of York pub in town is there?" "There is yeah"*, he informed me, *"It's over by the railway station."* Nigel had travelled to York by train...

We rang him again and sure enough he was waiting for us in the other Duke of York. So, not only did he have ten thousand men, he also had a couple of bloody pubs! To cut a long and tedious story short, after several more mobile calls to and from Nigel we managed to guide him towards us and eventually met outside the Roman Bath pub, in St. Sampson's Square. From the outside it looked a fascinating place and further research since has revealed that in 1930 it was discovered that this 18th century coaching inn stood on the site of some Roman baths. Inside, it's decorated with replica Roman stonework and even has its own museum downstairs. We fully intended to eat there, so we ordered a couple of pints of Theakston Best and another Coke for Kentley but in the end decided we didn't fancy the menu so off we marched again. This time we ended up in the 'Slug and Lettuce', on the banks of the River Ouse, where finally we got something to eat and I gorged myself on the excellent draft Peroni. We'd got ourselves a lovely table in an alcove overlooking the river; the huge windows were open allowing us to enjoy the perfect weather. Then, while Nigel and I were at the bar, Kentley decided to bugger off to the bogs and a couple of women sneaked in and nicked the bloody table for themselves! Reluctantly, we settled at another nearby and sulked for half an hour.

After eating at the S & L we moved on to the King's Arms down by the riverside for more beer, having by now given up all pretence of doing any sightseeing, especially as the last tour boat had just set off from its mooring a bit further downstream and was now gliding serenely past. Somehow or another we'd spent four hours eating and drinking and our next move would have to be back to Bootham Crescent for the 7pm kick off.

I'd been to York a couple of times before, most notably for the pre-season friendly against Leeds in August 2001. I'd sifted through my programme collection the other day to find the one from that game. It was a reminder of our Premier League days of course and among the Leeds players' names on the back of the programme were Nigel Martyn, Gary Kelly, Ian Harte, Olivier Dacourt, Lucas Radebe, Jon Woodgate, Robbie Keane, Mark Viduka, Harry Kewell and Lee Bowyer. Keane scored twice on the night in a 4 – 0 rout of the home side. As I studied the players on the pitch now, I wondered if any of their names would become as etched in our collective memory as that 2001 group. The side that started at York was:

Turnbull
Berardi Bellusci Bamba Taylor
Byram Bianchi Cook Mowatt
Morison Erwin

Subs: Horton, Wootton, Ajose, Drury, Purver, Dawson.

Goalkeeper Ross Turnbull only signed for Leeds a few hours before the game, although he had been with the squad as a trialist in recent days. He became the sixth signing of the summer and penned a two year deal. Chris Wood was supposed to have started this game up front but worryingly he succumbed to a knock during the warm up and was replaced by Steve Morison. It was a sort of 'Knock on Wood' moment. Adam Drury, the 21 year-old attacking full back released by Man City this summer, was still being assessed as a trialist, whilst academy graduate, central midfielder Alex Purver, got a rare inclusion in a first team squad.

The game was delayed ten minutes as a long line of Leeds fans was still queuing to buy tickets at the scheduled 7pm kick-off time. Eventually, the attendance was reported as 4,348 with there being said to be 2,313 Leeds fans in the tight little ground. www.footballgroundguide.com lists the capacity as 7,872 but I have no idea where they'd squeeze in the extra three and a half thousand. In particular, I can't see how the toilet facilities would meet that sort of demand; it was another one of those little brick sheds with bitumen walls. Purists would call this, 'a traditional ground'.

There was an odd smell of cooked chocolate in the air throughout the game but Jo and her chocolate brownies were nowhere to be seen so I assumed it came from the Kit Kat factory in Haxby Road, although the equally familiar stench of a few flares was far more easily identifiable as they landed on the pitch every few minutes. There were many familiar faces on the terraces as I looked around still pondering that chocolate smell. I said a quick, *"Happy New Season"*, to

@MOTForever and his mate, 'The Happy Chocker', and I had a long chat with John, aka @Mundial78.

Leeds began at a high tempo and looked far more dominant than at Harrogate the other night; York were restricted to a few half chances in the first-half. But, having said that, despite all the possession Leeds enjoyed, decent chances were few and far between. There was definitely more pace about this Leeds side than last season but still we seemed short of the nous to unlock a defence that only narrowly escaped relegation to the Conference last season. When chances did occur, Steve Morison missed them. But in the 35th minute, Leeds deservedly took the lead. Alex Mowatt exchanged passes with Charlie Taylor out on the left wing and then Mowatt's pinpoint cross picked out Sam Byram who leapt well above a defender and thundered a header past York keeper Michael Ingham.

At half-time, I braved those despicable bogs again and then returned to my spot behind the goal just as another bright blue flare was lobbed onto the pitch from somewhere at the back of the Leeds section up behind me. The sun was now disappearing behind the stands and we all went from very warm to very, very cold in an instant... all apart from Kentley who had stoically worn his favourite Liam Gallagher style jacket all day despite the heat. He was smiling smugly now as Nigel and I shivered in our shirt sleeves.

Leeds began the second-half unchanged and still they bossed the possession without creating too many difficult moments for the home keeper who was now plying his trade just a few yards in front of us. Steve Morison was a bit slow to react with one half-chance and then Berardi hammered a long range shot that Ingham expertly caught. In the 56th minute, Adam Drury came on for Erwin who'd become increasingly anonymous as the night wore on. It was early days but I couldn't see Erwin being a regular first team player this season. Drury was quickly into the action, playing up front on the left and first Ingham grabbed the ball off his toes and then dived smartly to his right to stop a close range header. Charlie Taylor was then thwarted as was Steve Morison when the keeper turned over a fierce point-blank volley. Chances were coming thick and fast now but a combination of inspired goalkeeping and poor finishing meant York were still in the game. Wootton replaced Berardi and Ajose replaced Mowatt as Leeds continued to press and the game moved into the final ten minutes.

There were two main features of our play last season that we saw time after time after time. The first was our lack of a cutting edge. That was seen not only in the paltry number of clear-cut chances we created in every game but also in a failure to convert many of the few we did carve out. To be fair, at York we did create a few good chances, particularly in the second-half, but once again we just didn't have the ability to bury them, although I accept that Chris Wood might have made a difference had he been fit; we all assumed he must be a top finisher. The second conclusion I came to last season, was that our defence was not good enough to keep out even the most average of Championship forwards. We'd signed six players this summer so far; two goalkeepers, two strikers, one midfielder and Sol Bamba, although Sol was a regular part of our defence as a loan player for the second-half of last season of course. Thus, our defence was inevitably going to be comprised of exactly the same names this season as last. Why would it suddenly become good enough to regularly keep clean sheets in the Championship in 2015/16 when it couldn't do it in 2014/15? It beats me. So often last season, our defence contrived to give games away through a moment of stupidity, naivety or inability to defend properly. We'd got away with a few such moments last Friday in Harrogate; we'd not be so lucky tonight. In the 80th minute, York equalised.

The miscreant this time was Scott Wootton. He backed off and backed off as Anthony Straker toyed with him on the York left wing. Then Straker got a yard of space and whipped over a cross that found full back Marvin McCoy at the back post as good as unmarked. It was a crisp finish from McCoy that highlighted yet again our defensive frailty. It was the last meaningful action of the match and, like Harrogate, it ended all square at 1 – 1.

After the game, there was the first sign that Rösler was maybe beginning to understand he had a problem with his defence. The Yorkshire Evening Post (YEP) reported him as saying:

"I'm just irritated that we didn't win. In the end all coaches want to win. The defence were much better than against Harrogate but we couldn't keep it up for 90 minutes."[1] It's that failure to keep it up for 90 minutes that cost us so many times last season. It's a complaint I regularly get from Mrs W too...

After the game, Kentley and I walked round to the main stand side of the ground where we'd left the car in that number '17' parking slot. Stuck on the windscreen was the biggest notice you have ever seen proclaiming: *"This is a private carpark. Please do not park here again without permission."* Well, it could have been worse...it could have been clamped or towed away. It was bad enough though because it was stuck on the windscreen with really strong sticky tape and try as we might we couldn't get all the glue off the glass. We decided to leave it a while and grab a coffee from the snack bar next to the club shop and then we stood with a few other fans waiting for the players to emerge, which they did one by one over the next half hour or so. Once again, just as I was at Wigan last season when I waited by the coach there with Shaun, aka @DoctorT1992, I was struck by how slight of frame all our players are; even Steve Morison looked boyish.

We actually followed the coach off the car park, partly to see where it was off to and partly because the huge rear lights were easy to see through our now very sticky windscreen. It was a major disappointment therefore when the bus turned off the A64 just outside York rather than carrying on towards Leeds as we were doing, to get on the M621. Gradually, a combination of furious windscreen wipers and a few drops of rain cleared enough screen for Kentley to peer through. Quite where the bus was going we never worked out; maybe a late meal somewhere or maybe they were stopping in a hotel for the night. I tweeted a picture I took through the murky windscreen and then we settled down to the journey home. It had been a good day out.

---

[1] *http://www.yorkshireeveningpost.co.uk/sport/leeds-united/latest-whites-news/york-city-1-leeds-united-1-rosler-irritated-by-late-equaliser-1-7361520*

The Battle of Eugendorf

The day after the games at York and Tadcaster, the not unexpected news filtered through that Neil Redfearn had resigned his post as Academy Manager. We'd all hoped the parting of the ways could be amicable; along the lines of the recent Salerno example perhaps. Sadly though, it was not and it looked very much as though Redders would have to take his place in the queue at the local courthouse to get his compensation. In a statement, Redfearn said: *"It is with great sadness that I am resigning from my employment at Leeds United with immediate effect.*

"I am desperately disappointed that Adam Pearson's 'offer' of a return to my old position as academy manager was not genuine and the club have since made my position untenable by refusing to let me take up my post at Thorp Arch."[1] I heard rumours the club even changed the locks to ensure Redders couldn't get in. For the first time, Pearson was implicated in something distasteful but my overall feeling was why, oh why could Cellino not just come to a deal with Redfearn and send him on his way with no ill feeling? Once again, it looked like shoddy man-management.

---

[1] *http://www.yorkshireeveningpost.co.uk/sport/leeds-united/latest-whites-news/ex-boss-redfearn-leaves-leeds-united-updated-1-7362104*

The Leeds squad flew out to Austria on Saturday 18th July; 25 players made the trip. Since even the injured Luke Murphy was there, it didn't bode well for their chances this season that Nicky Ajose and Chris Dawson were both left in Leeds, despite being fully fit as far as we knew. We then got news that Billy Sharp would not play in Austria as a deal was being finalised for the 'fat lad' with his home town club, Sheffield United; it was fitting that Sharp would join the Blades.

Kentley arrived at my place at 12:40am on Tuesday 21st July. I was driving as he'd come straight from work while I'd watched the last knockings of the Open golf on TV before grabbing a few hours' sleep. The golf had been delayed due to high winds at St Andrews which meant Monday became the final day. Zach Johnson eventually won the Claret Jug and a cheque for £1.1m, after a three-way play-off with Marc Leishman and Louis Oosthuizen; they all finished the regular rounds on minus 15…a familiar number to Leeds fans of course.

We arrived at Gatwick in plenty of time for our 6:25am flight to Munich and enjoyed an English breakfast in Wonder Tree, a recent addition to the Gatwick restaurants. Kentley insisted on paying for his share with a handful of 'shrapnel'; he'd obviously raided his piggy bank in readiness for the trip. It took the waitress a good five minutes to count up all the coins before concluding we were 25p short! I tossed in another couple of 20p pieces and generously told her to keep the change. She smiled politely.

The hour and forty minute flight was uneventful; the only surprise being the lack of Leeds shirts on board. I'd fully expected there to be dozens but we only spotted one lad in the light blue top from a few years ago. We did have one bit of luck on the plane though; the young lad sat next to us was *"half Austrian"*, he told us, and was flying from the south of England to watch his *"home"* team, Red Bull Salzburg, play Bayer 04 Leverkusen in a friendly. He was able to explain the best trains to get, how to buy tickets and where to head for. RB Salzburg would draw their game with Leverkusen 1 – 1, in front of over 30,000 fans.

With our Austrian friend's help, we made our way on the S8 train from the airport to Munich East and then onto a second train to the main station in Salzburg. It was a short walk from there to our hotel, the Grand Wyndham on Fanny-von-Lehnert-Straße. As always, Kentley was quick to find anything associated with Fanny...

Once in Salzburg, we saw Leeds shirts everywhere and in the centre of the old town the bars were packed full of our lads and lasses trying to combat the oppressive heat by swilling large quantities of Stiegl Goldbräu beer; and very refreshing it was too! At one point, while wandering around the old town, we got chatting with the self-styled 'Munich Whites', a small group of Leeds fans including Sean who lives and works in Munich.

I left Kentley to do all the timetables and schedules for this trip; he's usually spot on with the plans he makes based on the info he gets from the iPhone that's seldom out of his hand. He decided we'd need to set off from the hotel no later than 5pm for the train to the Eugendorf Sportzentrum, about 11 kilometres away...

At ten past five, Kentley was still in the shower and as I waited for him to complete his ablutions, I did think back to a brief conversation we'd had earlier with Heidi Haigh, the 'Follow me and Follow Leeds United' author; we'd spotted her and some mates in our hotel reception. It was around 4pm when Heidi told us they were just setting off for the match... perhaps we should have followed her... (This is not just thrown together you know!)

We strolled into the station at 5:19pm and surveyed the departures board; conspicuous by its absence was the destination, 'Eugendorf'. Kentley checked his iPhone and within seconds confirmed the next train to Eugendorf was due to leave at 6:18pm; the game was a 6:15pm kick-off. We quickly realised we'd have to grab a taxi from the rank outside the station. At the end of the day it was no great problem; there were plenty of taxis waiting for fares and the driver of the one we jumped into assured us it would only cost around 20 euros to do the journey up the A1 West autobahn. What he didn't tell us was that he was the deranged lost brother of Niki

Lauda; that he'd had a huge row with his wife before he came out this evening; and that he was suffering from a severe bout of painful haemorrhoids. Well, something was making him drive like his arse was on fire anyway.

The sight of brake lights in the road ahead is traditionally a signal to those following to slow down but for Niki's brother it merely triggered a response to give it more gas! We hurtled towards the slowing cars as if about to give them a mighty shove up the road like some sort of satanic stock car in a demolition derby. Then, at the very last moment, with Kentley and me both stamping on imaginary brake pedals and whispering *"I love you"* to our families; he suddenly threw out the anchor and almost stood the powerful Mercedes on its front bumper! I was in the back and the combination of Lauda's driving and the 30 degree heat outside was making the sweat pour off me. I swear I was a stone lighter by the time the little Sportzentrum ground came into view. I paid over the 22 euro fare and we both staggered gratefully away.

Once inside the ground it started to look more like a Leeds United game. There were a few Frankfurt fans sat in one end of the solitary grandstand but there were many, many more Leeds fans filling the remainder of the seats and standing 5 or 6 deep all along the touchline below. Most had a beer or two in their hands bought from a super-efficient mobile bar parked under the grandstand; if Carlsberg did football bars they'd definitely be like this one... The other three sides of the ground were virtually empty. There was a simple scoreboard on halfway on the opposite touchline and that was about it. Behind the single rail fence were open fields as far as the eye could see. There were lots of familiar faces already enjoying the evening sun and the draught Stiegl, and tuning up with a few Leeds songs. It wasn't long before we heard the new one about Uwe Rösler's grandad.

Rösler himself has assured fans throughout his English career that the story about his grandad bombing Old Trafford as a Luftwaffe pilot during WW2 is no more than a fan-made myth... but it does make a great story. It was new to us but was a favourite of Manchester City fans when Uwe played for them back in the mid-90s; he scored 50 goals for them in 152 games. It goes like this, to the tune of 'December, 1963 (Oh What a Night)' by the Four Seasons.

Oh what a night,
In late Feb-ru-ary 1941,
*Uwe's Grandad dropped a fu***** great bomb,*
On Old Trafford, What a night!

Whenever Uwe heard the song he couldn't help but give a little smile. In his autobiography, 'Knocking Down Walls'[1], he tells how the sound of Man City fans singing his name, relayed through the mobile phone of a friend at his bedside, helped him summon the willpower to keep fighting the cancer that struck him down in 2003. The thought of Uwe's grandad bombing the Stretford End was as attractive to Manchester City fans 20 years ago as it is to Leeds fans today!

We said hello again to the Munich Whites, now holding their huge flag; I had a quick word with Gary Edwards, the 'Paint it White' author; and I waved to and took a photo of Big Clive, Tim, Ozzie and Arthur who were all waving like mad up in the seats above us. Many fans had their shirts off showing their beer bellies and a pint in each hand as they soaked up the sun… and that was just the girls.

Silvestri
Wootton Cooper Bamba Berardi,
Bianchi Cook Mowatt
Byram Morison Sloth

Subs. Turnbull, Bellusci, Adeyemi, Phillips, Taylor, Erwin, Antenucci, Doukara, Coyle, Walters, Horton

So, no Billy Sharp, who'd be flying back to meet with Sheffield United the following evening; no Chris Wood, who still had that knock and no Luke Murphy, who was still recovering from knee surgery. There was a cracking atmosphere for this game even though there were only 1,100 in the ground. Leeds supposedly *only* brought 450 fans to Austria but it seemed like way more than half the fans in the ground were Leeds supporters. Even before the game began,

---

[1] KNOCKING DOWN WALLS, by Uwe Rösler with David Clayton, published by Trinity Mirror Sport Media, 2013

Phil Hay of the YEP had tweeted: *"Police seem a little anxious about this arrival from Frankfurt,"* alongside a photo of the riot police seemingly rounding up a group of fearsome looking Frankfurt fans.

From very early in the game, Leeds were pushed back by a strong Frankfurt side. Phil Hay tweeted again that with the exception of three players this was regarded in Germany as the strongest side Frankfurt could field. We'd already witnessed Harrogate and York getting behind our full backs so it was no surprise that Frankfurt managed it too; on a regular basis. As we've seen so often though, whatever our defence lacks in technical ability they almost make up for with sheer dogged determination and heart. Cooper in particular was throwing himself at anything goal-bound while the telescopic legs of Sol Bamba often intervened to snatch the ball off a striker's toe. Marco Silvestri was also showing why he is so well thought of for his shot stopping ability despite regular criticism of other aspects of his game.

As the half wore on, we were distracted momentarily as a number of sinister looking Frankfurt fans began pulling down the Leeds flags tied to the fence behind the goal to our right. There were murmurs of outrage from Leeds fans all around the ground but then we got the impression the flags had at least been returned and we all focussed on the game again. Leeds were slowly but surely playing themselves into it and it was the usually anonymous Tommaso Bianchi who seemed to be pulling the strings in the middle while Sam Byram looked dangerous on the right wing, just below where I was standing near the stairs to the upper section of the grandstand.

The closest the Germans got, was a shot that rattled the post after the ball had been bouncing around in the Leeds box for several seconds with bodies flying in all directions. Then, amazingly, Leeds went up the other end and scored. Byram went barrelling down the right wing and his low pass found Steve Morison. 'The Shift', dragged the ball from under a defender's boot and then lashed it home from 12 yards. The Leeds fans predictably went bonkers. The goal clearly spooked the Germans and Leeds were arguably the better side for the final 15 minutes of the half. As two very sweaty groups of players left the pitch for the sanctuary and shade of the dressing rooms, the score remained 1 – 0 to Leeds. *"How sh*t must you be we're winning away,"* sang the beery Leeds fans.

During half-time, I watched as Matty Pears put the subs through a warm-up routine; Peppe Bellusci didn't seem very happy. At one point he gestured to Pears as if to say, *"I shouldn't be doing this, I should be in the shade in the dressing rooms",* while later on he completely ignored Pears' instructions and got totally out of synch with the rest of the group. I could see Pears mouthing, *"Peppe...Peppe",* trying to get his attention. Bellusci struck me as one unhappy bunny. The friction generated when the Frankfurt fans removed the Leeds flags seemed to have dissipated now and there were a few Frankfurt banners hanging in their place. There was no sign of the gang of Frankfurt fans responsible or indeed the big group the riot police rounded up before the game. All was calm if still very hot and sweaty. It was the hottest July day ever recorded in Austria apparently. At one point, Kentley nudged me and pointed out a bloke in a blue cap that he reckoned was Aaron Cawley; the hooligan who floored Chris Kirkland up at Hillsborough a couple of years ago.

Leeds reappeared for the second-half with no changes but it looked as though we'd now adopted a 4 – 4 – 2 formation, with Casper Sloth dropping in behind Steve Morison and Alex Mowatt moving wide on the left, leaving just Morison and Byram further forward. Within a few minutes of the restart, Frankfurt should have scored, as once again they got behind our defence and around Silvestri only for Seferovic to clip his shot into the side netting. Then Rösler made his first changes and we were treated to a comic moment as the PA announcer called the substitutions. Imagine a badly sighted old geezer reading in stilted English with a very bad German accent: *"For zee Leeds United, zee player coming out of zee field is Bianchi Tomasso und zee player coming into zee field is Adeyemi Tom."* Then, *"und as well, zee player coming out of zee game is Sloth Casper und zee player coming into zee game is Antenucci Mirco".* We all chuckled at this and I could hear all sorts of, *"Don't mention zee vor",* type comments coming from the ranks of the Leeds fans. Three minutes later and the Germans metaphorically bombed our chip shop.

Once again we saw how easy it is to bamboozle this defence of ours. A free kick out on the Frankfurt left wing was clipped to the back post where Stefan Aigner rose unchallenged to head back across goal. This time Johannes Flum was first to react to stab the ball home from close range. I immediately looked for a reaction from Rösler and sure enough he turned straight to Rob Kelly on the bench behind him and muttered something that had lots of 'F's in it whilst slowly shaking his head in disbelief. On the pitch, the Leeds players were looking at each other trying to understand where these Frankfurt players had popped up from. It was embarrassing. Almost immediately we had another change and more giggling as the PA crackled again: *"Zee player now leaving zee game is Mowatt Alex und zee player coming into zee field is Taylor Charlie"*. I knew a tailor called Charlie once. On 71 minutes, Kelvin Phillips and Souleymane Doukara replaced Cook and Morison and by now Leeds's shape had all but gone and the Frankfurters were on a roll... Their winner came in the 74th minute. It was a bit of a Keystone Cops moment.

A quick move down towards the Frankfurt right wing corner saw them get behind Berardi for the umpteenth time and the ball was hammered low across the face of goal. Stefan Reinartz's first time shot was well blocked on the line by the diving Liam Cooper but the rebound came straight back to the German striker. He was now lying on the ground but he flicked his right boot at the ball and it ricocheted in off Scott Wootton's arse, past the flying figure of Marco Silvestri. Out of the corner of my eye, at that moment I was sure I'd seen a bit of a scuffle behind that goal as some Frankfurt fans appeared to be chasing someone out of the ground. A few other Frankfurt fans appeared to be gathering there and they seemed agitated...

There were many more substitutions but there was no further change in the score and the game petered out, while in the distance there seemed to be a much larger group of Frankfurt fans now standing in the sun; many with their shirts off. Meanwhile, in the field behind them, one man and his dog went about their evening stroll blissfully unaware of the plot being hatched by the small army of Frankfurt fans now lining that touchline; some new arrivals were mostly dressed in black and appeared to have their faces covered.

As the final whistle blew, almost all the Leeds fans on the touchline down below strolled onto the pitch and many tried to get selfies with the Leeds players. Then the calm broke as even more Frankfurt supporters appeared on the far side of the pitch and they were now facing a long line of Leeds fans, exchanging insults and challenges. It kicked-off in seconds when a couple of buckets were thrown and then both sets of fans could be seen bouncing up and down on their toes like kick boxers, exchanging blows. As soon as it became clear blood was being spilt, the riot police moved in. As they did, the Frankfurt Ultras, as we would later discover they were, jumped over the rail and fled into the field where the man and his dog had been walking peacefully just minutes earlier. They ran round the corner of the ground and disappeared from view while several Leeds fans were now running out of the ground to my right, presumably to head them off at the pass.

I waited for a long while and watched as a couple of Leeds fans guided a mate across the pitch towards us. He was bleeding from his mouth and nose and had clearly taken a punch or a kick to the face. Kentley went down to join the fans on the pitch at the end of the game and I'd now lost sight of him in the crowds. I made my way down the steps and waited. I spotted Mick and had a quick chat; he was one of many making his way to Oslo for the game there on Saturday.

Eventually, Kentley found me and regaled me with the full horror of what went on just outside the ground. There had been tens of these so called Ultras, many with black balaclavas covering their faces and carrying all manner of weapons, including batons, bike chains and knives. They'd attacked the Leeds fans that rushed out of the ground and had caused plenty of damage before the riot cops managed to separate the two groups. Kentley reported the cops had grabbed many of them and the rest had run off towards the town centre. It was like a battlefield now; one old fella, clearly dressed in Leeds colours, had been caught up in the rush and had fallen badly and he was now being lifted gently onto a stretcher, while the lad I saw with the bloodied face was propped against a wall looking dazed. There were police mini-buses and ambulances roaring away from the ground with screeching tyres and blaring horns and everywhere you looked there were riot police, fully togged-up in all the gear. We were trying to make for the station but of course since we'd come in Lauda's brother's taxi, we had no idea which direction to take. Most roads appeared to be sealed off by the police anyway, so for a while we just stood in small groups and waited. We were all watchful and nervous; carefully studying anyone who came too close, trying to see if they were our fans or theirs. No one was prepared to set off on their own for fear of being ambushed. It's been many, many years since I felt like that at a football match.

Eventually, a group of about a dozen of us set off towards town but after half a mile or so we came upon another line of riot police blocking our way. They were clearly on edge too and were all drenched in sweat underneath the heavy fabric of their protective clothes and white riot helmets; the temperature was still up in the high twenties even at close on nine o'clock. Two officers had set up a camera on a tripod in the grounds of a church overlooking the road and they were now filming us. I asked a good looking blonde female copper stood with the cameraman where we should head for but she said she had no idea. She explained in broken English that the Frankfurt fans had run into the town centre and that there was now trouble there. In the end she suggested we go back the way we came, cross two open fields and get to the station that way. Whilst chatting to the lady copper, I tried to ignore a gruff Yorkshire voice coming from somewhere in the group behind me suggesting I ask her if she fancied, *"a quick shag"*. We discussed this (the route we ought to take to the station not the quick shag) amongst ourselves and then half a dozen of us decided that was indeed the best course of action.

Kentley and I chatted with two lads from Driffield as we walked along together; they'd come over to Austria on their motorbikes and were planning another few days touring before returning home. I didn't get their names but they were really decent lads and we all bemoaned how this group of Frankfurt fans had spoiled the day for us all. We'd later learn that the police had ample chance to stop them in Salzburg earlier in the day when a gang had refused to pay the fare on a bus; the police were called and the Ultras were thrown off but bizarrely were allowed to continue walking to the ground. They didn't have match tickets and the riot police were expecting them but somehow the Ultras were allowed to storm the entrance, beating up a steward in the process. The rest we'd witnessed first-hand. Mistakenly, in the coming days, some press coverage would blame Leeds fans. Some of the video footage had shown Leeds fans fighting back. That was unfair; the older generation of Leeds fans went to watch a football match but they are a tough breed and if threatened will not run away. The younger generation, fuelled with plenty of Dutch courage, can be more easily provoked. But I'm ninety nine percent sure that had the Ultras been turned away from the ground by the police there would have been no trouble that night. Instead, we witnessed the 'Battle of Eugendorf'.

The one per cent of doubt I have about any Leeds fans being the cause of any trouble is due to an article I saw in the Sun a few days later. That alleged that the well-known hooligan, Aaron Cawley, was indeed at the ground, despite his life time ban. Cawley was pictured and videoed laying into some Frankfurt fans and it was even alleged that Cawley threw the first punch.[1]

On Wednesday, we had a day wandering around Salzburg, sightseeing, as our flight wasn't 'til 9:55pm. We went up in the cable car to the Festung Hohensalzburg, a medieval fortress that nestles on top of the cliff overlooking the city and spent much of the day seeking shade from the scorching sun. Some reports said the temperature was in the high 30s. We then got the train back to the airport where we discovered our

---

[1]   http://www.thesun.co.uk/sol/homepage/news/6559109/Football-thug-Aaron-Cawley-goes-on-Europe-rampage.html?CMP=spklr-_-S9SunSocial-_-TWITTER-_-TheSunNewspaper-_-20150724-_-News-_-213816057

flight was delayed by two hours. We spotted several Leeds fans waiting for the same flight back to Gatwick and the talk was all about the previous night. We spoke with Andy, a Leeds fan based in Brighton and he was convinced no Leeds fan went to the game looking for or expecting any trouble. None of us had seen the Sun article yet of course!

By the time we got back home it was almost 5am and we calculated we'd had just eight hours sleep in the previous 52... we were both knackered. On the OS, Uwe Rösler was raving about the team's performance saying: *"I think the players were terrific. We got exactly what we hoped for – we played against a team with very good ball possession.*

"We worked very hard against them and we worked extremely well in the shape. The longer the game went on, we adapted to their quality a little bit better..." I could accept that the players worked hard and we did look super fit but I was sceptical we were anywhere near their quality. Above everything else though, I still felt there was an elephant in the room we were all missing. That defence of ours was nowhere near good enough. To start the new season with it as it was suggested to me we were embarking on a Mission: Impossible. Leeds travelled to Oslo on Friday afternoon and turned out for the game against another Bundesliga side, Hoffenheim, on Saturday in front of a crowd of 2,824; almost exclusively all Leeds fans according to reports on Twitter. I listened to most of the commentary from Thom Kirwin on an internet audio stream. I have to say it sounded similar to the Frankfurt game; German efficiency and pace against a hard-working and very fit Leeds side. Leeds lined up for this one in a 4 – 3 – 3 formation again:

Silvestri
Berardi Bamba Bellusci Taylor
Adeyemi Cook Mowatt
Byram Wood Doukara

Subs: Cooper, Sloth, Phillips, Walters, Erwin, Antenucci, Morison, Turnbull, Coyle, Wootton, Horton.

Bianchi was out with a minor injury, Sharp had now gone and Murphy continued his rehabilitation; Rösler was adamant Murphy would not be fit to face Burnley in a fortnight. The game was played in Lillestrom SK's Arasen Stadion, a ground familiar to Rösler from his time there in 2002/2003. It was while he was there he was diagnosed with cancer and when he'd recovered it became his first managerial role. His memories of the place disappeared quickly though when Hoffenheim's Mark Uth hit a screamer after only two minutes. It was a quality finish; he had his back to goal initially but turned and struck the ball in one movement and it flew into the top right corner. Things got even worse in the 15th minute when Lewis Cook hobbled off; Kelvin Phillips took his place. Uth had another long range effort that clipped the bar and Sol Bamba was playing his usual heroic part in an overworked defence when he cleared off the line. Leeds's reply was a glancing header from Chris Wood who finally seemed to have shaken off his injury problems. Leeds grabbed an equaliser after 25 minutes; Mowatt's floated corner was nodded back across goal by a typical towering Byram header to find Doukara whose headed flick in turn found Adeyemi. Tom poked the ball home.

Leeds battled through to half-time and then again in the early stages of the second-half with Silvestri pulling off a number of fine stops. Cooper replaced Taylor Charlie (I must stop doing that) and Antenucci came on for Doukara but then the Germans were back in front. Substitute Steven Zuber turned in a low cross with Berardi once again in no man's land. The Germans saw the game out with little late drama.

I was getting used to Rösler's post-match euphoria; *"I thought the first 45 minutes were excellent,"* he said. *"We camped in their half – against tough opposition from the Bundesliga. "We looked very strong physically and sharp. We pressed them high and they didn't come out of their half. "We looked dangerous from set-pieces and we looked dangerous from open play. We had lots of chances – I'm very happy."* Obviously I didn't see the whole game... but Thom Kirwin must have been commentating on a completely different one.

Leeds flew home still without a win in pre-season other than the 3 – 0 victory at lowly Tadcaster. Most fans on Twitter were still suggesting we had a decent looking side and that pre-season results weren't important; I wasn't convinced.

It was all Yellow...

A couple of days before the Everton game, the brand new away kit was revealed in all its yellowness. So many fans had been calling for a yellow kit that Kappa would have been brave to go with anything else and predictably the new all yellow ensemble got a rapturous reception. The team would wear it against Everton.

The other thing the fans had been calling for, nay, yelling for, was a winger to wear the new kit. We had no real clue as to whether the club was trying to bring someone in or not but we were all conscious of Uwe's comment that our transfer business was only, *"95% done"*, and that left the door wide open for one more signing, or so most of us calculated.

The Leeds squad numbers for the new season were announced in the days leading up to the Everton game. It was said that wherever possible the players got the numbers they requested. Chris Wood unsurprisingly got number '9' which ruined another golfing pun for me. Had he got say, number '3', we could have joked about having a '3 Wood'. Surprisingly Scott Wootton would wear the historic number '4' once worn by Billy Bremner. A few fans suggested Wootton wasn't worthy.

I'd been playing golf on Friday afternoon with my lad Adam and was relaxing with a well-earned beer when I spotted a tweet from the YEP suggesting our search for a winger may well be over. It was alleged a deal to bring Brentford winger Stuart Dallas to Elland Road was almost complete. Dallas, a 24 year-old right footer who played most of last season on the Brentford left wing, was well known to Uwe Rösler, having played for the German at Brentford when he first arrived from Irish club Crusaders, back in 2012. The best news was that Brentford fans on Twitter were saying to a man they wanted Dallas to stay; suggesting they thought him a decent player. I liked the idea of having Dallas and 'Woody' in the same team; a couple of cowboys might just help us shoot up the league...

It was just like old times as I arrived in the Hoxton Mount car park, just after midday on Yorkshire Day, Saturday 1st August. I had a quick chat with the bloke on the gate who reminded me not to be late for the Burnley game the following week; that was live on Sky, a 12:30pm kick-off of course. I strolled down to the club superstore where I'd arranged to meet my old mate Nigel. He spotted me as I was trying on one of the new Kappa training tops. It was all very confusing. Kappa had labelled the new stock with their standard European sizes while the club had helpfully put them on hangers showing the UK equivalent which was one size smaller. Hence, I was sure I needed an XL Kappa size that was on an L hanger. Nigel studied me as I contemplated my own reflection in the full length mirror. *"I think you need the fat bastard size mate,"* he helpfully broadcast to the whole shop. Kev and Zack wandered by as I continued to ponder what size to plump for but they were far too circumspect to offer any advice. They'd later comment that they also saw me try on the new yellow away top in the body fit style and were pleased to hear I abandoned that idea. I acknowledged it had been a bit of a struggle to get it off again...think Houdini extracting himself from a straightjacket.

All the regulars were in the Pavilion; Nigel and I sat with Kev and Zack and later Ty, Martin and his three lads appeared. I spotted 'Acker' who'd introduced himself to me in the shop earlier as well. Everyone was in pre-season optimistic mood and the appearance of the team line-up on Kev's battered iPhone was universally acknowledged as the best eleven we currently had available for a 4-3-3 formation:

Silvestri
Berardi Bellusci Bamba Taylor
Cook Adeyemi Mowatt
Byram Wood Doukara

Subs: Turnbull, Coyle, Cooper, Sloth, Horton, Wootton, Phillips, Antenucci, Erwin, Morison.

It was the team I'd have plumped for and the only questions in my mind were whether the arrival of Dallas next week would mean he replaced Doukara for the Burnley game and who, if anyone, would make way for Luke Murphy when he was fit.

As in the previous two seasons, the Pavilion was only part open for the final pre-season game, suggesting they expected a similar sized crowd. We got just over 10,000 last season for the Dundee United game and only just over 9,000 for the Nurnberg game the year before that; everyone would be pleasantly surprised therefore when a figure of 17,057 was posted on the big screen during the second-half. 1,734 Everton fans had made the trip along the M62; no mean feat since I'd noted on my way up signs on the motorway proclaiming: *"M62 closed Junctions 4-5."*

Lynn and Mike and his little lad Benjamin, were in the row behind as Nigel and I squeezed into row GG, trying to avoid the stream of water falling from the roof; it was raining steadily and there appeared to be a drainage hole in the roof of the Kop right above our heads that I'd never noticed before. Nigel used his tiny Yorkshire flag as a makeshift headscarf to try to keep dry. The Elland Road pitch looked superb; it had been re-laid as usual over the summer and they'd now laid artificial grass all around the playing surface right up to the advertising hoardings; it actually made the pitch look narrower but I think it was just an optical illusion. Everything was set.

I ought to say at the outset that this was probably not the best side Everton could have put out. The back line in particular was made up of academy players with no sign of the likes of Leighton Baines, John Stones and Phil Jagielka, all of whom would turn out the following day at Goodison for Duncan Ferguson's testimonial game, along with several other established first team players. Four of the Everton defence were making their senior debuts. But equally, we did get to see Ross Barkley, Oviedo, Naismith, Mirallas and Tom Cleverley during the 90 minutes. So, exactly how this Toffees side compared in ability to the expected Burnley first choice team that we'd face seven days later was hard to judge. My guess was that Burnley would be a far tougher proposition but at the end of the day you can only beat what's in front of you and this we did.

It was a decent game and truth be told, Leeds looked good. Once again it was clear we were super fit; Alex Mowatt in particular kept running for the 80 minutes he was on and looked far leaner than he had done in the past as did most of the players who all sported the new body fit yellow away tops far more elegantly than I did in the shop earlier.

Leeds took the game to the visitors and Chris Wood was putting his height and bulk to good use holding up play and challenging in the air. Wood had the best effort of the first-half when he crisply hit a bouncing ball that the Everton keeper did well to parry away. Wood had the ball in the net just before half-time but he was well offside as he turned and stroked the ball past the keeper from eight yards. As Premier League referee Martin Atkinson brought the first-half to an end, the Leeds faithful stood as one and applauded the players off and there were many murmuring: *"That were a decent first-half, well pleased wi that."*

Everton came out for the second-half with a couple of changes and a lot more ambition and Silvestri was called on to make one of his trademark last-ditch saves as he dived full length to stop a McAleny header right on his goal line, grabbing it at the second attempt. It was the one time during the game I was reminded that we do lack concentration in that defence of ours every now and again as McAleny was left free as a bird in our box. But that was as close as Everton got and there was no sign of them getting down either wing and behind our full backs as we'd seen happen so often in pre-season. Once again, I was not sure if that was due more to an improvement in our defending or if it was a lack of ability by Everton.

Leeds took a deserved lead in the 57th minute and what a goal it was. Had it been Arsenal scoring this one it would have been all over Sky like a rash. As it was, we did at least get praise from www.metro.co.uk with a report and video of the goal under the headline: *"Alex Mowatt scores for Leeds United against Everton after incredible tiki-taka 10-pass team move."*[1]

All ten Leeds outfield players had a part in the 17 pass move that began on the Leeds right with Berardi. He played the ball up to Wood who chested it down to Mowatt who gave it back to Berardi. He checked and played it back to Lewis Cook who in turn moved it inside to Adeyemi. He touched it inside again to Sol Bamba who then played a neat triangle with Taylor and Doukara on the left wing. Bamba gave it back inside to Bellusci who then accelerated through the inside right channel before stabbing the ball out to Sam Byram on the wing. Sam and the Douk exchanged passes with Sam then racing into the box to play two short one-two wall passes with Alex Mowatt and Alex swept the ball past the keeper.

Uwe then made his first changes on 70 and 72 minutes with Leeds now looking comfortable and stroking the ball around confidently. Phillips replaced Cook and then Erwin replaced Doukara. It didn't seem to disturb our momentum though and in the 80th minute we doubled the lead. Tom Adeyemi showed some neat footwork as he weaved round a tackle before laying the ball off to Chris Wood, 25 yards from goal. Wood trapped the ball and then pulled the trigger and it looped up and over the keeper into the net off the underside of the bar. It took the slightest of deflections off a defender which caused the strange trajectory which may have deceived the keeper. That was no concern to Wood though as he stood with one arm raised saluting his first goal for the club. Just at that moment someone else was marauding down the Leeds right wing; a bloke covered in tattoos but otherwise stark bollock naked was approaching the Kop wearing nothing more than a smile. He did a couple of twirls and then slipped on the wet grass

---

[1] http://metro.co.uk/2015/08/02/alex-mowatt-scores-for-leeds-united-against-everton-after-incredible-tiki-taka-10-pass-team-move-5323459/

allowing two of the stewards to grab hold of him. Without any great struggle he was marched away to the north-west corner. There was no attempt to cover his modesty and all I can say in the bloke's defence was that the rain was bloody cold and that may well have frozen his assets...I heard someone say he appeared to have *"Ludo"* tattooed on his todger but I understand when he's excited it actually reads Llandudno...It would earn him a (pretty lenient I thought) one year ban from the club in case any of you fancy trying it in the future.

With the game safe, Uwe made three more substitutions, bringing on Wootton, Antenucci and Morison for Adeyemi, Mowatt and Wood. 'The Shift' should probably have got himself a goal as he tried three times to scoop the ball in from no more than two yards out but finally rasped it over the bar. No matter, this was an accomplished performance and at the final whistle the players got a well-deserved roar of approval. They could have done no more today but there was just that nagging doubt as to how good our opposition had been. In seven days' time we'd get a much better idea how fruitful the new season might be. 'FourFourTwo' magazine didn't rate our chances; their predictions suggested Wolves and Derby would end the season as top dogs with Brighton, Rotherham and MK Dons relegated. They had Leeds just missing the drop in 21st.

Two pieces of news that broke this weekend once again put football into context. While we were enjoying a pint in the Pavilion, at Oulton Park in Cheshire a pilot was killed when his Gnat aircraft crashed during an air display. The display was part of Chris Evans' annual 'CarFest' show that supports Children in Need. Then, on Sunday morning, we learned that Cilla Black had died overnight aged just 72. Only the previous night, Mrs W, Adam and I had watched an old Morecambe and Wise clip on TV, with Cilla and the two comedians doing their 'Bring Me Sunshine' song. Cilla Black had pretty much been around as a singer and TV personality as long as I've been following Leeds.

New season, same old issues...

O n the Tuesday between the Everton and Burnley games, it was hard to shift myself away from the TV. Sky Sports News HQ was well into its '92 Live' programme; they were visiting every one of the 92 league clubs during the day; a slightly more ambitious schedule than me completing them in just shy of fifty years! Not long before they went to Elland Road, the news popped up on screen that Stuart Dallas had finally completed the move from Brentford. The OS then carried the confirmation that Dallas had joined on a three year contract for an undisclosed fee. Tantalisingly, the last sentence of the OS piece reported: *"The winger could make his United debut in Saturday's 2015/16 season opener against Burnley at Elland Road this Saturday (12.30pm)."*

Shortly after 1:30pm, '92 Live' broadcast its visit to Elland Road; Richard Graves carried out the pitch-side interview with Adam Pearson. The Leeds director seemed in good form too, happy to confirm the Dallas signing and quite willing to joke about the fact that Massimo Cellino was an *"effervescent"* character and how, *"He's on holiday at the moment, we've got a lot done in the last two weeks!"* The most encouraging words he had though came right at the end of the interview as he told us: *"We have some serious people in place and we aim to be giving it a big go this year."* Perhaps 'FourFourTwo' magazine should have interviewed Pearson before they made their season's prediction... or perhaps not.

Hard on the heels of the 'Dallas in' news came a report from the YEP's Phil Hay of 'Morison out'. The YEP reported: *"Morison left Elland Road earlier today after agreeing to sever the last year of his contract. United spent several weeks attempting to remove Morison - one of their highest earners - from the wage bill and a settlement has been reached with 12 months of his deal remaining. The 31-year-old is now expected to complete a free transfer to his former club Millwall."*[1] I was slightly disappointed with that as I still felt he was a useful bloke to have around but it was the end of yet another failed striker in a long line of them at Elland Road; over to you Chris Wood. The reference to Millwall taking Steve Morison was a tad premature maybe as next up on the '92 Live' schedule was Millwall. Despite the best efforts of the Sky reporter to tease confirmation from their manager Neil Harris and Chief Executive Andy Ambler, they were stoic in their refusal to confirm the news other than to admit that a player was, *"next door having a medical."* It would be confirmed officially later in the day. So, for 'The Shift', his final moment in a Leeds shirt would prove to be that chance against Everton when he scooped the ball over the bar from a couple of yards out. Sort of appropriate really and somehow summed up his time with us. It had all been in stark contrast to how Neil Warnock suggested it might be back in February 2013 when he told us:

"We've never had a Morison since I've been here and he's not even fit yet.

"He'll be a legend here in a few years.

---

[1]   http://www.yorkshireeveningpost.co.uk/sport/leeds-united/latest-whites-news/leeds-united-morison-joins-millwall-after-leaving-whites-1-7392449

"The fans will love him to bits and say 'bloody hell that was one of Warnock's signings".[1] Funnily enough we do say something very similar…

Another former Leeds star we'd be seeing this season was Max Gradel; sadly not in a Leeds United shirt or even in the Championship but rather in the Premier League with new boys Bournemouth. It was reported that Leeds would benefit financially from Gradel's transfer to the Cherries as there was a sell on clause in his contract when he left Elland Road for Saint-Étienne. It was rumoured Leeds could expect to get around £500,000 based on the believed £7m fee Bournemouth had now agreed.

In the lead up to the Burnley game we were all getting giddy with excitement and expectation. There were very few Leeds fans who didn't expect a real push for promotion from the team but my concern was that a lot of the optimism had come on the back of that win against Everton. I still had doubts in my mind as to how strong that Toffees side was and if anything I felt we were all getting carried away. It wasn't just the fans though. In an interview on BBC Radio Leeds with Adam Pope, during the West Yorkshire Sport programme, Adam Pearson spoke positively about the forthcoming season just as he had done in the Sky '92 Live' piece the previous day. Twitter also quickly picked up a comment he made about the ownership of Elland Road. *"There only remains the stadium to bring back within its [the club's] portfolio of assets and I'm sure that will be…[hesitates momentarily]…it'll certainly be happening within the year will be my guess."[2]*

On Thursday, I sat riveted to my sofa (not an unusual thing in itself if you ask Mrs W) watching the 4th Ashes Test Match with Australia. England, or rather Stuart Broad with 8 wickets for 15 runs, bowled the Aussies out before lunch for just 60!

---

[1] *http://www.yorkshireeveningpost.co.uk/sport/leeds-united/latest-whites-news/leeds-united-morison-could-become-a-whites-legend-says-warnock-1-5438986*
[2] *Adam Pearson on West Yorkshire Sport on BBC Radio Leeds, 5th August 2015*

Then, in the afternoon, JR (Joe Root) reached a hundred to help England forge a huge first innings lead and make it odds on England would win the game to take an unassailable 3 – 1 lead in the series to regain the Ashes.

In the Centenary Pavilion, before the Burnley game, we watched on the big screens as England finished the job to win the match by an innings and 78 runs. England may have JR but Leeds now has Dallas (That's a TV pun in case you are too young to remember the classic TV drama 'Dallas' and central character, JR Ewing). There were no surprises in Uwe Rösler's first competitive line-up as Stuart Dallas was named on the left of the forward three with Doukara demoted to the bench; the only change from the Everton game. Sol Bamba had been named captain during the week.

Silvestri
Berardi Bellusci Bamba Taylor
Cook Adeyemi Mowatt
Byram Wood Dallas

Subs: Turnbull, Cooper, Phillips, Erwin, Wootton, Antenucci, Doukara.

Elland Road was buzzing; it was a lovely warm day and some pundits were talking of maybe 30,000 arriving for the game although I'd always been sceptical of that since it was live on Sky. There was a real feel good atmosphere too, largely on the back of that performance the previous week when we chewed up the Toffees. I sat discussing the merits of that optimism with George, Trevor and Steve and then Derek and Shirley when they arrived. Nigel, Martin and the boys, John and Alan all arrived in due course and eventually Jacqui too. We were all happy to note that the Club had finally seen sense and reduced the price of pie and peas back to a more sensible £3.80 after dallying with a ridiculous £4.80 the previous week; a move that saw a near total boycott of the dish! They'd put the price of entry to the Pavilion up to £3.80 as well mind you, but it was starting to feel more like the Pavilion we fell in love with a few years ago as the crowds rolled in. We even had the return of Peter Lorimer and Terry Yorath to entertain us. They were introduced by an announcer who, slightly tongue in cheek, mentioned he was aware we'd been a bit overlooked last season in the Pavilion... too bloody right we had! It was another sign of how normality was returning to this club of ours; in fact it was all slightly disconcerting at how they were finally starting to recognise us as valuable supporters. We're no longer used to it! Lorimer went for a 2 - 1 to Leeds prediction while the normally downbeat Yorath surprised everyone with a 2 – 0. I was sticking with the 1 – 1 prediction I'd posted in my YEP Jury article on Friday. The YEP runs a preview before each game, including the predictions of each of its Jury members and then runs the verdicts afterwards. It would be nice for my own credibility to start with a correct score.

Unusually, I left the Pavilion just after noon, a full half an hour before kick-off; I just wanted to sample the atmosphere. It was now hot; roasting hot. It reminded me of my few days in Austria and it crossed my mind that the Leeds players would at least have experienced playing in the heat quite recently. There were now thousands of fans streaming into the ground and for the first time I can ever remember there was a huge snaking queue lining up to buy the match-day magazine from a seller at the entrance opposite the Pavilion in Lowfields Road. Perhaps we would get 30,000 after all.

Inside, Elland Road looked magnificent in the glorious sunshine. Even more work had been carried out since the previous Saturday and now the walkway in front of the Kop had been painted in Leeds blue with two huge yellow badges either side of the goal. The paint was so new we could smell it in the air. Before I took my seat, I wandered along the front of the upper tier to find my old school mate Rob and his lad Pete and we had a quick chat; still not quite understanding how we could have failed to realise how near we'd been to each other over the last few seasons in these days of constant social media exposure...is it just me who is on Twitter all the time these days? Rob and Pete (who's the presenter of 'Drive Time' on '105 Capital Yorkshire Radio'), were planning to do the Reading game next Sunday so we agreed to touch base during the week and maybe meet up there too.

Just before the game, the Leeds compere interviewed four young mascots, over by the entrance to the players' tunnel, all decked out in the new yellow away kit. As he got to the second in line, a young lad, he asked: *"Are Leeds going up this year?"* The young lad thinks for a split second and then, to the amusement of everyone in the ground, tells the compere: *"Probably not. No!"* That lad knew it was 'Mission: Impossible' even at that stage!

As the game kicked-off, the sun was almost unbearable. There were a few small clouds slowly making their way over the stands and it was a wonderful relief each time the sun disappeared and then seconds later we'd be shading our eyes again as it reappeared.

The crowd would be announced in the second-half as 27, 672 – a figure that would also win me the 'Guess the attendance' competition on the LUFCTalk fans forum. I'd gone for a figure of 27, 563...getting good at these predictions! But in the first twenty minutes I was starting to think my 1 – 1 YEP forecast would be way off the mark as Leeds tore into Burnley and looked a good bet for the win; it must have been great viewing for the neutrals watching on TV, as well as for the hundreds of thousands of Leeds fans around the world. The more Leeds attacked, the more the fans roared them on and the full repertoire of songs was sung with gusto with the South Stand and the Kop alternating and then joining in together with a huge rendition of MOT. It was the sort of atmosphere that gave you goose bumps. Stuart Dallas looked every bit the missing piece of our jigsaw as he bombed down the Leeds left towards us in the North Stand. In the first ten minutes, Dallas could easily have opened his account for us as first he had a shot ricochet up onto the underside of the bar and then a back post half-volley well saved by Tom Heaton in the visitors' goal. At the other end, Bellusci was lucky not to give away a penalty when he clearly knocked the ball down with his arm but it went unseen by referee Kevin Friend. Then Peppe got in on the act up front as he burst forward to lash a swerving shot at the keeper from distance. Bamba and Berardi had opportunities too; Bamba probably should have scored with a back post header and Berardi with a ballooning shot that nearly took my head off. Mike bravely got a hand to the fiercely struck ball and then regretted it as blood began to drip from his torn thumb-nail. It was a feisty encounter between two teams going full tilt and it was surprising we got to half-time with only one name in the book, that of Sol Bamba. We were all getting nervous as Sol continued to debate the merits of his card with Friend for far too long but eventually, to our relief, he backed away. As the half-time whistle blew, the whole of Elland Road rose to applaud the efforts of both teams and the Leeds fans were well pleased with what they'd seen.

The second-half began slowly but then Leeds appeared to step up a gear and began to counter attack with pace but only when Burnley failed to bring us down. At one point, Lewis Cook seemed to be away but the experienced Scott Arfield put in a tackle any Leeds Rhinos' player would've been proud of to bring our man down. A booking was hardly the reward we might otherwise have had. Alex Mowatt had a good opportunity but pulled his left foot shot just wide of the post when many in the ground would've bet their season ticket on him scoring. Adeyemi then smashed a shot over the bar as did Chris Wood with an even better opportunity. Wood's decision making was giving cause for concern now as he clearly should have dinked this one over the onrushing keeper rather than trying to knock spots off the ball. In fact, it was about now I was beginning to wonder if our poor finishing would cost us the game. Wood didn't look strong in the air either; it was Sam Byram who was winning crucial headers to put Wood through on a few occasions but Wood just wasn't on fire.

In the 70th minute the first changes came. Uwe's move was predictable as Stuart Dallas was replaced; Rösler had commented earlier in the week that Dallas had not had as much game time in pre-season as he would have liked. It was a slight surprise though that it was Mirco Antenucci coming on and not Doukara. For Burnley, Sean Dyche replaced both his strikers as Lukas Jutkiewicz and Jelle Vossen made way for Marvin Sordell and ex-Leeds loanee, Sam Vokes. I was worried when I saw Vokes; former Leeds players have a habit of coming back and scoring against us as indeed Vokes did on his previous visit to Elland Road in 2013, when Burnley went away with a 2 - 1 win. But I guessed Massimo Cellino was equally concerned; we could all see Sordell wore the dreaded number '17' on his back.

Antenucci looked like a man with something to prove; within minutes of his arrival he was jinking his way through the Clarets' back line but his finish was just as wild as anything else we'd seen from Leeds today and his shot sailed into the South Stand. A few moments later though, he made up for that miss with a sublime effort that had us all dreaming, at least for a minute or two.

Mirco collected the ball with back to goal, just outside the south west corner of the Burnley area. He had Sam Byram outside and they were two on one but Mirco turned inside and managed to evade a lunging challenge before getting the ball onto his left foot. Then he curled the most delightful shot over the keeper and into the far corner of the net before setting off like a scalded hare towards the dugout to celebrate. All hell broke out near us as a big bloke in a blue T-shirt appeared from nowhere to jump on his mate stood next to me and they both swayed ominously. Had they toppled over, I swear they would have crushed me to death as they were both huge, twenty stone huge I guessed as my life flashed before my eyes. In self-preservation I grabbed a hand full of the blue T-shirt to steady myself and somehow we all stayed upright. Mike was doing his best to keep his damaged digit out of the way by holding it up in the air like he was giving a thumbs up signal. What a moment it was; it was Luke Murphy against Brighton on opening day two years ago; it was Billy Sharp last season against Boro; it was mayhem. This was going to be some celebration for the remaining eight minutes or so…

But I should have known better shouldn't I? I'd forgotten about Sam Vokes and I'd forgotten that more times than I care to remember these moments of elation with Leeds only last for seconds, let alone minutes. We are all singing our heads off and counting down the minutes as Burnley break down their right wing with George Boyd, another bloke with history against us. The noise is incredible and there are still folk hugging each other and fist pumping the air all around. Mike is still doing his one thumb jig. Boyd is being well marshalled by Charlie Taylor but somehow Burnley's new full back, Tendayi Darikwa, so new that his name is not even on the Burnley squad list in the programme, has got himself unmarked behind Boyd. We can hardly hear ourselves think as the noise in the Kop reaches new heights and we're all still bouncing up and down singing MOT. The ball is rolled back to the unmarked Darikwa and he lifts it first time into the middle; into that corridor of uncertainty that exists in and around our six-yard box where Jumbo jets have been known to disappear. This time, Sam Vokes has ghosted in there unseen and he rose majestically while Bellusci was half a yard away and too slow and Vokes headed the ball powerfully into the top corner. It was all just *so* Leeds United.

Leeds fans have seen this happen so often before that it wasn't actually that painful; just a terrible disappointment that we put behind us with a shrug of our broad shoulders. The real anger about it all was that our defence, the same defence of course that did this countless times last season, had cocked up again. How can we hope to challenge at the top of the Championship if we keep giving sloppy goals away and constantly fail to close out games we seemingly have in the metaphorical bag. Good as our young team was, this defence was still not fit for purpose.

It was a while after the final whistle, as Nigel and I sat silently watching Vokes and Bamba giving the post-match TV interview in the centre circle, that I remembered my 1 – 1 prediction for the YEP; at least it will look to their readers as though I know what I'm talking about. As big Sol gave a final wave to the few remaining fans, his 'Man of the Match' trophy tucked under his arm, Nigel and I made our way wearily up the steps to the exit.

After the game, I was encouraged by an interview Uwe Rösler gave to the BBC. He showed a great command of English as he commented on Stuart Dallas: *"He worked his nuts off for the team"* he said. More importantly though, he gave notice that he fully recognised the weaknesses we had in defence when he perhaps accidently let slip: *"We dropped a little in the back four; that is the issue we have to still work on* "[1]. I was pleased to hear that. I watched the replay of the game on Sunday night and was fascinated to hear the comments of studio guests Luke Murphy and Peter Beagrie. Both confirmed that a major part of the make-up of Uwe Rösler is his attention to detail, so again I trusted he'd deal with the problems we still had at the back. Beagrie joked: *"You don't want to play golf with him; he takes about 25 practice swings!"*

Our game having kicked-off early, I was able to listen to the BBC 5 Live coverage of the three o'clock games as I drove the one hundred miles back home. The commentary was from Bournemouth who faced Aston Villa, in the Cherries' first ever Premier League game. It was nil-nil in the 69th minute when Max Gradel came on for his debut. Sadly, Villa scored with a Rudy Gestede (he of Blackburn fame until this summer) header three minutes later to win the game. Around the country former Leeds men were scoring all over the place. Billy Paynter got one for Hartlepool as they beat Morecambe 2 – 0 and at Shrewsbury, Millwall came away with a 2 – 1 win thanks to a goal and a penalty won by Steve Morison. At Hillsborough, Tom Lees banged in a header for the home side as they beat newly promoted Bristol City. Elsewhere in the Championship there were predictably a fair few draws, with almost half of the opening weekend's games finishing level. The other winners, apart from the Wendies, were Birmingham, Wolves, Charlton, Hull, Brighton and perhaps the result of the day, newly promoted MK Dons who battered Rotherham 4 - 1 in Yorkshire. Our next Championship opponents were Reading, the following Sunday, and we'd hope to replicate Birmingham's win over them. Before that though, Leeds had a tricky little COC game, live on TV at Doncaster and before that I was on my 'Doing the 92' trail again with a trip to Northampton on Tuesday night. Their first round tie was against Blackpool. The season was well and truly underway.

Leeds United 1 Burnley 1 (**Antenucci (83)**, Vokes (86))
27, 672 (Burnley 1,719)

---

[1] *http://www.bbc.co.uk/programmes/p02z3789*

"You just don't seem to understand..."

The Burnley game was just the first of a hectic schedule of matches for me; I was doing Northampton Town on Tuesday, the Leeds game at Doncaster on Thursday, Carlisle on Saturday, Leeds at Reading on Sunday and Leeds at Bristol on Wednesday. I was hoping to squeeze in a trip to Oxford on the night before the Bristol game too…but I was still to raise that one with Mrs W!

Tuesday night I was in Northampton to see the Cobblers thrash a very sorry looking Blackpool, 3 – 0 to ease through to the COC 2nd round. Town were 3 – 0 up inside 29 minutes and it knocked the stuffing out of the Blackpool players and their few hundred intrepid supporters. Town looked a decent side and I decided Leeds would do well to avoid them in the next round if we got past Donny! My good buddy Red Russ organised the tickets as he lives in Northampton and we had a good old natter over a pint before the game. It was ground number 75 of the 92 for me.[1]

---

[1] *This game would prove to be a good pointer to the season ahead; the Cobblers would be promoted to League One while Blackpool would be relegated to League Two.*

Eight Championship sides had already crashed out of the COC this week; a sign that maybe promotion is far more lucrative than cup success. I for one though hoped Leeds would progress, either to face a Premier League side or maybe one of the 17 grounds I had yet to visit to achieve my '92'.

In the lead up to the Doncaster game, rumours persisted that Sam Byram was close to departing the club. This despite the news his agent was back in talks with us and Sam himself suggesting he had no thoughts of leaving in the short term. There were also rumours that Leeds were still chasing a few transfer targets of their own; a £1.5 million bid had apparently been turned down for 21 year-old Belgian winger Anthony Limbombe, although the YEP was now reporting that his current club, NEC Nijmegen in Holland, wouldn't sell unless offered, *"an astronomical amount."*[1] £1.5m sounded cheap to me for a bloke who scored 14 goals last season to help propel NEC to promotion.

I was teamed up with Kentley again for the Donny trip and we arrived at my usual parking spot on Lakeside Boulevard around 5:30pm. We wandered into the nearby Beefeater expecting to easily get a table and have something to eat there but it was not to be. They'd transformed the inside of the pub since we were last there and they now only served food in the restaurant section to the right as we entered. Predictably, they said every table was booked. There are plenty of places to eat near the Keepmoat though and we wandered over to Pizza Hut and got a table in there without drama. Eventually, Nigel bowled in and joined us. A pizza and a couple of beers later and we were ready for whatever Leeds would throw at us.

Leeds for once didn't quite sell out the ticket allocation for this one, although 3,394 of us took our places in an otherwise mostly empty looking Keepmoat Stadium. It was another game being featured live on Sky of course and the Leeds fans made their feelings plain about the missing thousands with an

---

[1]   *http://www.yorkshireeveningpost.co.uk/sport/leeds-united/latest-whites-news/leeds-united-consider-next-move-after-1-5m-bid-for-belgian-winger-rejected-1-7407098*

early rendition of, *"If you're watching on the telly you're a c***!"* and, *"Sky TV is f****** sh**!"*

Rösler made 5 changes to the side that almost beat Burnley at the weekend as he tried to strike a balance between resting players, knowing we had four games in ten days and yet still putting out a team capable of winning a Yorkshire derby. The team on the pitch looked to be about the perfect balance to me.

Turnbull
Berardi Bellusci Cooper Taylor
Cook Wootton Mowatt
Doukara Antenucci Dallas

Subs: Silvestri, Byram, Bamba, Murphy, Wood, Erwin, Phillips.

Thus, compared with the side that played Burnley, Silvestri, Byram, Bamba and Wood appeared to be being rested while we were told Adeyemi had a slight knock. Quite why Scott Wootton was preferred in a holding midfield role to Kalvin Phillips I was unsure although it started to make his shirt number (4) look a little less ridiculous. Liam Cooper was named captain, a role he performed several times last season of course. I personally would have started Chris Wood; it was clear for all to see last Saturday he needed some shooting practice but I guessed Rösler thought he was vital to his formation to play in the Championship on Sunday. Doncaster made just two changes from their game with Bury at the weekend.

Uwe Rösler was pitting his wits against his old strike partner, Paul Dickov, the Donny manager, who he played with at Manchester City; the pair are said to be great friends. At the weekend, Dickov's team made the headlines for a bizarre incident that took place in their league match against Bury at the Keepmoat. The game was all square at 0 – 0 with just seconds to go when Bury put the ball out after their player Nathan Cameron was injured. Then, in trying to give the ball back to the Bury keeper, Donny's Harry Forrester was a little over enthusiastic and the ball sailed right over the keeper's head into the net. After referee Eddie Ilderton discussed the matter with both benches, Dickov agreed to allow Bury to walk the ball into the Donny net unopposed, which they did;

Leon Clarke getting the easiest goal he will ever be credited with. The game ended 1- 1.

The playing surface looked fantastic, as they all do at this time of year of course, but the surrounding Astro Turf looked a mess with bits of yellow grass and weeds growing through it. It was a total contrast to the immaculate new surround at Elland Road we saw on Saturday. For fifteen minutes the Leeds players similarly outshone their League One opponents and the leading light was Mirco Antenucci who once again came out of the traps like a rocket propelled greyhound. Every time he got the ball it looked like something could happen, and in the 14th minute it did.

Charlie Taylor launched the ball up the Leeds left wing where Antenucci challenged for it in the air. It lobbed back to Stuart Dallas who in turn headed it on to Antenucci. Now 'Ant' was in a straight race with Rob Jones into the area and he won it. He shifted the ball onto his right foot and tried a curling shot towards the far post but the keeper was able to parry it away but only straight to the right boot of Lewis Cook and he steered the ball neatly into the now open net. Cook celebrated like a mad man for a few moments; it was his first senior goal and his team mates were obviously delighted for him. It was going to take a few moments for him to calm down.

The Leeds fans were also delirious with delight of course and we were all fairly relaxed at that point; it looked like it was going to be a bit of a stroll... Did I really just say that? For fifteen minutes the relaxed mood continued as we worked our way through our portfolio of songs and generally taunted the home fans. They were somewhat quiet, only rousing themselves when Charlie Taylor miscued a clearance straight to James Coppinger who lobbed Turnbull only to see Peppe Bellusci hook it back off the line and away to safety. Other than that aberration, Leeds looked comfortable. And then in true Leeds United fashion, it all fell apart.

Donny's Taylor-Sinclair took a short throw-in to Andy Williams, in the north-west corner over to our right. Williams played it back to Taylor-Sinclair and he spotted Cedric Evina who'd got away from Scott Wootton in the penalty area. Suddenly, Wootton wakes up and dashes over to cover Evina but the Donny man toe pokes the ball past him just before our man makes his tackle. With the ball now long gone, Wootton's lunge takes Evina down and the referee has probably the easiest decision of his career to make. Andy Williams takes the spot-kick and in typical Leeds fashion there is even more heartache as Ross Turnbull guesses right but then just fails to stop the ball trickling over the line under his body. It was as if those football gods were teasing us again...he'd saved it! Oh, no he hasn't. Once again it was already clear that this was going to be far from a routine away win. Then, seven minutes later, it was looking nigh on impossible.

Twelve months ago we were at Bradford's Valley Parade Stadium in a COC second round game when it all went pear-shaped. On that occasion Luke Murphy had a rush of blood to the head as he got himself sent off for two reckless tackles. Leeds battled manfully for over half that game with ten men and then took the lead with just a few minutes to go only to concede twice in the dying seconds to still lose the game. That was the classic Leeds game of ups and downs; joy and despair and it ultimately cost Dave Hockaday his job. This now felt very much the same.

Leeds were attacking the far end of the ground and Lewis Cook had just gone around the outside of two players on the Leeds right wing. Then, as he made to beat a third Donny defender, the ball just got away from him. Rather than let the defender hoof the ball into touch though, Cook, no doubt still with plenty of that adrenalin surging through his veins, lunged with both feet to try to rescue it. Instead, he left Aaron Taylor-Sinclair in a heap and the referee had his red card out quicker than a dying traffic warden with a parking ticket. Watching the replay the following day I winced when I saw the challenge; it was that bad.

I've lost count of the number of times Leeds have done this; shot themselves in the foot when in a winning position. That Bradford game was very obviously similar but there have been many, many more. Last season we gave away more penalties than any other side in the Championship, and in the first few games of that season we had numerous red cards that left us with impossible tasks. We had seven red cards in all. We also made numerous unforced defensive errors that gave away points all through the campaign; we just don't give ourselves a chance.

To be fair, in the remaining minutes of the first-half and throughout the second, Leeds more than held their own. Inevitably Doncaster amassed plenty of strikes on goal and dominated possession. But there were few moments of real drama for us and on rare occasions we even came close to nicking a result ourselves. On 67 minutes, Rösler made his first changes, sending on Chris Wood and Luke Murphy for Dallas and Doukara, neither of whom had been particularly 'visible' in their time on the pitch. Then in the 75th minute Sam Byram replaced Alex Mowatt to cheers from the Leeds crowd of, *"There's only one Sam Byram"* and then various warnings to Massimo Cellino not to sell our young star.

> *"He plays on the right, he's fu***** dynamite,*
> *I just don't think you understand,*
> *If you sell Byram, Sam Byram,*
> *You're gonna have a riot on your hands."*

Extra time came and went and then we faced penalties; COC first round games have to be settled on the night. I tried to persuade myself this game was going to be different, this time we'd get that bit of good fortune and win through. But deep in my heart something told me to be prepared for the worst. When was the last time we had any good luck? When I watched the TV replay a few days later, Uwe Rösler was asked before the game if his players had practiced penalties and his response was: *"You know what, Germans always practice penalties; you know that!"* When Paul Dickov was asked the same question he replied: *"The players stay out and practice penalties all the time so we did a little bit yesterday but it doesn't look good because I won the penalty competition!"*

Antenucci was first and buried his spot-kick comfortably. Donny replied in kind. The kicks were being taken in front of the Donny fans at the far end, so there was little we could do to assist but each time a Donny player lined up we shouted and hollered for all we were worth. The rain was pouring down by this time and conditions were not favourable but as they say, it was the same for both sides. Next up for Leeds was Luke Murphy; was this to be redemption for letting us down at Bradford? Well, maybe, just two steps and he lifted the ball into the top left corner of the net. Donny again replied in kind. Now it was Sam Byram's turn, with the Leeds fans chanting, *"There's only one Sam Byram"*, until just before he started his run-up. Sam's kick went two feet over the bar to wild cheers from the Donny fans. The Leeds fans showed they had no anger towards him and immediately chanted his name again while the other players consoled him. On the TV replay the following day I watched as Uwe Rösler turned away with a wry smile and a shake of the head, clearly disappointed at the way Sam leaned back when he struck the ball. *"Get your head over the ball"*, we were all taught from the first time we ever kicked a football. Donny scored their next kick without a problem. Up steps Chris Wood…

I was willing Wood to be a hero; to show us all he really could strike a football. It would do his confidence so much good for the rest of the season. But there was a certain inevitability that he'd miss. He's looked less confident each time I've seen him and even the celebration of his goal against Everton seemed to suggest he himself was surprised that one flew in the net. So, Chris Wood steps up, in the pouring rain, in front of the massed ranks of the Donny support all waving and shouting and jumping up and down. Wood skies the ball horribly, miles over the bar. A £3 million pound striker, miles over the bar… That must have hurt Uwe Rösler on so many levels. Doncaster had beaten Leeds on their own patch after a wait of 64 years and Leeds were out of the COC in the first round for the first time in their history. Leeds also became the 9th Championship side to bow out of this year's competition at the first time of asking. Where was all that optimism we experienced up to that 86th minute against Burnley now? As for that ball that Wood struck; NASA is still tracking it…

Doncaster 1 **Leeds United 1**, (**Cook (14)**, Williams (pen 31))
8,361 (**Leeds 3,394**)

Not pretty Reading

My game count grew quickly in the first few days of the new season. I was about to clock up number four as I journeyed to Carlisle on a cheap train ticket for their League Two game with Cambridge United. It was my 76th ground and what a game it proved to be! There were more twists and turns than a Cellino tax audit and the game ended in a 4 – 4 draw. I had a brilliant day out in the sunshine and even had time for a quick look round the county town of Cumbria itself. I wandered around the city agog at the sight of dozens of hen parties working their way from pub to pub; the girls all wore those huge platform shoes and short tight skirts, a combination that makes walking seem nigh on impossible. Like a dog walking on its hind legs; it can't do it well but you're amazed to see it done at all. The pubs all appeared to be former banks and that seemed to encapsulate the modern way; we no longer save for the future, rather we spend what we have living for today. At one point a couple of really drunk lads staggered past me and one made a bee-line for a posh-looking public waste bin. He propped himself against it, pulled out his todger and peed in it, oblivious to folk wandering by. I decided it was time to get my train home…

Early on Sunday, Mrs W and I packed the car and set off on the road to Reading. This was the first leg of a short break taking in our games at the Madejski later that day and Bristol on Wednesday night; I still hadn't broached the subject of Oxford on Tuesday for my next '92' game.

We had a trouble free journey and arrived safe and sound around midday at the World Turned Upside Down, a pub on Basingstoke Road where I'd been pre-match for every previous trip to the Madejski. It's renowned for its excellent carvery, although in previous years I'd always got there too late to try it. No problem this time though and we were among its first customers although there were already several Leeds shirts in evidence in the bar. When we'd finished eating, we took our drinks outside and sat at one of the wooden tables overlooking the road and it wasn't long before we were joined by many familiar faces. Derek and Shirley were first but hot on their heels were Adam, Conor and Karen, and then the usual car load of the Surrey and Sussex Whites, chauffeured by Simon W. Chris, Phil and his lad arrived a bit later, jumping out of a taxi… *"Christ Chris, have you come all the way from Leeds in that?"* I asked tongue in cheek!

True to form, Kentley texted to say he was, *"gonna be late"*, and he'd see us at the game, while Nigel was still wrestling with his suitcase which he'd arranged to leave in left luggage at the Madejski (he was staying in Cheltenham this week to be handy for the Bristol game) so we'd see him at the ground as well. A small group of us left the pub around 2pm to walk down Basingstoke Road to the ground; we were all just in shirt sleeves enjoying the stroll in the sun.

Nigel met me at the turnstiles and we wandered up to our seats. We chatted away, while out on the pitch some presentation thing was going on despite the Leeds fans trying to drown it out. In fact, we'd later learn that this was the first airing of a new Reading club song! Titled *"They call us the Royals"*; it was written by co-chairwoman Khunying Sasima Svrikorn and was being played over the Stadium PA… except the Leeds fans were making sure no one could hear it! If you really are that bored that you'd like to see the complete anthem then it's here in this piece from the Independent. Suffice to say they ran their article under the headline: *"Reading co-*

chairwoman pens excruciating new club song..."[1] Just to give you a taste, the pre chorus goes:
"Now we're here and we're strong, we're going to bring it on
  Can you hear when we shout "come on""... yes, exactly!
Rösler had been spouting on about how important it was to rotate his players during this opening run of games so it was no surprise to see six changes to the side that lost at Donny. Back in came Silvestri, Bamba, Adeyemi, Byram and Wood, while young Kalvin Phillips also got a rare start.

Silvestri
Berardi Cooper Bamba Taylor
Adeyemi Phillips Mowatt
Byram Wood Dallas

Subs: Turnbull, Wootton, Bellusci, Erwin, Doukara, Murphy, Antenucci.

In the pre-match chat going on around us, this was acknowledged as probably the best eleven available for a 4 – 3 – 3 formation, knowing that Lewis Cook was now suspended. There was the usual debate as to whether Cooper or Bellusci should partner Sol Bamba and one or two voices could be heard suggesting Ross Turnbull had shown he was possibly more solid between the sticks than Silvestri. Most also considered Antenucci was unlucky not to start after his fine performance in Doncaster. Reading came into the game having narrowly, many said unluckily, lost their opening game at Birmingham, but winning in extra time at Colchester in the COC. As Reading kicked off, attacking the goal at the far end, the stadium looked nicely full. The 'Mad Stad' can hold 24,200 according to www.footballgroundguide.com and we'd later learn that 21,581 were inside it today, including 4,131 Leeds fans; the biggest away following anywhere in the country this weekend.

At full time, Eddie Gray summed the game up with: *"that was pretty poor wasn't it?"* and Eddie's been involved in the game

---

[1] *http://www.independent.co.uk/sport/football/football-league/reading-cochairwoman-pens-excruciating-new-club-song-that-includes-a-rap-verse-10455625.html*

for six decades or more so he should know! Key moments were few and far between but the fact Sol Bamba escaped with only a yellow card in the second minute when he hauled back Hal Robson-Kanu was probably the most important. During a first-half of few chances, Stuart Dallas would have what proved to be our only shot on target all day as he fired into the arms of Reading keeper, Jonathan Bond. Nil – nil at half-time, the sides re-emerged to continue to shadow box throughout the second-half, with just a couple of decent efforts, one from each side that rippled the side netting. Murphy and Antenucci replaced Phillips and Mowatt in the 72nd minute and predictably 'Ant' put himself about but it looked like these sides could play 'til Christmas and not write a headline. The only moment that got us on our feet was when a picture of Reading Academy Manager, Eamonn Dolan went up on the big screen. Dolan was undergoing chemotherapy for cancer and this was an opportunity for all present to offer their support and good wishes. The Leeds fans, as they always do, stood and applauded genuinely.

The game ended as it began, goalless, and truth be told, Eddie was spot on. Neither team possessed the quality to unlock two very ordinary defences. Leeds in particular looked as bereft of creativity now as they did for large parts of last season. The only player who looked likely to create anything was Antenucci and it now seemed impossible for Rösler not to start him at Bristol. In the 'MailOnline', Uwe was already thinking about that game as he joked: *"Our recovery now is vital. We have to live like monks - no alcohol and no sex, the schedule we're having to go through isn't good. We have to rotate."*[1]

Argh! That 'rotate' word again; Leeds fans cringed at every mention of it, most just wanting to see our best eleven on the pitch every game, all game, and thinking the players should be quite capable and willing to play four games in ten days.

Reading 0 **Leeds United 0;**
21,581 **(Leeds 4,131)**

"Is there a fire drill?"

After the Reading game, Kentley, Mrs W and I spent an interesting few minutes back in the WTUD to use their Wi-Fi to submit my 'verdict' piece for the YEP football jury. There were still a few other Leeds fans in there and they were, by this time, very well oiled indeed! The locals were trying to watch the Man City v Chelsea game on TV and when the Leeds lads began to conga in front of the telly singing MOT at the tops of their voices it all started to get a bit fractious. I typed furiously on my laptop trying to get finished as quickly as possible. It all passed off peacefully in the end although when I returned at one point from a visit to the bogs, I found the Leeds fans had grabbed Mrs W and wrapped her in a huge Leeds flag whilst singing, *"She is Leeds, she is Leeds, she is Leeds!"* I hid round the corner enjoying the spectacle for a few minutes before making a rescue.

We bade Kentley farewell and made the journey along the M4 towards Bristol, to the village of Tolldown, where we were stopping for the next three nights in the Crown Inn; a lovely little country pub serving Wadworth beer. The following morning we spent at Dyrham Park, a National Trust property just along the A46 from the pub and we had a lovely time strolling around some of the 270 acres of ancient parkland as well as visiting the amazing roof restoration project going on at the mansion house. It was here that I finally got round to asking Mrs W if she fancied trying the Kassam that evening;

explaining that it wasn't a new coital position, rather it was the home of Oxford United. I'd researched the route and found there was a falconry centre just a few miles outside Oxford, called Millets Farm, where they had over 80 birds of prey including, most importantly, many rare owls; owls being a long held passion of Mrs W. There is very little Mrs W will not do for the promise of quality time with a beautiful bird with big eyes that comes alive in the dead of night... Come to think of it, I'm pretty much the same. So, after a magnificent full English breakfast at the Crown, we set off and then spent a fantastic few hours at Millets Farm, viewing the birds and watching a very entertaining falconry display by the excellent Joe, before heading to Oxford.

We discovered a Vue cinema right opposite the Kassam and Mrs W went off to see 'Paper Towns' while I wandered over to the football. Once again I'd chosen a decent game; Notts County took an early lead but then Oxford grabbed an equaliser before half-time and went on to win 3 – 1. Sadly, Mrs W would later describe the film 'Paper Towns' as: *"Rubbish!"*

We awoke on Wednesday morning to pouring rain but we still drove into Bristol to take the park and ride into town and then the little ferry across the harbour to the SS Great Britain; Brunel's magnificent propeller driven iron ship that's been moored in dry dock here since 1970. She'd been left to rust in the Falklands in 1937 but was finally returned to the dock she first left back in 1843. The late Sir Jack Hayward, former owner of Wolverhampton Wanderers, helped fund the return of the ship to the UK. She is magnificent and the museum attached to the ship is one of the finest I've seen. It was then time to head for Ashton Gate.

It was still pouring, so we decided to see if we could find a roadside parking spot near the ground. After circling round a few times and getting lost in the notorious one way system, we found a spot on Smyth Road, about a fifteen minute walk away. We met Keith outside the away end and as we stood there chatting all of the usual faces put in an appearance. Phil B was there, Martin and his lads arrived, Mike and Lynn who'd driven down from Leeds, and of course Nigel. It was a murky, damp old evening, but the mood was generally positive; most Leeds fans expected us to beat a City side that had lost all three of its opening games; 2 – 0 at Hillsborough, 4 – 2 at home to Brentford and 3 – 1 at Luton Town in the COC.

Rösler again plumped for rotation over consistency and this time made three changes from the side we saw start at Reading:

Silvestri

Wootton Bellusci Bamba Taylor

Adeyemi Phillips Byram Dallas

Wood Antenucci

Subs: Turnbull, Berardi, Mowatt, Cooper, Murphy, Erwin, Doukara.

There were murmurs from the Leeds ranks that Wootton had no place in a Leeds shirt and questions as to why the generally more appreciated Berardi was not at right back but other than that it was considered a decent side. I was pleased Antenucci was starting and I was guessing this was an experiment with 4 – 4 – 2, although it could equally be set out as 4 – 3 – 3 with Dallas on the left of the front two. My only concern was that there was no real visionary midfielder in there at all with both Murphy and Mowatt only on the bench.

Ashton Gate looked very different to my previous visits; there was now a big empty space to our right as we stood at the north end of the ground in the Atyeo Stand; the old West Stand having been demolished in preparation for the construction of a new one. At the far end of the ground, where we used to be housed in a low shed like structure, there was now another brand new stand that had only been opened for the previous game with Brentford. Notes in the front of the programme explained that the club had been forced to leave 2,000 tickets unsold for our game under advice from the Safety Advisory Group; that explained our paltry 1,300 ticket allocation which was predictably sold out. Ashton Gate will be a decent looking ground when the redevelopment is complete but as it currently stood, we were bound to hear: *"West Stand, West Stand, give us a song"*, at some point in the evening!

We'd also here the equally funny, *"Sh** stand, no fans"*, as we all pointed to the building site on our right.

Despite the lopsided look to the ground, the atmosphere was excellent; it was a typical football night with the rain drifting across the floodlights creating a misty haze. Leeds had their bright yellow kits on which contrasted starkly with the pillar box red shirts and white shorts of the home side. On the touchline to our left was the unusual sight of a female official; Lisa Rashid was the assistant on that side and within minutes of the start I could hear various comments suggesting she ought to, *"Get back to the kitchen"*, and, *"Who's the slapper with the flag?"* Encouragingly though, a loud booming male voice was heard to tell the offenders, *"Shut the f*** up with yer sexist crap you morons!"* The offenders stayed quiet for the rest of the game.

The first-half was played at a fair old pace, with City fulfilling their reputation as an all-out attacking side and Leeds reduced to counter attacking using the pace of Antenucci. Silvestri was the busier of the two keepers but looked solid enough and when he *was* beaten, Stuart Dallas was there to hack the ball off the line. Leeds' fans were doing their bit to spur on the side with non-stop chanting while the Bristol fans were strangely quiet. Then, in the 39th minute, the roof nearly came off the Atyeo Stand. Chris Wood moved at pace towards us and slid a perfectly weighted pass into the area for Antenucci. The keeper decided to come off his line, even though Antenucci was very wide and when Ant touched the ball past him he had no choice but to clip the Italian and bring him down. A roar went up demanding that referee Gavin Ward give us the decision and he didn't disappoint although the keeper did get away with a yellow despite our calls for red. Dallas picked up the ball and walked towards the spot but Antenucci was already there waiting and Dallas handed it over. Mirco drilled the penalty down the middle with Hamer diving away to his right; cue delirium all around.

That was pretty much the final action of the first-half and as the players trooped off I think every Leeds fan there was well satisfied with the performance and the score, even though the match stats would later suggest the home side was actually in the ascendancy for long periods.

Both sides emerged unchanged for the second-half and within seven minutes Leeds doubled their lead. It began when Bristol's Aaron Wilbraham was brought down heavily in midfield and we all panicked as the ref waved what looked to be a useful advantage to the home side that was now breaking quickly towards the Leeds goal. We breathed a sigh of relief when the move broke down though and suddenly the ball rebounded off Sam Byram into the path of big Chris Wood. He set off at speed and travelled fifty yards into the Bristol half before touching the ball to his left finding Antenucci again. Wood kept going though and soon had the return pass at his feet on the right side of the area. For a big man, Wood has surprisingly quick feet and in an instant he'd jinked to the left to side step a defender before lashing a left-footer into the far corner of the net. Cue more delirium and this time we all sensed we were now close to Uwe's first win.

It still looked very much like that as we moved into the final minute of normal time but by then Leeds had made two rather surprising substitutions; Antenucci and Byram were both withdrawn and Berardi and Mowatt had come on. It was clear that Berardi replaced Byram in a sort of right wing come midfield position but Alex Mowatt was playing his usual midfield role so that Chris Wood was now a very solitary figure up front. Bristol had made all three of their substitutions, including bringing on the dangerous Keiran Agard. There was still no sign of Leeds cracking though, despite Agard making a few dangerous runs and the home crowd clearly thought it was as good as over as they began to stream away in their thousands to a chorus from our fans of, *"Is there a fire drill?"*, so dramatically were the Bristol sections emptying. Then in an instant, everything changed.

Agard was suddenly on his own in the Leeds box, just a few yards below us; he pulled the trigger and the next thing we saw was the net rippling and Silvestri looking aghast at his near post as if thinking: *"How the hell did that get through?"* It had though and suddenly those Bristol seats were filling up again and the noise inside Ashton Gate was incredible. The

Leeds fans sensed this was going to be a nervy few minutes and we began to chant our own repertoire and then we all mouthed profanities as the PA announced, *"There will be a minimum of six minutes added time, six minutes of added time"*. *"Where the fu** has he got six minutes from?"* someone near us shouted angrily. Everyone was now on their feet urging their respective sides on and we could see the panic begin to flow through the ranks of those in yellow. Time and time again Leeds would just lump the ball out of defence up towards Chris Wood but every time he failed to get his head to the ball and instead it was knocked to a red shirt and the next Bristol attack would begin. Time after time a cross would be hoisted into the Leeds area and every time it was Sol Bamba throwing himself at the ball to clear it before we'd hammer it back up towards Wood. We resorted to trying to waste time too and Scott Wootton was yellow carded for taking too long over a throw-in. It was like the proverbial Alamo; every time Sol cleared our lines a chant of, *"Sol - Sol Bamba"*, went up from the now visibly worried Leeds fans. We were crying out for someone to take control out there. *"Put your bloody foot on the ball"*, I shouted to no one in particular but we soon lost it again and the ball was coming at pace back towards us. A header from Agard went just wide with Silvestri flapping at it and then a shot from Bobby Reid was blocked and bounced to safety. Wood then went in the book for a bad foul that had us all wincing even though it happened a hundred yards away. Bamba performed another heroic interception and the ball flicked away for a corner and up went the, *"Sol - Sol Bamba"*, chant again. The corner floated into our six-yard box, that notorious area where Leeds defenders fear to put their heads. Bellusci threw himself in the general direction of the ball but missed it completely and instead Marlon Pack glanced it towards the back post. Silvestri got to it but only managed to pat it down and it bounced back up behind Aden Flint who somehow flicked a boot at it to send it flying in the net.

The Leeds fans were silenced now. We'd seen this sort of thing happen so often in recent years that we just sort of accept it as, 'our lot'; it's just what happens to us. The home fans all around the ground were now on their feet saluting what they saw as a heroic effort by their boys. *"And you fu**** it up 2 – 0"*, was now echoing around the ground and I half expected our fans to join in, just changing the second word. We didn't, we didn't have the energy; we were drained, completely drained. It was a horrible feeling. There was only about one minute of those six extra ones left and soon the final whistle went and many Leeds fans slumped down in their seats, heads in hands. I did myself and the thought going round and round in my head was the single word, 'Why?' Why does this so often happen to us? Are we cursed? No of course we aren't, least not by any unseen abstract force. We'd given this game away, as we've given away so many in recent seasons. The names in our side keep changing but the malaise of not managing a game properly is never seemingly addressed. We were 2 – 0 up with 25 minutes to go and Rösler decided to take off Antenucci; he wasn't injured. He was replaced by the much slower midfielder, Alex Mowatt. Wood and Antenucci had worked well together all night and between the two of them we stood a chance of holding the ball up and even the possibility of scoring from another breakaway. Why change it? In the 85th minute, still 2 – 0 up remember, we took off Byram and replaced him with Berardi who we then played in Byram's role despite Gaetano never having played that role before to my knowledge. Why do that? Fundamentally though it was our lack of anyone with the ability to get the ball on the deck and put a foot on it to slow things down. Fingers were pointed at the goal keeping of Silvestri too and I have to admit he'd looked suspect all night; flapping at crosses and still on occasions kicking the ball dead from his hands. He was also beaten at his near post for the first goal and then gifted the ball to Flint for the second. In the coming days, the debate would rage fiercely on social media between those telling us Silvestri is a fantastic shot stopper albeit still young and inexperienced and others, like me, who'd seen just too many errors from the Italian in the last 12 months. He doesn't command his area, his punching is poor, he seldom catches the ball cleanly and he has this weak spot at his near post. Rösler was obviously aware of the problems he had with his keeper and he came out soon after the game to categorically tell us Silvestri would play against Sheffield Wednesday. I was worried. I've seen it happen too often before when a manager feels he has to show loyalty to a player only to then be let down again and have to withdraw the player in the full glare of another obvious error. We saw it graphically with Paul Rachubka a couple of years ago. He had four dreadful games when Andy Lonergan got injured in 2012 and to the fans he was clearly not up to the job. Yet still Simon Grayson stuck by him and picked him for the home game with Blackpool. In an appalling first-half Rachubka conceded three soft goals before finally, at half-time, being withdrawn and substituted by Alex Cairns. We never saw Rachubka in a Leeds shirt again. I hoped against hope we wouldn't see something similar on Saturday; we like a bit of déjà vu at Leeds!

As if we weren't feeling bad enough, Mrs W and I then had an appalling drive home as we battled with motorway closures and accidents. The M4 westbound was shut, so within a few miles of Bristol we were already stuck in miles of traffic that lost us half an hour at least. Then we saw the usual signs warning us the M6 was closed between junctions 11 and 12 but we're used to that and it normally only adds ten minutes or so to the journey. Not tonight though, as we were stuck for an hour or more with exit 11 completely jammed due to two lorries colliding. Then flashing signs warned us that junction 15 was shut so we came off at 14 to go through Eccleshall, only to find that the Eccleshall road was also closed when we got there! At that point, I looked skywards through the windscreen and said loudly: *"Go on then oh mighty one, what more have you got to hit us with?"* Mrs W shook her head at my unholy comment and then laughed uncontrollably until she physically shook as around the very next corner we met a complete blanket of thick fog and had to crawl through that at ten miles an hour. We finally arrived home at 2am. The events of the previous six hours tainted what, until then, had been a great trip away. I had a little over 48 hours though before I had to go again. As always I'd be ready, but I was expecting the unexpected.

Bristol City 2 **Leeds United 2**, (**Antenucci (39 pen), Wood (52)**, Agard (89), Flint (90+5)) 14,712 (**Leeds 1,307**)

More draws than M & S

There didn't seem to be quite the normal hype for the home game with the Owls and there was no talk of filling the ground. It was another live Sky game, our third already this campaign and neither side had yet set the Championship on fire. Leeds had drawn their opening three games while Wednesday had beaten Bristol City 2 – 0 on the opening day (as Leeds should have done of course), lost 2 – 1 at fancied Ipswich and drawn with Reading just as we did. There was clearly not much between these sides and a draw was always the most likely result.

Uwe Rösler continued to ring the changes and for this one he pleased around 80% of Leeds fans by bringing back Gaetano Berardi in place of Scott Wootton and pleased probably 95% of them by recalling Liam Cooper in place of Peppe Bellusci. Bellusci had become our Marmite player; you either loved him or hated him, but it had to be said that he'd not really let us down so far this season. There were rumours doing the rounds that a couple of Italian Serie A clubs – Atalanta and Bologna – were interested in signing him and the fact he was left out did nothing to dampen that speculation.

Silvestri
Berardi Cooper Bamba Taylor
Byram Adeyemi Phillips Dallas
Antenucci Wood

Subs: Mowatt, Murphy, Doukara, Turnbull, Wootton, Bellusci, Erwin.

Wednesday manager, Carlos Carvalhal, made six changes from the side that disappointed in midweek against Reading, presumably showing some dissatisfaction with that performance. He named Tom Lees as his captain in the absence of Glenn Loovens who was out injured.

The whole squad rotation issue came to the fore in the Pavilion before the game when comedian Jed Stone was again doing his stuff with Yorath and Lorimer. Yorath dismissed it as, *"utter rubbish"*, that players couldn't play four games in nine days on modern pitches but Rösler had hardly stopped complaining about this run of fixtures and was clearly of a different opinion. While we were in the Pavilion, news came through on various Twitter accounts saying that Leeds and Watford had agreed terms to sign Fernando Forestieri. He's the lad who took us apart last season at Watford, getting Bellusci sent off and scoring twice as we lost 4 – 1. In my mind, 'Fessi' was just the sort we needed to add a bit of a spark; a player with that magic touch to turn games in an instant. Most Championship games were so close it was only a mistake or a bit of magic that decided them, as we saw so often with many of our own games last season.

Looking round Elland Road before kick-off, it was clear that many folk we saw a fortnight ago for the televised game against Burnley hadn't turned up today; around 5,000 of them in fact. Wednesday brought 1,313 and the attendance was reported as only 22,597.

If ever there was a game that needed the magic of a player like Forestieri, this was it. Right from the start it was clear there was nothing between the sides and it really should have ended in a nil-nil draw. Leeds weren't helped when Kalvin Phillips was booked inside the first minute for a stupid tug on a Wednesday shirt. That meant he had to be super careful for the rest of the game. Berardi then clattered into Matias to get himself in the book as well and he was also left treading eggshells. The sole tactic Leeds had, was for Liam Cooper to aim long diagonal balls out to the right wing to Sam Byram and Rösler confirmed after the game this was indeed his secret ploy; saying he had to do this as his players were so tired! I assume he's not mates with Terry Yorath.

With the game in stalemate, we were really all waiting for that moment of magic and in the 37th minute it was Wednesday that provided it. A simple long ball was played over the top of the Leeds back four and Marco Matias got behind Liam Cooper just for an instant, beating the Leeds offside line. As the ball dropped behind Cooper, Matias let it bounce once before lifting it back over Cooper's head with his right foot. He then struck the ball with his left on the volley and it sailed over Silvestri and in off the underside of the bar. It was quite simply a breath-taking piece of individual skill and it left the Kop stunned and, for once, silenced.

At half-time, everyone was checking Twitter to see if that Forestieri deal had been completed; we were all hoping it would be and that we'd have him in our ranks by the time we went to Derby the following weekend. Without him, or someone else with magic boots, I couldn't see how we could get a result down there.

In the second-half, Leeds looked far more positive and created several openings in the early minutes only to suffer our perennial lack of accuracy as most shots flew into the Kop. By the end of the game we'd have recorded 20 attempts but only three hit the target. In the 56th minute, Rösler called for his 'M n M's as Murphy and Mowatt replaced the disappointing (again) Sam Byram and the booked Kalvin Phillips. That helped us move the ball via feet rather than those irritating long diagonal balls and Wednesday were by this time resorting to some agricultural tackling to keep us at bay. Tom Lees went in the book for a similar tug of the shirt to that which Phillips was punished for earlier. Lees was otherwise having a decent game and would later receive the Sky Man of the Match award.

Just after the hour mark, Leeds were level and it was another moment of magic. Stuart Dallas had now moved over to the right wing; a right footed player plying his trade on the right wing, with Mowatt, a left footer, playing on the left; *"Whatever next?"* I thought to myself sarcastically. Sol Bamba began the move in typically cavalier manner; going past two players with some neat touches from his telescopic legs. He passed to Mowatt who beat his man before slotting the ball through to Dallas. In true Eddie Gray fashion, Dallas dropped a shoulder, performed a neat nutmeg on one defender, and then left him and his mate for dead as he got to the by-line. He then squared the ball across for Wood to poke home from two yards and that was pretty much it for the afternoon; the game ended as many had predicted, all square.

I drove home listening to the rest of the football stories unfold on 5 Live, our game having been another early start of course. In the Championship, there were predictably several more draws including Forest at Bolton, Huddersfield at Fulham and MK Dons at Reading. The stand out result was at the Riverside, where Bristol won 1 – 0 to beat a Boro side tipped for promotion; it made our point at Ashton Gate look ever so slightly better. Later that evening, Cardiff beat Wolves 2 – 0, in the final game of this round of matches. Ipswich and Brighton were the early pacesetters with ten points apiece, whilst Rotherham were bottom with just one. Leeds were one of seven teams still unbeaten, along with Derby who, like us, had drawn all four games.

In the days following the Wednesday match, it became clear that the Forestieri deal had stalled; the Italian winger seemingly not keen on joining Leeds and saying he preferred to stay in the south of England. It was a blow. I really did feel we were in need of a boost and needed to add some magic to our hardworking squad. We were as good as most but probably no better than any and hence our recent results. We had more draws than Marks and Spencer and certainly more than any of those hen parties I spotted up at Carlisle the other day; they hardly had a pair between them!

As I continued my drive home, news began to filter through about yet another air disaster. A plane had come down during an exhibition at the Shoreham Air Show in West Sussex. The plane, a vintage Hawker Hunter jet, had crashed on the busy A27 road and ploughed into several vehicles. The crash site was only a matter of a few hundred yards away from the Brighton training ground. As details began to emerge, 11 people were reported to have died at the scene and the pilot,

Andy Hill, was critically ill in hospital; although the fact he survived at all was amazing. As so often is the case, the football world didn't escape and two victims were named as Jacob Schilt and Matthew Grimstone, both 23 year-old members of Worthing United's squad. They were travelling together to their Southern Combination Premier Division fixture against Loxwood that afternoon when their vehicle was tragically struck. Both men were supporters of Brighton, the club where Matthew was employed, most recently as a member of the Amex ground staff. The game was obviously postponed and on Sunday, Worthing United issued this heart-rending statement:

"Worthing United football club players Matt Grimstone and Jacob Schilt are both believed to be among the victims of yesterday's tragic Shoreham air show crash.

Grimbles was our first team goalkeeper, 23 years of age and a huge talent, quiet and reserved but a brilliant player with a huge potential to go further in the game.

Jacob, who was also 23 years of age, small in stature and a tenacious midfielder, also very skilful with an eye for goal.

They were both essential members of last season's double winning squad, the most successful season in the clubs history.

At this point we don't know how or if we will cope with this, Worthing United is a family, part of the football family; we have been moved by the number of tributes to them that we have received from our fellow clubs and from the public.

Our thoughts and prayers are with the families and the friends of Matt and Jacob".[1]

All COC second round ties played the following week held a minute's silence before kick-off as the football community once more came together to pay its respects.

Leeds United 1 Sheffield Wednesday 1 (Matias (37), **Wood (61)**). **22,597** (Wednesday 1,313)

---

[1]   http://www.pitchero.com/clubs/worthingunitedfc/news/official-club-statement-1479073.html

Rams, Romans and Jesus the Chopper

News broke this week that former Leeds director, David Haigh had now been jailed in Dubai following a conviction for a 'breach of trust' while representing GFH Capital as owners of Leeds United prior to the arrival of Massimo Cellino. There was inevitably talk that Haigh would appeal but for the time being he would serve a two year sentence, although since he'd already been incarcerated since May 2014 awaiting trial it was likely he'd be released before the end of 2015.

I'd known since the fixtures came out in June that I'd be missing the Derby game at the iPro Stadium. Despite amassing a sizeable quantity of Brownie points with Mrs W in recent months, there was no way I was brave enough to suggest I might miss her parents' diamond wedding anniversary celebrations in Edinburgh on the weekend of 29th August… which also just happens to be Mrs W's birthday! Hence, on Friday 28th August, Mrs W and I drove up to Edinburgh. To be fair, I wasn't that depressed to be missing the game, although it was the first time I'd not been at a competitive game live, since August 2013, more than two years earlier. There were loads of events going on in Edinburgh as the 2015 Festival season came to its conclusion and several big family dinners were also planned, so it was going to be an excellent few days and the game was live on TV anyway.

No sooner had we arrived, than we were off to a fringe event in the so called Underbelly in Cowgate, a tiny room in the bowels of Edinburgh. The show, 'Arms, Foil and Hogg', was a stand-up comedy act consisting of three Irish lads who were uproariously funny. It was also mildly nerve-wracking, as large parts of the show consisted of pulling members of the audience into the lime-light. Before and after the show we sampled several of Edinburgh's pubs in which my son Adam and I plotted where we'd be watching the Derby game the following day; it was yet another live on Sky TV game, this one with a peculiar 12:05pm kick-off time.

We continued our on-line research on Saturday morning and eventually, using a clever App that my techno savvy sister-in-law downloaded, we established that the game was more than likely to be shown in the Murrayfield Bar, at the bottom of Roseburn near where the A8 crosses the Water of Leith. A quick telephone call to the pub confirmed they had three satellite boxes and, yes, since there was only the Arsenal game at Newcastle that partly clashed with our game, they promised they'd put it on for us.

At the outset, I should say this arrangement did not prove ideal. The first surprise for Adam and I as we walked in was that all the seating had been cleared from the pub; there were just a few tables against the outer walls. The reason was that this pub is near Murrayfield Stadium where the Scottish national rugby union side play their home matches and that afternoon they were hosting Italy in a World Cup warm up game. Whenever Scotland play, this pub gets jam-packed for a couple of hours prior to kick-off. Today, they were scheduled to start at 3:15pm. The place was almost empty when we arrived but there were a couple of bouncers on the door even then.

Adam scanned Twitter to find the team line-up and soon we were both hunched over his iPhone trying to see where the name of Mirco Antenucci had disappeared to. Astonishingly, we eventually spotted he was only on the bench; replaced in the starting eleven by Alex Mowatt. The only other change from the Sheffield Wednesday starting eleven was the return of Lewis Cook in place of Kalvin Phillips, now that Cook's suspension was completed.

Silvestri

Berardi Cooper Bamba Taylor

Cook Adeyemi Mowatt

Byram Wood Dallas

Subs: Antenucci, Murphy, Turnbull, Wootton, Bellusci, Phillips, Doukara.

I've shown the side as a 4 – 3 – 3 formation but it could equally have been 4 – 5 – 1, with Wood up front on his own and the midfield packed to try to deal with the likes of Craig Russell, Tom Ince and Chris Martin in the Derby line-up. I was sceptical about leaving out Antenucci; I felt he'd been our stand out attacking player in recent games, indeed the only player we had who looked to have that spark of invention we were desperate for. I also wondered what Peppe Bellusci must be thinking as he again gave way to Liam Cooper. Maybe he'd be leaving us in these last few days of the transfer window. As Adam flicked through Twitter, we spotted that most people were convinced that the Forestieri deal was dead and indeed there was even talk he'd already signed for Sheffield Wednesday. The good news for Leeds, was that we were now being linked with another exciting forward; 22 year-old DR Congo winger, Jordan Botaka. His profile, like that of 'Fessi', seemed to fit my desire for a player with magic in his boots.

Just a few minutes before kick-off, the three screens in our bit of the pub were switched over to Sky's Championship coverage and we could see the Leeds players lining up on the pitch at the iPro. The commentary was booming out all around the pub, although we could see at the other end of the bar that the screens there had a different channel showing. There were by now a few Scotland fans at the bar, several in kilts, but none was showing much interest in the Leeds game or in Adam's Leeds Rhinos shirt. The Rhinos were playing in the Challenge Cup Final at Wembley later in the day and Adam was wearing their 2015 Cup Final replica shirt.

The atmosphere in the iPro sounded fantastic. Right from the start we could hear the Leeds fans going through their usual repertoire and I could picture in my mind some of the folk I know, doubtless singing their hearts out. Several had already sent me texts, including one suggesting: *"If you're watching on the telly you're a c***."* Mates eh? We'd see later that the iPro was pretty much full, with a reported attendance of 29,386, including 2,335 from Leeds. Throughout the first-half, Adam and I could only hear the Leeds fans and that was probably because in that period we bossed the game.

My fears about leaving Antenucci out were very quickly forgotten and Kentley summed it up pretty much when he texted: *"We've missed Lewis"*. Lewis Cook settled straight back into the side like he'd never been away and it was his familiar little driving runs that he makes from deep that seemed to be causing Derby most problems. He was clearly fired up and I momentarily held my breath as he lifted his boot very high to try to nick a bouncing ball. As Lewis's boot went up, the head of Richard Keogh went down and there was a sickening impact of studs on forehead. Thankfully, the referee saw it for what it was; a genuine attempt to get the ball and there was no sanction against Lewis other than the free kick. Keogh had a nasty looking cut though and there was a lengthy stoppage while he was bandaged up with a 'Kisnorbo' and given a change of shirt. It was four minutes before we were underway again.

Leeds took up where they left off and forced a string of corners and it was mostly one-way traffic. The only problem was that all our efforts missed the target and I was just starting to wonder if we'd pay for our usual lack of accuracy in front of goal. It looked like it would be nil-nil as half-time approached but then, in the 42nd minute, Leeds won yet another corner, albeit luckily. TV replays appeared to show that the ball came off Stuart Dallas last and Adam and I exchanged some raised eyebrows as the referee gave us the decision. Dallas himself took it on our left wing and just tapped it short to Alex Mowatt who gave it straight back. Dallas then clipped in a perfect right foot cross to find Tom Adeyemi in acres of space between two Derby defenders and he guided a perfect header into the corner of the net. Adam and I punched the air and then both looked round sheepishly wondering what the reaction of the locals would be. We needn't have worried; no one else seemed to be interested in the slightest! We noticed the pub was much busier by now though and there were loads of lads in kilts as well as a big group of blokes all dressed as Roman Centurions. We guessed they were on a stag do and as we scanned around the rest of the costumes on show we were pretty sure we'd located the stag; a long haired bloke dressed as Jesus, complete with a white bed sheet as a shroud and huge pieces of wood strapped to his arms and back with shiny black sticky tape by way of a cross. He looked well-oiled too!

While our game was on its half-time break, the Newcastle v Arsenal game commentary suddenly began booming out around the pub. We could see the game was being shown on the TVs at the other end of the bar. When our game restarted, the only commentary we could hear was *still* that coming from St James' Park and it stayed that way as the majority of folk now crammed inside the pub were watching the Arsenal game and not ours; the majority...but not everyone. Jesus was with us.

Jesus by now had spotted the Rhinos jersey and at every opportunity he was singing, *"We're Leeds Rhi-nos, we're Leeds Rhi-nos"*, at the top of his drunken Scottish voice while simultaneously twirling round like a bloody helicopter with those planks strapped to his arms! We were in serious danger of being decapitated if he came any closer! As we swayed out of the way of each revolution, a battalion of Centurions swayed in to try to grab him and pull him away. It was like a scene from 'Life of Brian'! Eventually, a couple of the biggest Romans got Jesus in a bear hug and as they dragged him away, still screeching, *"We're Leeds Rhi-nos"*, at the top of his voice, we spotted some writing inked on his bare back where his makeshift shroud had fallen away. It read simply: *"Jesus is dead!"*

We settled back down to watch the Leeds game and by this time a number of Centurions and some of the kilted Scots were also peering over our shoulders. Whether it was because we no longer had the support of Jesus we'll never know, but in the 48th minute, Derby levelled. To be fair, they'd come out for the second-half looking much more like the Derby we expected to see, with Tom Ince finally starting to get on the ball and pulling our defence around. Ince was involved in the move as Derby passed the ball around confidently, eventually finding Chris Martin right on the edge of the penalty area in the centre of goal. He turned first onto his right foot and then onto his left with Liam Cooper desperately trying to hang on to the Derby man much as those Centurions had tried to restrain our mate Jesus, but to no avail. Martin got himself the space he needed and he hit a low left foot shot into the corner of Silvestri's net. A few Centurions clapped us on the back saying: *"Och bad luck Leeds"*, before they returned to their beer and their marshalling of Jesus.

For the next twenty minutes or so, Derby pummelled us. They attacked us like Bristol did in those final few minutes at Ashton Gate and I was certain we'd eventually cave in, just as we did then. It was all one-way traffic and shots were raining in on the Leeds goal with Sol Bamba once again performing heroics, heading away crosses and blocking shots. Marco Silvestri also earned his wages with a couple of decent saves. Uwe Rösler decided to try something different and sent on his 'M n Ms' again, Murphy and Mirco this time, in place of Byram and Mowatt respectively and this time the substitutions did appear to strengthen rather than weaken us. Byram had once again been very disappointing, almost in a game of his own rather than part of the team and I did wonder if maybe we should have cashed in on him if there had been any offers made. I was sure his position would be in danger if the signing of Jordan Botaka was confirmed.

Antenucci just *looks* dangerous; he's all action and you can see defenders gird their loins whenever he appears. Within four minutes, Ant had sent over a curling ball for Chris Wood but, as so often this season, his heading has not been of the same quality as his footwork and once again Wood's header went over the top. A few minutes later, Derby made their next change and I wondered if the appearance of Darren Bent would be significant. As it happens, this time Bent made little difference and neither did a final change they made when Ryan Shotton appeared. Then, out of the blue, Chris Wood became a legend.

Adam and I had already expressed our satisfaction with a point and we both had our fingers and toes crossed that Derby couldn't repeat what Bristol did in the final seconds. Then Chris Wood took a pass from Lewis Cook. He had his back to goal initially but quickly shifted the ball to his left and took a couple of strides before turning and lashing a curling right foot shot that clipped the right hand post before rippling the net. There was an audible, *"Yes!"* from numerous Centurions as well as the two of us as the ball hit the net and we watched as Wood ran to the touchline and slid down on both knees. It was slightly surreal as the accompanying commentary was still the one from that Arsenal game, so we could only watch and not hear as Sky replayed the goal a couple of times.

The next few minutes seemed to last about an hour as Adam and I refused to accept we had the game won until the final whistle was blown. When it came though, we again punched the air and several of those Centurions were high fiving us and slapping us on the back before they began to make their way out of the bar and on towards Murrayfield. They'd enjoy that too; the home side walloped Italy 48-7. The beer would be flowing until the early hours and kilts would be twirling all over Edinburgh. I did wonder if Jesus was still standing by the end of the night.

Adam and I drank up and made our way back to the in-laws' where we then sat down and watched the Rhinos game, with the rest of the family. The Rhinos were unstoppable and ran up a historic 50 – 0 win over Hull KR, with Tom Briscoe becoming the first man to ever score five tries in a Challenge Cup Final. It was an amazing demonstration of the art of rugby league and it made an already fabulous day even better. Later that night, we had a big family meal in the splendour of a top restaurant in the city, washed down with a few beers and plenty of wine before returning to the house for a final couple of malts. If Carlsberg did Saturdays, they'd undoubtedly be like this one!

We had another big family meal at Mia, an Italian restaurant on Dalry Road in Edinburgh, on Sunday evening and then on Monday night we all went to Princes Street Gardens for the End of Festival Firework Concert. That was another amazing experience; watching fireworks and listening to classical music while sat on the lawn drinking Pimm's and looking up at the imposing structure of Edinburgh Castle. The castle sits atop the huge basalt mass of Castle Rock that rises some 260 feet above Princes Street and in the dark, lit only by the glow of the fireworks, it was some sight. We finished the night with a few beers in a couple of pubs in the city and it was in the Black Cat, a little pub on Rose Street that I spotted on Twitter that Leeds had signed Jordan Botaka. There was just one day to go in the transfer window and this looked to be our final move with no real talk of anyone going out. It looked as though Sam Byram was staying put. I'm sure I wasn't the only Leeds fan hoping that Botaka could provide that bit of magic that might be the final ingredient in this ever improving side. He does after all go by the nickname 'The Wizard'! We'd had so many false dawns in recent seasons that we were all nervous of getting too optimistic too soon but finally, it really did seem that things were looking up. Leeds sat nicely in 10th spot in the table after this result, with seven points; just three behind second placed Hull City and six behind the leaders, Brighton. Rotherham were rock bottom, with a single point still. Leeds were now one of only four sides still unbeaten in the Championship, the others being Brighton, Cardiff and Birmingham City.

There were some eye-opening Championship transfers in the closing hours of the window. Derby spent £10 million bringing Bradley Johnson from Norwich and Jacob Butterfield from Huddersfield, and Sheffield Wednesday not only got Forestieri but also his Watford team mate, Pudil. Watford also shipped out Matej Vydra to Reading. Burnley showed their intent too, as they swooped in for Joey Barton and Andre Gray, both players often mentioned as Leeds targets.

Leeds confirmed the Botaka deal on Tuesday and then reported that Nicky Ajose had left the club having come to a mutual agreement to cancel his contract. He immediately signed for League One club Swindon Town and would start scoring goals for fun!

Derby County 1 **Leeds United 2**, (**Adeyemi (43)**, Martin (48), **Wood (88)**) 29, 386 (**Leeds 2,335**)

Heavy metal it ain't; more like Limp Bizkit...

I spent the weekend of the international break on a little tour of the West Country. I'd spotted that Exeter City had a home game with current League Two leaders, Leyton Orient, on Saturday, while Bristol Rovers hosted Oxford United in a Sunday lunchtime game. These would be grounds 78 and 79 of my 92. Mrs W declined the offer, as of course she'd only recently been in Bristol with me for the City game when it peed down the entire day of the game. So, early Saturday morning, I set off on the 200 mile trip down to Exeter. Predictably, it was a nightmare journey that took me the best part of four hours thanks to a multiple car pile-up between junctions 17 and 18 on the M5. It was unfathomable how drivers can crash into each other when the weather is fine. It just added to my theory that drivers are less focussed when the sun shines.

I still arrived at St James' Park in plenty of time for kick-off and took my place on the 'Big Bank' with the rest of the home supporters behind one goal. With a capacity of around 4,000, the 'Big Bank' is the largest remaining all terraced standing area left in English football. Leyton Orient had got off to a flier this season, having won all five of their opening league games, so I fully expected them to beat Exeter who'd lost two of theirs. But that's why we watch football isn't it? Exeter won a penalty after only five minutes which they scored just down below where I was standing and they never looked back. They eventually ran out 4 – 0 victors.

After that game, I drove up to Bristol where I'd booked myself a single room for the princely sum of £39! I'd scoured the internet for a reasonably priced hotel around Bristol and the Almondsbury Interchange was the only one I could find under £80 or £90 a night. It had some dire online reviews and it looked a tad tired in the pictures but it proved to be perfectly adequate. You probably wouldn't take your other half there for a romantic weekend away, not if you were on a promise anyway, but for a one night stop between games it was perfect. My room was tiny and all the fittings dated from the 70s, including a well-worn and multi-cracked bathroom suite in 'mango' but it was clean, had a telly, kettle, bath and shower and despite being right on the busy A38 was quiet enough. It had a decent little restaurant and bar too and I spent the night in there with my mate San Miguel reading the Exeter programme and watching the X-Factor. Later, on the new Channel 4 show, Football League Tonight, I watched the rest of the day's lower league football. Former Leeds man Nicky Ajose held the limelight in a 3 – 1 win by Swindon, away at Crewe in their League One encounter. Ajose missed an open goal at one point but then made amends later with a goal and an assist. He's a decent player and I could see why various Leeds bosses had persevered with him but at the end of the day his talent is just too erratic and League One is probably his level. I watched in astonishment as another failed Leeds striker, Noel Hunt, scored a fabulous headed goal for Southend too, and then decided I'd had too many lagers as right in front of my eyes Hunt appeared to do a triple back flip as his goal celebration! My mate the Shrimper even messaged me a picture of the 'flipping Hunt'.

The following morning at breakfast, I was asked if I wanted to upgrade to a full-English… *"How much will that be?"* I queried. *"£2"* was the reply. I told you it was cheap! Having gorged myself on the excellent breakfast, I set off on the short journey along the A38 to the Memorial Stadium, home of Bristol Rovers. I parked up just next to The Wellington pub and then walked down the hill to the ground. It is, like Exeter's SJP, what I call a 'real' football ground. It was opened in 1921 as the home of Bristol Rugby Club and has only been used by The Pirates since 1996. The ground is dedicated to local rugby union players killed during the First World War, as evidenced by the stone pillar proclaiming this at the main entrance; hence the name, 'Memorial Ground' or latterly, 'Memorial Stadium'. There's one massive blue grandstand on the East touchline while the stand on the opposite side looks for all the world like a cricket pavilion. I was in the Blackthorn End, with the home supporters, a reasonably sized terraced area. As this was a local (ish) derby with Oxford United, there was a boisterous crowd of just over 7,000, including a good number from Oxford. Both sides had made steady starts to their League Two campaigns with Rovers newly promoted from the conference via the play-offs. I'd spotted in the Rovers programme that they'd signed Adam Drury as a non-contract player a few days earlier and wondered if he'd get a game. Drury, a former Manchester City junior player, had a pre-season trial with Leeds of course and we saw him come on from the bench at York.

It was another excellent game of football. After just 16 minutes, Rovers had a player sent off and they battled manfully to keep the scores level until Oxford were also reduced to ten on the hour mark. Then, somewhat ironically, Oxford took the lead! What a goal it was too, the Oxford number '4', Kemar Roofe, who I'd seen score and then also miss a boatload of chances in that game with Notts County a couple of weeks ago, smashed in a shot from all of 25 yards from the inside left channel to win the game. There was no sign of Adam Drury at all.

The Bristol game had been live on Sky and kicked off at 12:30pm, so I was on the road home just after 3pm. I spent the whole two hour journey listening to Radio 5 Live's preview of the Wales v Israel, Euro qualifier. It was the biggest game in Wales' recent history as a win would have guaranteed them a place at the Euro 2016 finals in France. They'd set this possibility up with a 1 – 0 win in Cyprus the previous Thursday. When I got home, I dashed in to catch the majority of the game on TV, only to then despair that they couldn't finish the job; it ended in a nil-nil draw, when the whole world had been convinced Wales would win. It was like watching Leeds really; failing to perform when everyone thought a win was a certainty. It was still a formality that Wales would qualify as they only needed a single point from their final two group matches one of which was a home game with Andorra.

England made sure of their place in France with a routine 6 – 0 win in San Marino, on Saturday evening, with Wayne Rooney scoring his 49th England goal, a penalty, to equal Bobby Charlton's record tally. In England's second game of this break, against Switzerland, Rooney then broke Charlton's record, scoring another penalty as the home nation won 2 – 0. Northern Ireland were also on the brink of qualification after a 3 – 1 victory in the Faroe Islands and a 1 – 1 home draw with Hungary, while The Republic of Ireland boosted their chances with a 4 – 0 win in Gibraltar and a 1 – 0 home win over Georgia. Stuart Dallas played all bar six minutes of the two NI games but I was certain he'd want to be involved against his old club, Brentford, at the weekend. Scotland, in the same group as the Republic, now looked unlikely to qualify as they lost 1 – 0 in Georgia and then 3 – 2 at home to Germany.

Another busy Leeds player was young Lewis Cook, who played the full 90 minutes for the England U19s as they won 3 – 2 in Germany, despite having Jonjoe Kenny sent off early in the second-half. Thankfully, Cook then only played six minutes as a late substitute in the U19s second game, in Croatia, where they drew 1- 1.

There wasn't much going on during the break in respect of Leeds; Paul Hart was named as our new Academy Manager, a role he held back in the 1990s, and an interview with Steve Thompson was published that added precisely nothing to our understanding of what led to his sacking last season. Perhaps

Steve himself still doesn't understand it. I then read that Adam Drury had already been let go by Bristol Rovers, just a week after they signed him and I wondered what that was all about. I re-read the full page piece in the Rovers programme which ended with Drury noting: *"I'm looking forward to playing for Rovers and I'm sure that I will enjoy my time here."* A week is a long time in football!

There was another legal claim looming against the club as we began to get details of how Lucy Ward was allegedly treated by Massimo Cellino. Ward was Neil Redfearn's partner and had been a leading figure on the academy staff for 17 years when she was removed along with her man a few weeks earlier. The MailOnline published a story this week suggesting that Ward was now bringing a dual case of unfair dismissal and sex discrimination.[1] The allegation was that Cellino, despite publicly appreciating the work Ward was doing for the club, decided that both she and Redfearn had to go and the Italian instructed Adam Pearson to find a way to get rid of her. They came up with a gross misconduct charge for Ward taking more than her allocated holiday allowance to enable her to do some work for the BBC during the FIFA Women's World Cup this summer in Canada. Ward appealed on the grounds she had permission but this was rejected by the club and now she was taking her case to an employment tribunal. Perhaps it was the fact she'd been at the club 17 years that irked Massimo, remembering how he considered that number so unlucky.

Ever since I learned about his apparently irrational fear of the number 17 (which I have documented ad nauseam in previous books) I've become aware of the seemingly disproportionate number of times it crops up in times of adversity and disaster. Only this week I read about another of those inexplicable cases where a double decker bus failed to get under a bridge; this time the roof of a bus was ripped off in Rochdale as a new driver took a wrong turning. The BBC reported that 17 people

---

[1]   http://www.dailymail.co.uk/sport/football/article-3228383/Leeds-looking-controversy-Lucy-Ward-Neil-Redfearn-pursuing-legal-action-against-Championship-club.html

were treated for injury when the number 17 bus collided with the bridge…[1] Make your own mind up whether 17 is unlucky or not. Oh, by the way, Brentford, who were our next opponents, sat 17th in the Championship this week…

Neil Redfearn himself was also in the news this week, as a possible successor to Paul Dickov, who was sacked by Doncaster Rovers.[2] Dickov, who plotted our demise in the COC this season of course, was not quite the first managerial casualty of the season; he was beaten to that honour by Dave Robertson, who got the push from League One Peterborough United, two days earlier. The reason for Dickov's sacking? Well, they had a poor start in the league and were in, ahem, 17th spot after their opening six games…

Virtually everyone was convinced Leeds would beat the Bees from Brentford. Of course there was the inevitable question as to how the international break would affect us; we have a record of coming back from such breaks in a far worse state than we were before them but this time felt different. The Bees had lost against both Burnley and Reading in recent games, whereas we'd managed solid, untroubled draws against both those sides. OK, Brentford had walloped Bristol City 4 – 2 at their place and we know how we messed up down there but even so most of us put that down to a rogue few minutes of panic. There was always that little fear though that we would do what we always do when things are looking positive; screw it up! I was also aware, from my own research that the last time Leeds won a home league game against the Bees, John Charles scored for us and it was before I was even born! Looking at our recent home record also revealed that Elland Road is not exactly a fortress these days and Mr Rösler's so called heavy metal football hadn't really changed that yet. Believe it or not, our record in Saturday home games in 2015 was abysmal; we had won just one game, against Millwall on

---

[1] http://www.bbc.co.uk/news/uk-england-manchester-34198572
[2] http://www.yorkshireeveningpost.co.uk/sport/leeds-united/latest-lufc-news/leeds-united-redfearn-in-running-for-doncaster-job-after-leeds-exit-1-7451916

St. Valentine's Day. Admittedly we don't get that many Saturday games, thanks to Sky TV but you had to go back eight home games, to Wednesday March 4th, for our last home win, against Ipswich.

On the morning of the Brentford game, I spotted on Twitter that there was yet another legal case being prepared against the club. In fact, reading the article delayed my departure about 17 minutes. This time it was our former fitness coach, Matty Pears. I'd been vaguely aware that Pears had not been around since pre-season and now the MailOnline was telling us that he too had been sacked.[1] Pears claimed he had permission from the club to attend his brother's wedding in Portugal during pre-season but apparently Uwe Rösler then complained about his absence. Matty P was accused of professional misconduct and after a hearing at the club he was dismissed. The MailOnline mischievously added that this took place: *"...two days before he was due a £10,000 bonus from last season."* *"Ah! That sounds like a Cellino cost cutting manoeuvre doesn't it?"* I thought to myself. Pears was now likely to take his place in the queue at the employment tribunal to sue for unfair dismissal. I wonder if there is an employment lawyer in Leeds who does bulk discount?

So, anyway, I set off a few minutes later than planned and by the time I reached the M6 I realised that was my first mistake of the day; once again the motorway was at a standstill. I rang home to ask Mrs W to find out what the problem was and after a quick look on the travel news on the Kindle she informed me there had been a big RTC at junction 16. The traffic crawled along for mile upon mile until I reached the scene of the accident which appeared to be a couple of cars that had had an altercation with the Armco at the side of the motorway. To be fair, the rain had been absolutely lashing it down all night and the roads were awash and it showed that my theory of the sun being the only cause of accidents was a bit off the mark. I

---

[1] *http://www.dailymail.co.uk/sport/football/article-3231300/Chelsea-Tottenham-scrap-playing-home-games-Wembley-new-stadiums-built.html*

cursed Twitter for making me set off later than planned; had I not spotted the Matty Pears news I may have got past junction 16 before the accident. Then I thought again; I might then have been *in* the accident!

It was gone 1:30pm when I finally pulled up on Gelderd Road, just outside the Bentley and Lotus showrooms, my latest parking spot of choice. By this time the rain had stopped and the sun was out and it was pretty busy everywhere; it being about an hour and a half later than my normal arrival time. There was a monumental queue for the Pavilion too, another thing I'm not used to seeing. Inside, I grabbed a beer and then joined Pete, Kev and Nigel for a chat. The usual crew were there and I managed to grab five minutes with Derek to check on arrangements for the meet at his and Shirley's home in Milton Keynes the following week. They had very kindly agreed to put on some food in advance of the MK Dons game as they live just outside Milton Keynes. When I returned to our table, Martin pointed out that Ty had arrived and being the friendly chap I am I went over to Ty and proffered my hand. Poor Ty was overloaded with bags and coats and all sorts of stuff and in the process of freeing his right hand to shake mine he dropped his Leeds United superstore plastic bag. There was a sickening crash and the unmistakeable sound of shattering china. Martin and his lads seemed to know immediately what had broken and they were soon holding up pieces of a shattered Leeds United mug. I was feeling terrible at this point but then everyone started to fall about laughing as the tale was told about how this was actually the second mug Ty had bought. He'd bought one on his previous visit to ER and that one had fallen out of the car boot and smashed! I was on the point of offering to get him another one as I felt it was partly my fault when he dashed off to the superstore, returning a few minutes later with a replacement having persuaded the store it was already broken when he bought it.

On the big screens in the Pavilion they had the Everton v Chelsea game on one side and the QPR v Forest game on the other but I hadn't taken much notice of either due to the mug incident. I did spot that Everton beat Chelsea 3 – 1 thanks to a Steven Naismith hat-trick; he'd only come on as a 9th minute substitute! Forest would go onto beat QPR 2 – 1 with two late goals largely thanks to QPR keeper Rob Green getting himself sent off. He's the one who once let his country down.

I didn't hear much of what Terry Yorath and Peter Lorimer had to say either; their little cameo with comedian Jed Stone also took place while the china mug incident was going down. I'd learn later though that Yorath was talking about the fear that many players show when they turn out at Elland Road because of the expectation of the home fans. It was one factor that might explain our poor home results in recent times although this was only our third game at ER so far this campaign so it was way too early to judge if it still applied to the current side. Uwe Rösler named an unchanged starting eleven from that which took the field down at the iPro a fortnight earlier and new signing Jordan Botaka was not even on the bench. Maybe this was a game for getting the 'Wizard' used to the Elland Road experience before he was sent out to cast his spells in public. I was disappointed that Uwe couldn't find room to include Mirco Antenucci in his side although pleased to see that the 'M n M's, 'Murph and Mirco', were both on the bench.

Silvestri
Berardi Bamba Cooper Taylor
Adeyemi Cook Mowatt
Byram Wood Dallas

Subs: Antenucci, Murphy, Wootton, Doukara, Phillips, Turnbull, Bellusci.

As the game kicked off, with Elland Road now bathed in autumnal sunshine and looking superb with over 25,000 in the stands, I couldn't help thinking this was another pivotal game, even this early in the season. We'd seemingly got a bit of momentum together with the win at Derby and we were unbeaten. If we were to have a good season you had to think we needed to now build on the good start with a win over Brentford and probably another against Ipswich on Tuesday night. Predictably though, Leeds did what they always seem to do when things appear to be looking up; they let us down and our miserable home run continued.

Leeds had a decent enough opening ten minutes or so with just a few glimpses of heavy metal football but then our game plan seemed to fade away and we became more Limp Bizkit[1]. Was it due to the expectation of a big home crowd weighing down the players? Was it the inevitable inconsistency of a very young side? Whatever it was, Brentford began to dominate possession and looked far more accomplished on the ball than we did. It wasn't helped by the fact that our normally assured and confident leader on the pitch, Sol Bamba, looked like he'd been out on the beer all night as he twice gave the ball away in dangerous areas. Then, after half an hour, he was in the spotlight again. A hurried clearance was hooked up the Brentford left wing to Alan Judge who then jinked inside leaving Sol Bamba scrabbling around on all fours. Judge slipped the ball to the Bees debutant, Austrian international Marco Djuricin, and he outfoxed Liam Cooper before firing a shot across Silvestri into the bottom corner. It was the first time this season Brentford had scored the opening goal in a game. That set the tone for the rest of the first-half and with the Leeds crowd now getting agitated believing that yet another of our frequent bubbles was about to burst, things didn't look good. As the half-time whistle went there was a chorus of boos from the Kop which was partly aimed at referee Nigel Miller for a less than satisfactory half but more at the Leeds players for a toothless first 45 minutes.

We were all pleased to see that Uwe Rösler changed things round at half-time by bringing on Mirco Antenucci for the struggling Alex Mowatt. Rösler would later comment that the substitution was a precaution as Mowatt had been struggling with a minor knock and had been the mystery player who we'd

---

[1] Founder member Fred Durst allegedly named his band Limp Bizkit, because he wanted a name that would repel listeners. According to Durst, *"The name is there to turn people's heads away. A lot of people pick up the disc and go, 'Limp Bizkit. Oh, they must suck.'* Source, *https://en.wikipedia.org/wiki/Limp_Bizkit*

been told before the game might not feature at all. Leeds were now playing in a clear 4 – 4 – 2 formation, with the Wood and Antenucci partnership resumed but it has to be said it didn't change our fortunes immediately and Brentford won a couple of early corners, albeit they came to nothing. In the 57th minute, Rösler made his second change, introducing Luke Murphy for Tom Adeyemi and suddenly Leeds seemed to have more structure to their play. It still wasn't heavy metal but at least it was a bit more Jaz Rock. Sam Byram suddenly came alive too and he was now frequently involved in a sort of inside right role. Still Leeds looked fragile at the back though; more fragile than Ty's Leeds United mug. In fact, Sol Bamba was not the only player to be having the proverbial 'mare' today. Marco Silvestri looked a bit shaky too. In the first-half he'd sprayed his usual clearance into touch while looking confused by some of his defenders' actions in front of him. Early in the second-half we all held our breath as Marco side-footed the ball out to where he thought Liam Cooper was heading but he put far too much on it and it went straight to Lasse Vibe instead. Vibe slotted the ball into the feet of Djuricin and with Sol Bamba doing his 'after you Claude' thing, almost waving Djuricin through, the Austrian had a clear shot on goal. Thankfully, probably due to the shock of how easily the chance had arisen, Djuricin clipped his shot against the post with Silvestri no more than an interested bystander. In the 62nd minute we all breathed another sigh of relief as the lively Austrian was substituted, with the Bees probably thinking they'd drawn the sting out of Leeds.

Gradually though, Leeds were getting on top. Numerous shots rained in towards the North Stand but our usual lack of prowess in the shooting department meant that more damage was being done to noses in the Kop than the Brentford net. Byram hit one way over the top, Wood put a header over and Luke Murphy smashed one high wide and not very handsomely into row Z. We were all waiting for one to fall at the feet of Mirco Antenucci; the one player we have who seems to be able to hit a ball accurately. It came in the 76th minute.

Chris Wood had just seen a near post effort deflected onto the post by Bees keeper (get it?) David Button and the Brentford area was suddenly a hive of activity. Lewis Cook battled for the ball which was cleared away but only as far as Brentford's substitute, Ryan Woods. Stuart Dallas nailed Woods and after a tussle won it back and quickly passed it forward to Chris Wood. Wood poked the ball through to Antenucci in the inside right channel and Mirco did the rest. The 'Beard to be Feared' performed a side-step that Jonny Wilkinson in his pomp would have been proud of, checked back onto his left foot and curled a sublime shot around the flying Button who was finally undone. It was very similar, if not as far out, as the goal he scored against Burnley on the first day of the season. Mirco raced over to the north-west corner twirling his shirt round his head before releasing it into the air as he took the plaudits of crowd and team-mates while showing off his now half-naked torso. It wasn't quite the physique Billy Sharp showed us last season but the celebrations were just as wild.

Elland Road was rocking now and baying for blood as Leeds pressed for the winner but time after time our shots flew over the bar or on rarer occasions were saved by Button. In the final seconds of added time, Antenucci was away on his own, behind the Bees' back line and we all thought he'd bury the ball in the net just below us to win the game. He ran with the ball from halfway but never looked confident as he tried to place his shot wide of Button. It wasn't wide enough and Button saved easily to his left and that was that.

After the game, Uwe Rösler alluded to that fear of playing in front of a passionate Leeds crowd. *"We lost our fearlessness and we made a mistake..."* he told the BBC. *"Then we were down on confidence and they scored. We looked like we were afraid to get on the ball; that can happen. We deserved to trail at half-time. The last 25-30 minutes we battered them in a football sense and could have won the game. I think it was a fair result for two teams who wanted to win."*[1] I couldn't argue

---

[1] *http://www.bbc.co.uk/sport/0/football/34160340*

with any of that and it was a joy to see both sides continue to try to win the game rather than attempt to run the clock down.

As I meandered back to the car after the game, most conversations I overheard had the phrase, *"we're still unbeaten"*, in them somewhere. In fact, we were still one of those four sides in the Championship yet to lose; Brighton, Cardiff and Birmingham had all won today while we were drawing. But it was patently obvious that draws alone are not good enough in the Championship; we'd now drawn five out of six but we all knew that in the unlikely event a team drew all their games in a season, they'd probably be relegated on 46 points. Nevertheless, if Leeds could manage to beat Ipswich, at Elland Road on Tuesday night, then a haul of 11 points from seven games would represent a satisfactory start. It would also be a bit of a coincidence that Ipswich were the last side we beat at ER, having had eight failed attempts since that Wednesday night last March.

After the Brentford game, Leeds sat 11th in the table, with Brighton, the team of the moment, four clear at the top with 16 points having beaten the side that started the day second, Hull City.

The big result of the weekend was a 5 – 1 thumping of Ipswich by Reading; the first four goal winning margin of this Championship season. Only two games had ended with a three goal margin out of the 70 games played so far, reflecting once again just how tight the division continued to be. So, Ipswich will be smarting; who did I say we play next? Ipswich Town manager Mick McCarthy and his assistant Terry Connor were both at Elland Road for the Brentford game and wouldn't have seen anything to frighten them too much.

Leeds United 1 Brentford 1 (Djuricin (29), **Antenucci (76))**
25,126 (Brentford 621)

Jigsaw

Determined not to get caught up in any more motorway chaos, I set off back up the M6 on Tuesday really early. I left the house at 2pm and was sat in the car outside the Bentley showroom on Gelderd Road ogling the motors by 4pm. I sat there listening to the radio for three quarters of an hour as I was sure the Pavilion wouldn't yet be open. There were frequent clips of Jeremy Corbyn, the new leader of the Labour Party, as he addressed the TUC conference. Then they had the author Frederick Forsyth on, talking about his memoires that he'd just published. Then they linked the two by asking Forsyth about Corbyn. 'He's a well-meaning bloke but he thinks there's a Utopia out there' was the gist of his reply... I went in search of my own Utopia, a Leeds win at Elland Road.

There weren't many in the Pavilion when I got there; Steve was there of course, I think he's got a room! It's probably why there's a shower in the gents; honestly, there is. Eventually George, Trev and Tony joined us and a bit later Jacqui and Mick arrived. The talk was all about whether Uwe would ditch his 4 – 3 – 3 and include Antenucci in his starting eleven. We were all convinced he had to but Uwe had said over the weekend that Mirco had asked not to play on the wing so it was difficult to fit him in the 4 – 3 – 3 if Chris Wood played and that was the formation he preferred. He even got a bit shirty with a reporter saying he didn't want to spend every interview debating whether he should play one or two strikers. In the end Uwe seemed to placate everyone by naming both Mirco and Luke Murphy in the side. It was therefore the side that finished the game on Saturday reasonably well but with Adeyemi in and Byram out.

Silvestri
Berardi Bamba Cooper Taylor
Dallas Murphy Adeyemi Cook
Wood Antenucci

Subs: Turnbull, Mowatt, Byram, Wootton, Phillips, Doukara, Bellusci.

Steve Hodge was doing the little compere spot in the Pavilion today and he interviewed the now usual pairing of Peter Lorimer and Terry Yorath. Hodge of course did a stint for Leeds on the pitch in the early 90s, playing 54 times and scoring 10. Yorath pulled no punches in his assessment of our performance against Brentford. *"Let's be honest"*, he began, *"we were crap"*. He then went on to say that in his opinion we had no leader at the club, no real captain, someone with real leadership qualities that the players respected and who could lead the troops into battle. We all assumed he meant a Billy Bremner type figure but we all also agreed they broke the mould when Billy passed on. There will never be another Billy Bremner. Yorath's outspoken comments certainly got the conversation going around our table and I did wonder if we would ever see him in the Pavilion again if his words got back to the club hierarchy. A bed shared with a horse's head was his likely penance.

Nigel and I wandered over to the ground and we took our seats just as the players were coming out. Elland Road was looking surprisingly well populated, with just over 21,000 inside, including 520 Town fans who'd made the long journey from East Anglia. The players formed two huddles either side of the centre circle and then when they broke away Marco Silvestri did his familiar routine of quick little steps and then his run and jump to touch the crossbar before clutching his right hand goalpost and giving it a quick peck like he probably greets his mother. I hoped he'd put the nerves he showed on Saturday out of his mind.

For whatever reason, Leeds never got started in this game. We were no worse than Ipswich but equally we were no better. It was another closely fought encounter with few moments of quality on show and it was always going to be a nil-nil draw. Either that or one side would profit from a mistake or a moment of brilliance. That's the way the vast majority of Championship games are decided. There was plenty of pace about the game as both sides probed for an opening but quality there was not. We were all a bit concerned that as early as the 6th minute Sol Bamba picked up a yellow card when he arrived about a day too late for a tackle out on the Ipswich left wing. After his poor game on Saturday the last thing he or we needed now was a red card. As we approached the half-hour mark, neither keeper had been given much to do. Then, in the 32nd minute, Leeds committed footballing suicide again.

A nothing ball bounced up high in the Leeds penalty area, just yards in front of me at the Kop end. There was no Ipswich pressure and it should have been a simple ball for Marco Silvestri to come and gather; except Marco wasn't moving. He was neither moving nor talking as Liam Cooper had a split second to ponder what to do with the bouncing ball. He decided there might be someone lurking behind him and he headed it wide of the post for a corner. Silvestri looked at Cooper and shrugged as if to say, *"That's OK, it's only a corner..."* But Leeds have a habit of compounding errors and with the Kop angrily blaming Silvestri for not gathering the ball we were all clearly nervous about what might follow. We were right to be nervous. As the ball floated across from our right, Silvestri could be seen stretching out to try to fist the ball away... but he seemed to miss it completely and in a flash the ball is lobbed back the other way and we all began to shout

"Nooooooooooooh" as we see the Ipswich defender Tommy Smith, unmarked by the post. Time seemed to stand still as we waited for the ball to reach the head of Smith and then the air was thick with expletives as his header rippled the net.

It was another classic piece of Leeds United non-defending; the whole episode, from conceding the corner to Silvestri missing the floated ball as it flew across his six-yard area; the Leeds player on the back post who was too slow to boot it away allowing an Ipswich foot instead to lob it back towards the other post; the fact that Smith was completely unchallenged as he rose to head the ball in the net over the huge figure of Chris Wood who'd raised himself no more than a millimetre off the ground. If anyone wanted a training video of how not to defend; they need look no further. The rest of the half played out to an audio backdrop of disgruntled Leeds fans bemoaning their lot with the name Silvestri and the words, *"useless twat"*, often uttered in the same sentence. In my mind I could hear the Twitter devotees getting their Silvestri jokes ready; *"They've nicknamed him Jigsaw in the dressing room; he falls to pieces in the box." "I think he's got Teflon gloves on; nothing sticks!"* and *"He's worse than Dracula at dealing with crosses!"* There were a few boos again as the players trooped off at half-time.

There were no changes in personnel during the break and the game became very disjointed in the early stages of the second-half with a few injury stoppages and with neither team able to get the ball down and under control for very long. Just around the hour mark, Uwe made his first change, as Sam Byram replaced Stuart Dallas and then ten minutes later another ineffective Tom Adeyemi performance was brought to an end as Alex Mowatt was brought on. Ipswich already had their game management heads on as they wasted time, seemed to go down far too easily for free kicks and then took an age over a couple of substitutions. The Leeds fans were getting more and more vociferous. A couple of times, Leeds tried to bring the ball out of defence but couldn't find a forward pass so they turned and pushed it all the way back to Silvestri. Each time, the Kop booed and gesticulated and a chant of *"Attack, Attack, Attack-Attack-Attack"* broke out and then, as if some of the fans realised this probably wasn't helping, someone started a *"We are Leeds"* chant and then MOT. The South Stand fans were doing their best to rouse the troops too but there was precious little happening on the pitch to keep the fans momentum going and each chant petered out quickly. Time was now running out and we could sense that our season was about to be transformed from 'unbeaten' to 'poor start'. That awful recent home record was looking like it was going to last at least into October; by then it would be over seven months since we'd seen a home win. Then, with five minutes of normal time remaining we were up on our toes as a ball was played through a static Ipswich back line and Sam Byram was through on goal in the inside right channel. He had a defender behind him but he looked to have the legs to get free and we were all waiting for him to shoot an angled shot past the keeper. Instead, Sam flies spread-eagled to the turf. *"Penalty"* is the obvious conclusion of 20,000 Leeds fans and the shout echoes around the ground and there is the usual cheering and hollering that always greets the award of a penalty to Leeds. But something is not right this time and we can see the referee running at speed towards Sam Byram with a yellow card held aloft like some sort of little glowing torch. Sam was being booked for a dive! All hell broke loose then as the reality began to sink in. A chant of *"The Football League's corrupt!"* and *"The referee's a c***!"* went up in quick succession and then, *"We always get sh** refs!"* You can tell how bad we thought this decision was as the ref is usually only branded a *"wan***"* not a *"c***!"* None of us really had any clue whether Sam had dived or not and even when Kentley, who'd come down to join us at half-time, scrolled through Twitter on his iPhone, there was no conclusive evidence. Half the posts seemed to say it was a stonewall penalty and half said dive. I've now watched the incident a couple of dozen times on videos on the internet and I still can't decide, so you can tell how difficult it was for the referee but on balance my best conclusion is that there was probably the most minimal of contact and Sam made a meal of it. Whatever, it's history now. We lost the game 1 – 0 and the debate over the penalty raged on Twitter for days. It helped fans avoid focussing on the real issue, which was that we didn't play very well at any time during the game. With the transfer window now closed and few if any further new names likely to appear in the loan window, I was concerned that we didn't have enough quality in our ranks even to ensure a mid-table finish this season. We still had the same fragile defence we've had all year; we had a goalkeeper capable of making basic errors; we seemed to make fewer chances than other teams; and we seemed to get fewer of *our* chances on target. One shot on target was all we registered against Ipswich. It was another dark, dark night at Elland Road. We'd end the day in 14th spot with 8 points, just 3 points off the bottom three but a whopping 11 points already behind table-topping Brighton. They were the only side to maintain their unbeaten record this Tuesday, with Leeds, Birmingham and Cardiff all losing. Middlesbrough and Burnley now joined Brighton in the top three followed by Hull, Ipswich and Cardiff. We looked a long way off the pace at this point and there was plenty of room for improvement; as everybody knows, that's the biggest room of all!

As I sped back down the motorways of northern England towards home, I listened to the Radio 5 Live summary of the night's Champions League coverage. Both Man City and Man United lost their opening games but the main news was that Luke Shaw had suffered a nasty leg fracture in United's 2 – 1 defeat at PSV Eindhoven. They played a clip of Louis van Gaal speaking about Shaw's injury and he sounded almost in tears. A few minutes later and I was almost in tears too as it was announced: *"Leeds United have been beaten at home by Ipswich tonight and news is coming through that Executive Director, Adam Pearson, has left the club..."*

Leeds United 0 Ipswich Town 1 (Smith (32))
21,312 (Ipswich 520)

MK Dons

A dam Pearson's open letter[1], published on the OS after the Ipswich game, gave no detailed clues as to why he was walking away. It was interesting though that he used the term *"taking a break"* rather than telling us he was going for good. What did that mean? As with all things Leeds United it didn't seem straight forward. There was social media speculation that it was just that he needed time to focus on his personal life (he was apparently going through a divorce) and on his interest in Hull FC, the rugby league outfit he owns. There was the inevitable speculation that Pearson had completed the job he went in to do – not that any of us knew what that was! Some reckoned he'd now found a buyer and would pocket a hefty fee from Cellino for that but no one seemed to be ready to move in. We did all know that Cellino had three court cases looming in Italy in October, so it was not beyond the bounds of possibility that our maverick Italian was

---

1

http://www.leedsunited.com/news/article/r3no0iv3tb6713tu2zrm71gs
g/title/an-open-letter-from-adam-pearson

preparing to sell before he was banned again. The 'Lucky 23' tax evasion case, the corruption case revolving around the building of the IS Arenas stadium in Cagliari and a non-payment of tax on player transfers in Italy were all being heard soon.

There isn't much time during a Championship season to pause for breath outside of the international breaks and so we didn't have long to think about that dire performance against Mick McCarthy's men before we were setting off for Milton Keynes. Over 6,000 Leeds fans were making the trip and initially at least I wondered if we might steal the league attendance record for the 'Stadium mk' from current holders Wolves. They took 8,800 to Milton Keynes in March 2014 and helped record a total crowd of 20,516 for the stadium, a figure only surpassed by a League Cup game with Man United that brought in 26,969 which you will be pleased to note the Dons won 4 – 0!

I'd bought a return train ticket for this trip several weeks ago for the very reasonable price of £17; the only downside being a 7:48am departure from Stafford. So, still sleepy, I settled down in my seat and watched as the fields sped by, the scene outside looking ever so slightly eerie as the morning sun tried to force its way through a heavy mist.

I had an invite to join Shirley and Derek and a few more Leeds fans for pre-match drinks and food at their home just outside Milton Keynes but arriving at Milton Keynes station at just after 9am I decided that was a bit early to impose, even though Shirley had assured me they'd be up and about any time after eight. Instead, I grabbed a coffee from the Pumpkin Café Shop on the station foyer and sat there with my plastic carrier bag containing my six cans of Red Stripe and a bottle of white wine I'd brought for the pre-match party.

I love just watching the world go by; it's the consequence of doing psychology and sociology as part of my degree all those years ago in Manchester. I'm just fascinated by people and the way the world works. This morning, passing through Milton Keynes Station, it was a little cameo of Saturday morning life in the UK. There was the inevitable hen party, presumably heading for London. This one was slightly weird in that there seemed to be one bloke amongst them, looking very awkward. Maybe it was the soon to be groom, although he appeared not to be specifically with the obvious bride to be who, despite being dressed in jeans like all the rest of the girls, wore a little bridal head-dress. No doubt once they arrived at their destination they'd all get their short flowery dresses and platform shoes on before tottering up the West End. There were the inevitable football fans, setting off for games all over the country. A couple stood nearby wore Man City scarves and were obviously going up north for the weekend as they carried suit bags and the wife had a black overnight bag. City faced West Ham at the Etihad later today. Bizarrely, a bloke wandered by in a Stoke City shirt, presumably doing the reverse trip to me and heading to the Potteries for their home game with Leicester.

I scanned the headlines on the newspapers stacked neatly on a news-stand outside the café, always a good way to keep up with world events. *"X FACTOR CHERYL AND RITA IN LESBO 3-SOME SHOCK"*, was the Weekend Sport's contribution while, *"CORRIE BLOODBATH"* was seemingly the most important thing going on according to the Daily Mirror. The big news of the moment was the migrant crisis, whereby thousands of Syrians were escaping the terror being waged by the so-called IS terror group in their country for the prospect of a new life in Europe. There had been some scepticism voiced that folk from many other countries were using the opportunity of the border chaos to make their own dash for a new life and the Daily Mail headline I could see suggested: *"4 OUT OF 5 MIGRANTS AREN'T SYRIANS."* I contemplated buying a copy of the Weekend Sport on the off-chance there were some photos to go with their main story…

Having finished my coffee and decided not to invest in a Weekend Sport, I hailed a taxi from the rank outside and headed to Chez Shirley and Derek. I lost about a pound in sweat in the four-wheeled sauna that doubled as a taxi and was happy to hand over my £13 to the Indian driver who proceeded to put a jacket on before driving off; presumably he hadn't realised I'd opened a window.

Shirley was hanging a Leeds United flag on the balcony when I got there so it would be easy to spot by guests as they arrived. Derek pulled into the driveway just after; he'd been despatched to buy extra burger buns as news had come through that Big Clive was calling in with seven mates. I've seen Clive at games myself in the past; often carrying cardboard trays piled high with hot dogs and burgers so I could understand Shirley's reasoning!

I was first to arrive, so after a tour of the house, Shirley, Derek and I settled down around their huge circular table on the patio and we cracked open our first beers of the day. It was a perfect way to enjoy pre-match drinks with mates. Over the next few hours around twenty or so arrived albeit all those journeying from the South met varying degrees of trouble on the M25 and several were delayed. Eventually though, Dave, Simon and Viv, Big Clive, Wayne, Cliff, Phil, Chris and little Harry and many more arrived and enjoyed the last of the summer sun.

Just after 2pm, Chris spotted the team news on Twitter.

Silvestri
Wootton Bamba Cooper Taylor
Murphy Cook Mowatt
Byram Wood Dallas

Subs: Turnbull, Berardi, Bellusci, Adeyemi, Phillips, Antenucci, Botaka.

So, there were three changes from the side that capitulated against Ipswich; Wootton, Mowatt and Byram starting in place off Berardi, Adeyemi and Antenucci. It was back to $4 - 3 - 3$ for Uwe with no place for the unlucky Mirco and we assumed Berardi was being rested. Rösler would confirm this to be the case after the game, saying that Wootton had done well when he came in at Doncaster so it was a luxury to be able to give Gaetano a rest. We got a first sight of Jordan Botaka as he warmed up with the squad down below us and Marco Silvestri was still first choice despite his clanger on Tuesday. Even Uwe had mentioned during the week that players could not continue to make mistakes without consequences and we were all sure that was a veiled warning to the young keeper to sort his act out.

There was a tad of confusion outside the stadium as I queued at 'gate number 1' as per the instruction printed on my ticket. Everyone in front of me was being turned away and sent to 'gate number 2'! I dutifully turned around and headed for gate '2'. At gate '2' there was a steward trying to turn us back to gate '1'! *"No, no"*, we tell him, *"your mate over there says we have to come in here!"* Eventually his mate arrives and explains: *"It's alright mate, they do this every game; it's a printing error."*

Stood inside the 'Stadium mk', it looked impressive; grey, but impressive. Leeds were later said to have had 6,297 fans there in a total crowd of 19,284, so just failing to beat that figure reached for the Wolves game in 2014. The place has an official capacity listed as 30,500, so there were still plenty of empty seats in the upper tier but with so many Leeds fans the atmosphere was electric. All we needed now was a decent performance and three points for a near perfect day.

Roared on by a raucous Leeds following that stretched all the way from the corner to my right around the one on my left, Leeds began brightly with Alex Mowatt having an early shot blocked and Charlie Taylor sending a shot from all of 35 yards past the post. But from then on, the home side began to dominate and the Leeds choir got quieter and quieter as all the action was taking place in the half nearest to us. For whatever reason, MK Dons were able to press forward and they fashioned numerous shots that peppered Silvestri's goal. It was just starting to feel like so many occasions in the past when Leeds have taken a huge following only for the team to let us down with a less than satisfactory performance when after half an hour, Charlie Taylor burst down the left wing, just inside the Dons' half. He ran right around the outside of Carl Baker towards the by-line and then from behind, Baker gets his timing all wrong and his sliding tackle clears our man out. The referee is only a couple of yards behind the incident and we can all see him bent almost double straining to keep his eyes on the two players while he makes his mind up. It seemed to take an age but eventually he threw out his right arm and pointed at the spot. As always, we celebrated the award of the kick like we would a goal, but then we we were all looking around to see who'd take the kick. Our number one spot kick man was Mirco Antenucci and he was sat on the bench. It was Chris Wood who already had the ball tucked under his right arm.

That game at Doncaster was still pretty fresh in our memories and even in the last few days I'd seen tweets reminding us that the spot-kick taken by Wood that day had still not returned to earth. Indeed, NASA was still trying to locate its orbit. Woody looked confident enough as he strode up to the ball this time though and he neatly side-footed the kick to the keeper's left as he dived away to his right; the left side as we looked on. Now we could celebrate properly! Once the initial cheering and fist-pumping had died down a new chant sprung up: *"All you need is Wood, la, la, la-la-la, all you need is Wood, la, la, la-la-la, all you need is Wood, Wood, Wood is all you need"*. 'All you need is Love', was released by the Beatles in 1967, decades before many of the lads now borrowing the tune were even born; I was ten years old and can remember it coming out.

The disappointment the Dons must have felt didn't appear to diminish their appetite for the game at all and they took up where they left off minutes earlier. They won four corners in as many minutes and we were all now urging our defenders to pick up their respective men and defend for their lives. The young lad stood next to me was clearly not a big fan of Scott Wootton and every time the ball went near the ex-Man U player, he'd get a torrent of abuse usually ending in, *"...you useless scum tw**!"* Then Scotty made a brilliantly timed tackle to give away another corner and his former abuser was cheering him madly and starting up a *"There's only one Scotty Wootton"* chant! Silvestri was making his abusers look a bit silly too as he pulled of another fine save to turn a shot onto the post.

The game was heading for half-time by now, and suddenly our man Charlie was careering down the left wing again. He burst through a tackle and just kept going round the outside of a second defender. This time he just let fly with his left foot and the ball arrowed across the face of the MK keeper and nestled in the bottom corner. How the Leeds fans loved that one! It all felt a bit like Fulham away last season when we ended up winning 3 – 0 despite being played off the park. The Dons shook themselves down once more and continued to press right up to half-time. At one point Sol Bamba clearly handled the ball in the area right in front of us, fair punched it away really, and the referee waved play on. This was clearly going to be our day.

At half-time, hundreds of Leeds fans gathered in the concourse behind our seats. The nature of the layout means that you can actually see through the back of the stand below the lower and upper tiers and Nigel and I were sat in row DD, quite near the top of the lower section. All through the half-time interval the Leeds fans chanted and banged on the metal barriers of the concourse. *"All Leeds aren't we!"* echoed around the stadium while one brave lad climbed across a beam high up in the roof of the concourse. All around us lads were trying to capture the antics on their mobile phones. The chanting back there was still going on as the second-half got underway.

Still the home side was driving forward but Marco Silvestri was as good today as he was bad on Tuesday and somehow he kept getting in the way of whatever the Dons threw at him. If Silvestri missed the ball it invariably struck the woodwork. Leeds were not without chances though as the full on pressure from MK did leave gaps at the back but as usual our finishing was dire. MK made their first two changes 12 minutes into the second-half bringing on Simon Church and Ben Reeves and while these changes were being made we could see hundreds of fans leaving the MK section over to our left and moving instead to the Leeds area next to it. A great long crocodile of fans made the move to a chorus of, *"You're just a town full of Leeds fans"*, and, *"You're Leeds and you know you are."* Several of them were now revealing Leeds shirts and scarves. Whether they were included in the 6,297 said to be the Leeds contingent, I have no idea.

A third MK substitution was made in the 72nd minute and then, a minute later, they were back in the game and my Scotty Wootton hating friend on my right was going ballistic. Chris

Wood limply lost possession in the centre circle and then Josh Murphy initially left Wootton for dead but our man didn't give up the chase and as Murphy reached the penalty area Scotty was right there with him again. Murphy got a yard of space though and hammered the ball across the face of goal, dissecting Silvestri and Sol Bamba at the near post and finding two MK attackers, either of whom could have tapped the ball home while both Liam Cooper and Charlie Taylor ball-watched. The crucial touch was applied by Simon Church. Finally, the rest of the stadium came alive, while all around me the only words I could hear were, *"Bristol City"*. Surely that wouldn't happen to us again would it? It all looked very similar to that dark night at Ashton Gate. Leeds were in panic mode again, thinking that the best form of defence was to keep launching the ball up-field even though we had eleven players behind the ball. Inevitably it kept coming back with interest.

Within minutes of the MK goal being scored, Leeds made their first change as Tom Adeyemi came on for Alex Mowatt. It was clearly a move to add some muscle to our midfield and to try to hold on to the three points. Then it looked as though the task would be made a little bit easier as the home side was reduced to ten men. Samir Carruthers tried to thread a short ball through to the right wing, deep in Leeds territory but Stuart Dallas read it and cleverly intercepted and then instantly touched it inside to Adeyemi. The problem was though, Carruthers couldn't stop and he ploughed into Dallas after the ball had gone, much as Lewis Cook did to get himself red carded up at Doncaster. Sure enough the referee reacted the same way and off went Carruthers for the last 13 minutes plus added time. There would be plenty of that too as the Leeds fans refused to send the ball back each time it flew into our section. If that friendly alien had been here again, he'd never have guessed that Leeds had one player more than MK did. If anything he'd have said it was the other way round as Leeds were pulled all over the place with some smart MK passing. Rösler sent on Peppe Bellusci, replacing Tom Adeyemi, deep into added time and we winced at the thought of the mad Italian centre back doing do something daft. Is he really the best we have in this sort of a situation?

In the final seconds of the game, MK won their 13th corner of the afternoon and this time up went their goalkeeper, David Martin. As the ball floated into our six-yard box, Silvestri was rooted to the spot on his line as the ball appeared to bounce against Liam Cooper and out to safety. Mirco Antenucci gathered it and eventually sent it down the right wing where Lewis Cook was now haring towards goal with David Martin doing his best to keep up. Initially of course the goal was empty and we were imploring Cook to try his luck from distance but he kept running and running until he reached the penalty area, still with Martin in close proximity. Another defender had also got back by this time as well and when Cook did eventually shoot the defender was able to deflect it away. Peppe Bellusci was following up but could only scissor kick the bouncing ball over the side netting. Had Cook spotted Peppe earlier and slid the ball inside to him instead of shooting, it was a certain goal for the Italian. There was time for one more MK attack but as that broke down the referee finally brought the game to an end.

By the skin of our teeth we got to the finishing line with our slender one goal lead intact. But this had been a mighty close run thing and I'm sure MK will have wondered how they had not got at least a point from it. As I sat on the train going home, I studied the other results from the afternoon's games. Top of the table Brighton had drawn 0 – 0 at Wolves while the team in second place now was Boro who had an impressive 2 – 1 win at Forest. Rotherham remained bottom on goal difference from Bristol City, despite the Yorkshire side pulling off the shock of the day beating Cardiff. Leeds were in 10th with eleven points, just three points off a gaggle of teams fighting for third spot on 14 points. Our next game was a tough looking one; second placed Middlesbrough at the Riverside, live on Sky TV next Sunday.

MK Dons 1 **Leeds United 2 (Wood (31, pen), Taylor (43),** Church (74))
19,284 (**Leeds 6,297**)

Deflated

"Sam Byram is the only one that maybe thinks Leeds is too small for him.
"He maybe thinks he deserves to be in a bigger team and a bigger club and maybe he's right. But when I hear that a player from Leeds, with his agent, that he thinks that Leeds is not big enough for him, that he wants something bigger, I felt really embarrassed."[1]

That was Massimo Cellino, speaking in his usual garbled language to Sky Sports in the run up to the Middlesbrough game. Cellino was commenting on continuing rumours that Sam Byram was wanting out of Leeds having been unwilling to sign the contract he'd been offered, rumoured to be at a reduced weekly rate to the one he was already on. It was an issue that appeared to divide Leeds fans right down the middle; don't they all? On the one hand, there were those who felt Sam was vital to our future and that Cellino was just reverting to type now his moderator, Adam

---

[1]   http://www.yorkshireeveningpost.co.uk/sport/leeds-united/latest-lufc-news/leeds-united-byram-too-big-for-his-boots-cellino-1-7475164

Pearson, had flown the coop. On the other hand, some fans pointed to the lack of form shown by Byram this season, the fact that no formal offer had ever been received and the fact it was now public knowledge that the Leeds wage bill was nearer £14m this season, down from over £20m a year earlier. That was said to be more manageable and sensible for a mid-table Championship outfit. I felt that if the new contract was around £10,000 or £12,000 a week as was rumoured then that was more than enough for a 22 year-old who was no longer guaranteed a start. It was something that obviously wouldn't be helping dressing room morale though and that was a concern. It was an issue not likely to be solved until the next transfer window opened in January.

One player definitely coming into Leeds was Will Buckley, the Sunderland winger. The BBC broke the news this week that the two clubs had agreed a 93-day loan deal and it would be signed on Friday 2nd October to ensure he'd be available right through to the New Year. Buckley was already training with Leeds but would not be available to play until after the Middlesbrough game.[1]

It was this week that I remembered I hadn't yet seen the Edinburgh Festival Joke of the Year winner, something I look forward to every year. I Googled it and was then disappointed. The winner was Darren Walsh with: *"I just deleted all the German names off my phone. It's Hans-free."* You can probably now share my disappointment. Scanning down the top ten I found number four far funnier: *"What's the difference between a 'hippo' and a 'Zippo'? One is really heavy; the other is a little lighter."*

To satisfy my football hunger this week, the only game I could find that was a sensible distance away was Notts County v Crawley Town. I'd already ticked Meadow Lane off my 92 but it was many years ago and I haven't actually got any evidence such as a ticket or a programme, so I decided to do it again. I'm pleased I did; it was another great game, with County coming back from a goal down to win 4 – 1. Before the match,

---

[1] *http://www.bbc.co.uk/sport/0/football/34321091*

I headed to the Notts County Social Club and persuaded Alan, the doorman, I was neutral enough to be allowed in. It's supposed to be for home fans only. It's the place I've usually been before each of our games at Forest. Chatting with Alan, he said he'd look out for me on Boxing Day when we were due at the City Ground. He also looks after the away end at Forest for their home games.

Boro was never going to be an easy game; they sat second in the table having won five of their eight in the league and this week they stuffed Wolves 3 – 0 in the COC, having made seven changes from the team that won at Forest at the weekend. Nevertheless, I travelled in optimistic mood. Last season no one gave us a hope; Boro sat top of the table when we went there in February but an early Alex Mowatt goal and then a defensive effort to rival Custer's last stand saw us steal all three points. I reckoned we'd need something similar this time although my researches also told me that since Boro had been at the Riverside, we'd only lost once in 13 visits. I love the Boro trip as it's always a chance to see our friends in Darlington; Sheila and Brian.

Mrs W and I drove up to 'Darlo' on Friday without drama and then on Saturday morning were in the car again en route for Newcastle. We were giving Sheila and Brian a lift, as they were doing the Newcastle v Chelsea game, a 5:30pm kick-off. Mrs W and I were going to spend the day shopping in Newcastle. But that plan came to an abrupt end as we suffered a blow out on the A1(M). I brought the car to a halt on the hard shoulder without any problem and then we began the process of changing the wheel. I used to drive 40,000 miles a year, every year when I was working and in all that mileage I never had a single puncture, so this was a new experience for me. Suffice to say, it didn't go well. I got all the wheel nuts off easily enough but could not budge the wheel; it was stuck fast. We were on the point of ringing for help when eventually a patrol vehicle pulled in behind us. The patrolman's guess was that the wheel was *"welded"* on with corrosion, even though the car was only twelve months old. His solution was to give the recalcitrant wheel a good *"bash"* with the spare and after several *"bashes"* it finally came loose. It was then a straight forward job to put the spare wheel on but since it was one of those space saver efforts, we decided to return to 'Darlo' and let Sheila and Brian do their Newcastle trip by train while we sorted out a new tyre. It was not a good start to our few days in the North East but S and B eventually got to their game and Brian was sanguine about the 2 – 2 result (Brian is a Chelsea fan) as Chelsea had been 2 down at one point. They'd not had the best of starts to the season and already media commentators were writing them off and suggesting Mourinho was likely to be sacked any moment.

Our game at Boro was a Sunday lunchtime kick-off and it was yet another one being shown live on Sky. Although I'd sorted the car tyre out on Saturday afternoon, I still decided to take the train to Boro; it would mean I could have a few pints. So, just as I did the previous season, I walked up to Darlington's main railway station at the top of Victoria Road, guided by the splendid clock tower that rises above the main entrance, bought my ticket and then made my way to platform 3.

The electronic boards were showing the 9:25am to Middlesbrough was *"On Time"* but as the clock ticked on to 9:27 and then 9:28, there was no sign of a driver for the two carriage train stood in the little siding labelled 'Platform 3'. I wasn't alone; there were about two dozen folk waiting on platform 3, many in red Middlesbrough shirts and scarves. We were all nervously surveying each other to see if anyone was panicking. Then, someone spotted the electronic boards were now showing our train as the one on Platform 2, another little siding adjacent to Platform 3. We all dutifully jogged around to the train on Platform 2 and climbed aboard. But no sooner had I sat down than I then heard a voice telling everyone that the train for Middlesbrough was the one now pulling into Platform 3! This was the Trans-Pennine Express via York. Up we all got again and once more we jogged around to Platform 3, looking for all-the-world like we were playing some sort of giant game of musical chairs! The scene on this train was chaotic. As I stepped up into a carriage, I was almost knocked back by the alcohol fumes! I hadn't yet twigged that this was the train from York and hence the one many Leeds fans would be on. At first I assumed the dozens of lads sprawled all over the carriage floor and sat on the tables were Boro fans but I soon realised my error as we got going and the lads in the carriage next door broke into a rendition of the new Chrissy Wood song:

"Oh, Chrissy Wood is magic; he wears a magic hat,
He should have signed for Wolves, but he said f*** to that!
He scores them with his left foot,
He scores them with his right,
And when we get pro-mo-tion we'll sing this song all night!"

Funny as this was, I can't condone the state these lads left the train in when we all got off at Boro. There were cans everywhere; some half full rolling about on the tables, spilling their contents all over the place and onto the carpeted floor. There were empty crisp packets and discarded sandwich wrappers strewn all over the place too. It was a right mess. Neither can I condone the abuse they gave one female passenger who had to force her way through when she boarded the train at Eaglescliffe. She didn't help, mind, when she lambasted them all as *"f****** p***heads"*!

I made straight for The Isaac Wilson, the Wetherspoon pub on Wilson Street, just around the corner from the station. Nigel and I have used this one for breakfast in the last few seasons. We both ordered a 'Large Breakfast' and I washed mine down with a pint of Silver Otter, a 4% abv ale, courtesy of The Otter Brewery in Honiton, Devon.

The Isaac Wilson was filling up rapidly and it was filling up mostly with Boro fans. So, with no sign of any of our Leeds colleagues, we decided to go back towards the station to seek them out; it wasn't difficult. The police and stewards had set up metal barriers outside Spensleys Emporium, on the corner of Albert Road and Zetland Road, near the station, so they could ensure only Leeds fans got in. Everyone was quizzed on the way in. The police, I have to say, were fantastic. Having asked if we were Leeds fans one copper explained: *"This is the place for you lads then, you can sing your happy songs and have a few beers without any worries in here"*. He was speaking the truth too. Inside the Emporium, it was jam packed with Leeds fans enjoying a typical pre-match session. The place was Spartan to say the least and very dark –

basically just a couple of large rooms with an old wooden bar – but it was perfect for our needs. I grabbed a couple of beers and then Nigel and I scrummaged our way through to a little annex that had a few tables and chairs and where we could at least hear ourselves think. It was about 11:30am when we arrived and over the course of the next hour or so it got more and more rowdy as our lads and lasses sank more and more ale. At one point the whole pub sang, *"Oh, Brian McDermott"*, over and over again as someone spotted Brian McDermott's double stood on the stairs leading up to the little balcony that overlooked the main floor space. Then, one lad started body surfing around the room, with everyone holding him up above their heads and passing him around and around until he'd decided he'd had enough. Then we could see through the archway between us and the main room that many of the lads in there were now throwing their beer in the air and everyone must have been getting drenched in lager and ale. It was all pretty boisterous stuff but there was no carpet in there and little to damage and hence the on-looking police and stewards seemed happy to let it play out.

We drank up and wandered outside with everyone else around 12:30pm and enjoyed a walk in the sun to the ground, going past one of the Boro pubs en route; The Lord Byron. As we did we sang, *"All Leeds aren't we"*, at the tops of our voices as the Boro fans looked on and our police escort ensured the two groups were kept well apart.

There was a new addition to the landscape around the Riverside this season; the huge rusting hulk of a ship. The 'North Sea Producer' was moored on Bex Quay, near the stadium. The ship, which returned to Middlesbrough in August this year after serving 18 years in the North Sea, had been a familiar sight when it was moored here for two years during a refit back in 1997. It even featured on 'Match of the Day' when the cameras picked out a banner on the ship proclaiming: *"Boro's Ravanelli's on the telly"*. The ship is now back awaiting its fate, as its role as an oil producing vessel in the North Sea has come to an end. It was still a magnificent sight.[1]

I'd walked along past the main entrance gates of the Riverside to get a better view of the ship and to take a few pictures but as I retraced my steps I spotted another surprising sight. Massimo Cellino, his sons, and another suit I didn't recognise, were stood outside the stadium smoking their fags! I couldn't resist the opportunity; I went up to Massimo and greeted him warmly with my hand outstretched. *"Come stai Signore?"* I asked. How are you sir? He shook my hand, giggled and muttered something totally unintelligible. As I looked in his eyes it seemed to me that the lights were on, but there was no one actually home. I wished him, *"Good luck"*, and went off to find Nigel again, not that I'd get any more sense from him!

Inside, the stadium looked magnificent. A crowd of almost 28,000 was packed inside, around a fabulous looking pitch that was soaking up the autumnal sunshine. Above the stand to our right, at one end of the ground, I could see the top of a steel gantry on that old ship, and guessed that was where they hung that Ravanelli banner back in the day.

As the players emerged from the tunnel on the opposite side of the pitch, the whole stadium erupted in a cacophony of noise. Kentley arrived just as the game kicked off and all around I could see the regular Leeds away day army of fans. Down near the front I spotted my old school pal Rob and his lad Pete who'd tweeted earlier that they were in Middlesbrough today. Phil B said hello too, he was just a row or two in front of us. I saw a few of the lads who'd been in the Emporium, swaying as they staggered up the steps. This is Leeds away!

When we'd seen the team on Twitter earlier, it raised more than a few eyebrows. We were all pleased to see Jordan Botaka make his debut but were less sure about the inclusion of Peppe Bellusci alongside Sol Bamba. In all, Uwe made five changes from the side that beat MK Dons last Saturday. I'll just repeat that; we made *five* changes to a winning side...

---

[1]   http://www.gazettelive.co.uk/news/watch-stunning-aerial-footage-boat-9897175

Silvestri
Berardi Bellusci Bamba Taylor
Adeyemi Cook Mowatt
Botaka Antenucci Dallas

Subs: Turnbull, Wootton, Cooper, Phillips, Byram, Doukara, Murphy.

To be fair, we'd been made aware that Chris Wood, the bloke with the magic hat, was carrying a knock and we knew he'd miss out – well most of us did. One lad we got chatting to on the walk to the ground was distraught when we told him; he'd boasted how he'd got 9/1 on a double of Wood to score and Leeds to win! The other four changes seemed to be part of Uwe's rotation plan.

The noise was incredible at the start, with the Leeds fans belting out MOT and joining in with the Boro fans as they sang: *"We all hate Leeds scum!"* It was possibly the best pre-match atmosphere I could remember in recent years and I'm sure everyone, like me, was expecting a ding dong battle to the final whistle. I'd forgotten the first rule of supporting Leeds though; expect the unexpected.

The game began at a phenomenal pace and both sides looked dangerous and then Boro sent a long diagonal ball out to the left of the Leeds defence. The ball was headed down to Christhian Stuani, a big white number '18' emblazoned on the back of his red shirt. He took on Charlie Taylor on the far side of the pitch, directly in line with where I stood. He turned inside Taylor, then outside and then he'd worked enough space to send the ball over to the back post. Peppe Bellusci seemed well placed to head it away but as he tried to glance the ball behind him he missed it completely. It hit David Nugent in the midriff but he was quickest to react and he swept it into the roof of the net before Berardi got his challenge in. Two minutes gone and we were a goal down. Once again, a marvellous atmosphere in front of a big Leeds following had lasted no more than the blink of an eye. It was another of those kicks in the teeth we get so often and it was only made worse by the sight of Nugent celebrating wildly right in front of us and not in front of his own supporters behind the goal. We were angry at him, angry at Bellusci, angry at the whole bloody world.

It was a bad goal to give away and would only serve to get more fans starting to question whether this defence of ours was ever going to make the grade. We were all thinking we knew the answer to that just a few minutes later when Sol Bamba almost put through his own goal. He chested a high ball firmly into the turf back towards Silvestri but it flew up towards the top corner and only a stretching Silvestri finger saved another embarrassing defensive cock-up. In between these defensive lapses, Jordan Botaka was showing that he was a decent footballer with some nice little triangle-passes on the Leeds right wing. But today was going to be all about this fragile Leeds defence that I've been worried about for almost 12 months. It just is not good enough and that begins with our weak and nervous goalkeeper.

Almost exactly on the half hour, Middlesbrough worked the ball out to George Friend on their left wing, down below us near the touchline. Botaka was with him but never got close enough to stop Friend firing the ball across towards Silvestri. Once again, I was right behind the flight of the ball and I was relieved to see it was going straight towards Marco with no Boro player in there to worry him. It would be an easy take. But it never got as far as Silvestri; flying head first towards the ball and his own goal was Bellusci and he somehow got his head on the ball to power it into the net at the near post. I could only assume there was no call from our meek and mild keeper and so Peppe felt he had to intercept the cross. When I watched the replay back during the following week, you could clearly see Bellusci, once he'd pulled himself up off the turf, mouthing an apology to Silvestri. *"Sorry Marco"*, he was saying, *"sorry Marco."* as he held up his hand literally and metaphorically. Did Silvestri shout? I'd wager he didn't. I stand only a few yards behind the goal in front of the Kop and I'm yet to hear Silvestri shout anything. Two defensive errors and two goals, other than that, there was nothing between these two sides. It was heart-breaking to watch how we were self-destructing yet again. I thought back to how this same defence battled so courageously to hold a one goal lead here last season and wondered how it was possible to go from so good to so bad in just a few months.

At half-time, Rob made his way up to join us and he, Nigel, Kentley and I discussed the first-half; a tale of two errors. Bellusci was taking most of the flak, though I still felt Silvestri should have taken command of the situation for the second goal. I couldn't defend a few wasteful passes Bellusci had made though or the very obvious elbow to a Boro player's head and we all wondered aloud why Cooper was only on the bench having played so well recently.

The start of the second-half saw Leeds have their best period of the game and for a while we all felt a comeback was on the cards. Boro played a very professional game though and every time Leeds looked like breaching their back line they'd bring our men down with a series of cynical fouls. From one resulting free kick, Alex Mowatt, his head heavily bandaged in 'Kisnorbo' fashion from an earlier challenge, curled a lovely shot over the wall only to see the Boro keeper, Konstantopoulos, claw it away, much as Silvestri had done with Sol's wayward chested pass in the first-half. In the 54th minute, the Leeds pressure should have resulted in a goal.

A Boro defender headed the ball away as far as Gaetano Berardi who shanked his volleyed shot off his shin. It bobbled through to Lewis Cook though and Lewis nonchalantly flicked it through the legs of a defender to Antenucci. Ant got in behind the Boro back line to slide it into the net. The Leeds fans went predictably barmy all around and for a split second it seemed we may yet scrape something from this game despite our costly mistakes, but I wasn't celebrating yet. Over on the far touchline I could see the liner on that side had not run back to the half-way line. He hadn't flagged either but he was clearly concerned about something. The referee, Neil Swarbrick, had also spotted something and was now running towards the liner. Some of the Boro defenders sensed there was a chance of redemption and several crowded around the officials as they discussed what had gone on. Uwe Rösler would later say how Leeds are *"too nice"*, as our players didn't join in the hassling of the officials to make any counter claim. After a few seconds, the liner finally held his flag aloft and the 'goal' was chalked off, presumably for an offside against Ant. Replays would later prove that the decision was wrong and the goal should have stood. We sang about the Football League being corrupt as we always do in such circumstances but it was no comfort and we all knew at that point that this would not be our day. Boro were no better than we were really but they were vastly more efficient; they took the chances we offered and they made no mistakes at the back; simples.

Our players didn't lose heart, even if the fans did and Botaka was starting to dominate the right wing. He sent over a fabulous inch perfect cross for Antenucci but with eight yards of goal to aim at he could only direct his header straight at the keeper with the long name; another great chance was gone. I knew perfectly well that had that chance fallen at the other end a Boro striker would have buried it. We had the German coach but they had the 'Vorsprung durch Technik'. With ten minutes left, it all became academic as Leeds pressed the self-destruct button yet again. Marco Silvestri tapped the ball out to Sol Bamba, just outside the Leeds area. Under no direct pressure but with Diego Fabbrini keeping a close eye on proceedings, Sol made to launch the ball out to the Leeds right wing. As he pulled his right foot back though, his left leg, his standing leg, slipped and he was left on his arse; that old position favoured by failed Leeds defenders through the ages. Fabbrini could hardly believe his luck as he strode forward, jinked to the right of Silvestri and fired the ball into the roof of the net. I was stopping up in the North East for a few days to take in the Hartlepool game with Bristol Rovers the following Tuesday and at that precise moment at the Riverside all I could utter was that immortal Chris Kamara phrase, once made to fanatical Hartlepool fan and Sky presenter, Jeff Stelling; *"Unbelievable Jeff!"*

At the final whistle there were no boos from the Leeds fans although immediately after Bellusci had headed into his own net he'd had a fair few aimed at him them. Now, as the players applauded us we merely applauded them back and then began our slow meander back to the town centre. That was a pretty distasteful experience too, as it always is here on Teesside.

Leeds fans heading back to the station end up going in the same direction as the Boro fans after the game, usually only separated by a line of police. It was the same this time as Kentley and I made our way back towards town. Suddenly, I spotted a coke bottle flying towards us and I shouted, *"look out"*, as a general warning to those in the vicinity. I was particularly concerned about the safety of a little lad who was being carried on his dad's shoulders; he'd be the most likely to be hit if another bottle came in our direction. Eventually dad lifted him down but several more bottles flew over before more police arrived on the scene to marshal the situation.

In the aftermath of the game, all the attention was on why Rösler felt the need to swap Cooper for Bellusci, with the Italian rightly given much of the blame for the defeat. In a lengthy interview on BBC Radio Leeds, Rösler responded to a direct question as to why Cooper was left out.

"Erm, I think, erm, we were forced today, or the circumstances dictated today that I needed to make changes and that is where I leave it today."[1] He then said he'd anticipated Boro would play in a similar fashion to Burnley at Elland Road earlier in the season and he pointed out that nine of the side that played then also played against Boro. Regarding Wood's absence, he reported that his injury was not serious and he should be fit to play, *"in the near future"*. Had Cellino instructed that Bellusci play? Some folk thought so.

My visit to the North East ended on Tuesday night with a trip to Victoria Park, Hartlepool, to see the 'Monkey Hangers' play Bristol Rovers. Hartlepool's captain was one Billy Paynter but even our banjo wielding former striker couldn't help the home side as they crashed to a decisive 3 – 0 defeat. For me, that was ground number 81 of the 92 and I probably enjoyed it more than the debacle at the Riverside two days earlier. Like my tyre on the A1(M) the other day, that Boro game just left me totally deflated.

Middlesbrough 3 **Leeds United 0** (Nugent (3), Bellusci (32 og), Fabbrini (81)) 27,694 (**Leeds 2,652**)

---

[1] *http://www.bbc.co.uk/programmes/p033pxyw*

Dreaming of Ola

On Friday, the eve of the Birmingham game, Mrs W, son Mark and girlfriend Chloe and I were at Broadhurst Park, home of FC United of Manchester. We were there to watch their National League, North Division game against Worcester City. It was my first City game of the season and I'd been looking forward to it ever since I spotted the fixture had been moved to the Friday night. It was a chance to see what all the fuss was about this new stadium of FCUM's as well as a chance to see my beloved City. I have to say the new stadium is superb. It's only small, with a capacity of 4,500 but it is brand new and of course it was funded by the fans; they run the club themselves. We spoke with one of the club directors, Kate, a former work colleague of Mrs W and she explained how the membership scheme works and how the club had come about. The original fan base was of course former Manchester United fans who became disillusioned with the Glazers' ownership and they broke away, set up their own club and vowed never to return to Old Trafford as long as the Glazers were in charge. The rise of FCUM in the first ten years of its existence has been phenomenal and now they have this fabulous stadium to show for all their efforts. We got talking with a couple of former Stretford Enders and their enthusiasm for their new club was infectious. They hadn't lost all their Man United credentials mind; I explained I was a Leeds fan and they made it plain that I'd never be on their Christmas card list and neither would fans of Liverpool who they seemed to detest equally as much. Weirdly, the other club they had no time for was A F C Fylde, who are in the same division as FCUM and Worcester this season. The reason for their dislike of Fylde seems to be the perception of how Fylde is trying to throw money at an all-out attempt to secure league football. FCUM see their club as altogether more of a community project to provide affordable football and a community asset for the local area.

The game itself was a tense affair in which City took a first-half lead through ex-WBA striker Lee Hughes. Hughes then lost the plot as he reacted angrily to a foul tackle and got himself sent off just before half-time. The second-half saw the kind of battling performance all Leeds fans are crying out for from our own team as City held firm in the face of an onslaught from FCUM, only to break away and grab a second goal in the final minutes. A crowd of over 3,600 made for a fabulous atmosphere.

I started to think this was going to be the perfect weekend as news came through on the car radio that Callum Watkins had scored a late try to secure Leeds Rhinos a place in the Rugby League Grand Final. Wins on Saturday for Leeds against Birmingham and England against Australia in the Rugby World Cup would be pretty much a dream scenario.

Leeds United's home record was becoming a worry though. We still had not won a game on home soil since March 4th, a 2 – 1 home win against Ipswich Town. Indeed, we'd won only three out of 15 games at Elland Road in the whole of 2015. Failure to beat Birmingham would stretch our winless home sequence to ten games and we hadn't done that since we were relegated from the old First Division in 1981-82. Uwe Rösler was yet to experience a competitive home win with the Whites. It was hardly the fortress Elland Road Rösler had spoken about creating. Was Uwe's position in any danger yet? Well, some fans thought so. It did seem to me, knowing Massimo Cellino's history, that we were maybe only one or two more defeats away from another eruption by our maverick Italian owner. It was interesting to see that in a column in the programme for the Birmingham game; he gave the dreaded chairman's vote of confidence to Rösler saying: *"I would happily appoint Uwe again."* That phrase could be taken two ways of course! I was not sure about Rösler anymore and I had a look back at his time at Wigan this week to see that he ran into a very similar situation there in his final weeks and months with Dave Whelan's outfit. A BBC Sport article[1] at the time pointed out that Wigan had managed only three wins in 17 games at the start of the 2014/2015 season and Dave Whelan told the BBC then: *"At Bolton last week we played well for 20 minutes and then we fell away. We didn't show any fight, determination, grit, and that upsets me and our supporters."* I'd heard exactly the same criticisms from Leeds fans about some of our recent displays.

In *his* programme notes, Uwe bemoaned the mistakes his team made at the Riverside and commented that other than those errors he felt we more than matched what he called the best team in the division. He inevitably focussed on the positives from that game, including the fact that his young team never gave up and the excellent debut of Jordan Botaka. He welcomed the loan signing of Will Buckley from Sunderland too; that was confirmed on the eve of the Birmingham game.

In the Pavilion, almost everyone was convinced we'd beat Birmingham; almost but not quite everyone. Terry Yorath surprised us all by going for a 2 – 2 draw! I'd plumped for a 3 – 0 win for Leeds and had even cleared out my William Hill online betting account of its last £4 on that 20/1 option. We were all nodding with approval when we saw the team sheet too. It was the side I think most punters would have gone for, with the obvious exception that Rösler had thrown Will Buckley straight in at the expense of the unlucky Jordan Botaka. I would have started with Botaka who seems to be the kind of unpredictable flair player who makes things happen and we don't have many of those. Antenucci was possibly the

---

[1] *http://www.bbc.co.uk/sport/0/football/29969583*

other missing name who many fans might have found a way of including:

Silvestri
Berardi, Bamba, Cooper, Taylor
Cook, Murphy, Mowatt
Buckley Wood Dallas

Subs: Turnbull, Byram, Wootton, Bellusci, Antenucci, Botaka, Adeyemi.

Everyone was pleased to see that Peppe Bellusci was left out after his howlers at Boro and it was now no surprise that Sam Byram was left on the bench as Rösler had come out this week and confirmed that Sam was, in his opinion, a right full back and that Berardi was his preferred man for that slot.

So, the mood amongst the Pavilion regulars was optimistic and jovial. None was more jovial than my mate Martin who at one point whispered in my ear: *"Watch when Nigel goes to put his jacket on, I've tied the arms up and stuffed his pockets full of rubbish"*. We all fell about laughing when it was Jacqui's husband Mick who we could see struggling to get his arms into the sabotaged jacket. Martin had picked the wrong coat!

A decent crowd of getting on for 25,000 was in Elland Road and we were enjoying what was probably the last of the autumn sunshine as we were being warned of the imminent arrival of hurricane Joaquin from Bermuda in the next few days. The pitch looked fine too despite the ravages of two Rugby World Cup games being played on it the previous weekend. There were still some tell-tale signs in the form of several battle weary paper Saltires amongst the litter hiding under the seats.

The game got underway to the usual soundtrack of the Leeds choir giving it everything to push the team on to that first home win of the season but the intensity of our support declined progressively as we witnessed another fairly limp performance from our heroes. Birmingham were giving a pretty good impersonation of Middlesbrough the previous week; sitting back and watching while Leeds passed the ball endlessly back and forth across the pitch. Another weak referee, Paul Tierney, was also allowing the Blues to get away with numerous tugs and trips as they, again like Boro, ensured no Leeds player would get close to their penalty area. Then, to the utter disbelief of the Kop, he booked Liam Cooper for what looked like a perfectly fair tackle just outside our own box. Nothing came of the resulting free kick fortunately. Then, just after half an hour, our world collapsed again.

Leeds were actually on a rare foray deep in Birmingham territory when Charlie Taylor was dispossessed in the south east corner, in front of the Cheese Wedge. The ball was worked forward and then launched towards us and over the top of the Leeds back line where Clayton Donaldson gave chase. He had both Sol Bamba and Liam Cooper with him but as he turned, our man Coops ran into Donaldson and, in trying to hoof the ball away, merely struck it at the Birmingham man and fell to the ground; the ball broke to Demarai Gray. Gray shifted the ball to his right and now had a yard on Cooper who was slow to recover from his collision with Donaldson. In an instant, Gray had lashed an unstoppable right foot rocket of a shot high into the Leeds net, beating Silvestri at his near post. It was defending befitting a pub league not the Championship.

Leeds continued to patiently pass the ball back and forth for the rest of the first-half and we were dominating possession by quite some margin but we were getting nowhere. Maybe a half-time cuppa and a pep talk from Rösler would get us going in the second-half. Fortunately, referee Tierney was having such a poor game that the booing heard at the half-time whistle was mainly directed at him.

There were no changes at half-time and that meant there were no changes in the way we played either. Another half an hour of tippy tappy football with no penetration ensued. Why does Rösler talk about playing heavy metal football and then oversee his side playing like this? It was a mystery to me.

Eventually even Rösler had seen enough and just before the hour mark he finally sent on Jordan Botaka and withdrew the very anonymous Will Buckley. Immediately Botaka had an impact and finally we had someone willing to carry the ball at the opposition; someone able to go past defenders. OK, he looks a bit like the Roadrunner when he darts forward and often his final cross was misplaced but boy did he light up the place. Now we had something to shout about and suddenly the place was rocking to the sound of *"We are Leeds"*, now it felt like home. You have to question Rösler's judgement that he preferred Buckley to Botaka in his starting eleven. Botaka is full of tricks and is well worth his nickname of the Wizard but his trickery is not just showboating; it worries defenders and forces them into hurried mistimed tackles and mistakes. Leeds had a purple patch of ten minutes or so, winning four corners in quick succession and then Lewis Cook thundered a shot that Tomasz Kuszczak could only beat away with his fists. This was more like it! Leeds tried to capitalise on the chaos Botaka was creating by bringing on Mirco Antenucci who replaced the increasingly sluggish looking Alex Mowatt and then Sam Byram was on for Berardi who seemed to have picked up a knock. All of Leeds good work was now taking place down that right wing. I was confident we'd pull this one out of the bag at any moment. Over on the touchline I could see the fourth official holding aloft the board signalling the three extra minutes just as the stadium PA burst into life with the same information. *"There will be three…"*

No one heard the rest of the announcement as it was drowned out by the noise from the Birmingham fans. Kuszczak had just launched a goal kick up-field and Liam Cooper had managed to head it sideways but only into the path of Birmingham's Jacques Maghoma. From where I was watching, a hundred yards away, the Leeds defence just seemed to open up and Maghoma was all on his own as he carried the ball away from us and then lashed a left foot shot past Silvestri. 2 – 0 and game over and all around the ground Leeds fans began to stream away in their thousands. They'd all seen enough. As always, I stayed until the bitter end, and I was even harbouring some ridiculous notion that we could still get two very late goals to rescue a point. Jordan Botaka hadn't given up either and he was now running riot on that right wing although his final shot or cross often fell well short of perfect. Nonetheless, he was a clear man of the match and he'd only been on the pitch just over half an hour!

As I wandered down Lowfields Road heading for the car, I picked up snatches of conversations as fans carried out their own post mortems on the game. One irate chap was adamant we'd soon be in the thick of a relegation battle. *"I'll tell you why"*, he spluttered, clearly not able to get his mouth working as quick as his brain, *"We've got f*** all at the back, f*** all in midfield, and f*** all up front. We haven't got a f****** clue"*. *"Botaka looked alright when he came on"*, his mate suggested, but that only made things worse. *"Yes, and f****** Rösler left him on the f****** bench for an hour!"* I hurried past them and picked up a discussion about heavy metal football.

Listening to Uwe Rösler, I can't deny that he was anything but honest in his assessment.

"At home we have to come up with something different, probably different team selections, and probably simplify our way of playing...we have to make sure that at both ends we are stronger, more competitive, mentally stronger.

"For some reason, at the moment we are conceding goals, teams don't need to work very hard to score goals against us...and we are not scoring enough goals..."

Yes Uwe, I'd say that just about covers it...Ten league games completed, almost a quarter of the way into the season and all the early season promise was now looking overdone in the extreme. Leeds sat 16th in the Championship, already 11 points behind the leaders Brighton who were still unbeaten. The most worrying fact though was that we were only three points better off than Bolton in 22nd, the first of the relegation spots.

So this wasn't to be a dream weekend after all. On Saturday night Australia comfortably beat England to ensure that the Aussies and not the Poms would go through to the quarter-finals in the Rugby World Cup. And then, to make matters even worse, in the new series of Strictly Come Dancing, Ola Jordan and Olympic 400 metre runner, Iwan Thomas, were voted off in the first round! I hoped someone would remember to buy me Ola's 2016 calendar for Christmas.

Leeds United 0 Birmingham City 2 (Gray (31), Maghoma (90))
24,601(Birmingham 898)

Brighton Rock, Not Leeds Heavy Metal

Duning the latest international break, Stuart Dallas helped Northern Ireland to qualify for Euro 2016 as they beat Greece 3 – 1 and then drew 1 – 1 in Finland. NI would join England, who beat Estonia and Lithuania and Wales, who despite losing 2 – 0 in Bosnia-Herzegovina, went through on the strength of their subsequent 2 – 0 win over the mighty Andorra and because Cyprus beat Israel . The Republic of Ireland faced the prospect of a play-off while Scotland were dumped out of the competition, despite winning 6 – 0 in Gibraltar.

I was using the break to get in another couple of grounds as I neared the end of my quest to complete 'The 92'. Mrs W and I drove down to Plymouth, on Tuesday 6th October, in time for me to see the Pilgrims' 2 – 0 home win over local rivals Exeter City, in the Johnstone's Paint Trophy. Then, after a few days in Plymouth, we drove to Cambridge. Cambridge United's Abbey Stadium was ground number 83 for me, and there I saw a 1 – 3 home defeat to Portsmouth, in a League Two game on a sunny October Saturday afternoon. It was another great atmosphere with Pompey roared on by 1,886 of their fans who'd made the trip up from the South; that was the biggest away attendance anywhere in Leagues One or Two that weekend.

We were fortunate to stop in a couple of fabulous old country pubs on this trip. The first one, The Ferry House Inn, nestles under the Tamar road and rail bridges, just outside Plymouth, and looks across the river towards Saltash; the old Saltash ferry building can still be seen next door to the pub. It was used for over 700 years prior to closing in 1961 when the road bridge was built alongside Brunel's magnificent rail bridge that was completed 102 years earlier.

For the Cambridge leg of our trip, we stopped at The Old Ferry Boat Inn, in a tiny village called Holywell, some 16 miles or so outside Cambridge on the banks of the Great Ouse. This is reputed to be the oldest inn in England (although if I had a pound for every time I've heard that about pubs I've been to then I'd have more than a few quid!) It is steeped in history though and is said to be built above the grave of a young girl who committed suicide back in AD1050 when jilted by the local woodcutter. The pub is therefore said to be haunted and I have to admit I did see a few ghostly apparitions while I was there although it may just have been the effect of the Greene King ale. It was a lovely spot and although we didn't see any, you can apparently often spot seals swimming in the river; they come all the way down from the Wash, some 50 miles to the north east.

Driving home after the Cambridge game, Mrs W and I were glued to the car radio. We were listening to the Rugby League Grand Final between Leeds Rhinos and Wigan. We knew our lad Adam was there, celebrating his birthday with a few of his mates. With 17 minutes to go, Leeds took a 22 – 20 lead and then we prayed they would hang on. When the final whistle went even Mrs W was punching the air. The Rhinos thus completed an amazing treble of Challenge Cup, League Title and Grand Final to give Kevin Sinfield and Jamie Peacock perfect retirement gifts.

In the other rugby code, this week saw the final group games completed and the World Cup quarter-final line-ups decided; Australia would play Scotland, Ireland faced Argentina, South

Africa would play Wales and the favourites, New Zealand, faced France.

I squeezed one more game in before our Brighton fixture; Worcester City had drawn their FA Cup 3rd Qualifying Round game at the weekend at Solihull Moors so I went to watch the replay. In front of a disappointing 600 odd crowd at City's temporary home in Kidderminster, City pulled off another miracle cup victory with a last minute Lee Hughes goal to set up a trip to Gateshead in the next round. It was already my 21st game of the season but the elation I experienced at the end when Hughes popped up to score was the best moment of the season so far. It's why we watch football; those sudden moments of joy that are as good as any drug fix...or so I imagine!

It seemed an awful long time since Leeds had taken centre stage in my life although it was only two weeks of course. But now our attentions finally turned to the Brighton game on Saturday.

Three likely starters on Saturday all returned from international duty in one piece; Jordan Botaka came back after starring for the DR Congo in a friendly against Gabon; Lewis Cook returned fit after playing two of the three England Under-19s games that saw them progress in the European qualifiers; and Stuart Dallas returned victorious having helped guide Northern Ireland through to Euro 2016. If I'd had my way, all three would've started against the Seagulls. I would also have started with goalkeeper Ross Turnbull instead of Marco Silvestri but news came through this week that Turnbull had broken an ankle in training and was effectively out for the rest of the season. Leeds had Charlie Horton available – he'd been away with the USA U23s as they began their Olympic qualifying campaign – but Leeds were also being linked with Southend goalkeeper, Daniel Bentley, as a possible loan target.

I'd already had my first contact from my Seagull supporting friends Vic and Audrey who'd messaged me to say they were visiting family in Norway this weekend but they were aware the game was being shown live on Norwegian TV so they'd be watching and hoping to, *"get the right result"*. I wasn't sure

Vic was aware just how big the Leeds support in Norway was and hoped he didn't celebrate any Seagulls' goals too boisterously!

As everyone was preparing for the next instalment of this already difficult season, no one foresaw where the next shipwrecking storm would come from but on Friday afternoon, a statement appeared on the club website:

"Massimo Cellino has called upon the Football League to re-think their strategy with regard to televised games after growing increasingly frustrated by the number of the club's rescheduled home fixtures. By the time we enter the New Year, United will have had four televised home fixtures and six away, taking the total to a joint league high of 10 following the recent changes made to December's games. The United chairman has now moved to express his disappointment at how he feels the club's stature is being unfairly "exploited", as well as outlining the steps he will take in a bid to make the League review the process. He said:

"Our loyal Season Ticket Holders are being unfairly penalised by the large amount of fixture changes. "They have already paid to attend these games but many are no longer able to and attendances are suffering as a result of this.

"This affects our revenue to a level where the club is losing money with each televised home game, as Sky's compensation payments are not enough to cover the losses in ticketing, retail and catering.

"We cannot just accept for our schedule to be changed with games moved to Thursdays and Sundays. We are a football club and tradition gives us a sense of belonging to our community.

"Our players need the passion and support of their fans at Elland Road – we should have the right to play there in front of our fans at the traditional time.

"We understand the value that Leeds United brings to the Football League, but we should be shown respect for that - we shouldn't be exploited because of it.

"We do not want to challenge the Football League or Sky, we simply want them to listen to us.

"We have used the correct channels in appealing to the Football League but the issues remain, so we have no choice but to take strong action to protect the future of Leeds United.

"In doing this we must be civil, show respect and remain within the rules. We must not be violent in our way of protesting.

"Football League rules state that clubs must make a provision for at least 2,000 away tickets to be sold. Therefore, in line with those requirements, we will be selling no more than 2,000 tickets for each away game from now on.

"We understand that this means a number of fans will now be unable to attend certain away games, but this is the sacrifice needed to make the Football League take notice - we have to vote with our feet.

"We are encouraging you, as supporters, to think before purchasing tickets for away matches – our silence, especially away from home, will demonstrate our disappointment.

"At away games our supporters are being taken advantage of because they travel in such large numbers.

"This unfairly benefits the home clubs, who increase the price of tickets, food and drinks for our fans.

"But again, the Football League are doing nothing to help us when they should be looking after their members – that is their responsibility to us.

"As a club we can no longer continue to be exploited like this and we are calling for change.

"If these issues cannot be addressed then I fear for the future of Leeds United, which is why I am taking this stance and calling for the fans to follow. The future of our club is at stake."

Massimo Cellino, on behalf of everybody at Leeds United Football Club."

On the one hand, it was a laudable attempt by Cellino to get the football authorities and Sky TV to have a hard look at the way they were treating Leeds and our fans. But on the other hand, was it right to penalise the fans by stopping some of them attending matches? It was the very thing Cellino was claiming was the result of Sky moving our games around!

Twitter was in meltdown, with very few fans prepared to accept that they had to share yet more pain to fight this particular battle that few thought was winnable anyway. To many it was another Mission: Impossible that Cellino was taking on. The Leeds United Supporters Trust even issued its own statement demanding Cellino reconsider his strategy immediately or make plans to issue refunds to thousands of membership holders, many of whom would no longer be able to get match tickets they believed their memberships would facilitate. Those hoping Cellino would eventually suffer another FL ban were disappointed when news came through that all three of the cases pending against him in Italy had been deferred until the New Year. It certainly looks like if you want to commit a crime, you'd best do it in Italy; you'll be dead before they prosecute you.

It was the main discussion topic in the Pavilion as we waited for the announcement of the line-up for the Brighton game. Terry Yorath was in there again with Jed Stone and Peter Lorimer and was as forthright as ever. When asked what he felt the main problems were he bemoaned the lack of a quality striker and also told the Pavilion punters the first thing he'd do was: *"Get rid of the centre backs, all of them!"*

When the team news came through, there were no significant changes despite Rösler having told us after the Birmingham fiasco that there would be. I was happy to see Jordan Botaka starting, with Will Buckley relegated to the bench, but less happy to see Tom Adeyemi replacing Luke Murphy. Charlie Taylor was missing too, he'd picked up a dose of glandular fever and his place went to Scott Wootton. Most fans couldn't understand why Sam Byram wasn't drafted in to that right back slot. After the game, Rösler explained how he felt Wootton had the better *"defensive qualities"*. That didn't go down well with the fans, very few of whom were members of the Scott Wootton fan club. The glaring omission for me though, was Antenucci; he was left on the bench yet again, with just Chris Wood up front.

Silvestri
Wootton Bamba Cooper Berardi
Adeyemi Cook Mowatt
Botaka Wood Dallas

Subs: Horton, Murphy, Antenucci, Byram, Buckley, Bellusci, Phillips.

I settled down for the game in my usual seat while Kentley struggled along the line to join me. Poor Kentley was on crutches having suffered a recurrence of a knee injury in a game of football the previous weekend He'd decided to get a seat near me as he didn't think he'd manage all the steps up to the back of the Kop where he usually stands. Kentley's injury was a blow as it meant almost certainly I'd be driving to Fulham on Wednesday. But first we had Brighton to see off.

For 14 minutes of the game, Leeds played well. It did seem that something had changed during the international break and we looked far more positive. There was none of that infuriating passing back and forth along the defensive line. Decent chances were still few and far between though and the shots we did manage seldom hit the target. Brighton had hardly had a kick at this stage but then suddenly Tom Adeyemi failed to make a tackle on halfway and the Seagulls were flying towards our goal at the Kop end. Beram Kayal slid the ball through and Solly March stole a, err, march on Scott Wootton to fire a left foot shot low into the far corner from 12 yards. The chance had come from nowhere in the first Brighton attack of the game but as we've seen so often, teams in the Championship are mostly deadly with the few chances they're given. It's just our players that seem incapable of putting chances away on a regular basis.

Leeds didn't let this setback put them off though and we continued to have the best of the possession. Just nine minutes later, we were level. Chris Wood toppled over like a felled giant redwood, out towards the Leeds right wing, about 25 yards from goal. Cook, Botaka and Alex Mowatt all stood around the ball as we waited for the free kick. Cook ran over it and on towards the box and then Botaka did the same, leaving Alex Mowatt to swing the ball into the middle with his trusty left peg. The ball was inch perfect; Liam Cooper meeting it in the six-yard box to glance a back header into the corner of the net. It was a well worked move that presumably had been worked on in training; mid-way through the first-half and all square again. In fact, only a few more minutes had passed before Leeds should have taken the lead. Tom Adeyemi was fouled this time, right on the edge of the Brighton box at the far end of the ground, the south end. The same three Leeds players once again stood over the ball and yet again first Cook and then Botaka ran over the ball leaving it for Alex Mowatt to swing it into the middle. You would have thought Brighton would have been wise to it now but no, steaming into the exact same position from where Cooper had scored was big Chris Wood; no one picked him up at all. Sadly, Wood's header was off target with the whole of the goal to aim at. That was pretty much it for the first-half and as the whistle went there was appreciative applause all around the ground and most Leeds fans trekked off to the bogs in a positive frame of mind. Kentley hobbled off in search of his usual half-time pie and coffee.

David Stockdale, the Brighton keeper, is a Leeds lad. He was in the youth system at Huddersfield Town and York City before joining Darlington and then Fulham from where he was loaned out on numerous occasions to various clubs. He'd been Brighton's first choice keeper since the start of last season. As he approached the Kop to take his place after the break, he gave a little Leeds salute. He was soon in the thick of the action too, as Leeds began the new half positively. Botaka was once again showing some clever footwork out on the right wing and then from a Mowatt in-swinging corner, Chris Wood just failed to direct a bouncing ball into the roof of the net. It had to go down as another miss by the big striker.

Then, just before the hour mark, Stockdale almost gifted his home town team a goal as he lazily swung a boot at the ball failing to appreciate how close Alex Mowatt was as the Leeds man closed him down. The ball ricocheted off Mowatt's left boot and hit the outside of Stockdale's right hand post. If we didn't have bad luck, we'd have no luck at all.

Uwe Rösler then made his first substitution; Will Buckley coming on to replace Stuart Dallas, presumably as Dallas was tiring after his recent exertions with NI. If anything, Brighton were now getting on top in the game and we had a lucky escape when a stinging shot from Solly March crashed against our crossbar with Silvestri well beaten. Rösler's answer to that was another substitution, this time Antenucci replacing Mowatt, Rösler's usual swap late in a game. Still Brighton got stronger though. Finally, Rösler sent on Sam Byram who replaced Jordan Botaka to the bemusement of most Leeds fans. Botaka was the one man who looked to be causing the Seagulls problems and he was actually keeping two Brighton defenders occupied most of the time. Why on earth take him off? And, days after Rösler told us Byram was a full back, he refused to play him when a full back place became vacant and then threw him on to replace a winger! It was just one more illogical Rösler substitution. At the same time, Brighton sent on Bobby Zamora, a proven goal poacher, to replace Tomer Hemed. Zamora is quality… and quality counts.

There were now ten minutes to go and the game looked to be heading for a 1 –1 draw, a result I think all Leeds fans would have gratefully accepted. Then, five minutes from time, disaster struck. Liam Cooper stuck out a leg to stop Kayal in his tracks but it left Coops rolling about on the floor in obvious agony. After several minutes of treatment he limped off and then we were dismayed to spot him being helped down the tunnel. He was clearly badly injured and we realised we'd be playing out the final few minutes with ten men having used all three subs. It also crossed my mind that Terry Yorath may soon get his wish; if Sol Bamba picked up a late booking now, then we may well see two of our centre backs missing for the Fulham trip!

The combination of Cooper's injury and the arrival of the deadly Zamora undid us. With just one minute left of normal time the alarm bell was truly ringing as Gaetan Bong (see what I did there?) strode into the Leeds box. He slipped the ball through to Zamora who stretched his legs to beat a very square looking Leeds back line and neatly dink the ball over the oncoming Silvestri. The ball floated agonisingly just under the bar and into the corner of the net. It was a fine example of the difference between Leeds and many other Championship sides. Brighton were clinical in their finishing – they had a couple of chances given them by Leeds and they ruthlessly stuck them away. By contrast, Leeds squandered the few droppings offered by the Seagulls.

Stockdale applauded the Kop and even threw his shirt to one lad down at the front before he jogged away; how brilliant would it be to have him, an obvious Leeds fan, working in front of the Kop every week?

The game ended with most Leeds fans streaming away wondering when our luck will change but this wasn't down to luck, not really; you make your own luck. Leeds had now gone 11 home games without a victory; a new club record and later that night Twitter was full of speculation that Uwe Rösler was in the last chance saloon. Rösler himself was clearly annoyed how Leeds had failed to see the game out; it wasn't as if this was the first time this season. He told BBC Radio Leeds:

"It can always happen that you make three substitutes and then get an injury. 4-4-1 is a training exercise to see a game out but we couldn't do it.

"I won't pick on a certain player. It's up to the players to look at it but the goal was easy to avoid. It's my job to stick with and support my players."

We'd end this round of games 18th in the table, 3 points above the bottom three; Bolton, Rotherham and Preston. Spookily, Rotherham were now managed by a certain Neil Redfearn, appointed just this week, while Preston were still under Simon Grayson. Another ex-Leeds manager, Neil Warnock, had also recently been appointed as a first team advisor by QPR. Leeds would face bottom club Bolton next Saturday at the Macron Stadium. Before that though, we faced a tricky trip to Fulham; Ross McCormack and all. Brighton were now four points clear at the top with 25 while Reading had crept up to second with 21. Boro, Birmingham and Burnley were also up there on 21 while sixth spot was held by Derby.

Leeds United 1 Brighton 2 (March (14), **Cooper (23)**, Zamora (89)) **22, 736** (Brighton 940)

Back to the Future!

I wandered downstairs and tapped my mobile phone. I had three text messages:

Kentley: *Ridiculous. What's the point?*

Rob J A: *Staggering news even by LUFC standards!*

Adam C: *Good God!!!!!!!!!!*

Something big was obviously going down at Leeds United this morning; no one sends texts to me about anything else!

The big breaking news was that Leeds had fired Uwe Rösler. The even bigger news (excuse this pun) was that larger than life, indeed larger than most things, Steve Evans was taking training at Thorp Arch and was expected to be named our new head coach before the day was out. I switched on the laptop and began to scroll through my Twitter timeline; within seconds I was rolling about laughing my head off as I read tweet after tweet containing jokes about *"Big Steve"* and the events of the morning at Elland Road. The best was: *"I woke up this morning so excited; only two more Leeds United managers 'til Christmas!"* Another one, from @paddypower read: *"Scientists have predicted that by 2017, you will never be more than 6 feet away from a former Leeds Utd manager. #lufc"* And they say we're not famous anymore!

Was any of this news a shock? No not really. I'd been convinced Rösler was on the edge despite the vote of confidence given him by Cellino the other day. The situation was so very like that of Hockaday last season; Leeds were losing too many games and there were too many excuses and broken promises coming from the coach. The sacking had maybe come a few games earlier than I'd have expected; I'd guessed he'd be given until November, just as he was at Wigan last season in similar circumstances. The fans were pretty much agreed; Rösler wasn't proving to be the great Messiah after all. Heavy Metal football had proved to be a vision he couldn't deliver and all the old failings – lack of creativity, sloppy defending, poor finishing, and unfathomable substitutions – were still just as prevalent as they were last season. It was time for a change; time to roll with 'Big Steve'.

Whether Evans was the right man for the job was an entirely different question. The persona of the man was totally different to any other coach Cellino had thus far turned to. McDermott, Hockaday, Milanic, Redfearn and Rösler were all pretty mild mannered blokes who preferred their teams to do the talking for them. Evans is a much more, 'in yer face' character. In fact, on the face of it, it was hard to see Evans working for a dictator like Cellino. He had as good as said so himself, this time last season when Rotherham played Leeds. In a Yorkshire Post article headlined: *"I could never work for Cellino says Evans"*[1] he'd explained how he preferred to be in sole control of all team matters. However, reading through the article again this morning, I was struck by the number of complimentary things Evans said about Cellino.

"... if you work for Massimo Cellino, you coach the players and get the results from the players he brings in or you pay with your job, that is the way it is. It is the foreign way of doing things and it does not make it right or wrong.

---

[1]   http://www.yorkshirepost.co.uk/sport/football/leeds-utd/leeds-v-rotherham-i-could-never-work-for-cellino-says-evans-1-6900768

"If you look at Leeds United and Massimo Cellino, where would they be if he had not have stepped in with his millions of pounds?"

On Monday afternoon, the YEP announced that Evans had agreed a deal with Cellino and would take charge of the team for the rest of the season. His first game would be at Craven Cottage on Wednesday night. Cellino said he'd dispensed with a *"gentleman"* in Uwe Rösler and employed a *"fighter"* in Steve Evans.[1] He even called him a *"Motherfu****"*. The Leeds website eventually posted confirmation that Evans was in place on a rolling contract until June 30, 2016. He'd be assisted by former Swansea City midfielder Paul Raynor, who has been with Evans throughout his managerial career. In fact, Raynor does most of the work with the players whilst Evans does the 'manager' bit. They had been entrusted with Mission: Impossible, keep Leeds away from relegation.

And we all settled down…for a couple of minutes. Incredibly, I then spotted the news that the Football League was banning Cellino again! The Football League statement read:

At its recent meeting, the Board of The Football League (with the exception of Chief Executive Shaun Harvey who declared an interest*) considered the position of Leeds United President Massimo Cellino under its Owners' and Directors' test.

In June, Mr Cellino was found guilty by a Court in Sardinia of an offence under Italian tax legislation relating to the non-payment of VAT on the importation of a Land Rover vehicle. This resulted in a fine of €40,000 and the confiscation of the vehicle in question.

Having considered detailed legal advice and the Court's reasoned judgment, as supplied by Mr Cellino, the Board determined that the decision of the Italian Court constitutes a disqualifying condition under the Owners' and Directors' test.

---

[1]   http://www.yorkshireeveningpost.co.uk/news/latest-news/top-stories/leeds-united-evans-is-a-fighter-rosler-was-a-gentleman-cellino-1-7523680

Mr Cellino has until October 28 to appeal against the Board's decision. Any such appeal would be heard by an independent panel.

It was just another manic Monday. It suddenly looked as if Cellino was trying to get all his work done and dusted before the ban came into force and hence the speed with which he'd managed to recruit Evans. Leeds fans didn't know whether to love or hate the Football League; half wanted them to ban him forever and half thought this was just another example of the FL getting their own back. Was this retribution for Cellino daring to defy them by placing that 2,000 limit on away ticket sales? Cellino clearly thought so and he told reporters exactly that. He also told them he fully intended to appeal the decision...well, he always does! He was adamant that under the rules of Italian law he was still innocent until all three levels of appeal had been completed and he refused to accept that he should be punished until that process was done. It was an argument that was ultimately rejected last time when his first ban was imposed. Those lads at @paddypower were working hard too; they came up with this within seconds of the FL announcement: *"Steve Evans has previously said he could never work for Massimo Cellino. It's a good job the Leeds Chairman has just been disqualified then!"*

The Leeds Fans United group was still plugging away in the background trying to raise funds with the intention of mounting a bid for a slice of Leeds shares. On the eve of the Fulham game, they held a meeting with Massimo Cellino and succeeded in persuading him to relent on his away ticket restrictions. No damage had been done and the restriction was lifted immediately. Cellino seemed genuinely surprised at the outcry from fans and this was a major feather in the cap of Dylan Thwaites and his LFU outfit. It would also serve to calm everyone's mood for that trip to Craven Cottage. What did we have to complain about now?

Kentley still had a lot to complain about; on the morning of the Fulham game he was undergoing various scans on his injured knee. He'd arrived for his 9:20am appointment on time but it was gone noon when he rang to say he was ready to be picked up. As he clambered into the car, having stowed his crutches in the rear foot-well, he was muttering about the shortcomings of the NHS while apologising if he smelled of garlic from his pizza the previous night. I'd watched with incredulity as he'd stood outside his mum's car spraying his clothes with deodorant!

We were following the MO of our previous trip to Fulham which was only a few months ago, in March earlier in the year. We drove as far as West Ruislip tube station; parked up, and then got on the tube heading into London on the Central Line. As we sat down, we reminded each other to make sure we got off at Notting Hill Gate where we needed to change for the District Line. We were headed for East Putney which was handy for our pre-match hostelry for the day, The Railway in Putney. Deep in conversation about the events of Monday morning, we suddenly spotted the signs for *"Queensway"* on the walls of the tube station we'd just pulled into; we'd somehow missed Notting Hill Gate! It was just a matter of hopping off the train (well, that was easy for Kentley with his crutches) and going back up the line one stop to get our District Line connection and then eventually we alighted at East Putney for the short walk down Upper Richmond Road.

The Railway was already buzzing with pre-match anticipation; we spotted Keith who'd also just arrived and we grabbed some beers and sat down with him at a table next to Derek and Tim. All the usual suspects were in there; Simon W, Wayne, Dave L, Mike H and big Clive, Shirley, Adam and Conor, Keith's mate Bob and his son arrived and joined us, Nigel eventually rolled in with talk of all the women he'd been chatting up during his latest little trip to London (he'd come down on Tuesday and was stopping a few days). It was a full house. I got through a few pints of the excellent Abbot Ale and one of Wetherspoon's Brunch Burgers and after that I was ready for anything.

There was general agreement that the team Steve Evans had picked for his first game was spot on. He'd made some comments already about how he'd seen a massive change in Sam Byram in the few days he'd been at the club and so it was no surprise to see Sam appear in the right back slot. I was pleased to see he'd found a way of accommodating both Wood and Antenucci up front too, albeit slightly disappointed that Jordan Botaka missed out. In all there were three changes from the starting line-up that failed against Brighton and we were amazed Liam Cooper took his place after limping off in that game.

Silvestri
Byram Bamba Cooper Berardi
Dallas Murphy Adeyemi Cook
Antenucci Wood

Subs: Wootton, Bellusci, Mowatt, Botaka, Buckley, Phillips, Horton.

We set off on the walk to Craven Cottage just before 7pm with a whole stream of fans, mostly Leeds. As we walked through Bishops Park we admired the views of the stadium floodlights reflected in the dark waters of the Thames. It had apparently been raining all day in London but by the time Kentley and I arrived it had stopped and it was now a crisp autumn evening. Kentley was still having to be careful where he placed his crutches though as the ground was still damp.

We went up to our seats and the three of us, Kentley, Nigel and I all squeezed into row LL, about half way up the stand at the Putney End with the nearest goal below us and to our right. As always, the sight and sound of almost 3,800 Leeds fans was something glorious to behold. There was a feeling of rejuvenation amongst the fans, reflecting the fact this was another new beginning under another new coach. Inevitably there was the hope that this would be *the one*. There was some negativity, but that was all reserved for Massimo Cellino. *"Time to go, Massimo"* was a chant we would hear on and off all night regardless of how things were going on the pitch below us. *"Sell the club and f*** off home"* was also heard at regular intervals.

Fulham had some decent players on show and were on a good little run that saw them gain a point in a nil-nil draw at Middlesbrough at the weekend as well as thumping QPR 4 – 0 not long ago. Ross McCormack was in the side as well as the deadly Moussa Dembélé. Ben Pringle in midfield is useful too.

There was no sign of former Leeds striker Matt Smith though, and Tom Cairney, he that was once told by Leeds he was *"too small"* to make a top footballer, was suspended.

The portly, not to say rotund figure of Steve Evans marched across the Craven Cottage pitch with the players and he must have marvelled at the scale of the Leeds following roaring on his team as he took his place in the dugout. I'm sure he was impressed and he'd also soon be impressed with his new charges too as they tore into Fulham with an eagerness we'd not seen in recent times. The 4 – 4 – 2 formation seemed to suit the players and Sam Byram looked much more like his old self bombing up and down the right side. *"He plays on the right, he's fu***** dynamite, you just don't seem to understand. If you sell Byram, Sam Byram, you're gonna have a riot on your hands!"* rang out from the Putney End even though there were rumours that Sam had already agreed a deal to join Southampton in the January transfer window. We all hoped the future would see Sam back to his old self on this 'Back to the Future Day'. October 21st, 2015, was the day Marty McFly and Doc Brown visited in the 1989 sci-fi time adventure sequel, 'Back to the Future II'. I'd have been happy to replicate the result from October 21st, 1999, when Leeds beat Locomotiv Moscow 4 – 1 in the Uefa Cup, but not October 21st, 2006, when Leeds lost 5 – 1 at Luton Town under caretaker manager John Carver. How times change eh?

The Leeds fans were in great voice and were soon on the back of a certain player wearing *"44"*. *"There's only one greedy bas*****!"* rang out from all around as McCormack dragged a long range shot wide and then got a dressing down from the referee for a niggly foul. In the 18th minute we were all up on our toes as Chris Wood touched the ball into the path of Stuart Dallas and he absolutely thrashed it at goal. We were convinced it was going in but somehow Joe Lewis in the Fulham goal palmed the shot away. It was the first of several world class saves Lewis would make. This was all starting to look very good, very good indeed…

Too good in fact; whatever Steve Evans had managed to cover in the first few days of his reign, I don't think the session on 'cutting out sloppy defending' had come up yet. Suddenly, the ball was shifted inside to Dembélé, he who's more deadly than Ebola, and he's racing towards the Leeds goal down below us. He brushed past Liam Cooper with the greatest of ease and then escaped from a tentative tackle by Adeyemi. He managed to keep just a yard ahead of Sol Bamba all the way to the six-yard box and Gaetano Berardi had an 'after you Claude moment'. Finally, just as Sol lunged towards him, Dembélé scuffed the ball towards goal from the corner of the six-yard box and somehow the tame shot found a way past the scrambling Silvestri. Marco should have stopped it; end of. For all the changes that had gone on at Leeds this week, that defence had altered not one iota. It was still as dodgy as Kentley's right knee.

There were only 22 minutes gone, so there was plenty of time but I don't think many Leeds fans thought at that precise moment we'd get anything from this game. I certainly didn't.

Fair play to Leeds, we didn't let our heads drop and we kept playing with a nice tempo and shape and carved out a few half chances. Lewis Cook was looking just as sharp as usual but today his final pass was much more effective. On Saturday, against Brighton, almost all his little runs ended with him losing the ball. Today, he was far more productive. Dallas dragged a shot wide and Cook put Berardi in for a tremendous right foot shot that Lewis again turned away, low to his left. The keeper was in inspired form. Fulham had to resort to some fairly agricultural tackling too and both Dembélé and O'Hara were already in the referee's book.

At half-time, most of the talk was about how good we looked but how that one defensive lapse could well prove costly. Silvestri was not popular. The bloke next to me pointed at Kentley who was sat with his crutches and told me: *"The lad with the sticks would be a better bet in goal than that tw** Silvestri"*. I wasn't convinced; I've not seen Kentley play...

The second-half started well for Leeds and still Lewis Cook was pulling the strings, assisted by Luke Murphy. Stuart Dallas was also having his best game in a Leeds shirt. Evans wasn't hanging about though and 12 minutes into the new half, he brought Murphy off and sent on Jordan Botaka. It was a positive looking substitution.

Botaka was instrumental in Leeds winning a couple of corners which he then took and from the second, Leeds finally got the break they needed. As the ball flew across the area, Sol Bamba shaped to chest the ball down but it was flicked away from him by the hand of Ben Pringle. There was no argument from Pringle as the referee pointed to the spot.

There were however a few arguments going on in the Putney End as it appeared that Chris Wood was going to take the kick. He held the ball tightly whilst talking with Mirco Antenucci who also looked interested in adding to his own goal tally. As Antenucci wandered away, clearly having lost the argument, we all held our breath. We'd seen Wood sky that penalty over the bar at Doncaster; NASA was still searching for that one. We'd also winced when he dinked one down the middle at Milton Keynes; fortunately the keeper that day dived away and the little dink worked. Now Wood was taking on a keeper who was clearly at the top of his form. The whistle went; Wood strode up and clipped the ball right footed towards the keeper's left hand side ...and the net rippled. We knew Lewis wasn't far from saving it though as the ball had bobbled off him as it made its way into the net. Several replays on Kentley's iPhone eventually explained it. Lewis got both hands to the ball but could only deflect it up and over his head and into the side netting. Phew, that was close. I then decided that the bloke next to me was totally wrong in his estimation of Kentley's abilities in goal as he nearly dropped the phone when one of his crutches slipped to the floor and we all did a sort of Rhumba shimmy to keep him on his feet!

The majority of Leeds fans were not bothered how the penalty went in, they were just happy they could now celebrate and for once our play had actually deserved the equaliser. I was even thinking we might yet go on to win it, so well were we playing. Fulham were looking very ragged by this time and their manager, Kit Symons made two quick substitutions. It didn't change the flow of the game though and Leeds were still rampant; when was the last time I said that? Chris Wood had now picked up an ankle injury and he was replaced by Will Buckley. Antenucci fired in a couple of shots and then Stuart Dallas was denied by another world class save from

Lewis as his right foot shot bent towards the top corner. We were now into the last ten minutes and Fulham made their final change, bringing off Dembélé. Antenucci then bent one of his trademark left foot curlers towards the top corner of Lewis's net and once again the keeper somehow managed to finger-tip it away for a corner. The man was just unbeatable. Fulham were now hanging on and were trying to break up the play any way they could. Dan Burn got himself booked for the home side and then Luke Garbutt and Lewis Cook got involved in some hand-bags and both had their names taken. Kalvin Phillips made a late appearance replacing the hard working Stuart Dallas but the game ended in the 1 – 1 draw. I was happy enough with that. I'd always felt this game was a sort of freebie for Evans; far more important was the outcome at Bolton on Saturday. The Trotters were in serious trouble at the bottom of the table with just a single win in 18 games stretching back to last season. If Leeds were to convince us they were not going to be embroiled in a relegation battle this season they had to be beating the likes of Bolton; it was an early season six pointer.

It was a long journey home but Kentley kept me awake with his constant chatter and his iPhone DJ'ing and I finally dropped him off at his home sometime after two in the morning. I wasn't that tired and when I got home I sat and flicked through my Twitter timeline whilst enjoying a large tumbler of Glenkinchie. Steve Evans had won over the majority of our fans with this performance and a very plain speaking post-match interview. It had been a good day on planet Leeds; a very good day.

Fulham 1 **Leeds United 1** (Dembélé (23), **Wood (64, pen)**)
19,969 **(Leeds 3,789)**

Good Evans, another penalty point!

We quickly moved on to the Bolton match. I'd considered, for all of a nanosecond, missing this game and going instead to Gateshead where my beloved Worcester City were playing in that FA Cup 4th Qualifying Round tie. City were giving off all the signs that they may well get involved in another incredible cup run, just as they did last season. But, at the end of the day, the lure of Leeds was just too great because I was convinced we'd beat the Trotters soundly as we embarked on this new dawn under Steve Evans. Bolton were such a poor team that even their manager, Neil Lennon, had talked about their lack of quality in the days leading up to the game. He'd also demanded that the Bolton board either, *"sack him or back him"*, as he knew he needed to bring in some new faces if they were to avoid going the way of Wigan; down to League One. They did manage to bring in one player this week; Shola Ameobi, the 34 year-old former Toon striker. His claim to fame was that he'd made more Premier League appearances as a substitute than any other player. He only signed for the Trotters the day before the game, on a short term contract but he went straight into their squad and would start on the bench against us.

Mrs W drove Kentley and me up to Bolton; she was meeting an old school pal for coffee and dropped us off at the Beehive pub around 12:15pm. We had a meal in the restaurant part of the pub with Nigel and chatted with Chris and Phil M who were sat at the next table. As the pub filled up, there were the usual manic queues at the bar but Kentley quickly sussed that as long as we kept ordering food, the waitress would also kindly bring our beers to the table thus avoiding said queues! So, we took our time and eventually topped off the meal with a couple of ice cream sundaes. Went down well with a few pints of IPA I can tell you....not!

We bumped into Pete, aka PockWhite, Martin and '+15', Nick and Karen and many others from the regular away day crew. The best spectacle of the afternoon though was the 'table surfing' going on at the other end of the pub that we stumbled upon as we left. We could see a huge crowd of folk about three deep all around a couple of Formica topped tables joined together end to end. Everyone had their mobile phones trained on the action. The table tops were swimming in beer and a couple of lads were taking turns to launch themselves on their bellies so they 'surfed' along from one end to the other. Each 'run' was prefaced by a crescendo of cheering and then as the lad took off, the onlookers would all leap up and down cheering and throwing more beer in the air! Despite the mess it was creating – although most of the beer was being soaked up by the lads' jeans to be fair – the security and bar staff watching on seemed relaxed enough to let the game continue without penalty. We watched, fascinated, for a good few minutes before wandering out of the pub and setting off to the ground.

Steve Evans named an unchanged starting eleven for this one, although we'd learn later that Jordan Botaka may have got a run out had he not fallen victim to illness on the eve of the game. Steve Evans told reporters that Botaka was sent home to try to ensure the rest of the squad didn't catch whatever it was.

Silvestri
Byram Bamba Cooper Berardi
Dallas Murphy Adeyemi Cook
Antenucci Wood

Subs: Horton, Wootton, Bellusci, Mowatt, Phillips, Doukara, Buckley.

Souleymane Doukara took Botaka's place on the bench. Kentley's ticket was for the lower tier while Nigel and I had upper tier tickets so we bade farewell at the entrance and went our separate ways. Nigel and I were up on row 'OO' which was ten or so rows from the very top and we were to the left of the goal below us. It looked a very long way away. Leeds had sold their allocation of tickets and 4,419 voices greeted the Leeds players as they marched out of the tunnel away to our left. On the other three sides of the stadium there were lots of empty seats, a clear signal that the Trotters' fans were not happy with their lot.

Almost from the start, we could tell it was not going to be the easy ride many of us hoped for. Leeds were just not 'on it'. For the first nine minutes, it was mostly Bolton driving towards us although they got caught offside a couple of times and didn't fashion any meaningful chances. Then we noticed that Trotters' striker Gary Madine was down holding his head and eventually Bolton rolled the ball out of play. Madine is a dangerous player and initially I thought it was good news (for us, not Madine obviously) that Madine was heading off down the tunnel. Then I spotted who was replacing him and I was immediately nervous; Shola Ameobi was trotting on to the pitch. I've lost count of the number of times something like this has happened when a substitute player has proceeded to score against us. The most famous occasion in recent years was up at Barnsley on New Year's Eve, in the 2011/12 season. Ricardo Vaz Te, on that occasion, stepped off the bench after quarter of an hour when Jacob Butterfield was injured and then rifled in a hat-trick as the Tykes beat us 4 – 1. Seeing Ameobi lope across the pitch made me think of that terrible winter's day again.

For the next twenty minutes or so the two sides traded corners and Mirco Antenucci did a passable impression of Luciano Becchio as he was caught offside needlessly a couple of times. From one of the Leeds corners, sent over by Luke Murphy from the right wing, Tom Adeyemi was unlucky to see a right foot volley crash against an upright but that was as close as either side got to opening the scoring. Then, just after the half hour, it was time for the regular match-day piece of schoolboy defending by Leeds.

There was no real danger as Liam Feeney sent over a high cross from the Bolton left wing and we all expected Marco Silvestri to catch the ball. Ha! I made that up. Of course we didn't *expect* him to catch the ball, he never does, but 99 keepers out of a 100 would have done. Instead, our keeper did an impression of a flappy thing as he launched himself towards the ball but only succeeded in knocking it behind for a corner. Berardi was clearly calling to him to let it go. It was just one more in a catalogue of errors to be laid at Silvestri's door this season. But Leeds then decided to 'go large' and make a complete Horlicks of dealing with the corner. It was a terrible corner, just scuffed low across to the near post but somehow both Luke Murphy and Stuart Dallas contrived to miss it as they also tried to marshal a Bolton player out of the way. The ball continued to bobble across the area through a gaggle of players of both sides until it arrived at the right boot of, yes you've guessed it, Foluwashola 'Shola' Ameobi. Ameobi puts his laces through the ball and it is past Silvestri and nestling in our net in the blink of an eye. Bugger!

It was the 7th time in eight games we'd conceded the opening goal and in six of those games that first goal had come on or around the half-hour mark. It was enough to knock the stuffing out of us and for the rest of the half it looked very much as if it had. Leeds were poor; very poor.

I was sure Evans wouldn't accept that performance and equally sure someone would pay for it by being subbed at half-time. Sure enough, only ten Leeds players appeared initially for the second-half and, as I mentally checked them off, I soon realised it was Luke Murphy who was missing and Alex Mowatt who was now waiting on the touchline to be ushered on by the referee. Murphy had been anonymous in that first 45 minutes. It seemed to do the trick; Leeds were suddenly looking much brighter and our passing and movement was much quicker. Antenucci had a decent angled shot crash into the side netting as we tried to help them get going with some *"MOT"*s and *"All Leeds aren't we"* chants. Then Tom Adeyemi was in the thick of the action again as he cut inside onto his left foot and hammered a shot towards goal. Nigel and I were stood right in line with the ball and I was already up on my toes ready to celebrate as it appeared to be curling away from the keeper into the corner of the net. At the very last second, Ben Amos stuck out a hand and diverted the ball onto his left hand post and it was eventually hacked clear. Bugger again! This was much better though and the pressure was clearly building although we were all conscious there was only 20 minutes left to avoid the unthinkable; losing to the worst side in the division, the one that had won just a single game in 18 attempts.

We very nearly went two down in the 70th minute when another Bolton sub, Stephen Dobbie, cut inside and thumped a shot towards the bottom right corner as we looked on from nigh on a hundred yards away. Silvestri amazed us all this time by diving to his left and knocking the ball away to where Gaetano Berardi collected it and he prodded it further up the line to Alex Mowatt. Mowatt steadied himself, looked up and then launched the ball down that left wing towards where Bolton's Prince Gouano was marking Antenucci. Gouano stumbled and for a split second Antenucci stopped, no doubt expecting the ref to blow for a foul. But no whistle came and now Antenucci was racing towards goal with the ball at his feet. Mirco checked as he reached the box to cut inside another Bolton defender and that just gave the recovering Gouano time to catch up with the speedy Italian. But Gouano was behind Mirco and Mirco was pulling the trigger...

Antenucci never got to pull the trigger as his back leg was clipped by Gouano for an obvious penalty and then, as we all celebrated wildly as if Christmas had come early in the Franking Sense South Stand, the referee held up a red card to Gouano whose work was done for the day. We celebrated some more.

There was still the small matter of who was going to take the kick. Chris Wood was clearly the nominated penalty taker but none of us wanted him to take this one; we hadn't been impressed with the one he took on Wednesday night in London, the one that bobbled in off the keeper. And of course there was that other one that was still in orbit several miles over Doncaster. Antenucci had hold of the ball and he was clearly telling Wood he'd won the kick himself and he'd take the kick himself thank you! Wood eventually moseyed away with a shrug. It was a nervy moment and, to make things worse, Ben Amos in the Bolton goal was waving his arms and shuffling back and forth along his line like a demented table football goalie. Antenucci waited, and waited and then hammered the ball straight down the middle as Amos dived to his right. Thankfully, the ball crashed into the netting and Mirco was now stood on the by-line saluting the Leeds fans like a ship's captain on the bridge. He looked the part too with his big bushy beard if you've ever seen the film, 'Titanic'.

Against ten men for the last twenty minutes we ought to have roasted the Trotters but truth be told, we were not good enough. We had plenty of pressure but our final ball was too often wasted. Will Buckley replaced Stuart Dallas shortly after we equalised and he had a handful of chances to get in a decent cross but each time it was badly miscued. Sam Byram had several runs down the right wing but infuriatingly he was far from *"dynamite"* and more often than not he messed up. Steve Evans was shouting at him from the touchline and waving him on but still he did that thing where he stops on a sixpence, flicks the ball with his right foot behind his left and then looks for support inside or behind. Alex Mowatt curled a free kick over the wall in the dying seconds but it was easily dealt with by Amos and that was that. Another 1 – 1 draw salvaged from the jaws of defeat with the help of another penalty kick.

As the players came towards us at the end to thank us for our support, I was appalled to see the venom with which a few Leeds 'fans' were shouting and bawling at them. One lad was up on the shoulders of a mate and gesticulating wildly towards our players making exaggerated 'wan***' signs and sticking up two fingers. Another chap making his way down the steps towards the exit was leaping up and down shaking his fist at them and shouting obscenities and about how they were all *"fu***** useless c***s"* and how they wouldn't get his support until they started *"to play with some passion"*. It was horrible to witness and I'm sorry, no matter how badly our lads play, that is no way to show support for our great club. We ought to be above that sort of stuff. To be fair, the vast majority of our fans merely applauded the players and no doubt optimistically expected it all to be different next time.

I met Kentley at the exit and we wandered across to McDonald's where Mrs W was parked. As usual it took for ever to get away from the traffic chaos that always follows a game at this stadium, it's another example of piss poor planning considering it was built as recently as 1997. (The toilets are another example too; totally inadequate.) Kentley tuned his iPhone into Steve Evans giving his post-match reaction and we listened as he explained how he was frustrated by the failure to score against ten men.

"I'm frustrated and I will certainly go home disappointed. These fantastic Leeds United fans behind the goal will also go away disappointed because for me it is two points we have given away. Reflecting on the whole performance, I don't think we started in the same way as we did at Fulham and we looked half a yard off it all over the pitch in the first twenty minutes

"The goal was a poor goal to concede and it should never be a corner because we should deal with it. Then Stuart Dallas couldn't clear and Tom Adeyemi loses a runner and we had three errors for the goal, really.

"But the difference was the final ball. We got to the by-line on seven, eight or ten occasions in that second-half and Chris Wood's movement was absolutely fantastic and you have to stick it on his nut. If you do that and the big man doesn't score, then the issue is with him. But his movement was fantastic"

I wasn't sure about the 'big man' scoring had the ball reached his 'nut' but the rest was refreshingly honest. Having heard Evans' take on the game, I turned to my mobile and called up the BBC Sport Football website, going straight to the FA Cup. I nervously scrolled through the games until I came to Gateshead v Worcester City and then I exclaimed at the top of my voice: *"They've only gone and fu***** done it; Gateshead 1 Worcester City 2."* City were in the first round draw!

Bolton 1 **Leeds United 1** (Ameobi (32), **Antenucci (pen, 71)**)
18,178 (**Leeds 4,419**)

"We're Leeds United; we've all had enough!"

The few days between the Bolton and Blackburn games were filled by the usual media speculation about what was actually going on at Elland Road. No one really knew but it was fun to speculate. The Independent no less published a couple of online articles claiming to have had an interview with Cellino.[1] The article had David Haigh's name spelled wrong and it reckoned Cellino drove an *"Audio X5"* (someone on Twitter joked that 'Audio' might be Italian for 'Audi') but if the rest of it was correct then it was more grim reading for Leeds fans. It talked about the impending employment tribunal that Lucy Ward was still intending to bring and claimed Cellino's response to questions about her dismissal was: *"I don't know Lucy Ward"* and then he blamed Adam Pearson, saying he dealt with it! The article also claimed there were approximately 30 legal demands for payments outstanding in Cellino's in-tray. We didn't really learn anything new from The Independent though and it

---

[1]   http://www.independent.co.uk/sport/football/football-league/massimo-cellino-the-ugly-truth-about-the-way-italian-runs-leeds-united-revealed-a6709711.html

looked to me like someone inside the club was leaking information to try to get at Cellino. Meanwhile, Massimo had confirmed his lawyers had submitted the appeal papers to the FL over his latest ban and we all sat back and waited for that to play out.

An article from 'thedailymail.co.uk'[1] was even more damning of Cellino, claiming there were currently eight legal cases against him or the club pending. These included; the Lucy Ward discrimination case; the unfair dismissal case over Nigel Gibbs; a potential illegal payment alleged to have been made to Ross McCormack's agent when Ross went to Fulham; another payment to the same agent over the transfer of Lee Erwin from Motherwell; the Enterprise shirt sponsorship battle; the Macron kit deal saga; various issues surrounding the loan of Adryan in 2014; the failure to pay various taxes on two player transfers while at Cagliari; and charges of embezzlement and false representation in the rebuilding of a stadium in Sardinia. Was that eight? Oh, and that excludes the ongoing import duty case appeals in Italy as well. Even the staunchest Cellino supporters, of which there were still a few amongst Leeds fans on Twitter, were starting to have doubts that Cellino could survive in the face of all those charges. To me, it seemed a matter of 'when' and not 'if' he had to accept defeat and sell his interest in the club.

Rumours that Luciano Becchio might be on his way back to Leeds were dismissed by Steve Evans on the Monday before the Blackburn game, as he told reporters *"That's news to me"*. Becchio was apparently a free agent and had played for Evans at Rotherham of course but I was sceptical he'd be much help to us as it was now years since he'd had any sort of prolonged run of games.

Monday night saw the draw for the First Round of the FA Cup and I sat glued to the TV waiting for ball '49' to come out of

---

[1]   *http://www.dailymail.co.uk/sport/football/article-3292301/Leeds-owner-Massimo-Cellino-remains-defiant-despite-mounting-rap-sheet-cloud-controversy-club.html?ITO=1490&ns_mchannel=rss&ns_campaign=1490*

the drum. It was a long time coming but eventually Worcester City's ball emerged to set up a tie with Sheffield United at Bramall Lane. All I needed now was for the game to be moved from the Saturday to either the Friday or Sunday to avoid a clash with our trip to Huddersfield.

I was joined by son Mark and his girlfriend Chloe for the Blackburn game; picking them up from Altrincham before making another tortuous trip up the M60 and M62 to Leeds. We all joined the usual folk in the Pavilion before the game where once again Terry Yorath was vocal in bemoaning the lack of quality in the Leeds ranks. When we got to our seats in the North Stand, Kentley was already there, having made his own way to Leeds. We were all really buoyant; convinced we'd see a powerful Leeds performance in response to Evans saying how our recent home record was a *"disgrace"*. If that didn't do the trick then Cellino had some ideas too. He'd installed lemon trees in the club reception for good luck and had apparently taken charge of pre-match music; he sent the players out to D:Ream's 'Things Can Only Get Better'.

Evans, on the eve of his 53rd birthday, named an unchanged side from that which started at Bolton.

Silvestri
Byram Bamba Cooper Berardi
Dallas Murphy Adeyemi Cook
Antenucci Wood

Subs: Horton, Bellusci, Wootton, Mowatt, Buckley, Botaka, Doukara.

It was disappointing Botaka didn't get a start and that Charlie Taylor was still not recovered after his illness but other than that few in the Pavilion criticised that team selection.

The Leeds players all gathered together in their usual huddle while the Blackburn players stood waiting, the Rovers forwards taking the opportunity to discuss how they would start the game no doubt. It was a Blackburn kick-off with Leeds choosing to kick towards the South Stand in the first-half as normal. Jordan Rhodes touched the ball and then set off towards the Leeds goal at the Kop end as did Craig Conway on the left hand side. Meanwhile, Blackburn worked the ball out to their right wing, first with Chris Taylor and then Tom Lawrence. They'd made four passes before Lawrence sent the ball over into the Leeds box looking for Rhodes. Sol Bamba was with him though and got his head to the ball but it was the merest flick that knocked the ball behind him. Sam Byram was ducking to head the ball away but Sol's touch meant Byram was too low and the ball flew over his head towards the back post where Craig Conway was now all alone. Stuart Dallas spotted the danger but he spotted it a few milliseconds too late. Conway had time to chest the ball down and then thump it past Silvestri from about seven yards out, just before Dallas slid across. Once again that defence of ours had shown itself to be totally unfit for purpose. The near 20,000 crowd was stunned. Over in the dugout, Steve Evans turned to Paul Raynor to ask what had happened; I don't think Evans even saw the goal! At that moment I was even more sure that our defence needed to change; I'd been convinced it was our weak point right from pre-season of course. Why were we still persisting with the same names? These were the same names that had been conceding soft goals throughout 2015. As the ball hit our net, exactly 16 seconds of the game had been played. This was as bad as it could get…well, nearly. Six minutes later we were two goals down and the game was as good as finished as a contest. Once again our mission this season looked impossible. At 1 – 0 all Leeds fans, as I did, still felt we could win this game and we were soon singing *"All Leeds aren't we?"* and deriding the Rovers' fans with *"You're just a small town in Burnley"*. The clock had ticked on just another five minutes and Leeds were on the attack when we lost the ball and Ben Marshall slid a pass down the Blackburn right, in front of the East Stand, to Tom Lawrence. He carried the ball from half way and was now ahead of Berardi who'd been supporting Leeds in attack just seconds earlier. Lawrence easily went round Liam Cooper who immediately adopted the default Leeds defender position of 'arse on turf' and then, as Sol Bamba lunged in, he touched the ball inside to Jordan Rhodes. Rhodes had scored four goals in his last three games against Leeds and we all knew how deadly he was. Rhodes had Sam

Byram in close attendance but the wily Rhodes has been there before and a couple of touches got him half a yard of space and he turned and arrowed a shot through Byram's legs and past Silvestri into the corner of the net. Twelve games without a clean sheet for Leeds and the first goals Blackburn had scored in four. This was now a disaster.

As the second goal went in there were a few boos around the ground and then gradually the anger turned towards Massimo Cellino who was sat in the East Stand. *"Time to go, Massimo"*, rang out all around Elland Road. *"What the f*** is going on?"* soon followed. You know things are bad when we sing that.

As the clock on the big screen ticked over to 17:00 applause broke out in memory of Skye Thompson, a 17 year-old Leeds fan who died this week. Skye, a season ticket holder on the Kop, gave an improved life to four people as an organ donor. It was also a moment to remember long time Leeds fan, John Cave, aka Jailhouse John, who also died recently. John had followed the Whites since the 1940s. For one minute we focussed on them and not the feeble effort our team, their team, was making out there on the pitch. We were happy to focus on any distraction by now and we had another one on the half hour mark as a picture of a missing person, Shaun Howson, was displayed up on the big screen. A bloke in front of me sarcastically shouted: *"Aye, there's eleven more gone missing out there an all!"* Very little was happening, for either side out on the pitch. Sol Bamba picked up his fifth booking of the season, meaning he'd miss the Cardiff match on Tuesday night but it no longer seemed very important to be honest. We'd have Bellusci or Wootton in there no doubt and it was hard to see how that could make us any worse; Sol had to take the blame for the first Blackburn goal today.

As the half-time whistle blew, more boos came from the Kop but even that was half-hearted. Mark and Chloe disappeared off to the concourse while Kentley and I slumped down in our seats in silence.

Steve Evans only left it five minutes into the second-half before making his first change. Jordan Botaka replaced Tom Adeyemi. It was a surprise to me that Botaka hadn't started and as soon as he was on we looked more positive; the 'Wizard' always looks like he might produce some magic. Little in the way of chances came our way though and the game was meandering along with Blackburn content to sit on what they had. The Leeds fans knew the game was done by now and we spent the rest of the evening protesting against Cellino and Sky TV. A prolonged, *"Sky TV is f****** sh**"*, rang out followed by, *"Thursday night, what the f***"*, as we let the TV viewers know exactly what we thought about Thursday night footie. Another, *"Massimo, time to go"*, followed and then a rendition of, *"Sell the club and f*** off home"*. Then, almost with a sigh, we all joined in as a chant of, *"We're Leeds United, we've all had enough"*, broke out. That was heard just before the end of Ken Bates' regime and then again before GFH sold out to Cellino. The Leeds family had spoken; it was time for Cellino to pass the baton. Over in the South Stand they amused themselves by singing, *"Let's pretend we scored a goal"*, and then counting down from ten before all jumping up and down and going berserk as if we really had scored a goal. It was good to keep in practice as surely we'd get another one sometime soon.

There was still a game going on of course, in a fashion, and Evans was still trying to make something happen. Wood was replaced by Doukara on 68 minutes with the Leeds fans booing Wood as he went off and then Mowatt replaced Cook with five to go. Leeds created bugger all though and to be fair neither did Blackburn. The game ended 2 – 0, just as it was after five and a half minutes. At the final whistle there were more boos and I have to say that was all I wanted...more booze, anything to take away the pain of this most feeble of displays but some of the stuff coming from Leeds' fans towards the end of the game was unacceptable. A couple of times Silvestri caught the ball to a chorus of sarcastic cheers and there were ironic cheers for Doukara too. That won't help. Neither will the chant of, *"What the fu***** hell was that?"* directed at the few Leeds players who ventured towards the Kop at the end of the game.

Back in the car, Mark tuned in to Radio Leeds and we waited for Steve Evans to be interviewed. He was obviously having plenty to say in the dressing room as they had to extend the show until well after 10:30pm before they got their man. I expected Evans to be foaming at the mouth but he was surprisingly candid although we learned very little about how he planned to turn around the good ship Leeds. It would take some doing as she was listing badly.

When I got home, after another dire journey due to various problems on the M62, it was 12:30am but I still fired up the lap top and, with large single malt in hand, I scrolled though my Twitter timeline. Almost all the fans' anger was directed at Cellino. A few pointed out that eleven players in white ought to search their consciences too but in the main the feeling was that Cellino's ownership was the root cause of all the problems at the club and indeed in the universe generally. There was some cause for optimism for those who wanted him out the following day, as various publications suggested Cellino himself may well have had enough.

"I'm losing my balls," Cellino told The Times, who reported rumours of renewed interest in the club from Red Bull. *"Ten years ago, I had more balls, but since I came here it's been a nightmare. Now I have a low quality of life. I feel shame when I walk to the shop to buy cigarettes if we lose a game.*

"I convinced my family to come here and they have run away.

"It's like being at a party where you're not welcome. It's killing me. Every night I lie awake, asking myself, 'Am I good enough?'."[1]

But in case anyone thought Cellino would be going any time soon he added: *"You think I can sell a club in five minutes? Who gets hurt in the meantime? Last season someone sent me a lot of bullsh**ters."* I couldn't see anyone buying out Cellino; the reckoning was they'd need to pay something like £40m just for him to walk away without being out of pocket. Was Leeds United worth £40m to anyone?

Leeds United 0 Blackburn 2 (Conway (1), Rhodes (6))
19,666 (**Blackburn 520**)

---

[1]   http://www.irishtimes.com/sport/soccer/english-soccer/massimo-cellino-considering-ending-his-leeds-nightmare-1.2411376

Leeds Fans United

At precisely 6:09pm, Friday 30 October, Phil Hay of the YEP tweeted: *"Astonishing breaking news tonight: Massimo Cellino has told @LeedsFansUtd that he is willing to sell them his majority stake in Leeds United"* We knew Cellino was having a meeting with various fans groups to discuss the ongoing strategy in fighting the way Sky TV was changing match dates and times. What we had no inkling of was that Dylan Thwaites of Leeds Fans United (LFU) would use the opportunity to explore again the possibility of LFU getting a stake in the club. Cellino was so fed up that he apparently told Thwaites he'd be willing to sell up to a fans group at no profit to himself assuming the fans group could come up with the asking price; whatever that proved to be. Predictably social media went berserk with fans glorying in the imminent demise of the man they saw as the root of all evil and new pledges of money began pouring into LFU again from fans desperate not to miss this chance to own a bit of their club. LFU announced that they'd need some time to consider the ramifications of this latest twist and promised to make a further announcement the following week. My guess was that the ever unpredictable Cellino would have changed his mind by then. It seemed to me that there was absolutely no chance of LFU raising the necessary funds from ordinary fans to meet what was still expected to be an asking price of forty or fifty million pounds just to secure Cellino's stake, remembering that GFH still held a 23% shareholding too. My guess was LFU would reopen their discussions with the half dozen or so groups they said were waiting in the wings when they first set up some nine months earlier. One or more of those groups acting in concert with LFU might have the necessary financial might and could conceivably have the resources to then further invest in the club to run it on a day to day basis. LFU could then still take a small share in the club to allow it a voice on the board which was always their main aim. Some fans were immediately wary that Cellino had only sought to publicise the fact that he was now ready to sell and that a bidding war might break out as all the usual culprits came out of the woodwork. Within a few hours there were rumours of Cellino having meetings in London with potential buyers. Former Southampton Chairman, Nicola Cortese was the first big name to be mentioned in the press. LFU immediately tried to obtain an exclusivity agreement with Cellino to stop any other bidders in their tracks. Dylan Thwaites told the Yorkshire Evening Post on Monday: *"At our meeting on Friday, Massimo was absolutely clear that he was only selling to fans. Indeed, when we asked if we could involve any of the other third parties we have been working with, he was adamant that he would only sell to Leeds fans.*

"This clearly gives us an exclusive position. Of course, as professionals we need this signing and we expect to have that shortly."[1] Good luck with that I thought!

Cellino then came out and said that because of the strength of feeling against him at the Blackburn game, he'd decided to cease going to the matches. He didn't confirm whether this was for the time being or for good. Many fans saw this as yet another small victory and even more signed up to LFU.

---

[1]   http://www.yorkshireeveningpost.co.uk/sport/leeds-united/latest-lufc-news/leeds-united-fans-group-warns-of-hostile-reaction-to-rival-takeover-bids-1-7547966

Meanwhile, I was making use of my Leeds United free weekend by ticking off another couple of football league grounds; numbers 84 and 85 out of 92. On Saturday I was at Leyton Orient to see them beaten 1 – 0 at home by Accrington Stanley and then the following day, accompanied by my good mate Kentley who was still operating on one leg, I was at Victoria Road, home to Dagenham and Redbridge who lost 2 – 0 to the Hatters of Luton Town. I was getting used to the London Midland service from Stafford to Euston.

Ahead of the Tuesday night game with Cardiff City, Steve Evans lamented the lack of true characters in his squad. He told the YEP:

"The fans are knowledgeable enough to know that there's not a player in the dressing room who Steve Evans has signed."

Asked if he had any strong characters in the dressing room he responded: *"There's some but there's not enough; I'd be telling a lie if I said that all the players in this squad fit playing for Leeds United in the Championship."*[1]

Leeds were looking for any little help they could find to try to jerk the team out of this current trough and prior to the game with the Bluebirds – a side we'd not beaten since 1984 – Leeds turned to the Good Lord. Back in 1967, Don Revie allegedly summoned a gypsy from Scarborough to Elland Road to exorcise the curse Revie believed was preventing his side being successful. Now, over 50 years later, the centre circle and dressing room were 'blessed' with holy water by Monsignor Philip Moger of St Anne's Cathedral, Leeds, at the request of Massimo Cellino in a bid to revive our fortunes. I'd have preferred him to concentrate on those six-yard areas myself. Presumably Massimo believed a gypsy spell had a limited shelf life of only 50 years. Either that or maybe he'd decided the lemon trees weren't working. Remember, it would be eight months to the day on the Wednesday after this game that we last won at Elland Road.

---

[1]   http://www.yorkshireeveningpost.co.uk/sport/football/football-headlines/leeds-united-evans-blasts-squad-ahead-of-cardiff-encounter-1-7549436

Britain was in the grip of a pall of fog that was causing travel chaos at the airports and on the motorways. It had been foggy down at Dagenham on Sunday and it was still hanging around as I set off up the motorway on Tuesday afternoon. With the chaos I experienced on the M62 last Thursday still fresh in my mind, I decided to use the M1 for this one and I had a trouble free run that got me to Elland Road at exactly 4:45pm, three hours before kick-off.

I still wasn't first in the Pavilion; Ian English is always there in his wheelchair and Steve, one of the three lads from County Durham, must sleep in there! George and Trevor joined us later, together with Jacqui and Mick from Hampshire, Derek and Shirley from Milton Keynes, Si from somewhere else 'darn sarf', Nigel, Martin and the boys, and loads more I've probably forgotten to mention. We all listened intently to Lorimer and Yorath, wondering if 'Tel' would have anything derogatory to say about the team today. He certainly did! He went through them all; *"Well, we need a new goalkeeper don't we?"* he began, *"and two new centre backs".* He moved through the team; *"and a striker, we don't have a striker who is any good and Wootton, he's not good enough for Leeds United."* We sat, mouths gaping open, hardly believing what we were hearing. Peter Lorimer looked slightly embarrassed and then very embarrassed as Yorath continued; *"Peter won't like this but honestly, we're just crap and let's face it; we'll remain crap until this owner leaves Leeds United."* Despite how crap Yorath thought we were, he still managed a 2 – 2 forecast for the game, while Lorimer hoped for a 2 – 1 Leeds win. In the knowledge that Cardiff came to Leeds on the back of four straight clean sheets, that Leeds only had one clean sheet all season and that we hadn't scored a goal from open play since 19th September, more than six weeks ago… I strolled over to the Coral counter and confidently placed my one pound bet on Leeds to win 4 – 0 at 66/1…

Nigel and I wandered over to the ground just before 7:30pm, I was determined not to miss the one minute's silence and the playing of the Last Post, this being our designated Remembrance game. I had a chat with young Zack who hailed me as I walked by and then went over for my now usual pre-match chat with Rob and Pete; I told them if we lost today I was ceasing that particular ritual!

Elland Road had lots of empty seats but a crowd of 17,914, with the help of only 184 from Cardiff, was not bad for a foggy November night, especially since Leeds had that eight month home win drought. The teams lined up around the centre circle and it was noticeable that while the Leeds players linked arms, the Cardiff players mostly stood with their hands clasped in front of them, heads bowed. It was the first body language signal I picked up and I liked it. Steve Evans had been distraught over the Blackburn defeat and pledged again to get Leeds fired up and *"Marching on Together"*. He'd shown the team a motivational video before the game about Nick Vujicic, a man born with no legs or arms but who now gives inspiring talks on how to overcome adversity. Check it out on the link below; it's an amazing film.[1] I tell you what, if that didn't inspire our lads, nothing would and it wouldn't matter how many priests visited Elland Road or how many lemon trees we planted, if that failed we were doomed!

Evans made a couple of changes to the team that wilted against Blackburn; Sol Bamba was suspended while Tom Adeyemi was prevented from playing by the terms of his season long loan from the Bluebirds. So, in came Peppe Bellusci for the first time since his horror show at the Riverside and Alex Mowatt came in for Adeyemi. Terry Yorath's favourite full back, Scott Wootton, replaced Sam Byram who disappointed on Thursday. Liam Cooper took the captain's armband as he did so often last season. Charlie Taylor had still not returned after illness. The word was that Leeds were on the point of signing Liam Bridcutt, the out of favour Sunderland midfielder, on a loan arrangement but he wasn't signed in time to play against Cardiff.

Silvestri
Wootton Bellusci Cooper Berardi
Dallas Cook Murphy Mowatt
Wood Antenucci

---

[1] *http://ed.ted.com/on/QpfmsLex*

Subs: Horton, Byram, Doukara, Botaka, Buckley, Phillips, Sloth.

Cardiff had several recognisable names in their squad; former Leeds player, Lee Peltier is a regular full back for them these days and of course the likes of Morrison, Noone and Whittingham had all damaged us in the past as had the huge imposing figure of Kenwyne Jones. He was on their bench alongside Sammy Ameobi, younger brother of Shola, who scored for Bolton against us the other day.

After a minute of silence, a lone trumpeter played the Last Post. It was a haunting moment, the mist still swirling around the ground, like so many ghostly shapes caught in the glare of the floodlights and that familiar lament filling the otherwise silent space of Elland Road. Whether it was the damp air or the nerves of the trumpeter I don't know but a couple of times his notes were not as crisp as they should've been. No matter, it was a fitting tribute to our fallen heroes from the forces.

Leeds looked much more positive from the first whistle and looked comfortable in the formation they were playing. Luke Murphy was rampaging around the centre of the pitch like we hadn't seen since those opening minutes at Bradford last season; I hoped he'd reign himself in just a tad to avoid repeating what happened that similarly misty night! Lewis Cook was back to his best; gliding along with the ball or harrying the opposition and miraculously coming away with it without seemingly tackling his man, just stepping in and running away with it. How does he do that? At the back we looked composed enough with neither Wootton nor Bellusci giving any cause for concern. Up front Chris Wood was looking more mobile than usual too. Cardiff looked like a team slightly bemused by the vigour of this Leeds team; perhaps they'd only studied the video of the Blackburn fiasco. Whittingham was soon in the book for a foul as Cardiff struggled to keep Leeds at bay. Having said that, clear cut chances were few and far between, with a Stuart Dallas left footer from the edge of the box being the best effort from either side in the first-half. When the half-time whistle blew, there was generous and sincere applause from the Leeds fans and even leaving the pitch the Leeds players seemed to have the more positive body language as they jogged down the tunnel while the Cardiff players meandered off.

The second-half began in similar vein, although if anything Cardiff now looked to be upping their game. They won a couple of corners and were now having long spells of possession. Still Leeds were in their faces all the time though and still Lewis Cook would often steal the ball away like some sort of magician performing an illusion. Cardiff were the first to twist as Sammy Ameobi replaced Craig Noone on the hour mark.

Winning games in the Championship is easy. I'm convinced of it. All you need to do is make no mistakes and then either wait for one from the opposition, or find a moment of brilliance yourselves. There never seems to be much between the sides, so most games tend to be won either by taking advantage of mistakes or coming up with some magic. I suppose that's the nature of the game. Today, it was finally our turn to come up with a moment of magic.

A long clearance was won in the air by Stuart Dallas and Antenucci was onto the knock down like a terrier with a rag doll, wrestling the ball away from a defender and then scuffing it inside to Alex Mowatt about 35 yards from goal. Alex looked up to get his bearings, took one touch and a couple of steps nearer goal and then unleashed a left foot shot that soared into the top right of Marshall's goal with the Cardiff keeper left scrambling along his line trying in vain to reach it. Elland Road exploded! It always does when we score a goal but it is a long time since we reacted with quite such an explosion of joy! Think Billy Sharp at Huddersfield last season and it felt a bit like that! The players all tumbled on top of Alex Mowatt as he slid down on his knees in the north-west corner while the Cardiff players trudged wearily back to their positions. There was fear though, even at this moment of excitement; to concede this victory now would be another huge blow to our confidence and as the game restarted you could feel the tension amongst the fans. Everyone was now willing our players to fight even harder for every loose ball, every header, to close them down at every step. We winced as Peppe Bellusci went beyond the cause as he nearly decapitated

Scott Malone over on the Cardiff left wing and got a yellow card. In the Premier League, do that against Chelsea at Stamford Bridge and you'd probably be having an early shower. We winced again as we spotted the ginormous figure of Kenwyne Jones jogging on to replace Alex Revell and he and Ameobi were soon linking up to give our defence more to think about. Cardiff forced a couple of corners and Silvestri was again showing that, whatever his shortcomings, he can stop shots. Cardiff made their final change as Pilkington replaced Whittingham and then Leeds twisted by bringing on Byram for Dallas. The fresh legs of Byram were immediately sprinting down the Leeds right but, as so often, Sam stopped and cut back inside and the chance was gone. But then we were all on our toes again as Sean Morrison, under pressure from Wood, got his back pass horribly wrong. Wood was onto it in a flash and cleverly knocked the ball past Marshall to the right while Wood skipped past him to the left. He had two Leeds players begging for the ball to be laid across the face of goal, a goal now only protected by a single Cardiff defender. Instead, Wood had a rush of blood to the head and he slammed an angled shot into the side netting. We all sank back down wondering if that would be proved to be a costly miss in the final few minutes.

It wasn't. Leeds did their best to break up the flow of the game by substituting first Phillips for Mowatt and then Doukara for Antenucci and then saw out the four minutes of added time without any major drama. We had done it; the huge cheer at full time was one mainly of relief but also appreciation of a performance befitting Leeds United. Whether it was the pre-match blessing by Monsignor Moger, that amazing motivational video or the lemon trees, Leeds had come out and given it some boll**** tonight. The question now was; was this a turning point in our fortunes or just a one off?

The win lifted us back up to 17th place in the table with 16 points from 15 games; one point and one place above the Terriers from Huddersfield. Guess where we were heading on Saturday?

Leeds United 1 Cardiff City 0 **(Mowatt, (63))**
17,914 (Cardiff 184)

Town and City

Chris Powell paid the price for a poor start to the season by Huddersfield Town. The Terriers sacked their manager following a run of one win in seven with their Chief Executive, Nigel Clibbens telling the BBC he wanted *"a change of direction."* Powell was the fifth Championship manager to be sacked this season and was quickly followed by the sixth when QPR removed Chris Ramsey, despite the 'R's sitting comfortably in mid-table. Neil Warnock was put in temporary charge there. Huddersfield was our next destination and we were told Town's Academy Manager, Mark Lillis would be in temporary charge at least until after the game with Leeds.

I was just absorbing that news when Twitter suddenly burst into life with a story claiming that Massimo Cellino had now changed his mind about selling the club to Leeds Fans United. Another quick search of the BBC Sport website soon fetched up the relevant statement made by LFU:

"We've been informed by the lawyers of Cellino he no longer wishes to sell to Leeds fans. Our insistence on him confirming his verbal offer of exclusivity in a legally binding agreement

has forced transparency on his motives. It is much better that we identify this insincerity now before we spend our shareholders' money."[1]

That was that then. Well, at least until he changed his mind again. Leeds fans on Twitter seemed to be divided, as they always are of course. Half seemed surprisingly pleased that LFU would not be the next owner of their club while half were already organising more 'Cellino out' protests in case he harboured any thoughts of now staying on. The 'Cellino In' group even set up a Facebook account 'In Cellino We Trust', and quickly recruited over 2,000 followers.

For what it's worth, I felt it could be as simple as Cellino seeing that the side could win football matches after all and hence he'd prefer to ride out the storm in the hope the Cardiff win was a turning point and not another false dawn.

Sky TV must have been delighted that Powell was sacked as it gave a whole new line of interest for their TV show; yes folks, the Leeds game at Huddersfield was yet another live on TV game with another ludicrous 12:30pm kick-off. The only good news about that kick-off time was that it did mean I'd be able to see the Worcester City FA Cup tie at Bramall Lane, which was a normal 3pm kick-off. I'd calculated I'd have to leave Huddersfield no later than half-time though, to ensure I didn't miss the start of the City game. This would be a first for me as I'd never left any game early, ever! Cup fever had well and truly taken hold in Worcester, just as it did the previous season when we disposed of Coventry and took Scunthorpe to a replay. I'd even been interviewed live on BBC Radio Hereford and Worcester ahead of the game.

In other news: Lee Erwin was back at Leeds after returning from his brief loan spell at Bury; Leeds announced that Steve Evans had organised a friendly game at Wycombe on the first Friday of the next international break to keep the players sharp; the Liam Bridcutt loan was now 'in the balance' with the Sunderland man having several options although Steve Evans was still hopeful he'd choose Leeds; Peter Lorimer was

---

[1] *http://www.bbc.co.uk/sport/0/football/34721028*

lambasted by the 'Cellino Out' fans for a piece he wrote in the YEP in support of Cellino; oh, and there were rumours of an investigation into possible match fixing during three Leeds games last season. Just your average day on Planet Leeds really... As to the match fixing allegations, I could think of plenty of games in which the goals we gave away could far more easily be explained if match fixing was involved!

Saturday came and I was back on the road heading for Huddersfield by 7:30am. For once I had a trouble free run and I found a parking spot near the ground by 9:30am and eventually I braved the weather and went for a walk round the ground to take a few photos. It was really windy and every now and again the rain would come down in torrents. I met Si as I was wandering around the John Smith's Stadium and we had a quick chat and then as I doubled back I bumped into Phil B. As Phil and I chatted we could see a magnificent rainbow as we looked away from the stadium towards the town centre. We wondered which side would come away with the proverbial pot of gold later.

I took shelter in the bogs on the concourse at one point as another deluge poured from the sky and I was met in there by the sight of a couple of discarded sombreros propped up in the basins. Another sombrero was on the head of a bloke at the other end of the trough and I had to laugh as he chatted to a mate adding the phrase, *"I take my hat off to him for that"*, at the end of the conversation! The prevalence of sombreros was in honour of Steve Evans who famously wore one together with Bermuda shorts, T-shirt and sandals when Rotherham went to Elland Road at the end of last season.

Evans named an unchanged starting eleven, which meant Sol Bamba and Tom Adeyemi could only find places on the bench and once again there was no starting slot for Jordan Botaka. Sam Byram and Doukara were missing altogether. Lee Erwin was straight onto the bench following his return to the club.

Silvestri
Wootton Bellusci Cooper Berardi
Dallas Cook Murphy Mowatt
Antenucci Wood

Subs: Horton, Bamba, Adeyemi, Phillips, Erwin, Buckley, Botaka.

This was Huddersfield's Remembrance Day game and so proceedings began with the traditional one minute's silence with the teams lined up around opposite sides of the centre circle. The Leeds players all linked their arms around their neighbour's shoulders while the Terriers stood mostly with their arms down by their sides looking, as Cardiff had done the other night, a pretty ragged bunch.

After all the rain we'd had in the previous few hours, it was a surprise to see the stadium bathed in bright sunlight as Leeds kicked off. Nothing much happened for ten minutes and then Leeds won a corner on the right wing; Luke Murphy trotted over to take it. Out of the corner of my eye, as I watched Murphy standing over the ball, I could see the Leeds players darting about in the area and then suddenly two of them seemed to collide. Both players fell to the ground but only Scott Wootton bounced straight back up. Our other player was Liam Cooper and he was now prone on the deck holding his head. Watching the incident back on the Sky TV recording it was a sickening collision. Both of them turned to dash in opposite directions but unfortunately neither realised where the other was and as they collided both heads bashed together. Cooper was down for five or six minutes and it was clear he couldn't continue. Sol Bamba was soon stripped and ready to resume his place at the heart of the defence after all.

The only other 'incidents' of the first forty odd minutes were a couple of rash tackles by Scott Wootton, who may have still been a bit dazed and therefore not quite as sharp as he should have been. Wootton got a yellow card for his first tackle and was lucky not get a second and an early bath when he did it again. Martin Crainie got a card for a similar indiscretion as some typical 'derby day' challenges were made by both sides.

A mammoth eight minutes of added time was announced due to the various stoppages and I was looking at my watch trying to work out if I could still make it to Sheffield if I stopped to see the first-half out. I'm glad I decided I could, just.

After about four of the allocated eight minutes, Scott Wootton had the ball deep in our own half, over on the Leeds right and he launched a speculative ball up that wing. Stuart Dallas just got a yard ahead of his marker as the ball came down over the head of the Huddersfield player who'd misjudged the flight of the ball. Dallas cushioned the ball inside to Chris Wood who gave it straight back and Dallas was then away on his own towards the Leeds right wing corner. In a flash, he sent the ball across the face of goal and there was Mirco Antenucci flying in to hook it home. It all happened in a couple of seconds and many fans must have missed it altogether as they'd already have been down to the toilets or the snack bars. The rest of us celebrated like crazy as did Mirco and the rest of the players down on the pitch. Mirco was twirling his shirt around his head as he's done before and we could see the referee shaking his head and pulling his yellow card out for the usual sanction for showing joy on a football pitch. Mirco even had a matching yellow undershirt on but the referee was unmoved and not for changing his mind.

Many more fans took that as the signal to go off for their half-time break but I stood where I was; knowing I'd have to leave for good in a few minutes' time.

Huddersfield restarted the game eventually and had a look of resignation as they lamely knocked the ball up field. Leeds were suddenly fired up by the goal though and none more so than Mirco. A long ball was lofted up the Leeds left wing and suddenly Mirco was all alone behind the Terriers' defence, much as Dallas had been moments earlier. He sprinted towards the by–line, jinked past goalkeeper Joe Murphy and then squared the ball across the face of goal. From where I stood, a hundred yards away, it looked like Antenucci had shot at goal and I joined in with a gasp of annoyance as the ball seemed to ricochet back off a Huddersfield defender. But then we could all see the ball arriving at the feet of Chris Wood and in a flash Wood struck the ball and the net was rippling again! Two bloody nil! Two goals in the space of a couple of minutes had suddenly transformed the balance of the game. *"How sh*t must you be, we're winning away"*, belted out from the ranks of the Leeds fans and then: *"In yer cup fin-al, two-nil, in yer cup fin-al two-nil"*, as we all continued to bounce around punching the air. Finally the referee brought the first-half to an end and in the chaos I looked at my watch again. It was 1:30pm.

I said cheerio to Nigel and jogged down to the concourse and over to the nearest gate. A lady steward was stood by it. I asked her if she could let me out and I explained: *"No, I don't want to come back in."* Some Leeds fans nearby looked at me strangely as I dashed outside and off up the road.

I listened to the second-half of the Leeds game on Radio Leeds as I sped down the M1 and I punched the air again as Alex Mowatt struck another one of his trademark long range left-footers to put Leeds three-nil up. I was still nervous even then but gradually as time ebbed away and Marco Silvestri seemed to be having one of his better days, I started to relax and at the final whistle we still had that three goal advantage. What a result! It was Leeds going away with that pot of gold after all! *"Now, if only Worcester City can match that score-line it will be the perfect day"* I thought to myself.

I arrived in Sheffield at 2:45pm and dropped the car in the first 'Football Parking' car park I came to. It was right in front of the Grosvenor Casino on Duchess Road, about a ten minute jog from Bramall Lane. Inside the ground I was blowing a bit as I climbed the final set of steps and was grateful to pause for a moment as a steward stopped me going any further. *"Wait there mate, they're doing the minute's silence"* he told me.

I'd done it! I'd made kick off. There was an electric atmosphere in the 'Redbrik Upper' stand as over 2,000 Worcester City fans roared on their non-league heroes. The rest of the ground was pretty sparsely populated and the official attendance was later given as only 11,108. I'd forgotten what an impressive stadium Bramall Lane is; looking around from my position high above the pitch, just to the right of centre behind the goal City were defending it was hard not to admire the old place. Everything was red of course, even though the Blades were playing in almost all white pinstripe shirts these days and not those historic bold red and white stripes. City looked resplendent in their blue and white. Inevitably, the home side had the bulk of possession but City were not outclassed and appeared to be defending well. But then a few quick passes got Che Adams into the City box and

Sam Miniham brought him down. It was a clear penalty. Jose Baxter scored from the spot despite our efforts to put him off.

For the rest of the first-half and 35 minutes of the second, City defended heroically and created a couple of great chances themselves. Sadly, we just couldn't find a decent finish and then, as the City boys tired, the Blades cut through us twice more and the game was up; we'd matched the score from the John Smith's Stadium but it was 3 – 0 to Sheffield United. Had he been needed, Billy Sharp was on the Blades' bench. There would be no pot of gold for City this season.

Leeds victory at the John Smith's was clinical although not totally dominant. We'd put away three of our four shots on target but the Terriers bossed possession 63% to 37% and had 19 attempts to our eight. We all knew we couldn't get carried away but the Steve Evans reign had started well.

There was no rest for the Leeds players who were not involved in international action; there was that friendly at Wycombe on Friday 13 November to keep everyone sharp. I wouldn't be there, as Mrs W and I were off to Gran Canaria for a week of sun but 1,800 Leeds fans would make the trip.

Leeds were back up to 15th after this round of games, firmly in mid-table with the likes of Wolves, Fulham and QPR. We had 19 points, 6 more than the best of the bottom three, Charlton Athletic, and 9 points outside the playoff places. The top six, were Hull, Brighton, Burnley, Middlesbrough, Derby and Birmingham. The stand out result of the day, just pipping ours, was a 5 – 2 win by Birmingham at Fulham. By Sunday morning the news had broken that Fulham had sacked their manager, Kit Symons, the seventh Championship manager to bite the dust this season. I was sure there would be more.

Huddersfield Town 0 **Leeds United 3 (Antenucci (45+4), Wood (45+6), Mowatt (54))**
17,118 (**Leeds 3,831**)

Another false dawn

In the week leading up to the next international break, most talk on social media was speculation; speculation about who Cellino might be talking to with regards to the sale of his stake in the club. LFU was being phlegmatic about the situation, openly stressing they wouldn't criticise Cellino for pulling out of the deal they felt they'd secured, just in case he changed his mind again. In the meantime, the bookies favourite appeared to be Mike Farnan, long-time Leeds fan and the man who tried unsuccessfully to wrest Leeds from GFH before Cellino sneaked in. Farnan was then the lead figure in the consortium known as Together Leeds. As we saw back in April though, Farnan had been caught on the hop when another name from that consortium, Adam Pearson, moved into Elland Road as CEO. So, I thought it unlikely those two would be getting together again any time soon even though Pearson had long since ejected. Another name in the frame was Steve Parkin but it soon became clear that his interest was only to *invest* in the club, possibly alongside Cellino, rather than go for a controlling stake. In a YEP article back in 2013 Parkin seemed to have said then that he was not prepared to risk too much of his retirement pot when he told the paper: *"It has been underfunded for so long, it would need £40-£50m. I would be mad keen to get involved but my family would not be happy if I put that amount of money into the club. I wouldn't, it*

is just too risky."[1] So the rumours rumbled on and on. The papers were even speculating on who the next Leeds manager might be if Farnan got involved. David Moyes, former Everton and short term Man United head coach was said to be Farnan's preference; Moyes having recently been sacked by Real Sociedad.

Meanwhile, elsewhere in the Championship, manager number eight got the elbow as Blackburn finally parted with Gary Bowyer. Blackburn had only managed three wins so far this season, the same number as Leeds of course and one of them was that 2 – 0 humiliation we suffered at Elland Road just a couple of weeks earlier. Former Norwich and Villa boss, Paul Lambert would eventually be named for the Ewood hot-seat. It made a few people sit up and take notice of the ambition being shown on the other side of the Pennines as they compared the appointment of Lambert with Evans at Leeds although Lambert himself would be gone by the end of the season.

There was still no sign of Liam Bridcutt at Elland Road yet as that saga also rumbled along; other clubs were now said to be chasing his signature but Steve Evans was still saying talks were ongoing.

I managed one more new ground this week before we flew off to Gran Canaria; I drove down to Gillingham on Tuesday night to watch their JPT second round game with Yeovil. The men from Somerset won through after a penalty shoot-out. That was ground number 86 of 92.

Mrs W and I flew out to Gran Canaria late on Friday morning; Friday 13th as it happens but we arrived safe and sound at our hotel in Las Canteras on the north east corner of the island and, having dropped our suitcase, went for a wander and then ate at a restaurant on the sea front. The weather was perfect; even as we enjoyed our evening meal in the open air it was still around 24 degrees. We were in good spirits in more ways than one as we tumbled back into the hotel room after a few beers and I was keen to check how Leeds had got on at

---

[1]   *http://www.yorkshireeveningpost.co.uk/news/steve-parkin-rising-from-the-coalface-to-change-leeds-s-skyline-1-6045631*

Wycombe in that friendly. Having finally got the Kindle hooked up to the hotel Wi-Fi, I was soon scrolling through Twitter and could see that Leeds had come through a satisfactory work out at Adams Park, beating the home side 2 – 0 with goals from Erwin and Byram. The Leeds side was: **Silvestri (Peacock-Farrell 86), Wootton, Bamba, Bellusci, Berardi (Byram 45), Botaka, Bianchi (Sloth 45), Adeyemi (Phillips 60), Buckley, Doukara, Erwin.** Other subs: **Murphy, Mowatt, Antenucci.** The closing stages saw a first senior outing for young goalkeeper Bailey Peacock-Farrell, who only signed professional terms this last summer. A crowd of just 2,216 watched the game including 767 travelling Leeds fans. In the weeks to come, Kentley would rib me something chronic about, *"missing yet another game"*, and he'd tell me that for sheer atmosphere, this was one of the best games he could remember; there was no pressure I guess and the fans really enjoyed themselves.

As I was taking in the details of the game though, various tweets were starting to appear about something happening in Paris; some sort of terror alert. For the next few hours, Mrs W and I watched BBC World News as the full horror of that awful night was played out in front of our eyes. It would not be until the following day that the initial death toll of 129 would be established and the full ramifications for the world would not become clear for months. I will *never* forget where I was on the night of the attacks of course as I am sure folk all over the world will never forget either and nor should we…

On our return to Manchester, we witnessed one of the funniest things I've ever seen. Walking through the airport towards the luggage reclaim area, there were huge signs proclaiming how Manchester had been voted 'Best UK Airport of 2015'; nothing funny in that you may think. I've always found Manchester to be one of the best organised airports I've used. This time, we were directed to carousel number '5' and we noted that a flight from JFK New York was also designated for the same carousel and indeed the bags had already started to arrive for that flight. There was no sign though of any of that flight's passengers, while we recognised many of the folk who'd been on our plane, stood waiting. Round and round went the carousel and each time it went round, more and more bags from the JFK flight were on it. The bags were now so tightly packed on the conveyor belt that one or two began to topple off, scattering folk in all directions and threatening to crush any small child in the way. An old lady swayed wildly as a big black case caught her with a glancing blow on the way past but her daughter grabbed her and pulled her to safety. Still no one was claiming any of the bags and still more were piling on the belt. Then, another of the bigger cases caught the wall on the way back outside through the little hatch and suddenly there was a tsunami of bags and cases and golf bags crashing into each other and piling up at the far end of the carousel! It was like an earthquake as the biggest bags got pushed together and up into the air before toppling on to the floor. A few of the menfolk, yours truly included, dashed forward to try to stem the tide but as fast as we tried to pull the bags clear more came and we all quickly gave up reasoning that it was no way to die; crushed under a jumbo sized suitcase. Then, one bright spark thought to hit the big red emergency stop button and finally the carnage was halted. By this time though there was a mountain of cases piled up against the wall and I couldn't help but burst into fits of laughter. We then spotted that the Gran Canaria flight had been shifted to carousel '4' and a couple of hundred passengers made a mad dash for the prime spots. Once again it was the survival of the fittest as we all elbowed our way to the new location. It was like a scene from a Carry On movie! Carry on round the crazy carousel. In fact it reminded me a bit of life at LS11. Good job you got that award this year Manchester.

Back home and scrolling once more through Twitter, the only breaking news on Planet Leeds was that, predictably, Cellino did appear to have changed his mind again and the YEP was reporting that he'd now decided *not* to sell the club after all, at least *"...until he knows Leeds will be safe in the Championship come the end of the season."*[1]

It looked as though he was trying to wrong-foot both the 'Cellino In' *and* the 'Cellino Out' brigades both of whom were limbering up ahead of protests to be made before the Rotherham game. For me, I was convinced more than ever he was just waiting to see how far up the table Evans could get us, just in case there was still a shot at the play-offs; Cellino knew full well that to sell up now and then see us promoted would be the worst agony of all for him. After all, in the TV series and the film versions, Mission: Impossible is always achieved!

The day of the Rotherham game dawned with a blanket of snow over most of northern England and it had suddenly turned bitterly cold. As I drove up the M6 the temperature on the dashboard read 4.5 degrees...a far cry from the 30 plus we had in Gran Canaria. It was so cold that it was no wonder the 'Cellino out' protest only attracted a handful of fans outside the ground and they soon adjourned to the warmth of the Peacock.

In the Pavilion, Terry Yorath was again doing his best to slag-off most of the Leeds players. He told us how in his opinion, *"None of the back four are any good".* Someone called out that Berardi had done OK but Yorath was adamant that even Gaetano was no use. *"If Berardi's a good full back then I'll go outside and show my backside in Elland Road"*, he told the Pavilion punters. There were lots of heads shaking in response to that and then one table began to boo the former Welsh international as he turned his attention to Steve Evans. *"He's a scruffy bastard"*, Yorath began, *"and I didn't like it when he was giving it large to the Huddersfield fans after we scored".* Most of us had actually loved that show of passion and emotion from Big Steve!

---

[1] http://www.yorkshireeveningpost.co.uk/sport/leeds-united/latest-lufc-news/leeds-united-massimo-cellino-puts-sale-of-club-on-hold-1-7582159

I did laugh out loud at one point while listening to Jed Stone interviewing Yorath and John Hendrie. In response to Yorath's jibes about the *"scruffy bastard"*, Stone remarked, *"Well, we've just heard that Steve Evans has been awarded the 'Manager for a Month' award for Leeds United..."* Yorath then told us how our awful back four would, *"never keep a clean sheet in a million years"*, but when asked by Stone for a prediction he replied: *"Three-nil Leeds"...*

I went over to the ground earlier than usual to make sure I was in place for the tributes to the victims of the Paris terror atrocity. Boy was it cold outside; the wind was biting our faces as we stood in silence and then applauded as the French national anthem, *'La Marseillaise'* blasted out with the French flag lighting up the big screen. Frenchman Sol Bamba placed a wreath on the centre spot before joining the line of Leeds players stood in the centre circle. It was an emotional and poignant tribute that was taking place at grounds all over Britain; bag searches at the turnstiles were the first practical ramifications of the Paris nightmare.

Sol Bamba was not in the 18-man squad; he'd suffered a broken toe down at Wycombe and would be out for a few weeks, so Steve Evans named the same starting eleven that began the Huddersfield game, with Liam Cooper having recovered from his collision there with Scott Wootton.

Silvestri
Wootton Bellusci Cooper Berardi
Dallas Cook Murphy Mowatt
Antenucci Wood

Subs: Horton, Adeyemi, Erwin, Byram, Doukara, Botaka, Buckley.

Rotherham made *nine* changes to their side from the one that lost 5 – 2 last time out to Ipswich, and they included two debutants; the aggressive Leon Best up front and full back Stephen Kelley.

And so another Yorkshire derby kicked off with the same managers on the touchline that we saw in this fixture at the end of last season; they were just in opposite dug-outs this time. I felt it was vital Leeds came out of the blocks quickly and got at Rotherham before they could settle; I was disappointed that Jordan Botaka didn't start as I felt he could have been the wild card to upset the Millers. As it was, it was a cagey first-half with the best chance falling to Alex Mowatt who mishit his back post shot into the ground and Lee Camp scrambled across his line to palm it away. There was little else to keep us warm in that first 45 minutes. In my YEP Jury piece, written and submitted this week from the hotel in Gran Canaria, I'd written;

"So, if we really have turned a corner, we ought to win this one but I am sure all Leeds fans will be nervously awaiting the outcome. We often get to a place similar to this full of optimism only to see it disintegrate in front of our eyes!"
Although I knew full well how we so often fail to capitalise on a bit of momentum, I still predicted a 4 – 0 win for Leeds; I'd even stuck a couple of quid on it but that bet, and all the optimism Leeds fans felt going into the game was about to go the way it had gone so many times before.

It was the 54th minute and Leeds were attacking; a long ball from Bellusci found Antenucci, busy on the left wing. But Mirco was easily dispossessed and the ball was knocked up towards Joe Newell on the edge of the Leeds box. At this point, Newell was surrounded by three Leeds defenders. Somehow he scrambled the ball out left to Toffolo who in turn passed to Richie Smallwood. The Rotherham man looked up and presumably couldn't believe his eyes as he spotted Joe Newell was now not surrounded by anyone; he was free as a bird on the edge of our six-yard box; that Bermudan Triangle that has seen Leeds defenders going missing for years. Predictably, Smallwood's cross was inch perfect and Newell rose unchallenged to steer the ball wide of the helpless Silvestri. I couldn't help but think of those words spoken by Terry Yorath two hours earlier. *"None of the back four are any good"*. Two clean sheets had lulled us into thinking our problem defence was sorted but now we knew differently.

Evans left it ten minutes before making his first changes; sending on Botaka and Adeyemi for Dallas and Murphy but truth be told we never looked like breaching the Rotherham defence. There was a distinct lack of quality about everything we tried and Botaka didn't even see the ball for his first ten minutes. We resorted to pumping long balls up the middle trying to find the head of Chris Wood but we all knew he wouldn't win a ball in the air as long as his arse pointed to the floor. In the 73rd minute, some heat was generated on the pitch if not in the stands, as Leon Best smashed an elbow into the nose of Gaetano Berardi and he could then be seen smirking as Berardi got up and pushed him to the ground. We got excited as we saw the red card for Best but inevitably it was followed by another one for Berardi for retaliation and so there would be no one man advantage for us.

With five minutes left we got another chance to see Lee Erwin who replaced Lewis Cook as Evans threw caution to the wind. But Erwin made little impact and Rotherham saw the game out without too much drama. Their 905 fans were all that could be heard at the final whistle as the Leeds fans drifted away hunched against the cold and resigned in the knowledge that this team of ours just isn't good enough. They keep teasing us with a couple of decent results every now and again but those are the exceptions not the rule. After the game I listened in the car as Steve Evans was honest enough to admit we didn't play well. He told Adam Pope from BBC Radio Leeds that we had no quality in the final third although he couldn't fault the players' energy and commitment. The post-match interviews focussed more on a bizarre tale about Neil Redfearn, the Millers manager being refused a parking space. For the second time in a week Leeds were saying there was no chance of 'Parkin' at the club.

I felt as depressed as I could remember as I drove back down to the Midlands. There are only so many times that we can be teased like this believing we are better than we are. I'd lost count of the number of times I'd seen a little run of good results from Leeds and decided, 'this is it', believing finally we were on the up; we'd turned that metaphorical corner and would go on a run that would see us challenging for at least a play-off spot. Countless times I've thought that and countless times we've then capitulated tamely against poor opponents. I wasn't sure how many more times I could fall for the con.

Leeds United 0 Rotherham 1 (Newell, (54))

25, 802 (Rotherham 905)

"We're f***ing sh*t!"

It was a quiet week in Leeds. We learned that American goalkeeper Charlie Horton had left the club to return home for personal reasons following the death of his grandfather. That left us with even less goalkeeping cover than we had before with Ross Turnbull still injured. I'm sure we were trying to rectify that in the final few days of the emergency loan window but in the event the only move was the arrival, finally, of Liam Bridcutt. Steve Evans had somehow persuaded Bridcutt that Leeds was a better move for the Sunderland man than Cardiff who thought they'd landed the combative midfielder themselves. Whether it was part of the deal or not we don't know but Will Buckley returned to the North East in what looked like a bit of a swap. Bridcutt would go straight into the squad for the trip to Loftus Road, with Leeds only having the bare minimum number of fit players available. Bridcutt had of course played against Leeds for Sunderland last season in our FA Cup defeat at the Stadium of Light and was well regarded as a defensive midfielder.

On Tuesday, I was a Crewe Alexandra supporter for the day as I took my place on their official coach down to Colchester and ticked off ground number 87 in my quest for 'the 92'. We travelled in luxury on the coach usually reserved for the Port Vale first team and when I explained to the folk on the coach what I was doing they were all really interested and friendly despite me also confessing to be a Leeds fan. They told me in no uncertain terms that had I said I followed The Vale or Stoke City they'd have thrown me off at the next service area! At Colchester I was treated like a minor celeb as they allowed me to go pitch side for a chat and some photos and then the game proved to be another great example of lower league football. Crewe were down and out with an hour gone, 2 – 0 down and struggling but the introduction of the veteran Ryan Lowe changed the game and Crewe stormed back in the final half hour to win 3 – 2. These days I invariably get more entertainment from these games than I do from trips to LS11.

Saturday morning dawned crisp but fine and I was climbing aboard the 06:48 from Stafford expecting to meet Kentley on the train. Having sat down, my phone beeped; Kentley had missed it! He arranged to get the next available London Midland train from Stoke which would get into Euston about an hour later than me. We agreed to meet at the pub.

Stafford station was undergoing some sort of a refit and so there had been no café and no newsagent stall open. All I'd been able to find to read for the journey was a copy of Thursday's Metro newspaper and all I learned from that was that Lewis Hamilton was allegedly shagging Rita Ora.

My train started to fill rapidly as we made the first few stops and by Milton Keynes it was standing room only throughout the carriage. One middle-aged woman squeezed in alongside me and then apologised for squashing me against the window as she hauled her very attractive grown-up daughter onto her lap; I did think about offering...

Everyone in the carriage seemed to be coughing their guts up and the bloke sat behind me was sneezing his head off. Each time he sneezed, I'd do that thing where you try to only breathe out and not in. I briefly thought about the Leeds players waking up in their swanky London hotel and I absentmindedly wondered if they had any idea what we fans go through to support them. Sneezy behind me sneezed again and I felt the blast of what I hoped was only cold air on the nape of my neck, just as we entered a long tunnel. My ears popped as we came back into the light a few seconds later. This was not pleasant. Suddenly, Sneezy lets out another ear piercing sneeze and he loses control of the black-currant cough sweet he'd been sucking. It looped over my head and into the gangway between the seats where those standing just had time to duck out of the line of fire like the most expert of Dodgeball players. Everyone was weaving out of the way until one old chap at the back of the line got his timing all wrong and he did a little skip to leap over the projectile. Instead, he only managed to land on it, crushing it underfoot with a sickening crunch like some kind of giant purple cockroach. It was that sort of a journey. Finally, the arch of Wembley stadium appeared through my window as the sun broke through to begin melting the frost on the ground outside; we were nearly there. As we alighted at Euston, I spotted Sneezy trying to clear the mucus from his nose on a soggy paper tissue, much of which was then left plastered to his face. I hoped he was travelling with a close family friend who would mention this to him before he arrived at his ultimate destination.

I took the tube to Victoria and then an overland train, two stops up the line on the Southern service to Caterham, emerging in the sunshine at Clapham Junction. As it was still only 9:30am, I stood and peeped over the wall outside the station to watch as the trains came and went, in and out of the station. It was just like, err, Clapham Junction, with trains on the move every few seconds while overhead a long line of planes queued on the flight path into Heathrow and behind me the traffic rushed along the road. Welcome to London folks! I couldn't stop humming The Jam's 'London Traffic' as I wandered up and down St John's Hill for half an hour, waiting for 'The Falcon' to open.

According to the Guinness Book of Records, the bar counter in the Falcon is the longest in the UK, and it's overlooked by a stunning stained glass window depicting a falcon. MC Escher, the artist involved in the bar's design, is best known for his strange graphic works depicting surreal, impossible perspectives; I saw an exhibition of his works in Edinburgh earlier this year. As to being the longest bar in the UK, well, it's another one of those, 'If I had a pound' jobbies.

The pub doors were opened by an attractive blonde girl in blue denims, (not that I particularly noticed) who then took her place behind the bar. I ordered a full English breakfast and my first pint of Bombardier and then sat on a stool that looked out onto the high street. Gradually, over the next few hours, the Leeds family arrived, including Simon who'd arranged the venue and his lovely wife, Viv, who joined me at the table. By the time Kentley bowled in at noon, the place was rocking, not only with Leeds fans but also with a few Newcastle fans on the way to their game at Palace. Some friendly banter took place between the two sets of supporters at various times during the afternoon. Chris came up with, *"You're just a small town in Sunderland"*, which took a bit of effort to sing in time with the usual tune.

Another highlight was watching 'Soccer AM' on the screen in the bar. Leeds United supporters were the 'Fans of the Week' in the TV studio, while the 'You Know the Drill' competition pitted Jimmy Bullard against Leeds striker, Chris Wood. Predictably, our big centre forward missed several open goals and looked anything but a top striker but he still somehow managed to win 3 – 2 against a clearly very unfit Bullard.

This all served to keep us entertained while we slowly drank the pub dry and then we all filed out to make our way back up the road to the station and onto the 14:01 headed for Shepherds Bush. As we stood in the carriage waiting for the doors to close, one lad spotted the team selection pop up on his Twitter feed. He proceeded to read out the line-up while the rest of us cheered wildly between the names. Suffice to say *"Scott Wootton"* got a more muted reception than did either of *"Charlie Taylor"* or *"Liam Bridcutt"*, both of whom seemed more popular choices,

Silvestri
Wootton Bellusci Cooper Taylor
Dallas Bridcutt Cook Mowatt
Antenucci Wood

Subs: Peacock-Farrell, Byram, Adeyemi, Murphy, Doukara, Botaka, Erwin.

Charlie Taylor thus returned after his bowt of glandular fever, just in time to resume his left back position with Berardi now suspended, while Bridcutt replaced Luke Murphy. Bailey Peacock-Farrell got the nod ahead of Eric Grimes as the goalkeeping back up with Charlie Horton now back in the USA. Former Leeds managers Neil Warnock and Kevin Blackwell were in the Rangers dug out.

Loftus Road looked almost full as the game kicked off and Leeds, backed by 3,220 noisy fans, looked fired up. Liam Bridcutt was putting himself about from the start but was unlucky to find himself booked as early as the 7th minute when he appeared to win the ball fairly from Junior Hoilett.

This was another game that would alarmingly highlight the failings of our current squad; an inability to take chances up front and an inability to defend headers in our own box. The first issue was amply demonstrated by Chris Wood, just before the half hour mark. A wayward back pass put Wood clean through in the inside left channel and he easily rounded Rob Green, the QPR keeper. But rather than shoot with his weaker left foot with the goal at his mercy, he took the ball on a few more steps giving defenders the chance to surround him before he finally lashed at goal with his right. Predictably, the ball ballooned over the bar from a tight angle. Voices were muttering, *"Three million quid?"* all around me for the next few minutes as heads shook in disbelief. That was probably the only moment of note in a forgettable first-half of football, certainly from a Leeds perspective. QPR just shaded the first 45 minutes.

I was fairly confident at this point that my nil-nil prediction was not going to be far off the mark come five o'clock. Neither of these sides had been scoring many goals in recent weeks, indeed QPR had failed to score in five of their previous six games, including their last four. Their main striker, the dangerous multi-million pound valued Charlie Austin, had been out injured for their previous game and it was announced on Friday that he'd play no part in the match. That now looked to be a bit of gamesmanship by the Rangers' management as after 57 minutes Austin came trotting onto the pitch as part of a double substitution by the home side. All Leeds fans were immediately nervous and with good cause. Kentley turned to me and joked about Austin scoring with his first touch…

You would have thought that the alarm bells would have rung for Leeds and that players would have been given specific responsibility to deal with Austin's arrival in the game but within seconds a ball was curled into the Leeds box and Austin was only inches away from making deadly contact. The ball went for a corner this time. Then we watched in utter disbelief as the right wing corner floated right into the heart of the Leeds penalty area where Charlie Austin was all alone, eight yards from goal. Austin made perfect contact with his head and the ball flew past Silvestri to ripple the net. It was a near replica to the Rotherham goal last weekend when Joe Newell was allowed a similar free header to nick that game against us.

I just could not believe what I'd witnessed. It was worse than schoolboy defending and this against the bloke who is probably the most dangerous striker in the division. In any other walk of life, heads would roll for such a dereliction of duty.

It was as if the Leeds players knew full well the enormity of the crime they'd just committed and for the next few minutes we were completely outclassed as QPR ripped into us and continually fed Austin who was hungry to add to his tally. The only Leeds player earning his keep now was Marco Silvestri who pulled off a number of world class stops to keep the score at 1 – 0. Surprisingly, Steve Evans waited a full ten minutes while the QPR assault continued before making his first change and for me it was too long overdue. I felt Jordan Botaka should have been on from the start to give a lacking in confidence QPR something to think about. By now it was really too late, as the home side, backed by a vocal following of a near capacity crowd, were cock-a-hoop. Botaka replaced a lack-lustre Alex Mowatt and then a few minutes later, Lee Erwin replaced Antenucci. That didn't go down well with the Leeds fans who felt it should have been Chris Wood making way. *"You don't know what you're doing"*, belted out from a section of the Leeds crowd over to my right while a chorus of booing was heard from most areas. There was a brief chant for Sam Byram too, he was sat on the bench and would once again not feature at all; his contract negotiations were rumoured to be continuing behind the scenes and Evans had intimated he was reluctant to use the young full-back until it was clear he wanted to be at the club.

It was all too little, too late and just as happened last week, we failed to get the ball out to Botaka often enough for the winger to do any damage. The final ten minutes was probably our best spell of the game but we still failed to worry Rob Green in the home goal overly much. The match ended in another 1 – 0 defeat, with a large section of the Leeds fans singing, *"We're f***ing sh*t"*, while others tried to drown them out singing, *"We are Leeds"*, and shouting angrily at fellow fans who were berating the players. In front of Kentley and me, a fight broke out between a couple of young fans who'd been criticising the players and a couple of older lads who'd turned on them demanding they, *"Shut the f*** up and support the f***ing team or f*** off home you bellends!"* It was a miserable end to a game we ought not to have lost. Yes, we'd been outplayed but Silvestri had done his job well and but for that single moment of stupidity by the defence we'd have all been moseying away pleased enough with a point away from home. Charlie Taylor was very good and looked like he'd never been away and Bridcutt looked useful while Silvestri pulled off some excellent saves. But, apart from those, the rest were poor.

My mood was even worse than last week when we'd similarly peed away a point against Redfearn's Rotherham. That two more ex-Leeds managers were in temporary charge of QPR today, Warnock and Blackwell, seemed to make this latest set-back even worse. All the way home, despite Kentley chatting incessantly about everything from his BMW to his job prospects, all I could think about was how our defence wasn't fit for purpose. I was so annoyed to think that I had been aware of this fact since pre-season yet still we persisted with those same names that were giving soft goals away all last season. Admittedly, I knew full well that we had other problems, we had problems all over the pitch but I could not stop myself believing that, poor as we were today, we'd given away a point that few other teams would have lost in similar circumstances. We were not learning from our mistakes and I started to think that relegation was the inevitable end product if we continued down the same path.

Steve Evans said all the right things after the game and no one could say he wasn't being honest as he told us: *"I don't think we have that many good players and we certainly don't have many very good players at this level."*[1] Whether that sort of talk would inspire his charges to do any better, I was unsure and with the loan window now firmly shut we had to get through the next seven games with the meagre squad we currently had. The sight of Leeds fans fighting amongst themselves also hadn't improved my mood. Throughout the game we could see Massimo Cellino sat at the front of the directors' box, wrapped in a blue and white QPR blanket to keep out the cold; I wondered what he made of it all? It was another U-turn by Massimo that he was there at all of course, having promised not to be present at games after the barrage of abuse he received during the Blackburn fiasco. There were, *"Massimo, time to go"*, chants during this game too but they were probably so few because it was not widely known the Italian was present.

Leeds ended the weekend in 17th spot in the table with 19 points, exactly half the number that top of the table Brighton had. Our next opponents, Hull City, were 4th with 35 points and the word was that Rob Snodgrass was almost fit to turn out for them after a long lay-off. As I said farewell to Kentley, stepping off the train back at Stafford, I began to think about the prospects of Snoddy humiliating us next Saturday. It would be so typical of what tends to happen to us!

QPR 1 **Leeds United 0** (Austin (58))
18,031 (**Leeds 3,220**)

---

[1] *http://www.bbc.co.uk/sport/0/football/34887085*

The pie's the limit!

The stark contrast between what Leeds United *could have* achieved and what we had *actually become* was highlighted this week as news came out that Manchester City had sold a 13% stake in their club to a Chinese consortium for £256m. That put a value on City of around £2bn. Meanwhile, at Elland Road, Leeds had decided to impose a tax on pies and we were worth, maybe one donkey!

Yes, the latest act in our Flying Circus was the imposition of a £5 premium on tickets for the South Stand to include a voucher that could then be redeemed at the ground for food and drink. It was a similar idea to the entry fee charged in the Pavilion, whereby a voucher is given that can then be exchanged for £3.80's worth of food or drink. The problem is, there are other places to go before the game and so it's down to choice whether the fans go in the Pavilion or not. But the South Stand pie tax was mandatory; if you wanted to sit there it now cost you £5 more than before, unless you would have bought a pie and a pint there anyway, in which case you were quids in. From the club's perspective it was a way of guaranteeing additional revenue... unless of course fans voted with their teeth!

Not turning up at all was always unlikely but plans were put in place for a walkout protest during the Hull City game. South Standers were asked to walk out in the 17th minute for a period lasting 17 minutes; 17 being that number that sends shivers down Cellino's spine... although many fans were questioning whether he even had one!

One disgruntled fan decided he'd had enough of Cellino and so put him up for sale on eBay. Itv.com reported the details:

"For sale, one used football club owner, desperately in need of a new home. Will bring the following qualities to your football club: False promises, outright lies, contempt for fans, bullying of club staff, the worst signings in your club's history, a new 'head coach' every 13 games and injury faking players."[1]

By the eve of the Hull game, some 40 bids had been received and the offer price had reached £1,060! It was unclear how this offer of slavery could be fulfilled and eventually eBay pulled it.

The '17 on 17' idea once again split the fans down the middle. The Supporters Trust came out and backed the walkout while Leeds Fans United distanced itself saying it did not wish to make an enemy of Cellino (in case the Italian again decided to offer his shares to them). I felt it unlikely many would walk out unless we were already a couple of goals down like we were against Blackburn. If that happened, I could see almost everyone walking out... and probably never going back.

Championship manager number nine got the elbow this week as Steve Clarke was sacked by Reading while QPR announced that Jimmy Floyd Hasselbaink was to be their new permanent manager; Jimmy finally leaving Burton Albion after doing amazing things with them in recent seasons. Leeds fans were not sleeping at night thinking about us getting Steve Evans and the 'R's getting Jimmy.

---

[1]   http://www.itv.com/news/calendar/2015-12-03/angry-fans-put-leeds-utd-owner-massimo-cellino-up-for-sale-on-ebay/

Saturday arrived and the UK was being battered by storm Desmond. By the time I arrived in the Hoxton Mount car park the wind was definitely storm force and outside the Pavilion it was actually possibly to lean into the wind at 45 degrees and not fall over. It would make for an interesting game and my thoughts strayed back to that incredible day at Yeovil a couple of years back when Stephen Warnock floated a free kick into the net from 50 yards.

It was the same old fayre in the Pavilion; John Hendrie came past our table and told us all to cheer up. *"Och, yous look like yous all sh*t yerselves lads"*, he joked. On the little stage in there, Terry Yorath once again lambasted the team, with big Chris Wood taking most of the flak this week. *"To play on your own up front you have to be a really good centre forward... and Chris Wood is not a really good centre forward"* he sighed, shaking his head.

Steve Evans made just one change to his starting eleven; Tom Adeyemi came in for Mirco Antenucci as part of a five man midfield.

Silvestri
Wootton Bellusci Cooper Taylor
Bridcutt
Dallas Cook Adeyemi Mowatt
Wood

Subs: Peacock-Farrell, Byram, Antenucci, Murphy, Doukara, Erwin, Botaka.

Word was filtering through Twitter before the game that the latest round of contract negotiations with Sam Byram had ended in rejection by the youngster. That was taken as the reason by most as to why Wootton continued to keep Sam out of the team. The new offer of a one year deal on the same money didn't do the trick and we were all resigned to losing Sam in the New Year.

From early in the game, it was apparent that this was a sort of 4 – 1 – 4 – 1 formation, with Liam Bridcutt operating just in front of the back four; helping out the defence when under pressure and picking up the ball and driving forward when not. It worked wonders! We also kept the ball firmly on the deck throughout the first-half which was essential as the wind continued to gust around the stadium. There was rubbish all over the pitch but for once, not in white shirts.

There was a huge contingent of Hull fans over in the West Stand, at the far end from us but they were already very quiet as Leeds turned on the style. We were quick to get in the faces of the Tigers whenever we lost the ball and then swift to attack as soon as we had it back. Time seemed to be racing by and soon the Kop was counting down the last few seconds as the time on the big screen went from 16:50 to 17:00. We waited to see how many would leave. It looked as though they'd misunderstood the '17 on 17' as only about 17 actually walked out. There seemed to be some sort of scuffle over there as well as Stewards moved in to separate a few fighting Leeds fans; presumably the meat and potato faction taking issue with the peppered steak supporters. We sang, *"Get yer pies out for the lads"*, during a lull in proceedings.

On the pitch, Alex Mowatt fired in a left-footed free kick but it came to nothing while former Leeds man, Alex Bruce hobbled off to be replaced by Curtis Davies as more fearsome Leeds tackling left its mark. Then, in the 29th minute, the Leeds pressure paid off. Bridcutt broke up a Hull attack and pushed the ball to Lewis Cook who was off like a little jack rabbit. So often when he does that he then disappoints with a poor final ball or even more often gets caught in possession, but not today. For once, everyone was doing exactly what they're paid to do. Cook slid an inch perfect ball inside the full back for Stuart Dallas to run onto in the south west corner. Dallas sent it first time along the ground towards the near post and there was Chris Wood to clip it neatly into the roof of the net as he arrived milliseconds before the keeper and a defender. It was a classic counter-attack goal very similar to the ones we scored at Huddersfield a few weeks ago.

Just as we did at Huddersfield, we continued to press the foot down firmly on the throttle and within minutes we ought to have doubled the lead. A headed clearance by Hull only reached Tom Adeyemi and he headed it back towards the edge of the box. It should have been meat pie and drink for Hull defender Harry Maguire but the ball slipped under his foot and Alex Mowatt was left with only Hull keeper, Allan McGregor to beat. Alex struck it well and had McGregor beaten all ends up but the ball cannoned back off the crossbar instead of ripping into the net. Still Leeds piled forward though and on the stroke of half-time we won two corners in quick succession. I was debating with my fellow Kopites when we last scored from a corner and the closest we could come up with was the Adeyemi header at Derby. That was from a Dallas cross after taking a short corner. This time Alex Mowatt lofted a left foot in-swinger into the heart of the Hull box which was headed away under a challenge from Chris Wood. It fell on the right boot of Lewis Cook who struck it back towards goal through the crowded box and McGregor did well to parry it to his left. Tom Adeyemi was scrambling to get to the rebound and in the process lost his left boot but still managed to sweep the ball with his right into the roof of the net. Elland Road erupted as only Elland Road knows how while all the Leeds players tumbled on top of Adeyemi right in front of the big screen which beamed the pictures back to us, a hundred yards away. Seconds later the half-time whistle blew and once again the ground echoed to the sound of Leeds fans' delirium.

Once again, Leeds' unpredictability was almost so extreme as to be predictable. Virtually everyone had written off our chances in this game well before kick-off, yet here we were 2 – 0 up and half way to my pre-match bet. As the second-half got underway, Mike began a chant of, *"Dave wants four"* that got a modicum of support in our section of the Revie Stand; everyone wanted that pint I'd promised them if I won!

In recent seasons, Leeds have seldom managed to put two good halves together. Even at Derby earlier this season and the Cardiff game come to think of it, after a blistering first-half we usually revert to type and give up the momentum in the second. This was to be no exception. I suppose it's inevitable really; Hull were a decent side and their boss, Steve Bruce had been around long enough to know how to turn a game around. They were bound to be more of a threat after the break. The post-match stats would reveal that Leeds bossed the first-half with 58% of the ball, ten shots and six of them on target. By the end of the game Hull had amassed 60% of the total possession and Leeds had added just one more shot giving the clue to Hull's second-half domination. It was another huge disappointment that we only lasted six minutes of the new half before conceding and worse than that it was yet another poorly contested header in our six-yard box. Scott Wootton was beaten on the Hull left wing and Ahmed Elmohamady climbed all over Charlie Taylor to force a header past Silvestri. After the game, Steve Evans would say he was convinced Taylor had been fouled but for me it was another case of us not being good enough in the air in that vital area of the pitch. That was three headers conceded in three consecutive games in that mysterious black hole in the middle of our back line.

Hull threw the kitchen sink and Rob Snodgrass at us in the second-half, Snoddy coming on for his first league action in many months after a long injury. He got a tremendous reception from the Leeds fans while Sone Aluko, who he replaced, was booed all around the ground as he walked off having niggled his way through the whole game.

Byram replaced Mowatt on 74 minutes and Sam also got a great reception with a rousing chant of *"There's only one Sam Byram"*. Luke Murphy replaced Stuart Dallas in the 80th minute and then in added time Doukara came on for Chris Wood. In another sign as to how 'together' this squad is, it was Doukara who effectively saw the game out for us, keeping the ball in the north east corner for several minutes to run the clock down and constantly turning to the Kop to encourage us to keep the noise levels up. When the final whistle blew the roof nearly came off, and not just because of storm Desmond! The roof took some stick over in the South Stand concourse too as pie rage broke out among some so-called fans. It was rumoured that £15,000 of damage was done and we wondered what penance would be paid for that. No pies for a few weeks I'd wager. Massimo wouldn't be happy at more maintenance expense but he wasn't at the game so it would be a while before he knew about it. His absence meant there were only a couple of *"Massimo time to go"* chants during the game.

It was a vital three points that just eased the tension that little bit in typical Leeds United fashion. We are most likely to win when it seems least likely and vice versa. After the disappointment of the previous two defeats this was probably just enough of a lift to keep our spirits up to go again. They've been teasing us like this for years.

We'd end the weekend back in that 17th spot in the table with 22 points from 19 games and a goal difference of minus 4. This time last season we had 23 points with a goal difference of minus 3. I'm sure if I could be arsed to look back to the three or four years before that I'd see similar stats; *"plus ça change, plus c'est la même chose"*, as they say in the streets of Beeston.

I knew we'd been battered by the 'Codheads' in that second-half and I wasn't prepared to get too carried away on the back of one decent half of football. I was happy to acknowledge that the new formation had worked well though and that Liam Bridcutt had been a revelation. There was clearly plenty of team spirit in the squad too. After the game, Steve Evans again scoffed at suggestions that Cellino had been in the dressing room at QPR dictating tactics, reminding us that he'd walk out if ever that happened. As with everything at Leeds, it all seemed very fragile but some folk were already getting carried away with the smell of success and were telling anyone who'd listen that we'd turned the corner and now, *"the pies the limit"*; next up, Charlton Athletic at the Valley.

During Sunday we learned the devastation that had been caused by storm Desmond across the North West. Over a month's rain had fallen in less than 24 hours and vast tracts of land were submerged under water. The worst floods were centred on Carlisle and I was horrified to see the TV pictures of the town centre and the football ground several feet under the brown swirling water. I'd been there enjoying some late summer sunshine as recently as August when I witnessed that amazing 4 – 4 draw between Carlisle and Cambridge United. 5,000 homes were now flooded and hundreds of thousands of homes were without power for several days; all this heartbreak for so many families just three weeks before Christmas. Pies and football no longer seemed very important watching all that on the news.

Leeds United 2 Hull City 1 (**Wood, (30), Adeyemi, (45)**, Elmohamady, (51)) **24,962** (Hull, 2,591)

Valliant Effort

The FA Cup 3rd round draw was made on Monday of this week and I was hoping for an away draw at Newport County, the only one of my five remaining '92' to have survived this far. It took ages for ball number '21' to come out of the pot but when it did it gave us a home tie against Rotherham. Not the glamour tie we wanted but an opportunity at least to right the wrong done by losing to Redfearn's side a couple of weeks ago. Revenge was a distinct possibility.

Other than that it was a quiet week with just the news from Italy that Cellino had survived another court case as he was acquitted over non-payment of tax on a couple of player transfers during his tenure at Cagliari. On Twitter the 'Cellino out' brigade was disgusted while the 'Cellino in' group celebrated. They'd all forgotten this was nothing to do with the current appeal going before the FL which was over his alleged tax dodging on the import of a Range Rover to Italy. He'd been fined 40,000 euros on that one and the FL had already banned him subject to the result of an ongoing appeal that seemed to be taking for ever.

Kentley decided to drive all the way to Charlton instead of our usual ploy of leaving the car outside the capital and getting the tube in. We dropped the BMW in a car park in Victoria Way SE7, about five minutes from the Valley and headed straight to Charlton station. It was already 12:15pm but we'd agreed to meet a few folk in the Lord Moon of the Mall, just off

Trafalgar Square, one of our regular watering holes for London games. We weren't going to have much time there as the next train wasn't until 12:47pm and the journey took around half an hour. In fact it was about twenty past one when we bowled in. Thankfully, Adam and Si had got a few beers lined up and despite having only 40 minutes before we had to set off back to Charlton, I still managed a decent quota of three pints of the excellent Doombar and finished off Adam's last pint of Coors, lightweight that he is! As always the Lord Moon was rocking and all the usual away day faces were there. There were also a few Stoke fans in there en route to their game at West Ham later in the day.

Adam, Si, Kentley and I joined the rest of the Leeds conga as it snaked its way from the pub back up to Charing Cross station and onto the 14:09 Gravesend train. Inside, the carriage was rocking, literally, as Leeds fans belted out their anthems to a backing track of the heavy beat of two lads thumping their fists against the carriage roof. A few locals returning from their Christmas shopping spree in town looked on disapprovingly. A lad called Gary recognised me and had a chat before I slumped into a seat at the end of the carriage as the Doombar began to play with my senses!

The Valley is a modern looking stadium these days but it retains its very traditional location in amongst the streets of terraced houses; it suddenly appears out of nowhere. Considering the whole place has been redeveloped since the 1990s though, you have to say the away entrance and turnstiles are 'rustic' to say the least. Most fans were frisked on the way through but I had a chuckle as the spotty youth charged with checking me just looked me up and down and waved me through. I'm starting to think I need to toughen up my appearance. Once through the ridiculous little turnstile block, we then had to fight our way through the masses queuing at the bar. It was chaos! It did mean you could have a quick chat with old friends as you made your slow progress though.

Steve Evans named an unchanged starting eleven for this one, even though he had Gaetano Berardi available again after suspension; the Wootton haters were not amused.

Silvestri
Wootton Bellusci Cooper Taylor
Bridcutt
Dallas Cook Adeyemi Mowatt
Wood

Subs: Peacock-Farrell, Murphy, Doukara, Antenucci, Berardi, Byram, Botaka.

It's always hard to change a winning side but I still felt that against a team lacking in confidence, as Charlton must surely have been, we could have been more aggressive and maybe include Botaka from the start to run at them and test their resolve. Charlton were rooted in the bottom three, having lost their previous two games but they'd taken an early two goal lead against top side Brighton last time out before having a man sent off and eventually losing 3 – 2. As with any Championship game this one was hard to predict.

*"Support the f****** team. Don't waste your time with that (the protests). You have a good team which doesn't deserve to be where it is. I tell you the truth. I wish we win but if we don't win today I'm happy anyway. I don't give a f***. You have a good team. You give an excuse to the players to play s***."[1]*

It was the unmistakeable language of Sig. Cellino of course and you'd be forgiven for thinking he was addressing Leeds fans. In fact he wasn't. Cellino came face to face with a group of Charlton fans protesting against their owner, the Belgian, Roland Duchatelet outside the Valley. They'd been chanting, *"We want our Charlton back"*, and were handing out leaflets bearing the legend, 'Made in Charlton, destroyed in Belgium' as they stepped up their campaign to remove Duchatelet. The 68-year-old Belgian also owned Belgian Pro League side Standard Liege, Spanish club AD Alcorcon and German outfit Carl Zeiss Jena, while his son Roderick was president of Hungarian side Ujpest. Duchatelet sacked the Addicks popular manager, Chris Powell, soon after his arrival and two of his

---

[1]   *http://www.yorkshireeveningpost.co.uk/sport/leeds-united/latest-lufc-news/leeds-united-cellino-tells-angry-charlton-fans-support-the-team-1-7621308*

successors - Jose Riga and the incumbent Luzon - had previously had stints in charge at Standard. Charlton fans believed they'd become the forgotten part of Duchatelet's football empire.[1]

The first-half of this game was another of those that will not linger long in the mind of even the most ardent Leeds fan; very little happened. The Addicks had an early chance when a shot from a tight angle went through Silvestri's legs but the ball skimmed along the goal line and missed the far post. The usual early Wootton yellow card and a tame Alex Mowatt free kick were the only other memories I had.

At half-time, I made my way to the toilet block outside the away end. It was a tortuous struggle with hundreds of fans pushing and shoving to try to make progress either to the bogs or the bar. It has to be said the set up just does not cope with 3,000 Leeds fans. At one point, I spotted Jo E in the queue coming towards me and as we crossed she handed me a little package of folded tinfoil which drew some alarmed glances from folk nearby. Inside the bogs there were lads disproving the theory that we blokes can't multi-task as they stood at the urinals with a pint in each hand.

Back in the stand, I opened my secret parcel and was delighted to see it was a couple of pieces of lemon drizzle cake. Jo is a superb cook and her cakes have taken on legendary status at Elland Road. Sadly, Kentley had spotted my contraband and was now drooling over my shoulder like a hungry dog so I had to hand over a piece to him. It would keep us going until we could grab a curry in town later.

Early in the second-half, Evans withdrew Wootton and sent on Berardi and Leeds suddenly looked a much more positive outfit. Wootton looked annoyed at getting the hook and exchanged angry words with Evans as he left the pitch. After the game Evans told reporters his response to Wootton was: *"You're on a yellow son and you might get a red!"*

On 64 minutes, Jordan Botaka replaced Alex Mowatt and by this time Leeds were dominating the game with wave after

---

[1] *http://www.bbc.co.uk/sport/0/football/31503903*

wave of attacks; it was as dominant a display as we'd seen from Leeds for many a month but for all the chances we created we were lacking that bit of class needed to stick the ball in the net. At the other end, the home side was reduced to the odd breakaway but could easily have snatched all three points had Silvestri not pulled off a stunning left hand save from Ricardo Vaz Te, a name that strikes fear in the hearts of all Leeds fans.

It was a thrilling last half hour and the noise from the Leeds fans as we urged our lads on was incredible. At the final whistle we were as exhausted as the players but we generously stood and applauded them as they took their bows. Evans told the BBC after the game: *"I was delighted with my lads. I told them in the dressing room to look how the Leeds fans applauded them at the end. The difference between now and when we lost at QPR (1-0 two weeks ago) was incredible. The fans are behind them now because they played for the shirt, played for the badge - that's what the fans want. If we had left The Valley without a point then the Charlton players and staff should go home wearing balaclavas because it would have been a robbery."*[1]

In a curry house just up the road from the ground, we reflected on another Jekyll and Hyde performance from Leeds; impotent in the first-half, rampant in the second. The only thing missing in that last half hour was a clinical finish. Tom Adeyemi missed a couple of real sitters while Lewis Cook hammered a goal bound shot against Chris Wood's huge backside. You could say it was just one of those days but good chances are so rare in the Championship, you can't afford to squander them. Nevertheless, a point away from home is not to be sneezed at. Next up was an altogether more difficult looking trip to Wolverhampton Wanderers. For now, Leeds were stuck in 18th spot in the table, with 23 points from 20 games, exactly the same record we had this time last season.

Charlton Athletic 0 **Leeds United 0**
15,867 (**Leeds 3,129**)

---

[1] *http://www.bbc.co.uk/sport/0/football/35013658*

Byram, the Wolves and Peppe's pants

S ky TV decreed that our trip to Wolverhampton would take place on a Thursday night; 17th December. Cellino must have been having kittens! It was not the most popular move amongst Leeds fans either and was sure to attract plenty of vocal condemnation at the game. For Kentley and me it was no great problem of course as neither of us was working. I'm retired while Kentley was in what we could call 'a period of contemplation' following the end of his degree course. Wolverhampton was also the shortest trip of the season for us, being just 37 minutes down the road from Stoke.

Kentley was driving again and he picked me up near junction 15 of the M6, bang on the appointed time of 3pm. On the radio they were talking about the passing of Gareth Mortimer, 'Morty' of the Welsh band Racing Cars. The 17th had not proved a lucky day for the 'They Shoot Horses Don't They?' vocalist. That is a phrase that often comes to my mind when thinking about Leeds these days; there is just so much wrong at the club and seemingly no hope of long term success that, like a badly injured horse, perhaps someone should shoot us and put us out of our misery.

We parked up as recommended by West Midlands Police (WMP) in Faulkland Crescent, next to where the Leeds coaches park. We'd walked about fifty yards when the alarm triggered. We strolled back and Kentley clambered over the little fence around the car park. I waited by the fence having discovered it wasn't *that* little and it had some sharp pointy bits along the top edge. Kentley reset the alarm and hopped back over the fence and off we went down the road again. The alarm went off once more. Back he goes again and this time he spends ten minutes faffing about with the doors, windows and the boot lid before then doing what every young lad would do in that situation. He rang his dad! This after he'd confessed in the car to having forgotten that today was his Dad's birthday! I should also point out that Kentley's degree is in automotive electronics and he works weekends in the family garage business. The eventual conclusion was that they had no idea why the alarm was going off so Kentley disconnected the battery and that fixed the problem, albeit temporarily.

Finally on our way, we walked into the town centre. I'd already seen tweets from the WMP saying there was no designated pub for Leeds fans, *"because of all the Christmas parties going on"*, so it was a matter of wandering the streets trying to find a hostelry without a *"HOME FANS ONLY"* notice in the window. The WMP also tweeted that the pub we used last season, The Prince Albert, and the one we used previous to that, Walkabout, had both closed, so that reduced the options a bit. Police twitter accounts are becoming the go-to resource for match day information about where to park and drink and the West Yorkshire force even has a dedicated football account - @LUFC_WYP. They'd tweeted earlier: *"It's Thursday, game day?!Course @LUFC has to be one of 10in10, they've been on TV more than the John Lewis Xmas ad"*, referring to the fact that tonight's game was number 9 in Sky's ten Championship games in ten days schedule. Nice to see Old Bill has a sense of humour these days!

We tried the Britannia Hotel but they had the home fans notice up and then we spotted a Wetherspoon pub just a bit further along Lichfield Street, opposite the Grand Theatre; 'The Moon under Water'. No notice and no security on the door yet although it was still only 4:30pm. Neither of us was wearing Leeds colours anyway so we could probably have got in anywhere but it's always nice to know you're in a place where at least they are not actively discouraging your mates to enter. There was one table of Leeds lads already in and wearing colours but as the evening wore on and the security chappies arrived to take up their positions on the door they were politely asked to cover up. All a bit pointless I thought and the lads were clearly not too chuffed either. When they left, they chanted, *"We are Leeds"*, at the tops of their voices! There were plenty of gold and black Wolves tops around the pub.

Once again Sharp's Doombar was available and went down well with a Wetherspoon Gourmet Burger as we discussed the upcoming game. Jo E, Martin and Rob appeared at the table next to us later in the evening but Jo was sans cake on this occasion. Shame, would have gone down well as dessert.

Just before we left the pub, Kentley pulled up the team on his iPhone. There was one change from the side that started on Saturday at the Valley and a couple of changes to the bench.

Silvestri
Wootton Bellusci Cooper Taylor
Bridcutt
Byram Cook Adeyemi Dallas
Wood

Subs: Peacock-Farrell, Bamba, Murphy, Coyle, Doukara, Antenucci, Mowatt.

The inclusion of Sam Byram instead of Alex Mowatt was a strange one. All the talk surrounding Sam recently had been about how he was still refusing to sign a contract and Evans had intimated that until he did it would be difficult to include him in his plans. That aside, what the change did do was to up the pace and stamina down the flanks and add Sam's undoubted ability in the air too. Quite how significant the change would prove to be would only become apparent once the game got underway.

Leeds had not managed to sell out their allocation for this game although we still had 2,169 noisy fans spread along the lower tier of the Steve Bull Stand. Predictably, our first target, even before a ball was kicked, was Sky TV. We told them they were, *"f****** sh** "*, and how Thursday nights were the same and I did wonder how this backing track to their footage was going down with the Sky management. They probably don't ever watch TV of course and certainly not on a Thursday night...

The atmosphere at Molineux is always good. There is something about the colour scheme of black and gold that just looks right, especially in the glare of the floodlights. The huge North Bank to our right was nowhere near full but it was still a mightily impressive sight while the noise coming from the South Bank at the opposite end of the ground was nearly a match for our own efforts.

I don't think many Leeds fans thought we'd win this game, I certainly didn't, but within the first six minutes we were starting to dream as Chris Wood won a header and directed the ball straight to Stuart Dallas about 22 yards out. Dallas took the ball on his chest and then hit it cleanly on the volley with his right foot and Carl Ikeme in the Wolves goal had given it up, knowing he had no chance of getting across to it. Instead of rippling the net though, it cannoned off the outside of the post and ran away to safety. Bugger! Those Wolves fans up in the South Stand went quiet though as they, like us, wondered, *"Where the f*** did that come from?"*

Sadly, that proved to be the last we saw of Leeds as an attacking force until just before half-time. Wolves though were suddenly carving through our butter-like defence with an ease that was very worrying. The goal-scoring machine that is Benik Afobe had just missed a decent chance, latching onto a defence-splitting through ball but he pulled that one wide. Seconds later though he scored and Molineux went mad.

A long through ball was headed inside and it neatly bisected Bellusci and Cooper to find Afobe running in behind both of them to slide the ball under the body of Silvestri. Bugger again! It was another shocking goal to concede that made us look like a school third team. Now Molineux was rocking to the sound of, *"He's Benik Afobe, he scores when he wants"*, and I for one thought he might well decide he wanted a few more. There were still only ten minutes gone and for the next twenty it was non-stop Wolves pressure as they cut through us at will but somehow failed to increase their advantage. They won four corners in that period too but again failed to capitalise. In fact, in the whole of this period, the only Leeds player looking anything like decent was Stuart Dallas. He was up and down the pitch like the proverbial Duracell bunny and without his defensive work we'd have been sunk without trace. On the half hour mark, Tom Adeyemi went down with an injury and a few minutes later it was clear he couldn't continue. Over on the touchline we could see the unmistakeable figure of Souleymane Doukara warming up.

We'd started the game with the 4-1-4-1 formation that had been Evans' preference since the Hull game but as soon as Doukara came on, that changed to a more traditional 4-4-2, albeit with Doukara playing slightly in behind Chris Wood. The fact that Doukara began to put himself about from his first seconds on the pitch seemed to give everyone a boost and he and Bridcutt were both clearly tasked with winning the ball back whenever we lost it. Every time Doukara won a fifty-fifty challenge, a huge roar of approval went up from the Leeds contingent and suddenly it looked a different game. Two minutes before the break we were level.

Doukara won the ball deep in our own half, right in front of us near the west touchline and he passed inside to Lewis Cook. Cook did a bit of a hop and a skip and then slid a perfect ball right through the centre of the Wolves defence to, of all people, Sam Byram. Sam's first touch was a bit heavy but the ball went straight to Chris Wood on his left and although Wood's first touch was also not great he managed to poke it back to Byram with his second. Sam was now behind three Wolves defenders with just Ikeme to beat but Chris Wood's momentum was driving him right across Sam's line of fire. Mindful of the fact he got in the way of Lewis Cook's effort at Charlton, Wood now launched himself into the air with all the grace of a ballerina on a pogo stick and somehow managed to dive over Sam's shot which nestled in the corner of the net. Watching the goal back, from the moment Doukara won the ball this was a thing of beauty; a goal any Arsenal side would have been proud to score. The South Stand was now emptying quicker than a Glasgow pub that's run out of ale as the Wolves fans sought solace in their half-time Bovril while we were all jigging up and down singing, *"There's only one Sam Byram"*. It's a funny old game!

A choir from a local church sang carols on the pitch at half-time to get us all in the festive spirit – even though the weather was distinctly spring-like with the temperature in double figures. I had daffodils daring to pop their heads through the soil in my garden and a tree in blossom, so peculiar had this autumn weather been. As the teams came back out for the second-half I wondered if they could spring a similar surprise.

Within seconds of the restart we were starting to think we possibly could. Wolves now looked asleep, it was Leeds with the hot butter knife now and it was Sully wielding it. Suddenly, Doukara was through and sliding the ball to his left for Chris Wood to run on to, we were all willing him to, *"Hit the f***** thing"*, but he dillied and dallied and then when he did eventually strike it, Ikeme was able to smoother it out for a corner. For a £3 million striker it was a shocking miss and almost three thousand Leeds fans were now holding their heads in their hands muttering, *"F*** me, how's he missed that?"* Fortunately for Wood, events out on the pitch were moving quickly and within a few minutes Leeds were pressing forward again. Scott Wootton began this move with a simple short ball down the Leeds right wing to Stuart Dallas who turned it, first touch, inside to Doukara but kept running past him and was able to collect the Douk's back heeled pass in his stride as he bore down on goal. Three Wolves defenders seemed only mildly interested in Dallas's progress and allowed him to get to within fifteen yards of goal before he unleashed a thunderbolt of a shot that beat Ikeme at his near post. It was another sublime move that had us all scratching our heads and wondering why we couldn't do this all the time. I have to say the Wolves defending for both goals was worse than anything we'd seen from our own boys this season but even so, the precision of our passing and the movement to create the space was top drawer.

There were still forty minutes to go, so we knew Wolves would get chances but looking up at the South Bank I got the distinct impression that their own fans thought this was over.

Wolves had the odd bit of possession but the only time they looked like breaking through us, Peppe Bellusci made sure they didn't with a blatant professional foul. We did get nervous when Adam Le Fondre made an appearance as a substitute though; he's hurt us more than once in the past and was soon in the action up front. Chris Wood also continued to miss chances that my granny would have put away in her heyday. He thumped a close range header straight at the overworked Ikeme with the whole goal to aim at and then lamely hit a right footer straight at the keeper when clean through on goal. He was having one of those days; a 'Billy Paynter' we'd call it. He wasn't alone though as Byram and Bridcutt sprayed some wide as well but Wood's were the most glaring and we did pay £3 million for him to do this job. Gran would have done it for a cup of Horlicks!

Almost exactly on the hour mark, we were celebrating again and this time, with a two goal advantage and half an hour to go we really were starting to dream. Chris Wood tried to cross the ball from the left but his effort was blocked and the ball came back to Charlie Taylor. Taylor spotted Sam Byram at the back post and launched a long cross towards him. From where we stood the cross looked way too long but amazingly Sam managed to leap and get his head to it and the ball looped over Ikeme in to the opposite corner of the net. 3 - 1 and surely that would be enough? Well, not quite. We had a little spell of ten minutes or so when Wolves really did look dead and buried and looking across to the South Stand there were even folk leaving, for good this time. But that man Le Fondre was out there and Nathan Byrne was now on having replaced the ineffective James Henry. With ten minutes left on the clock, it was Byrne who brought Molineux to life again as he latched onto a long left wing cross to volley home from beyond the back post. It was another case of leaving a dangerous player unmarked in our box and another piece of video for the defensive coaches to study in the morning. It was far too soft, Andrex toilet tissue soft. The home crowd was now in full voice again and we were constantly checking the clock that looked down from the very top of the South Stand. It seemed to have stopped, so slowly were the minutes going by. Both teams made their final substitutions, with Alex Mowatt replacing Dallas for Leeds and still the stadium was rocking with the noise from both sets of fans. Marco Silvestri was now the centre of attention as the Wolves pressure mounted. He was out at the feet of Le Fondre at one point and then when he jumped up with the ball he towered menacingly over the little striker with the Leeds fans egging him on. This was a side of Silvestri we'd never seen and he seemed to love his new found confidence. He cleanly gathered a couple of crosses and then took an awkward shot that bounced up just in front of him. Again the Leeds fans roared their approval. The board went up signalling 5 minutes of added time and we prepared ourselves to go again but the final minutes were dealt with expertly with a bit of time wasting and then the referee brought it to an end.

Steve Evans came over with the rest of the players while Doukara and Byram were ushered into the centre circle for Sky's Man of the Match presentation. While they were being interviewed, the Leeds fans first sang, *"There's only one Sam Byram"*, and then, even more loudly and clearly, *"Sky TV is f****** sh**"*, echoed around the famous old stadium. Meanwhile, the rest of the players were all stripping off their shirts and throwing them to the Leeds fans and Peppe Bellusci even peeled his shorts off and threw those to one lucky lady in the front row. Peppe stood proudly in his black speedos and a white undershirt while Steve Evans gave us a few fist pumps just as he did up at Huddersfield not long ago. This man was winning over the fans slowly and surely; we love a bit of passion and we love to celebrate a hard fought victory.

After the game, Evans admitted that the first 35 minutes were not good and he knew he had to change it round but he'd been confident that Doukara would do a job for him and so it proved to be. The big man now had quite a decision to make as to who to include in his starting eleven against Simon Grayson's Preston North End on Sunday afternoon. The optimism was building and another win in that game would set us up nicely for the Christmas and New Year games.

Wolves 2 **Leeds United 3** (Afobe (10), **Byram (44 & 60)**, **Dallas (51)**, Byrne (81))

19,592 (**Leeds 2,169**)

Santa slays Preston with early Xmas gift

These were busy days for me; the Wolves game was the first of three in four days. I had the Friday off but on Saturday I took the 06:48 train to Euston heading ultimately for Barnet and their game against Crawley Town. It was my 88th ground as I neared the end of my '92' journey.

On the train, I went through the usual rituals I'd developed over many trips with London Midland during the year, including trying to spend more time breathing out than in; my feeble attempt to avoid the flu germs being spread by the legion of folk who spent the whole journey coughing and snorting. I also read The Metro cover to cover again, this time learning only that Jose Mourinho would still pick up £250,000 every week until he gets another job (he was sacked this week by Chelsea) and that Red Bull F1 boss, Christian Horner, married Geri Halliwell earlier this year. Fortunately the day got better and the game, despite starting slowly, eventually burst into a six goal thriller with the Bees winning 4 - 2.

Sat in the Pavilion on Sunday, ahead of our game with Preston, I liked the look of the 66/1 odds on a 4 – 2 win for Leeds, so my regular quid went in that direction. I was quietly confident Leeds would get a comfortable win as long as they could reproduce the form shown in that second-half at Wolves. For that to happen though, I really felt Steve Evans had to pick the side that was on the pitch during that magical spell and that meant starting Doukara. When the team was announced on Twitter just after 2pm, Doukara was listed on the bench.

Silvestri
Wootton Bellusci Cooper Taylor
Bridcutt
Byram Cook Murphy Dallas
Wood

Subs: Peacock-Farrell, Coyle, Bamba, Phillips, Antenucci, Mowatt, Doukara. Ex-Leeds man Neil Kilkenny was on the bench for the visitors.

It was basically the same *starting* eleven as at Wolves, with Murphy stepping off the bench for Adeyemi who was still recovering from a virus, though I doubt he caught his in cattle class on the London Midland 06:48. For now, I had to accept the fact that Evans had seen this formation do the job against Hull City at Elland Road the week before, so I just had to keep the faith. I was becoming increasingly frustrated though that Wood was offering us nothing as a lone striker.

Messrs Lorimer, Hendrie, Yorath and compere Jed Stone were all in festive mood as they gave their little preview of the game to the Pavilion punters. The usually miserable and Scrooge-like Yorath had clearly had a glass of Christmas cheer or six as he went for 3 – 0 Leeds, while Lorimer was more conservative with 2 – 1 and Hendrie, *"a comfortable 2 – 0"*. I think 95% of Leeds fans went into Elland Road this time expecting a *comfortable* win.

The problem with Leeds, as we all know, is that we've become accustomed to seeing the unexpected; if we expect a win we often lose and if we expect a defeat we often win! Another feature of Leeds games is that returning former Leeds heroes tend to do well against us and sat in the manager's seat in the Preston dug out was Simon Grayson. Neil Kilkenny was there as well and Peter Ridsdale was in the ground somewhere, not that he's a returning hero of course. He was still acting as Chairman of the Lancashire club despite having been banned as a company director until April 2020 such is the ludicrously hypocritical state of the beautiful game these days. Days when Mourinho is paid a quarter of a million quid despite being sacked and Blatter and Platini were banned for eight years by FIFA's ethics committee for an unauthorised £1.3m payment made by Blatter to Platini in 2011. With our own Massimo

Cellino's various court cases still ongoing it was hard not to believe the game is just riddled with greed. I wonder what Jimmy Hill thought about it all? He of course was, to some extent, the man who paved the way for the huge amounts of money footballers now earn and indirectly therefore for the vast amounts of money swilling around in the game. It was he who successfully ended the Football League's maximum wage in 1961. Hill passed away this weekend at the age of 87.

It was chilly inside Elland Road and the wind was blowing again, albeit nowhere near as bad as it was for the Hull game. Chilly, but still incredibly mild for mid-December, and with hardly a sign of any frost so far this winter it was easy to believe the forecast that this was likely to be the warmest December in over 100 years. It was great for travelling footie fans but confusing for gardeners and the daffodils!

Preston came to Elland Road in decent form with just one defeat in eleven and in that period they'd managed impressive victories over Burnley and Forest and a goalless draw at league leaders Brighton. They'd posted seven clean sheets in that spell too and sat only two places below Leeds with just one point less. However you looked at that recent record, it was impressive. And the way the game started it was clear my 4 – 2 bet didn't really have legs.

As early as the 2nd minute, Silvestri pulled off an excellent save at the foot of his right hand post to turn away a vicious shot by Paul Gallagher. That woke us all up and there was an immediate chant of, *"Marco Silvestri"*, from down near the front of the Kop. Marco's performances lately had made him more of a hero than the villain he was seen as at one time in LS11. It was a wake-up call to the team. Before we'd even seen ten minutes' play Silvestri had made two more excellent stops as Preston continued to dominate. The only excuse we could give our players was that Preston had the benefit of two extra days of recovery after their previous game, Leeds having played as recently as Thursday thanks to our friends at Sky. We'd also heard that the team coach didn't get back to Elland Road until 3am Friday morning due to various road closures so that wouldn't have helped either. Gradually, Leeds shook off the cobwebs though and for twenty minutes it was a pretty even affair. Then, after almost exactly half an hour we got our early Christmas gift, as Santa arrived, disguised as referee Gavin Ward.

Scott Wootton launched one of his trade-mark long diagonal passes up towards Chris Wood and the ball bounced midway between him and the Preston keeper, Jordan Pickford, just outside the Preston area. Both men appeared to get to the ball at the same time, Wood with his head and Pickford with an outstretched arm. There was a huge cry from the South Stand for a foul by the keeper on Wood as the two collided and the ref immediately gave a free kick. He then pulled Pickford to one side and began taking down his details for what we assumed would be a booking. Then, incredibly, the ref held up a red card and Pickford, after a brief protest, was walking off! We waited several minutes for Preston's reserve keeper, 17 year-old debutant Mathew Hudson, to ready himself and for Grayson to decide who they'd sacrifice to get the young keeper on. They chose John Welsh. The details about the age and inexperience of the Preston keeper soon got round the Leeds fans as social media sites were viewed on mobile phones and that meant for the rest of the afternoon young Hudson was subject to jeers and cat calls whenever the ball came near him; anything to try to play on the lad's nerves. It didn't seem to be affecting him though as he calmly saw out the rest of the first-half.

In the bogs at half-time, there was no great optimism that Leeds could beat ten men. *"We're f****** useless against ten usually"*, one lad broadcast to his mate. At the other end of the trough I could hear someone cautioning that, *"They're a lot f****** better than I thought they'd be"*, and he wasn't referring to Leeds.

When I got back to my seat, I'd half expected to see Kentley. He'd told me he was going to be here and he'd told me he was going to get a seat near me; there were plenty that seemed available but he was nowhere to be seen and I'd not had a text either.

The second-half kicked off and we just about had time to settle down after the break when…WE F****** SCORED! Well, *we* didn't score exactly; Santa was back, this time masquerading as Alan Browne, the Preston defender. Stuart Dallas got round the back of the Preston defence down the Leeds left and he hammered the ball across the face of goal. Quite what Browne was doing I'm still not sure to this day having just watched another replay but he planted a solid forehead on the ball and it fair rocketed through the grasping gloves of young Hudson. It was just what we needed, a helping hand, or forehead, to get us off the mark. I realised my 4 – 2 bet was now pretty unlikely but I thought Leeds might well go on to get four or even five. As for the young goalie, the Kop cruelly sang, *"One Nil and it's your keeper's fault"*, in the hope it would shatter the lad's confidence and help us get those three or four goals we were sure would follow.

It didn't happen. Leeds huffed and puffed for the next few minutes and Preston resorted to some very agricultural tackling to keep us at bay but we didn't really create anything of note in the remainder of the game. In fact if anything, Preston came more and more into it. Grayson's team would end the afternoon with five yellow cards to add to the red one they got in the first-half and a foul count of 17 to our nine. It wasn't only cynical tackling though, they also began to boss the game, despite having one fewer player than we did; you'd honestly never have known had you dropped into Elland Road during the second-half.

Talking of dropping in, mid-way through the second-half Kentley arrived! He looked suitably sheepish as he explained the reason for his late appearance; for some reason he had in his mind this was a 4:30pm kick-off! The upcoming Forest game is scheduled for 4:30pm and hence that was probably what caused his confusion. He'd been sat at home scrolling through Twitter at around 2 o'clock when he'd spotted the team in a Phil Hay tweet and it had struck him as odd it was being announced so early! Then he checked and realised the error of his ways!

The game wasn't actually that riveting anymore and the most interesting spectacle was the arrival on the pitch at the Kop end of a solitary magpie with a broken wing. Back and forth he hopped, at one point taking up a position on the goal line while Hudson was out patrolling his area. Normally, a solo magpie is thought to be bad luck; one for sorrow and all that, but with this one we didn't know who the bad luck was for!

Not long after the hour mark, Steve Evans sent on Doukara for Luke Murphy, presumably in an attempt to replicate the form we saw at Wolves. It didn't happen. The Douk we saw today was more like the old Doukara, the one most Leeds fans thought was a *"lazy useless bas****"*. On 83 minutes, Antenucci came on for Chris Wood who got a surprisingly good round of applause as he left the pitch. Kentley and I both looked at each other and rolled our eyes; he'd been very poor again we thought. The final change was more to waste time than anything else as, deep into injury time, Kelvin Phillips got a few seconds, replacing the excellent Stuart Dallas. It ended 1 – 0 to Leeds and we all breathed a huge sigh of relief. At the end of the day three points is three points and I couldn't fault the work ethic of the players who may well have suffered some reaction to the Wolves game and the late arrival home. We also put in some strong tackles ourselves and at one point three tremendous Leeds challenges, one after the other, got the Elland Road crowd roaring their approval; we love and value commitment to the cause above almost anything else!

As I wandered down Lowfields Road back to the car, most fans were just happy we'd picked up the three points while some were getting giddy noting we were only five off the last of the play-off spots. For me, I was angry the team had played so badly and I couldn't ever remember feeling so down following a win. I reasoned that if we played like that at Forest we'd get tonked. Evans made much of the fact his team were dog tired, particularly because they didn't get back to Leeds until the early hours on Friday but he promised they'd turn up at Forest on the 27th *"fresh as daisies"* after a good Christmas break. Two days after the game, the FA's Regulatory Commission upheld Preston's appeal over Pickford's red card and it was changed to a yellow and I started to think maybe our luck was changing; had the ref seen it as yellow and kept him on the pitch I'm not sure we'd have won the game, so poorly did we play. That magpie was definitely on our side!

Leeds United 1 Preston North End 0 (**Browne, (og 46)**)
22,641 (Preston, 894)

Poor quality Wood in Forest

C hristmas came and went in a flash; a sure sign of old age. Time seems to fly by faster and faster the older I get. Boxing Day felt peculiar too, with no football to watch thanks to those meddling TV schedulers at Sky. Everyone else in the Championship, and most of the other divisions for that matter, played their games in the traditional 3pm Boxing Day slot; fathers and sons all over the country enjoying the special feeling of wearing that new footie shirt, bobble hat or club scarf to the match. Some games were postponed due to the continued wet weather that left huge areas of the North East and North West devastated with more floods. Blackburn's game with Boro was called off as were many other games in the Manchester region, while the centre of York was now under water as were parts of Leeds city centre. The weird warm weather had brought the side effect of heavy rain and rivers all over the North were bursting their banks. All the other Championship games went ahead, with Derby the big winners; they went top of the table with a solid 2 – 0 win over Fulham. Boro remained second but now with a game in hand of course, while the other four play-off spots were filled by Hull, Brighton, Burnley and Ipswich. Leeds would start the game at Forest the following day in 13th, eight points behind Ipswich.

The Forest game may have been moved back 24 hours but at least it was not that far away. We'd escaped the worst of the wet weather too, so it should have been a straightforward blast along the A50. Kentley was predictably a few minutes late arriving at our usual pick up point so I took great pleasure in reminding him he'd promised to be on time. In fact, so engrossed was I in pulling his leg over it that I automatically turned right and joined the M6 rather than turning left onto the A500! We were a couple of miles down the motorway before I suddenly realised what I'd done. Thankfully, Sally Sat-Nav came to the rescue and plotted a new, though rather long-winded, alternative route to Nottingham via Uttoxeter.

Forest is one of those trips I've now done every season since I started this writing malarkey and so I knew exactly where to park, just down the road from the Notts County Social Club which was once again a designated watering hole for the travelling Leeds fans. We wandered in not long after 2pm and there were already plenty of familiar faces at the bar. Derek got Kentley and me a Coke each and, after saying hello to Shirley, Chris and Phil, we sat down in one of the little booths with Si and Connor. Jo E and Carmel arrived a few minutes later and Carmel brought out a plastic tub crammed full of mince pies which she handed round. They were gorgeous; on a par with Jo's chocolate brownies… I have to say that in case Jo ever sees this! (I'm in enough trouble as it is for once referring to her as 'Little Jo'…)

The main topic of conversation was whether Big Steve would change things around or not today. He'd hinted that he'd use all his regular first teamers during this next spell of three games in seven days but when Connor spotted the team on his phone, it was the same eleven who'd started against Preston. There were a couple of changes on the bench, with Tom Adeyemi fit again and Casper Sloth getting a rare seat in the 18 man squad. Kelvin Phillips and Alex Mowatt dropped out altogether; Alex having a minor groin strain apparently.

Silvestri
Wootton Bellusci Cooper Taylor
Bridcutt
Byram Cook Murphy Dallas
Wood

Subs: Peacock-Farrell, Coyle, Bamba, Sloth, Adeyemi, Antenucci, Doukara.

As I've said before, while the team continued to get the right results it was hard to criticise Evans' team selections but there were question marks hanging over this side. Scott Wootton had few fans amongst the Leeds regulars while Luke Murphy's name also came in for regular stick. The elephant in the room though was Chris Wood. He'd got himself into a bit of a goal drought in recent games; missing chances that a top striker really ought to have been burying. He was our top scorer at the time, with seven, but most of us thought he'd missed as many as that again. Quite how long Evans could persist with him as our lone striker was debateable; it was not as if we were creating boatloads of chances, so each one missed was potentially costly. Maybe he'd turn it around today we concluded.

I joined Kentley, Si, Connor, Jo and Carmel on the fifteen minute walk from Meadow Lane to the City Ground. It was drizzling, chilly and dark but that just added to the atmosphere. We took our places in the lower tier of the nattily named Money Shop Bridgford Stand with the other 1,900 or so Leeds fans and over to our left, in the same stand, was the core of the Forest support. They were armed with flags adorned with various legends including, *"FOREST ARE MUCKING FAGIC!"* which I thought was very polite. The ground looked just about full and we'd see on the big screen later on that the attendance in total was 27, 551, only around three thousand short of its capacity. The Leeds fans were noisy and very early in the piece we let rip with a welcoming chant for the Sky TV people; *"Sky TV is f****** sh**"*, belted out round the ground. Someone amongst the Leeds ranks then spotted another Forest banner over to our left with a big picture of Brian Clough and Peter Taylor printed on it and suddenly, *"There's only one Don Revie"* filled the air. Yes, this was what Boxing Day football should be like... but, as we reminded those TV schedulers, this was not Boxing Day, it was a *"f****** Sunday night"* and it was, *"F****** sh***!"* Leeds were doing their best to take our minds off that little fact though as we served up possibly the best start to a game this season. We pegged Forest back in their half for the first 15 minutes and dominated possession but only had one Stuart Dallas shot to show for it all and that one flew past the post. It looked as though the ref had it in for us too as he booked Sam Byram for a dive in the Forest box, although mobile phones all around us were soon buzzing with the news that it was indeed a blatant dive. Sam has form for this kind of thing and could give Tom Daley a run for his money. I reminded anyone who'd listen that this was the ref, James Linington, who controversially sent Sam off at Watford at the start of last season for no good reason along with Peppe Bellusci for a much better one.

In times gone by, this scenario of total domination was usually followed by a major calamity by the Leeds defence and we'd find ourselves a goal down... In the 17th minute we found ourselves a goal down. Did someone mention '17' again?

Forest's Matt Mills brought the ball out of defence at the far end of the ground and launched the ball over the top of the Leeds back line. Forest striker, Nelson Oliveira was chasing after it but Peppe Bellusci looked to be in control as he stretched a leg out towards the ball. For some inexplicable reason, Marco Silvestri was also loping out of his area and suddenly memories of Marco and Peppe getting in a right old tangle at Cardiff last season flashed in front of our eyes. On that occasion it was big Kenwyne Jones who waited for our two prize clowns to screw up before picking up the loose ball and stuffing it in our net. Bellusci's outstretched leg didn't quite stretch far enough and he missed the ball and stumbled over and Oliveira was on it in a flash. He easily touched it past Silvestri and stroked it into the empty net. We hadn't conceded that many goals this season to be fair, but almost all of them had been the result of individual errors; if we'd have had a decent defence we'd have been nigh on invincible. Oh, we'd have needed a striker who could score as well. If Massimo was watching this game somewhere he would have winced if he he'd noticed the big white '17' on the back of Oliveira's shirt.

I guess the Leeds players are so used to this sort of disappointment that these days it never seems to affect us too much and it would be the same this time. We picked up exactly where we'd been before the goal and continued to dominate possession. By the time the half-time whistle went though, we still hadn't registered a single shot on target. Charlie Taylor had been possibly our most adventurous player, bombing down the left wing and slinging the ball across but there was seldom anyone there and when there was, unfortunately it was Chris Wood. Possibly Wood's best chance was a header that he got too far under, sending the ball miles over the bar. You would have thought Wood would have felt at home at the Forest...

It was more of the same in the second-half with Leeds now attacking the goal just yards away at the Bridgford End. Liam Bridcutt was the architect of every Leeds attack, breaking up any Forest foray and slipping the ball to Cook or Murphy who'd then feed either Charlie Taylor down the left or Scott Wootton on the right. The main target in the middle now seemed to be Sam Byram who had gradually come more and more central, possibly realising that we could be here 'til next Christmas if we waited for Chris Wood to get to the ball. Byram had a couple of towering headers before the best chance of the evening fell to that man Wood again.

A clever ball over the top put Wood in the clear in the inside right channel with Forest keeper, Dorus de Vries, suddenly finding himself in no man's land. The ball bounced up perfectly for Wood and he just needed to side foot it gently over the stranded keeper and it would have dropped deliciously into the net. Instead, Wood tried to smash the cover off the ball and it ballooned way up into the Bridgford Stand into the arms of the delighted Forest fans. Wood had this sort of mystified look on his face as if some unseen force had taken control of his right boot. But we all knew that was bollox and the man was just f****** useless. All around me Leeds lads and lasses had their heads in their hands and some were now angrily gesturing to Wood to *"fu** off"* and to Steve Evans to, *"Get the useless twat off the pitch"*. Meanwhile, Wood trotted back towards half-way with those strange outward pointing feet of his leading the way.

Forest were still being restricted to odd breakaway attacks but they looked far more likely to score again than we did of finding an equaliser, despite the fact we were almost constantly in possession of the ball. Luke Murphy saved our blushes as he headed the ball off the line following a Forest corner and then, on the hour mark, Evans made his first change.

We all leaned forward, peering out towards the fourth official holding up the substitutes board hoping to see the number '9' in red alongside the number '11' of Souleymane Doukara in green. We could see it was the Douk coming on but the number in red was '23' and that meant it was Lewis Cook coming off, thus switching the formation to a classic 4 – 4 – 2. It was a Forest sub, Jamie Ward, who made more of an instant impact though as he stung the fingertips of Marco Silvestri with a powerful drive from outside the box. Finally, with just ten minutes of normal time to go, justice was done and Leeds got the equaliser we so richly deserved.

Charlie Taylor ran the ball out of defence up the Leeds left wing and then touched it to Doukara expecting it straight back as he made to overlap. But the Douk cut inside instead and played a quick one-two with Mirco Antenucci who'd replaced Stuart Dallas three minutes earlier. The Douk then tapped the ball inside to Sam Byram, 25 yards from goal and Sam took two touches before lashing a low right foot shot into the bottom corner of the net. Oh boy that was a moment! Sam ran towards us with his arms outstretched and soon the rest of the team had joined him as we all went mental celebrating our equaliser. The Forest fans were finally silenced and they must have feared the worst as straight from the restart Leeds were on the attack again.

Scott Wootton got behind the Forest back-line and squared the ball across to Antenucci who let the ball run across his body before stabbing a left foot at the ball. It sliced agonizingly past the left hand post. That man Wood had another chance too as it looked impossible to miss from a couple of yards at the back post but he got his legs in a complete tangle and merely kicked the ball against his own ankle to let the keeper swoop and collect it. The game was now being fought out at a frantic pace and Forest broke away and smacked the ball against an upright with Silvestri beaten. It must have been a great game for the TV audience. Lewie Coyle got 20 seconds or so at the end of the game, coming on for his debut first team appearance and it ended all square 1 – 1.

The nature of our performance was very encouraging and at the end Steve Evans came across to us with the players and did his now familiar cheerleading antics and we lapped it all up. This man had somehow moulded us into a difficult to beat and confident unit. Certain players were now looking a million times better than they did under Uwe Rösler... blimey, I'd almost forgotten about him. Players like Marco Silvestri had come on leaps and bounds and the young keeper was now displaying a far more assured presence in the box and Sam Byram seemed to have regained his old mojo. The introduction of Liam Bridcutt by Evans also seemed to be a masterstroke; he was without doubt the glue that held us together, that piece of our jigsaw that had been missing for so long.

In the car, travelling back along the A50, we listened to Steve Evans giving his post-match interview; Kentley having cleverly linked his iPhone into the car media system.

"If it's a boxing match the towel would have come in. For all our dominance we made a mistake on the breakaway.

"Some of our play in the second-half was exceptional. We opened them up a number of times and on another day we go on to win."[1] I couldn't argue with that. Now, Derby County...

Forest 1 Leeds United 1 (Oliveira, (17), **Byram, (80))**
27,551 (**Leeds 1,890**)

---

[1] *http://www.bbc.co.uk/sport/0/football/35144283*

Sky's the limit

Leeds were unbeaten in December with one game to go; Derby County at Elland Road. There was even talk that Steve Evans was in line for the Manager of the Month Award rather than the Manager *for more than* a Month Award he'd already achieved much to most people's amazement. The Derby fixture was seen as another chance to assess just what sort of a turnaround Evans had achieved; a win or even a draw against one of the best in class would surely signal we'd turned that mythical corner.

Good as December had proved to be, everything about Leeds remained fragile. In theory, the Derby game could be the last time we had the benefit of Liam Bridcutt, the man who'd undoubtedly been central to our recent good run. His initial loan was up at the end of the year and there were still rumours that Brighton had the hots for him and that Sam Allardyce, the Sunderland boss would prefer Bridcutt to be sold rather than loaned out again. Leeds fans were all pretty much resigned to the likelihood that Sam Byram would be moving on too, the assumed final contract offer having been rejected amidst rumours that his Dad and his agent wanted the lad out of the 'madhouse' they believed Leeds United to be under Cellino. And then there was Cellino himself. We all knew he was capable of rocking our boat so violently that the waves would engulf us and if we thought we were safe for a while, the eve of the Derby game provided a firm reminder that calamity was never far away.

The Derby game was another live on Sky offering; it was the tenth match chosen already this season, that's 40% of our games. The day before the game, news broke that Cellino, who was back in Miami for Christmas, had ordered the Elland Road staff to refuse entry to Sky personnel, effectively preventing them setting up for the broadcast. The FL soon issued a statement confirming they were aware of the issue and that they were trying to make contact with someone in authority at the club. The statement ended with a thinly veiled threat:

"Under Football League regulations, clubs are required to provide access to the League's broadcasting partners for the purpose of setting up and filming any matches that are selected for transmission. Failure to do so will lead to a club being charged with misconduct."

That got the pro and anti-Cellino factions in a total frenzy. The pro-Cellino folk applauded the Italian maverick for taking a stand against Sky and the FL, with the movement of the Brighton away game to a Monday night being cited as the final straw. The arguments remained the same as when Cellino tried to get the authorities attention by restricting away ticket sales. He was adamant that Leeds were being penalised financially every time a home fixture was televised, as the £100,000 compensation payment did not come close to the revenue and profit lost by the fall in the attendance. His calculations suggested our attendance fell by more than 3,000 whenever a game was on TV. He was also purportedly fighting on behalf of the fans, who were often not able to use their season tickets when games were rescheduled. The Derby game was a good example; I knew of many fans who would have been there had the game remained an afternoon kick off on the Bank Holiday Monday rather than the Tuesday night when many folk were back at work. There was also the issue of fans buying train tickets, even plane tickets and booking hotel rooms for games they couldn't then attend.

The anti-Cellino faction's argument was simpler; Cellino was a complete nutter who through another ill-thought action had potentially jeopardised the club's chances of promotion as we would now surely suffer another deduction of valuable points. All day Monday, Cellino stood firm and by the Tuesday morning, now only hours before kick-off, it looked as though the game would not be shown although the FL had confirmed that come what may, the game would go ahead.

I was on my own for this trip, with only the car radio for company. It was informing me that storm Frank was on its way to the UK threatening to dump even more water on the North of England, while in South Africa, England's cricketers were well on top in the First Test, closing the fourth day needing just 6 wickets to win. Then came the news that: *"The screening of the Leeds United versus Derby game this evening will go ahead as planned as the club has finally agreed to allow Sky TV cameras into the ground"*. I would later read the statement the club had posted on its official website which explained how it had *"reluctantly"* allowed the cameras into the ground. The statement reiterated the recent run of fixture changes whereby four consecutive games were rescheduled to facilitate the showing of three of them live on TV. It noted:

"Leeds United Season Ticket holders have had enough of these fixture changes, the players and staff have had enough, and Leeds United Football Club has had enough." [1]

It remained to be seen if retribution would be extracted by the FL for the delays caused to Sky's preparations. A little later, in an interview with Steve Evans he added his not inconsiderable weight to the argument that it was unfair on Leeds that Derby would arrive with 30 hours more recuperation after their previous game than Leeds would have after the Forest trip.

It was the main topic of conversation in the Pavilion which was hardly surprising, although it was somewhat ironic that a live feed from Sky was being shown on the big screens in

---

[1]

http://www.leedsunited.com/news/article/tmkq6kplrq2613jrdaw1vsf4 e/title/club-statement-sky-sports there. Other topics of conversation included the death of Lemmy, lead singer and founder of the iconic rock group, Motorhead, and of course the likely team selection. Lemmy's death cropped up because it thwarted a betting selection for Kev who explained that his office was running a competition to guess which celebrities might cough their clogs during 2016. Incredibly, Kev had chosen Lemmy amongst his selections only the other day. Having died four days too early though, the 'Ace of Spades' vocalist was now a void choice!

When the team was announced, there were two changes from the starting eleven at Forest:

Silvestri

Wootton Bamba Cooper Taylor

Bridcutt

Byram Adeyemi Murphy Dallas

Wood

Subs: Peacock-Farrell, Coyle, Doukara, Antenucci, Phillips, Cook, Bellusci.

Hence it was Adeyemi in for Cook and Bamba finally back in for Bellusci who was presumably being punished for his cock-up at Forest. Bamba appeared with the captain's arm band that Liam Cooper had worn for the previous few games. Derby had old Leeds favourites Stephen Warnock and Bradley Johnson in their eleven and the dangerous Chris Martin and Tom Ince on their bench. Warnock wore the captain's armband for the Rams.

The first signs of storm Frank were in evidence as Nigel and I walked across to the ground with a strong wind blowing and the first drops of rain driving in towards us in the North Stand. It was the last game of 2015 and I took the opportunity to pop over to see Rob and Pete to wish them an early Happy New Year before taking my seat in row GG. There were a few regular faces missing, no doubt stymied by the game being moved away from the Bank Holiday but equally there were some new faces. Jo pointed out one bloke a couple of rows in front of us who appeared to have a pair of flying goggles sewn into the back of his headgear. He was giving it large, as they say, right from the off and looked to have had more than a few sherbets.

Derby failed to sell out their full allocation of 1,900 tickets but still had a good looking following of around 1,500, over in the West Stand. The South Stand gave them some early stick noting: *"Forest bring more than you"*, and, *"Top of the league, half the stand"*, referring to the vast space they hadn't filled. The home sections were nowhere near full either and the attendance would later be reported as just over 23,000. I reckoned that would have been nearer 30,000 had this game been played on the Bank Holiday when most folk weren't working. The £100,000 from Sky would go nowhere near to fully compensating the club for that loss of revenue and profit. The TV viewers would have been well pleased with the entertainment though as the two sides traded early blows. They would possibly have been less enamoured with our usual greeting for the TV show though as we reminded everyone what we thought of Sky TV and how it was, *"Killing football"* and was *"F****** sh** "*.

Leeds looked comfortable in the early minutes and it reminded me of the game at Forest just two days earlier. We just needed to avoid any sloppy defending and we were in with a shout of some points here. The sloppy defending arrived just as that thought was circulating in my mind. I said during pre-season that this defence was not good enough and with every game we seemed to get a reminder suggesting I was spot on.

Stephen Warnock, out on the Derby left wing laid the ball square along the edge of our box in front of the Kop and we then watched with dropping jaws as Jeff Hendrick sold Liam Bridcutt half a dozen dummies, nutmegged Sol Bamba and then calmly clipped the ball past Silvestri. Bridcutt had his hand in the air appealing for handball rather than actually trying to get goal-side of Hendrick while Scott Wootton, head still bandaged with a 'Kisnorbo' following the clash at Forest, looked on as if watching a move being rehearsed on the training pitch. Was Sol match rusty? Well he certainly looked it as he took up the traditional Leeds centre back position; flat on his arse on the turf. Was Liam Bridcutt expecting a Bellusci like challenge? Who the hell knows? The result was we were 12 minutes into the game and were already a goal down, as we had been in 15 of our 23 games this season. It was the 25th goal we'd conceded too and I was hard-pressed to think of any good ones that had been earned rather than gifted.

The next half hour saw some decent football played by both sides. Adeyemi got a couple of half chances with headers but neither troubled the Derby keeper, Lee Grant. Some tasty tackles were flying in too but another very unpredictable referee, Mark Heywood, seemed only to consider Leeds challenges worthy of cards. Byram, Bridcutt and Murphy were all shown yellow. The inevitable chant of, *"The Football League's corrupt"*, belted out from both ends of Elland Road. It was the 41st minute before the first Derby name was written on Mr Heywood's yellow card with Hendrick cautioned for a cynical foul on Adeyemi near half-way. From the resulting free kick though, Leeds were level.

The free kick was lofted towards the Derby goal where Lee Grant came as far as the penalty spot to punch the ball away from the head of Liam Cooper. He then chased to the edge of his area to try to beat Byram to the ball but Sam got there first to touch it past him and hit it back towards goal. It cannoned back off a defender's leg though and rebounded out to where Stuart Dallas was now steaming in. Dallas, spotting that Grant was still not quite back to his line, tried to curl the ball over everyone towards goal but Grant just managed to stretch a hand up to swish it away again. This time though it fell perfectly for Sol Bamba on the six-yard line and Sol swept it home. The celebrations were manic as big Sol raced over towards the bench pointing manically to Doukara and Antenucci who jumped up and hugged the goal-scorer. The South Stand turned towards the Rams fans and sang enthusiastically, *"One – nil and you f***** it up"* over and over as the folk from the East Midlands sank into their West Stand seats. Meanwhile, in front of us in the Kop, our friend with the weird hat with the goggles had leapt out of his seat and jumped over the advertising hoarding onto the pitch. He literally only bounced over and then got straight back in his excitement but a steward spotted him and within seconds reinforcements had arrived and goggle-hat was escorted away. Elland Road was positively shaking with the noise now and when the half-time whistle blew it erupted again in cheers and applause as we hailed our heroes as they trotted off. This Leeds team had something about them and the only disappointment was it had taken us half a season and two head coaches to unlock it.

The second-half continued as the first had ended, with Leeds giving as good as they got and the crowd roaring them on into every attack, every tackle and every 50-50 challenge. There were no changes to the teams at half-time but there had been a change of referee, as Mr Heywood had succumbed to a hamstring injury. Fourth official, Richard Clark took the whistle and I have to say Clark looked far more assured than his predecessor. Derby's Cyrus Christie was booked early in the second-half to roars of approval.

Just after the hour mark, Chris Martin replaced Darren Bent for Derby and Lewis Cook came on for Adeyemi and it was Cook who had more impact on the game as he immediately began to make those trademark darting runs between Derby defenders. The visitors then had a spell of five minutes camped in our area as they won three successive corners but Leeds survived and then suddenly we were breaking down the right wing in front of the East Stand towards the Kop. The ball went out off Bradley Johnson's head and a quick thinking ball boy threw it straight to Sam Byram who immediately took the throw to Lewis Cook. Cook sidestepped a challenge to steer the ball back to Sam Byram and Sam's burst of pace took him around the outside of his marker. His pin-point cross had just enough on it to beat a defender and Chris Wood was on hand to nod the ball past the flailing Lee Grant. Cue delirium all around again as Wood veered off towards the northwest corner where a number of the Leeds subs had been warming up seconds earlier. They all joined the players in a group celebration and there was a definite look of relief on the face of big Woody. The look turned to anguish a few minutes later though, as shortly after the restart he was gripping his right thigh as he sat on the turf and he'd eventually limp off. You could say the excitement of Wood had only lasted a few minutes, something I'm well used to at my age…

The South Stand was now taunting the Derby section with shouts of, *"You're not bouncing anymore"*, while all around the ground Leeds fans were making merry as we started to dream of an unlikely double over what has often been a bogey team of ours.

Wood was replaced by the eager looking Doukara but a minute later Derby retaliated by bringing on Tom Ince for Andreas Weimann. Whereas no one had particularly noticed Weimann, it was hard to ignore the introduction of young Ince. To start with, Leeds fans were already chanting, *"You're Dad's a c*** and so are you"*, at the tops of their voices, but Ince was quickly into the action and looked very sharp, you might almost say..., 'incisive'. Within two minutes of his arrival, he'd levelled the score. I often wonder if we sometimes give players an extra boost by chanting obscenities at them. I remember Ryan Giggs taking some stick from the Kop in a League Cup game some years ago, just before he rammed the ball in our net. He then wheeled away with his hand cupped around his ear suggesting he couldn't hear us anymore. Now Ince was doing the same. A long ball was headed away by Leeds only to find Bradley Johnson. He threaded it though to Johnny Russell who flicked it first time into the path of the speedy Ince. The flick completely fooled Sol Bamba and in a flash Ince fired into the far corner before Liam Cooper could get a challenge in. Watching the replay I'm still unsure whether it was poor defending or sheer brilliance from Derby.

The last few minutes were frantic as first Derby and then Leeds had little spells of pressure where both in turn looked likely to snatch victory. Kalvin Phillips got a late run out replacing Sam Byram for no reason I could ascertain and that was that, it ended all square 2 – 2; probably just about right.

Leeds thus ended the year 12th in the table with 31 points and unbeaten in December. One year earlier, almost to the day, Leeds had tamely lost 2 – 0 at Derby to end that year 20th in the table with 24 points. That day, Stephen Warnock was in our side and others in the squad included Rudy Austin, Billy Sharp, Michael Tonge, Montenegro, Del Fabro and Adryan. That's progress I reckon!

Leeds United 2 Derby County 2 (Hendrick (13), **Bamba (42), Wood (71),** Ince (78)) **23,027** (Derby 1,490)

Pos	Team	Played	GD	Points
1	Middlesbrough	23	22	49
2	Derby	24	22	48
3	Hull City	24	17	44
4	Brighton	24	7	44
5	Burnley	24	11	41
6	Ipswich	24	4	40
7	Sheff Wed	24	7	36
8	Brentford	24	3	36
9	Birmingham	24	2	36
10	Cardiff	24	3	34
11	Wolves	24	-1	31
12	Leeds	24	-2	31
13	Reading	24	1	30
14	Forest	24	1	30
15	QPR	24	-2	30
16	Blackburn	23	2	28
17	Preston	24	-2	28
18	Fulham	24	-2	27
19	Huddersfield	24	-8	25
20	MK Dons	24	-12	22
21	Rotherham	24	-13	21
22	Bristol City	24	-21	21
23	Charlton	24	-21	19
24	Bolton	24	-18	17

The final Championship table of 2015 had Leeds in 12th spot.

Leeds limp with no Wood

In the run up to the MK Dons game at Elland Road, Steve Evans reported that Wood was only *"50-50"* to start, following his early departure from the Derby game. *"We won't take any chances"* Evans claimed. *"No, neither does fu***** Chris Wood"* I mused to myself.

It was the main conversation topic in the Pavilion before the match; if Wood wasn't fit, would Evans change his favoured formation to 4 – 4 – 2 and play both Antenucci and Doukara or would he try Doukara in the target man role? The adventurous amongst us wanted Leeds to show more attacking intent in a home game against one of the weaker sides in the division while the more conservative punters favoured the straight swap. In the event, Evans picked Doukara to plough the lone furrow up front.

Silvestri

Wootton Bamba Cooper Taylor

Bridcutt

Byram, Cook, Murphy, Dallas

Doukara

Subs: Peacock-Farrell, Coyle, Bellusci, Phillips, Erwin, Antenucci, Adeyemi.

That amounted to two changes in the starting line up from the Derby game with the Douk in for Wood and Cook in for Adeyemi.

The build up to this game felt much like that for Rotherham a few weeks ago. Then, Leeds faced a lowly side following two good wins against Cardiff and Huddersfield and Leeds fans expected, or maybe I should say hoped for, a convincing victory to prove we'd turned that mythical corner. We failed of course. This time, against fifth from bottom MK Dons we had exactly the same anticipation. Win this and surely we were on our way towards the play-offs? How many times had we thought that in recent years? But the Mission: Impossible no longer seemed that unlikely.

It was a dark and dingy Saturday afternoon in Leeds; it was still mild at around ten degrees but a fine rain had been falling constantly ever since I left the house earlier in the morning. It was that sort of rain that Peter Kay goes on about; the sort that, *"soaks yer through"*. As I took my seat in the 5th row of the Kop, I pulled the hood of my cagoule over my head and was resigned to getting a good soaking.

MK Dons were in all red and that made me think of Middlesbrough for some reason; Boro sat top of the table as today's games kicked off and they were playing second placed Derby who they would go on to beat 2 - 0. The Dons started the game as if they *were* Boro!

For 15 minutes, Leeds were on the back foot and indeed were having trouble staying on that one as the Dons moved the ball about purposely and Leeds resorted to some robust tackling to keep them at bay. A few free kicks were given away and MK had one player limp off to be substituted following a characteristically physical challenge from Liam Bridcutt. Bridcutt was giving his all as usual and I did wonder if his exuberance meant he already knew this was his last game for us; his initial loan ended immediately after this match. Other than Bridcutt, most Leeds players struggled; Sol Bamba was having one of those games when nothing goes right and he constantly had to repair the damage he was causing himself through sloppy passing and poor decision making. The Leeds crowd had already gone quiet as the half hour mark came and we all realised this was not going to be the easy victory we all expected. By this time, Bamba was in the book, having had to resort to bringing down Nicky Maynard when he was clean through and we'd also escaped two penalty claims as referee Jeremy Simpson seemed to be in a benevolent mood. He was obviously a 'Homer' Simpson... Twice, Charlie Taylor took the legs of a Dons' forward right on the by-line in front of the Kop and the stony silence from the Leeds fans told you everything you needed to know. Then, in a flash, we were a goal down for the umpteenth time this season.

Another sloppy Leeds pass, this time from Sam Byram, gave away possession deep in the MK Dons half and Samir Carruthers came away with the ball. He easily went round Bridcutt despite the loan man trying his best to bring him down and then slid the ball forward to Nicky Maynard on the right wing, in front of the East Stand. Cook, Byram and Dallas were all jogging along with mild interest at this point and then Charlie Taylor and Liam Cooper both failed to get close enough to Maynard to prevent him sliding the ball along the edge of our box. Two Dons players were steaming onto the ball and the first was Robert Hall who let it go across his body before side-footing it just inside the left hand post giving Silvestri no chance. It was a well-crafted goal from the Dons' point of view but another case of not being on our toes from Leeds'. *"Here we go again"*, was no doubt in every Leeds fan's mind. Predictably, as the half-time whistle blew there was a chorus of boos from the home crowd, something I'd hoped we wouldn't hear again this season.

Steve Evans had obviously seen enough too and he gave the ineffective Luke Murphy the hook at half-time, sending on Mirco Antenucci, as finally we switched to the more attack minded 4 – 4 – 2 approach. It has to be said we were mildly better in the second period but far too often our final pass went astray and we reverted to that infuriating MO whereby the defence passed the ball amongst themselves for minutes on end without ever spotting an incisive forward run from anyone. Inevitably the ball would go back to Silvestri and he'd launch it up-field and with no Wood in sight we'd lose possession. It really did bring a new meaning to the phrase: *"No Wood, no penetration"*. As we reached the hour mark, Leeds had still not registered a single shot on target, with Charlie Taylor coming closest with a left-footed free kick that clipped the outside of David Martin's left hand post. It was a shocking statistic against one of the worst defences in the division. Steve Evans reshuffled again, this time resorting to Lee Erwin who replaced the tiring Doukara. Still Leeds toiled away and still we wasted opportunity after opportunity with sloppy final balls. Lewis Cook broke through at one point and seemed certain to score but yet again his rushed effort was miles off target. Someone up behind me moaned and then told his mate: *"We could play 'til next Christmas and we ain't gonna score."*

With 15 minutes left, Evans played his final card as he sent young Lewie Coyle on for Stuart Dallas. It had a look of desperation about it as the right-footed Coyle took up station at left back to allow Charlie Taylor to play on the left wing. It struck me just how tiny Lewie Coyle is but fair play; he and Taylor got stuck into the action as finally Leeds showed some urgency as the clock ticked into the final few minutes. Antenucci was now busy all over the pitch and he had a shot blocked at the near post while at the other end Marco Silvestri pulled off a stunning save, diving to his right to push away a powerful drive from Maynard. Sam Byram was playing as an out and out right winger now and a close range shot was blocked and went for a corner. Charlie Taylor rushed across to take it in the north east corner. His first effort was headed straight back to him and then, after setting himself, he launched a high looping cross back in towards the penalty spot. We all groaned as we could see no Leeds player within spitting distance of the man under the ball, the Dons' Anthony Kay. He rose unchallenged and seemed to be sending a cushioned header back to his keeper but David Martin was on his knees in the centre of his goal while the ball was heading towards his left hand post. Incredibly, the ball took two or three bounces and nestled in the corner of the net! I've looked at the replay a thousand times and still don't understand what the defender was doing; it was more Peter Kay than Anthony Kay! Never the sort to look a gift horse in the mouth, the Leeds fans went bonkers and immediately a chant of, *"Sign him up, sign him up, sign him up"* started at the back of the Kop and was soon spreading right around the ground. It was an astonishing own goal the likes of which I've never seen before. MK Dons made sure the game didn't get even worse for them with a string of timewasting ploys as players started dropping all over the pitch holding their heads, a sure way to get the ref to stop the game these days as they are all petrified of letting a bad head injury go untreated. When the game ended there were no boos, only resigned applause, recognising that we'd had a huge slice of luck in a game in which we failed to record a single shot on target from our own efforts. We'd witnessed another of those moments in Leeds United history that would be filed under, 'false hope'.

After the game, Steve Evans was angry about the lack of ability his side had shown.

"I don't think we played until around the 80-minute mark, and we were gambling a bit then and chasing the game," Evans said. *"We won enough tackles, we won enough of the ball, but our quality on the ball today was way short of what we would expect and what we've worked on. We're very grateful for the own goal, it looked bizarre to me and the kid probably couldn't do it again if he tried it another hundred times. We'll take the point and move on."*[1]

In the car going home, I listened as Adam Pope interviewed Evans. He seemed confident Bridcutt wanted to stay with Leeds and that the club had an agreement in principle with Sunderland to ensure he'd be with us until the end of the season. For me, that was vital; Bridcutt had been one of few players to show up today and it was no coincidence our unbeaten run of seven games coincided with him slotting into that role just in front of the back four.

Bad as today had been, our luck had held and they do say in this game it's far better to be lucky than good.

Leeds United 1 MK Dons 1 (Hall (30), **Kay (87 og))**
24,356 (MK Dons 407)

---

[1] *http://www.leedsunited.com/news/article/p9wvatnivczq178rkzmg3jr yf/title/mk-dons*

Mustapha Carayol

In the week following the MK Dons disappointment, Leeds fans on Twitter didn't quite know which way to turn. The first issue was Liam Bridcutt. The way he walked around the pitch after the Dons game, waving and applauding to the crowd, was taken by many as a signal he'd be leaving. Even after Steve Evans and Bridcutt himself had been interviewed saying that they very much hoped Sunderland would allow an extension of the loan until the end of the season there were still fans lambasting the club for a lack of ambition. It was almost as if certain 'fans' wanted us to lose Bridcutt just to support their argument that Cellino was destroying Leeds. I was no supporter of Cellino and I still felt there was ultimately no way on earth he could be a long term successful owner of the club, but I was sure as hell not going to turn everything the club did into a chance to berate the bloke. After all, we all only really want one thing; success on the pitch. Liam Bridcutt was the most influential player we'd seen in a long while and his inclusion had transformed the look of the side and our results over the last couple of months, despite the odd blip like that MK Dons performance. It was with relief therefore that I read on Tuesday 5th January that an agreement had been signed, sealed and delivered to keep Bridcutt at Leeds until the end of the season and there was said to be a purchase option at that point too.

The Twitter keyboard warriors then had to find another battleground of course and as usual there was plenty going on at Elland Road for them to scrutinise. Head of Recruitment, Martin Glover had left to go to Sunderland to re-join Sam Allardyce whom he'd also worked with at West Ham and Blackburn. That was hardly a surprise knowing the long relationship they'd had in the past and the obvious increase in salary Glover would secure at a Premier League club. But for those Cellino out agitators on Twitter it was seen as another bloke leaving Leeds due to not being able to work with the mad Italian or even Cellino kicking him out.

The winter transfer window was now well and truly open and it was transfer speculation that was causing Leeds fans the most angst. On Wednesday 6th January, a rumour broke on Twitter that Bournemouth had secured a deal with Leeds for the signature of Lewis Cook for the sum of £10 million. The only 'source' for this revelation seemed to be a tweet by @petter_andre, a well-known supporter of the LFU movement and vocal anti-Cellino campaigner. He tweeted: *"Cook to Bournemouth deal has been provisionally agreed...£10m plus add ons, personal terms to be agreed and medical to pass. #LUFC ½"* Leeds fans on Twitter were once again polarised. The 'Cellino out' brigade took the tweet as gospel and vowed to step up their campaign to oust Cellino from the club. Once again Leeds were selling their best players so the owner could line his own pockets without any thought to what is best for the team on the pitch. On the other side, the defenders of Cellino demanded to know where @petter_andre had got his information from and they made it clear they felt he was making it all up to discredit Cellino and whip up more support for LFU. The battle raged on most of the evening, with the usual sources of confirmation, Adam Pope of Radio Leeds and Phil Hay of the YEP remaining quiet on the subject. Then, finally, Phil Hay emerged to tweet: *""From Cellino:" Not true. I'm not selling Cook. He is happy in Leeds and I'm proud of him!"#lufc"* And that was that, at least for the time being everything calmed down again and @petter_andre went very quiet, some thought he may even have been set up. Someone I very much respect also sent me a direct message confirming the Phil Hay line and even suggested that Cook's father had wanted the record put straight that no such deal was in place and Lewis had no intention of leaving Leeds for the foreseeable future; however long that is in football these days!

We would have to get used to rumours about transfers both in and out for the rest of the month until the window slammed shut. In the run up to the Rotherham FA Cup tie, Steve Evans confirmed that he'd enquired about the possibilities of either Peter Crouch at Stoke or Jack Grealish at Villa joining Leeds but again Phil Hay reported that Evans had been told neither was available. Evans had been known to want Norwich's out of favour striker Kyle Lafferty for many months and it was reported again that talks were ongoing but it seemed Norwich wanted an immediate sale while Leeds wanted a loan with a purchase option, as is Cellino's preferred MO. In terms of possible transfers out of the club, rumours persisted that Sam Byram was the most likely to leave and it was just a matter of waiting for the biggest bid, while Evans confirmed that overseas offers had been received and refused for Peppe Bellusci. The fact that such offers had been turned down disappointed a lot of Leeds fans who were desperate to see the back of Peppe despite his recent better form.

Kemar Roofe, a player I'd seen a couple of times this season playing for Oxford United was another potential target. I'd been impressed with him and saw him score some incredible long range goals while on my 'Doing the 92' trail. But when news came through on the eve of the Rotherham game of our next acquisition, it was a name no one had been talking about.

Mustapha Soon Carayol was a winger on the books of Middlesbrough and he joined on a loan basis until the end of the season. Unusually, Carayol was contracted with Boro until the summer of 2017 but it was believed that Cellino must have been satisfied that he could be transferred permanently if he proved his value to us. When we spotted the team line-up for the game with the Millers, Carayol's name was there.

Silvestri
Coyle Bellusci Cooper Taylor
Byram Bridcutt Murphy Carayol
Antenucci Doukara

Subs: Peacock-Farrell, Phillips, Dallas, Cook, Wootton, Bamba, Bianchi.

That meant four changes from the side that struggled so much against MK Dons. Carayol, Antenucci, Murphy and Lewie Coyle for his full debut were in and Dallas, Cook, Wootton and Bamba were all on the bench together with the returning Tommaso Bianchi, now recovered from his lengthy injury. In the Pavilion, as the news of the team spread, there were plenty of nodding heads. This was clearly the 4 – 4 – 2 formation so many fans had wanted us to go with at home. In the Rotherham side were former Leeds men Paul Green and Frazer Richardson and on their bench was a certain Alex Cairns, the young keeper allowed to leave Leeds last summer.

It was another miserable dark and wet afternoon in Leeds and a paltry crowd of just over 16,000 turned up; the South Stand was not even open, although all the flags were still displayed there giving some kind of background colour to our view from the Kop.

There was some initial encouragement as Carayol got himself involved right from the off and he was clearly tasked with getting the ball into the box at every opportunity. It was great to see him taking defenders on and whipping the ball across even though there was, as yet, no end result. For forty five minutes, there was little 'magic of the cup' on display as two ordinary teams struggled on a very heavy Elland Road pitch in the swirling rain; rain that was once again drifting in towards us from a south westerly direction. I was cursing my decision to leave my cagoule in the car.

We were just getting ready for a sit down as half-time approached and a group of girls stood in the row in front of us was disappearing off to the concourse as two consecutive Leeds corners came to nothing. Nigel and Kentley were debating whose turn it was to go and get the coffees as the ball was clipped out towards Charlie Taylor on the Leeds left wing by Liam Bridcutt. Taylor challenged for a header and then Luke Murphy slid in to knock the loose ball to Carayol who had a big rip in his shirt on the right side of his chest from a previous clash. He was thus very distinguishable from the similar looking but bigger figure of Sully Doukara. Taylor sprinted towards the by-line as Carayol poked the ball through to him but instead of firing the ball across, Taylor cut the ball back sharply to Carayol who was now in a few yards of space right on the left corner of the Rotherham box, as we watched from afar. Carayol took one touch and then absolutely lashed the ball into the roof of the net, with Lee Camp, the Millers' keeper diving in vain with the ball already long past him. It was without doubt one of the best strikes I have ever seen at Elland Road; up there alongside that Bradley Johnson rocket against Arsenal a few years ago. An idiot fan sprinted onto the pitch while the Leeds players were celebrating and gave us a few moments of mirth as he danced and weaved his way around some stewards before they finally grabbed him and walked him away. Why would someone pay good money to go to a game and then miss the second-half and probably get banned?

Within seconds, the half-time whistle blew and the whole of Elland Road was on its feet saluting the goal and an excellent debut performance from Carayol that had thankfully wiped the memory of the rest of the first-half from our minds. Nigel lost the debate about the coffee and went on his way while Kentley and I sat and planned our trip to Ipswich; that game coming up as soon as the following Tuesday.

The second-half saw Rotherham come more into the game and the longer it stopped at 1 – 0 the more I was thinking it would be 'just our luck' if Rotherham grabbed an equaliser and we'd have to fit in a replay. Having said that, the defence, with Bellusci and Cooper in the middle and young Lewie Coyle and Charlie Taylor either side, was seldom stretched. With twenty minutes to go, Steve Evans replaced Mustapha Carayol with Stuart Dallas and the debutant Ghanaian got a huge ovation from everyone bar one bloke behind me who was shouting to him, *"slow down, take yer bloody time"*, as Carayol appeared to him to be not wasting enough time as he jogged off!

A few minutes later Rotherham made their final substitution by bringing on Matt Derbyshire, often a thorn in our side in the past, while Leeds threw on Sol Bamba for a limping Bellusci and then Lewis Cook for Murphy. It was still tense of course, as we knew full well how capable we were of handing a gift wrapped goal to any side and the same bloke up behind me was now moaning about Sol Bamba coming on, describing him as *"a fu***** accident waiting to happen"*; I don't think any Leeds fan really knew which they preferred out of Bellusci and Bamba but this chap was definitely in the Peppe camp! Stuart Dallas very nearly settled the game and put us at ease when he rattled a shot against the crossbar and Liam Bridcutt nearly got Sam Byram in at the back post as Leeds looked the most likely to score but we continued to have that slight doubt. No one wanted a replay at Rotherham.

The clock on the big screen had by now ticked onto 89:00 and most of us were jogging on the spot either from the nerves or the cold as Marco Silvestri kicked a long ball up towards us in the North Stand. Mirco Antenucci tried to trap the ball but it bounced comically right under his boot and then over the Millers back line. Former Leeds man, Frazer Richardson was on hand to shepherd it back as it rolled towards the edge of the box where Lee Camp was stooping to pick it up. But Souleymane Doukara was there as well, lurking on Richardson's shoulder and quick as a flash the Douk had stuck out a toe and nudged the ball through Camp's hands. It was then an easy task for Sully to tap the ball into the now unguarded net and then saunter casually over to the corner flag in the north-west corner where he proceeded to treat it as a punch-ball with a few right-left combination punches.

The 2 – 0 score line was a much better reflection of the game and we could all relax for the final few minutes of added time and begin to wonder who and where we might get drawn in the next round. The last time we managed to get through the 3rd round we were rewarded with a trip to Manchester City of course; something like that would be nice. As I tiptoed through the gents bogs underneath the North Stand at the end of the game, trying to find a trough that was not blocked and cascading a waterfall of pee on to the floor, I could hear a few optimistic voices singing, *"Wem-ber-lee, Wem-ber-lee, we're the famous Leeds United and we're off to Wem-ber-lee"*, and that sounded nice too!

While I jogged back to the car (it was still drizzling incessantly with that Peter Kay rain), I started to think about how our luck seemed to be changing. There was definitely a different feel about this club of ours at the moment. Only a couple of months ago, it was Leeds defenders falling over themselves to offer gifts to opposition forwards every game and that was usually how we were losing. Now, we had had two errors in our favour within a week; that fabulous own goal last week and now a classic 'After you Claude' moment between Lee Camp and Frazer Richardson. I thought about all the times Silvestri had tangled with one of his own defenders in the past to give away dolly goals. Yes, something different was in the air. Was it that Evans had got us working so hard that we were finally getting the benefit of that other old adage – *"The harder we work the luckier we'll be"* – or was it maybe down to that visit to Elland Road by Monsignor Philip Moger of St Anne's Cathedral? Remember him? He blessed the Elland Road pitch at the request of Massimo before the Cardiff game; our results since then? P12 W6 D4 L2. Results prior to that possibly pivotal moment were: P15 W2 D8 L5. Make your own mind up. I daresay Steve Evans would put a word in for his own efforts too, in reshaping the side and bringing in Bridcutt and Carayol and he'd point to the fact we were now unbeaten in eight games. He may have just missed out on the Manager of the Month award for December (Boro's Aitor Karanka got that) but having served 15 games under Massimo Cellino he was now in gold watch territory!

Another stern test was next up as we faced the long trip to Portman Road, Ipswich, on Tuesday. Wonder if Monsignor Moger would be free to join us? We'd not had much luck at the home of the Tractor Boys for a few seasons.

Leeds United 2 Rotherham 0 (**Carayol (45), Doukara (90)**)
16,039 (Rotherham 1,344)

No defence

On the Monday evening after the Rotherham game, I watched as ball number '27' was pulled out of the plastic bowl by Ian Wright, in the One Show studio on BBC1. We'd been drawn away to either non-league Eastleigh or Bolton who would have to replay after drawing their first game 1 – 1 down at Eastleigh's Silverlake Stadium near Southampton. Leeds fans all over the country were asking *"Where's Eastleigh"* and I could feel a new T-shirt design coming on. Most fans were praying that Bolton could see them off in the replay for the not insignificant reason that we'd get a bumper ticket allocation there whereas the Silverlake only holds just over 5,000 in total!

The cup draw and everything else going on in the world on this particular Monday was overshadowed by the news of the death of pop legend David Bowie, at the age of just 69. He'd been struggling to fight off liver cancer for 18 months and finally lost the battle just a few days after the release of what would prove to be his final album, 'Blackstar', which included the track, 'Lazarus'. The track begins: *"Look up here, I'm in heaven, I've got scars that can't be seen, I've got drama, can't be stolen, everybody knows me now."*[1] Most of his fans took that to be him writing his own epitaph...

I held my hand out and asked *"How you doing Tim?"* shaking his hand vigorously. He just had time to answer, *"I'm alright..."* and then all hell broke loose! I'd spotted Tim stood on the end of the row in front of where I was headed and I'd stopped just to say hello. We'd got the timing all wrong today – probably a result of an extra pint at the excellent Dove Street Inn on the outskirts of Ipswich. I'd travelled down with Kentley in his BMW this cold and damp Tuesday and we'd spent a very pleasant couple of hours in there with Keith, Nigel and Andy the Shrimper. Jo E, Martin and Rob were in there too and we chatted with them before finding a free table at the back of the pub. Andy was just meeting for the beers as he lives in Ipswich and wasn't going to the game but the rest of us had trudged to the ground thinking we were in plenty of time. We'd miscalculated though as we'd forgotten there are always monster queues at the turnstiles at Portman Road and had taken another twenty minutes to get from the end of the queue into the ground. Hence it was bang on kick-off time as I shook hands with big Tim.

I hadn't even noticed that the game had started really and it was just the almighty roar from all around that caused us to look down to the pitch. At the far end of the ground the Leeds players were now celebrating wildly and quite obviously we'd scored. By the time I glanced at the digital clock above the goal at that end of the ground it was showing *"00:24"*. Doukara had actually scored in the 12th second of play! Having now watched a video of the goal a few times I can report that it went like this:

Leeds kicked-off with Doukara touching the ball forward to Sam Byram who then played it back to Liam Bridcutt. Bridcutt knocked it further back to Liam Cooper who took a couple of touches and had a quick look up-field to see what was on before clipping the ball left footed some 50 yards up towards

---

[1]   https://uk.news.yahoo.com/david-bowie-secretly-cremated-report-043512827.html

the penalty area at the Bobby Robson Stand end. It was aimed at Mustapha Carayol but it was headed away by Luke Chambers towards ex-Leeds man Jonathan Douglas. Douglas is facing his own goal and his first touch is really poor, allowing the ball go get away from him a couple of yards, just enough in fact for Sully Doukara to muscle his way in. The Douk took one touch and then simply passed the ball into the bottom right corner of the net. It was the fastest goal scored in the FL so far this season.

Kentley had managed to witness it and he was able to give a brief description at the time but there were plenty like Tim and me who'd missed it. Until this point we'd only scored one goal in the first 15 minutes of any game this season and that was Cook's 14th minute opener at Donny in the League Cup. It certainly got the Leeds fans going and the noise we generated for the next few minutes was incredible. It was another of those magical moments that define why we do all this travelling in crappy weather.

Steve Evans had shuffled his pack again for this game against an Ipswich side that was nicely placed in sixth spot in the table. Wootton, Cook and Mowatt all returned to the side with Lewie Coyle, Luke Murphy and Mirco Antenucci dropping back to the bench. It was back to a 4 – 1 – 4 – 1 formation, with Chris Wood still not considered fit enough to resume his position at the top of the pack.

Silvestri
Wootton Bellusci Cooper Taylor
Bridcutt
Byram Cook Mowatt Carayol
Doukara

Subs: Peacock-Farrell, Coyle, Bamba, Murphy, Antenucci, Phillips, Dallas.

When we'd seen the team on a Twitter feed in the pub earlier, there was a general feeling that since the one up top system hadn't worked with Doukara playing it in the MK Dons game, why would it work in this one? Well, I guess Steve Evans was purring when the Douk stroked that ball into the net after 12 seconds!

Sadly, that was as good as it got though. Leeds were bright for about fifteen minutes and could possibly have had a second in that early spell but then gradually Ipswich got to grips with the game and truth be told they pretty much dominated it. They scored a goal at either end of the second-half to win it 2 – 1 but the stats would show they dominated possession and had 17 shots to our paltry 4 and 7 corners to our 2. Having said all that though, if Leeds could defend, we'd have at least grabbed a point; both the Ipswich goals were carbon copies of goals that have been flying in our net for the last two or three seasons. The first was created by Ipswich left-winger Ryan Fraser who sped past Scott Wootton to whip in a cross that was met by the head of Luke Chambers. Charlie Taylor was putting up minimal resistance as Chambers headed home. The second was even worse, as this time Fraser went past Peppe Bellusci and then found Brett Pitman all on his lonesome in our six-yard area to head home. We are seemingly unable to prevent crosses coming in – presumably because our full backs are not good enough - and then we are totally unable to compete in the air in our own area. I said it at the start of the season; if we continue to do what we have always done we will continue to get what we have always got; soft goals conceded in our six-yard box. It was without doubt the elephant in our room as it had been for years.

Ipswich Town 2 **Leeds United 1 (Doukara (1)**, Chambers (50), Pitman (90))

19,140 (**Leeds 1,259**)

It looked as though the Ipswich defeat was the end of our dream of promotion this season. The defeat left Leeds in 15th spot in the table, 12 points adrift of Ipswich and Brighton in the last of the two play-off spots. Only a miracle series of results would get us in amongst those places come the end of April.

In the transfer window, the latest Leeds signings also looked to be made with more of an eye on future seasons than this one, as it was announced we'd signed the 19 year-old McKay twins, Jack and Paul from Doncaster. The twins' father is football agent Willie McKay while their elder brother Mark is an agent with ExelFoot. The two lads can hardly go wrong can they? Jack is a striker and Paul plays at centre back.

Another face to join Leeds this week was Paul Bell, who left Sheffield Wednesday to join Leeds as the club's new Executive Director. Bell had previously had a spell as Commercial Director at Leeds prior to joining Wednesday and he boasted: *"During my previous time here, I helped the club reach its strongest commercial footing for nine years – an achievement which I am incredibly proud of and something I am aiming to build on this time around."*[1] Good luck working with Massimo sir; I wondered how long this one would last.

And then on Thursday we got the news we all expected. Twitter announced on various accounts that a deal had been agreed with Everton for the signature of Sam Byram for around £4m plus add-ons. This term *"plus add-ons"* was there to try to persuade folk the real fee would be much larger so that in a case such as that of Sam Byram, the fans would nod sagely and mutter, *"That's a decent price that is"*. Predictably, the keyboard warriors on Twitter were having their day, as many wheeled out the *"selling club"*, *"Cellino's a c*** and wants to kill the club"*, arguments while the more sensible realised that if Byram was aware he could double or treble his salary and maybe play in the Premier League as early as this season, then wild horses would not be strong enough to keep him at Leeds. It was also believed that Sam's family had just about had their fill of Massimo Cellino and wanted their lad out of the mad house for good.

On the night Leeds lost at Portman Road, there were a few eye-opening results. Of the bottom four sides in the Championship, Charlton lost 5 – 0 at Huddersfield; MK Dons lost 5 – 0 at home to Burnley; Bolton lost 3 – 2 at Sheffield Wednesday; and Bristol City lost 1 – 2 at home to Preston. It was no surprise therefore that Bristol City then parted company with manager Steve Cotterill while Charlton sacked

---

[1]

http://www.leedsunited.com/news/article/1t0j8xmk5t3f61lzfm5nyn3ik 5/title/united-appoint-new-executive-director their interim boss, Karel Fraeye. He was replaced with Jose Riga, who managed to keep the Addicks in the Championship at the end of the 2013/14 campaign. The bloke would deserve a medal if he could achieve that again. It was most definitely squeaky bum time in the Championship but, for the time being at least, we were still well clear of the bottom four.

I had a ticket for the FA Youth Cup game at Elland Road on Thursday night in which Leeds faced the talented Manchester City youngsters; a side rumoured to be worth more than the Leeds first team squad. In the event I awoke on Thursday morning with a severe bout of man flu and I decided to give the game a miss. Leeds lost 5 – 2 and were totally outplayed by all accounts.

By the time Saturday morning dawned, I was still suffering and with the weather now more traditionally icy than of late I took the decision to miss the trip to Hillsborough too. The game was to be shown live on Sky TV anyway, so I reasoned I was doing the sensible thing for once in my life. When I told Mrs W I wasn't going she almost passed out with shock and I think I even caught her thumbing through the yellow pages looking for undertakers' numbers; she thought this must be the end!

I have to say it was a very pleasant and relaxed way to watch a game. I settled down in front of the box with a mug of blackcurrant Lemsip laced with Glenmorangie and a packet of Strepsils and watched the third test between South Africa and England before switching over to our game. England skittled South Africa out in their second innings and would go on to win the game before the end of this, the third day. That was the four game series secured with a 2 – 0 lead.

Steve Evans tinkered again with his team for the Hillsborough game and back in came Murphy and Dallas, with Alex Mowatt missing out and Sam Byram still presumed to be on his way to Everton, although that deal was still not completed and the latest rumour was that both West Ham and Newcastle United were now also interested.

Silvestri
Wootton Bellusci Cooper Taylor

Bridcutt Murphy
Dallas Cook Carayol
Doukara

Subs: Peacock-Farrell, Antenucci, Adeyemi, Bamba, Coyle, Erwin, Mowatt.

I've shown the line up as a 4 – 2 – 3 – 1 formation because that's how Sky showed it. There was no Tom Lees in the Wednesday side but they had the dangerous Forestieri and Hooper up front and due to injuries a third choice keeper in Lewis Price. Perhaps we could put some pressure on him and force an error I wondered. At least we were now getting used to our own keeper looking much more solid in recent games, despite the defence in front of him often going missing in action. That last sentence would come back to haunt me!

As the game kicked off, with Daniel Mann and Don Goodman doing the commentary, I was still confident we could at least nick a point from this game but I knew it all depended on us not making our usual errors at the back. As they say, there would be no defence for that.

As early as the first minute of the game that defence of ours was already showing the jitters. Forestieri smacked the ball against the crossbar but was adjudged offside. Replays showed Fessi was very much *onside*. Perhaps this would be our day I was thinking; maybe the officials are on our side for once. I was still thinking it a few minutes later when Peppe Bellusci blatantly pulled down Forestieri in our box but referee Anthony Taylor seemed oblivious.

After the initial fifteen minutes, when the home side looked rampant and every bit a top six side, Leeds started to grow into the game. Indeed had Lewis Cook been an experienced striker and not a young midfielder, we could have gone in a couple of goals to the good. I lost count of the number of times he found himself in the opposition six-yard box but only managed to 'swing and miss' as the ball slid past him. The other highlight of an entertaining first forty five minutes was the sight of Wednesday manager Carlos Carvalhal engaged in a verbal battle with Steve Evans over another dubious refereeing decision from Anthony Taylor, a late choice for the game with

Kevin Friend crying off ill. By the end of this game Taylor must have wished he hadn't answered his phone.

The general consensus of the Sky team was that Leeds had edged the first-half in terms of the quantity and quality of chances created. There was the usual caution though that a team that fails to take its chances often goes on to pay the penalty. Within five minutes of the restart that old football proverb came back to haunt us once again and with the bad luck we suffered I just knew Monsignor Moger wasn't at Hillsborough.

In the 46th minute, Marco Silvestri palmed a long range shot away for a corner when it was clear for all to see it was going well wide; it was needless. Predictably, when the corner came across, Leeds did the Keystone Kops thing again as the ball bobbled around before Forestieri stabbed it back across goal. Eventually, after another goal-line scramble, Gary Hooper prodded it over the line. As Don Goodman said on commentary, it was plain and simple, *"poor defending"*.

I was just coming to terms with that disappointment when, just a few minutes later, that annoying fella 'Fessi' Forestieri hammered a long range shot at Silvestri. It was the sort of shot Marco had been gobbling up in recent weeks but whether it was the memory of that needless corner, or whether it was just coincidence, this time he allowed the ball to bounce away and that man Hooper was on hand to stab it in the net again. Without the help of Monsignor Moger, I felt that was the end of our chances of getting anything from this game and indeed this season and once again it was down to us handing out gifts to the opposition. I was suddenly feeling in need of another Lemsip and another large nip of Glenmorangie.

There has long been a feeling among Leeds fans that the FL and indeed the whole world is in concerted determination to keep Leeds in the FL and out of the Premier League. This is achieved, fans argue in their cups, by various skulduggery and sleight of hand by referees and linesmen. I hasten to add I do not subscribe to such conspiracy theories but 12 minutes from the end of this game I did feel the need to give it more serious consideration. If it isn't a conspiracy, at the very least you have to admit we are one of the unluckiest sides ever to play the beautiful game. Steve Evans had by this time sent on Mowatt and Antenucci for Carayol and Murphy respectively, to try to change our luck but sadly our luck just went from bad to atrocious.

Leeds won a free kick out on the right wing in the 78th minute, and as the players lined up for it Wednesday made their first substitution. The board went up showing it was number '45', Fernando Forestieri who was coming off. Fessi was intent on wasting as much time as he possibly could and he was still sauntering towards the touchline as Alex Mowatt waited over the ball. The camera then switched back to the free kick and Anthony Taylor could clearly be seen blowing the whistle telling Mowatt to proceed. Alex lifted a high ball to the back post where Liam Cooper was able to nudge the ball over the line with his chest. Game on!

Well, no, not game on at all. Forestieri had still not left the pitch and he was now aghast that Taylor had signalled the goal. He had his arms outstretched wide and was pleading with Taylor to reconsider. We Leeds fans have seen a thousand controversial decisions over the years but I'd be hard pressed to think of one that has ever gone in our favour. We just knew this 'goal' would be chalked off. Sure enough, after a discussion with the fourth official, Taylor changed his mind and disallowed the 'goal'. It was technically the correct decision of course as the game cannot, according to the rules, restart until the substitution is complete but unlucky or what?

Steve Evans rushed down the tunnel as soon as Cooper 'scored' but the cameras were now on him as Paul Raynor tried to explain what had gone on. After the game, Evans was a clear convert to the conspiracy theory as he could speak about little else than the howler by Taylor. Evans suggested the Premier League referee should never step on a pitch again.

That was pretty much it. Wednesday saw the game out comfortably with the stuffing well and truly knocked out of us and at least until the afternoon fixtures they were now firmly in the top six. For Leeds, this surely had to be season over.

Sheffield Wednesday 2 **Leeds United 0** (Hooper (47&50))
23,909 (**Leeds 3,530**)

One midfielder Toumani

Although still wracked with man-flu, on Monday night I managed to continue my '92' challenge with a trip to Newport County whose FA Cup 3rd round tie with Blackburn had been postponed on the day we saw off Rotherham. I travelled down on the 13:40 Shrewsbury to Milford Haven train, calling at Newport and a thousand other stations en route either side of the Welsh border. I felt like crap and it reminded me of all those train journeys I'd made down to London following Leeds, when it was me trying to avoid breathing in the germs of the other flu laden passengers. This was pay-back!

It was a pleasant ride; this is the line I'd use if going to Cardiff and most of the stops along the way are full of football memories for me. Not long after pulling out of Shrewsbury, I passed the Shrews' 'New Meadow' stadium where I did ground '71' last April (2 – 0 win v Dagenham and Redbridge); The next stop was Church Stretton where both my lads played many times against the local 'Magpies' when turning out for Market Drayton. Then it was Ludlow, with the race course on the left just before the station. After that, Leominster, where I played against the local grammar school many times, albeit with the oval ball not the round one. On the approach to Hereford, I could see the floodlights of Edgar Street, where I watched the great John Charles play many times against my home team Worcester City, back in the early 70s. All these memories floated through my mind as my germs floated around the carriage with every sneeze, cough and blow of my dripping nose.

I'd arranged to meet @PCOX74 in Newport, a Leeds fan born and bred in South Wales. What a great lad he is! We met in Wetherspoon's in the city centre and sat together at the game putting the world of Leeds United to rights in the three hours or so we had in each other's company.

There was no cup shock here sadly, although Newport will still be kicking themselves for missing a great opportunity to cause one. Rovers took an early lead from the penalty spot before they then had a man sent off for a nasty foul that left Medy Elito on a stretcher. The Amber Army were on their feet when their side equalised with a 25 yard screamer but then at half-time Rovers brought on Jordan Rhodes; both Coxy and I knew what that would mean having seen the big number 11 on the scoresheet against Leeds many, many times. Sure enough, with fifteen minutes left, it was Rhodes who headed the winning goal for ten man Rovers, while five minutes later the home side missed an even easier header at the other end.

As I sat on the train going home, with the whole carriage to myself, I flicked through Twitter to see what was happening on Planet Leeds. There was still no confirmation that Sam Byram had signed for Everton and indeed the rumour was that the club had now agreed a similar or better offer from West Ham and it was now down to Sam as to which offer he took; Sam's family had roots in Essex and that was now the expected destination.

The following day, Bolton beat Eastleigh 3 – 2 to set up a 4th round FA Cup tie with Leeds at the Macron Stadium on 30th January. I was pretty much resigned to be missing it as I was due at my best mate's 60th birthday party in Worcestershire at 7pm that night. Maybe I could do the first-half?

Lots of Leeds fans were this week condemned to missing the home game with Middlesbrough. It was announced it was to be the 13th Leeds United game to be shown live on Sky this season so far. It was moved from Saturday 13th February at 3pm to the following Monday night. Immediately there were overseas fans of the club complaining bitterly that with fewer than four weeks to go before the game they were already committed to flights and hotels. A huge contingent of Norwegian fans was hit by the change as well as many Irish supporters, not to mention large numbers of season ticket holders who couldn't get time off for week-day games. The FL tried to deflect the flak it was getting by reporting that Sky approached them back in December for this game but it could not be agreed and announced due to a legal challenge being made by the club. It looked on the face of it that Leeds had missed a great PR opportunity by not telling us back in December the game had been requested by Sky and that they were challenging the request in law. That way, the club would have got the support of the fans who maybe wouldn't by then have stumped up for their flights and hotels, as well as showing they were still trying to make a stand.

Sam Byram was finally announced as a Hammer with ridiculous staged footage of him putting pen to paper distributed across the air waves; it was clearly a completely blank piece of paper he was pretending to sign.

It had not been a good few weeks for ageing rock legends. Hard on the heels of Lemmy and David Bowie, this week also saw the deaths of Eagles guitarist, Glen Frey and drummer and founder member of Mott the Hoople, Dale Griffin. Bowie of course had written Mott's biggest hit, 'All The Young Dudes'. All four of these rock and pop icons left us in their late 60s... a sobering thought for a bloke like me who would turn 59 in a couple of months!

On the transfer market, Leeds pulled out a wildcard on the eve of the Bristol City home game with the announcement of the signing from Brentford of 28 year-old Toumani Diagouraga, a defensive midfielder. When we were all expecting, or perhaps hoping to see a new centre back or striker, there was the inevitable joke going round that we now probably had at least one midfielder, Toumani...

The signing of Diagouraga had not been completed in time for him to debut in the Bristol City game, a good job really as none of us could pronounce his name but we'd all decided to use the name the Brentford fans gave him... 'Dave'. There was even talk of a new chant, *"All Dave Aren't we?"* and I was up for that one. Although the season was seen by many as already over, more than 20,000 still turned up at Elland Road to witness this one, significantly more than watched Rotherham's FA Cup demise a couple of weeks earlier. Steve Evans resisted the temptation to throw Wood straight back into the fire, although he was fit and ready. Evans said he needed Wood for the bench... (And a few nails too I presumed!) It was the same starting eleven as for Hillsborough:

Silvestri
Wootton Bellusci Cooper Taylor
Bridcutt
Dallas Cook Murphy Carayol
Doukara

Subs: Peacock-Farrell, Bamba, Antenucci, Wood, Adeyemi, Phillips, Coyle.

Bristol had beaten league leaders Middlesbrough in their previous league game and pushed West Brom all the way in a cup replay this week, so they were clearly no pushovers. But the game was seen as a must win by most fans if we were to avoid talk of the 'R' word for the next few weeks. City sacked manager Steve Cotterill of course after their recent 1- 2 home defeat by Preston and arrived at Elland Road under the temporary charge of former Leeds defender John Pemberton. Pemberton joined Leeds in the summer of '93 and quickly became a cult hero with his 100% attitude. He was in the side that lost in the League Cup Final to Villa in '96. It was in my mind that we don't do well against returning former heroes...

Following a forgettable goalless first-half in which Bristol carved out far more opportunities than we did, the Kop broke into a spontaneous round of booing as the players left the pitch. Liam Cooper, who was on the edge of the penalty area at the Kop end, turned round and appeared to mouth, *"F*** off"*, towards us bringing more abuse and pointed fingers from the crowd. It was a reminder that everything at Leeds was still very fragile, even the relationship between fans and players. The regular Leeds match-goer had suffered too long to tolerate too many more inept performances like we saw in that first-half; a first-half in which we failed to get a single shot on target against a side that had the fourth worst defensive record in the division. The low point of the first forty five minutes was a 19th minute free kick from Mustapha Carayol that nearly decapitated someone in the back of the South Stand.

Kentley went off at half-time to get the coffees and returned cleverly balancing three cups in a sort of Pisa tower. It was ironic therefore that Nigel then poured half the contents of his all down his front, staining his already 'well worn' Leeds scarf a lovely shade of coffee brown. It was sort of appropriate really as Leeds first-half performance was more dirty brown than Mighty Whites.

Evans left it just nine minutes into the second-half before making his first change. Predictably, Chris Wood trotted on while slightly less predictably, Mustapha Carayol walked off. Lewis Cook moved to the left while Wood and Doukara shared the load up top. Within five minutes of the change, Leeds had scored.

Wood was involved in the start of the attack, eventually feeding the ball out to Stuart Dallas, wide on the right wing in front of the East Stand. Wood trotted into the middle. Dallas toyed with his marker until he got a yard of space on his left foot and then whipped the ball across to Wood. Big Chris had his back to goal and a defender close enough for a prostate exam but somehow the ball struck the big striker in the midriff and bounced a couple of yards away. Doukara was onto it in a flash to sweep it low into the corner of the net. The mood changed in the blink of an eye as the Leeds fans celebrated all around and Sully jogged over to the dugout where he jumped into the arms of Sol Bamba. It was relief more than delight we all felt but it still felt pretty good!

Steve Evans summed it up perfectly when he told us in his post-match interview: "*The first-half was like going to the dentist. It wasn't pleasant and it was a long 45 minutes. It was a scrappy game. We were poor in quality all over the pitch in that first-half - it was lazy and sloppy.*" Whatever criticisms you can lay at the door of Evans, not telling it like it is cannot be one of them. We were desperate for some inspiration from somewhere to reignite our season. Maybe 'Dave' could provide it at Brentford.

Leeds United 1 Bristol City 0 (**Doukara, (50)**)
20,441 (Bristol 641)

Keep Calm & Carayol!

I was driving for the trip down to the Bees of Brentford and was joined by my usual co-driver and navigator extraordinaire, Kentley. It was a relatively uneventful journey apart from the usual scare when Kentley suddenly announced he was, *"Well desperate for a wee!"* as we hurtled down the M40. As usual, he was none too fussy where we stopped as long as we did stop! His chosen point of relief was a little layby just along the A429 off junction 15. That accomplished, on we went and we were circling Griffin Park looking for a parking slot around 2:15pm. We found a tiny car park on Windmill Road near Brentford station and worked out it should only cost us £6 at the advertised rate of £1 per half hour, until the regulations ceased to apply at 5:30pm. Obviously, we sat in the car and waited until the clock ticked past 2:30pm. It was then slightly weird that every £1 we dropped into the slot seemed to be worth exactly 43 minutes and not the stated half hour! £4.50 was all it took to get us to 17:46 on the meter although neither of us was sure the car wouldn't be clamped when we returned after the game.

We headed first for the Magpie and Crown, a fine old real ale haunt that dates back to the year 1614, although the pub was totally rebuilt in the 1920s. It's mentioned in a peculiar poem attributed to one Alfred Pearce entitled, 'Fifty Pubs on Brentford's High Street', in which he tells a convoluted story that incorporates the names of all of Brentford's fifty pubs as they were in 1948 when he wrote it.[1] It was Keith who'd mentioned the pub a few days ago although it was only by chance that Kentley and I stopped by as it was the only place we could find serving food. It was a bit of a shock therefore when Keith suddenly appeared in there although he was heavily disguised with a fetching blue woolly hat and at first we didn't recognise him! Nigel joined us later and we worked our way through a selection of the real ales on offer, including East London's 'Pale Ale', Butcombe Bitter and Wild Card Brewery's 'Jack of Clubs', a potent ruby coloured ale.

The time fairly flew by in the 'Pye' and it was a bit of a wrench to leave there at all but around 5pm we decided we'd better get a bit closer to the ground. Nigel staggered off to his hotel to check in and get some food while the rest of us headed to the New Inn, one of the four pubs located on the corners of the ground. I was doubtful Nigel would make it to the game at all as I totted up in my head how many pints he'd already got through!

The New Inn was bustling and mostly full of Leeds fans when we arrived; some folk were already on the point of leaving to work their way around the other three pubs around the ground although one of those, The Royal Oak, was closed for some reason. The other two are The Griffin and the Princess Royal. Jo E and Martin were just off to *"do the tour"* as we arrived. All the regular Leeds 'away day' folk were in the New Inn or so it seemed and spirits were high. A pint of Doombar was the order of the day and then that was me done for the day with that long drive home to accomplish after the game.

Kentley was first to spot the team news on Twitter and the only surprise was the fact that new boy 'Dave' was only on the bench. Chris Wood for Carayol was the only change from the eleven who lined up against Bristol on Saturday. That did at least mean we were going 4 – 4 – 2 in a slightly more attacking approach than of late.

Silvestri

---

[1] *http://www.brentfordhistory.com/2013/11/01/magpie-and-crown/*

Wootton Bellusci Cooper Taylor
Dallas Murphy Bridcutt Cook
Wood Doukara

Subs: Peacock-Farrell, Coyle, Antenucci, Carayol, Diagouraga, Phillips, Adeyemi.

Sol Bamba was missing altogether and the word was he'd gone home to Paris for *"family reasons"*. It was not thought there was anything sinister in this and he was fully expected to be back in time for the Bolton game. It did mean we were a bit light in the event of any injuries to defensive players though.

It was a miserable wet and windy evening in West London and Leeds' play during the first-half didn't do much to cheer us up. The only positive thing I can report is that Kentley, Nigel and I had a fabulous view of the proceedings, as our seats were in the front row of the upper tier, looking right down on the roof of the net at the Brook Road end where Leeds were attacking in the first-half; not that we saw much attacking from our boys. We were not getting much luck either, as big Chris Wood limped off after only 19 minutes to end that experimental forward partnership before it really had time to find its feet. It looked like a recurrence of the hamstring injury that had side-lined Wood in recent weeks. Wood's replacement, Mirco Antenucci, then proceeded to test the linesman's arm far more than the goalkeeper below us, getting caught off side way too many times for my liking. He did bring out one fine save from the Bees' keeper, David Button though, as he curled a right-foot shot agonisingly towards the top corner.

We were a frustrating team at the time; we were working hard and were doing a decent job in closing down the opposition and winning possession back but then, when we had the ball ourselves, we were just plain sloppy with it. Time after time a Leeds move started with promising intent only to break down as a player made a poor pass, got caught in possession or unleashed a shot miles off target. It was starting to frustrate the hell out of our travelling support. By contrast, Brentford's passing and movement looked slick and clever and they would smoothly move from defence to attack. That defence of ours still has lots to learn too and on the half hour mark it parted like the Red Sea at the bequest of Moses. I was stood right in line with Sam Saunders as he collected the ball just on half way from a wayward Liam Bridcutt header and he then ran and ran and ran straight towards the Leeds goal at the far end of the ground. The movement of the Brentford forwards pulled our defence all over the place and we could see the pitch open up and our goal look about a mile wide as Saunders lashed a low shot into the bottom corner. For some reason this defence of ours doesn't actually concede that many goals (about 1 a game on average) but boy do we concede some sloppy ones! Watching a replay of the goal on the internet the following day, a circle of no less than six Leeds United players could be seen surrounding Saunders, tracking him like some sort of human UFO until the Brentford man pulled the trigger. No one tried to tackle or block him or even bring him down.

At half-time, there was more muted booing as the players left the pitch down in the corner below us but then the majority of the Leeds crowd turned on those abusing the players and tried to encourage the men in yellow to better things in the second-half. And to be fair, we did look marginally more professional after the break with Sully Doukara going close a couple of times.

On the hour mark, we got our first sight of 'Dave', as the former Bees favourite, Diagouraga, replaced a misfiring Luke Murphy who is looking more and more out of his depth at this level. The talk in the disgustingly inadequate gents at half-time was mostly about him and how he's, *"only a League 1 player at best"*. Diagouraga put himself about and does look a useful prospect although he was clearly a defensive minded player when what we were crying out for was someone with vision going forward. With the game seemingly going away from us, Evans made his final change by bringing on Muzzy Carayol for a very tired looking Stuart Dallas. It was a last throw of the dice, presumably looking for another long range shot like Muzzy conjured up on his debut. 'Keep calm and send on Carayol'. Thankfully, Evans got it spot on! A mishit clearance out of the Bees box went straight to Sully Doukara but he was tackled and the ball rolled free to Carayol. Muzzy turned and curled a lovely first time shot beyond Button into the far corner of the net from just outside the box.

At the end of the day, Leeds were well worth the point, as Brentford, despite being far more accurate and precise with their passing, didn't really create much more than we did and the stats were pretty much even. Once again the feeling at the end of the game was one of frustration; if we could've just tidied up our play a bit we'd have been getting far better results than we actually were.

Once again, in a post-match interview for TV Yorkshire, Steve Evans was nothing if not honest in his assessment of the game: *"Conditions in the first-half were really tough I think. At the start of the game there's a swirling wind and driving rain getting into the faces of the back four and goalkeeper so that makes it tough. I don't excuse our passing of course, if you're passing on the floor you can get around the wind and the rain. Losing Chris Wood was another factor I think that's a blow to us but we didn't really seem to perform at any level; we didn't close people down as sharp as we can and when we got the ball and got the opportunity to counterattack, a good team, then we gave away the ball too sloppy and misplaced passes."*

That pretty much summed it up for me, particularly in the first-half. Second-half, Evans thought we were the better team, although he bemoaned the fact that by then the swirling wind and rain which had been in the faces of *his* team first-half had abated, as if Brentford had, *"wrapped it in a box and put it in a cupboard"* as Big Steve put it.

At the end of the day, a point at Brentford was a decent point and especially since we'd played so badly. As Kentley and I drove the 160 miles or so home, we kept returning to the central fact that, good as this team of ours was in parts, it was still desperate for a driving force in midfield and some real quality in the final third of the pitch. There was less than a week to go in the transfer window and hope was fading that reinforcements were on the way.

Brentford 1 Leeds United 1 (Saunders (27), **Carayol (84)**)
10,051 (**Leeds 1,632**)

AWOL (Absent Without Leeds!)

I was sat in a former RAF canteen building that was these days the café at Croome Court, a National Trust property in deepest rural Worcestershire. I was having afternoon tea with Mrs W. I chuckled as I read one of the advertising flyers: *"Expect the unexpected. Incredible innovation, devastating loss, remarkable survival and magnificent restoration. All in one place"* It could have been a slogan advertising a documentary on Leeds United rather than a huge country house that had fallen into disrepair. It was 3:20pm and Leeds were already a goal to the good at the Macron Stadium in the 4th Round of the FA Cup.

I'd been getting regular texts from Kentley and my lad Mark since late morning, presumably to make me feel even more 'homesick'. Mark rubbed it in when he texted just after midday to tell me he'd arrived at the pub: *"Comfortably pitched our tent in the Beehive – everyone's asking after my "famous" father... Missing in action! Beer's flowing – we all love Leeds!"* A few minutes ago Sully Doukara had popped up to score his fourth goal in six games and he was having a stormer by all accounts.

Steve Evans had finally gone with both Doukara and Antenucci in the line-up, with Sol Bamba and Toumani

Diagouraga joining Antenucci as the three changes from the side that began at Brentford. Liam Cooper and Chris Wood were out injured while Diagouraga, not unexpectedly, got the nod ahead of Luke Murphy who'd been poor on Tuesday night.

Silvestri
Wootton Bellusci Bamba Taylor
Diagouraga Bridcutt
Dallas Cook Doukara
Antenucci

Subs: Peacock-Farrell, Coyle, Sloth, Murphy, Adeyemi, Erwin, Carayol. Sol Bamba was captain in Cooper's absence.

The formation shown here is the one Thom Kirwin tweeted, although I wasn't sure he hadn't got Ant and Douk the wrong way round. No matter, it looked a decent side to me and the hope was presumably to free up Lewis Cook to roam a bit further forward than usual now that we had two solid defensive midfielders in Bridcutt and 'Dave'.

It was half-time as I switched on the TV in our room at Puckrup Hall where we were stopping the night; Leeds were now 2 – 0 up, with 'Dave' having scored on his full debut. I managed to persuade Mrs W that we needed a little rest before going down to join the other guests so I lay on the bed and watched as the BBC reported the minute by minute developments in all the FA Cup games.

The reason for me being in Tewksbury in Worcestershire and not the Macron Stadium in Bolton was the occasion of my best mate Malc and his wife Di's joint 60th birthday party. I've known Malc since I was about 12 years-old and we'd been best man at each other's weddings. I'd been tempted to do something daft like watch the first-half and then drive down but the timings and the likely traffic chaos around the Macron would have rendered the plan likely to fail miserably and probably end in divorce. So, there I was in the Puckrup Hall Hotel watching news of our game on the BBC. Later, I would be dressing up as 'Danny' from Grease the movie, with my oversized sideburns and my T-Birds fake leather jacket, while Mrs W tried to be Olivia Newton-John. It was a 50s themed party if you hadn't already guessed. Another large group of residents at the hotel this night was the first team squad of the Exeter Chiefs Rugby Union Club. They had a game against the Worcester Warriors – another love of my sporting life – the following day and I was initially encouraged when Mrs W informed me she'd seen them all in the bar. Sadly, when we went downstairs after the football had finished, I saw that they were indeed all in the bar ... but they were all drinking bottled water and not gallons of beer. My only other hope was that the noise of the rock and roll band Malc and Di had laid on for the evening would keep them all awake into the small hours! Whether it did or not I will never know but the Chiefs ran out comfortable winners over the Warriors on Sunday afternoon.

"...and there has been a goal at the Macron Stadium" the announcer cried. Darren Pratley had just got one back for Bolton. At the same time my 'phone beeped to signal another text from Kentley: *"Same old Leeds"* it began, *"Should be Okay though, Leeds as a club would be really low if we lost this lead in front of 7k."* He was referring to the fact that Leeds had an amazing 6,630 fans behind them; just failing to sell out the entire allocation by a couple of hundred tickets. I couldn't help thinking back to that Bristol game again though, when we similarly conceded in the last few minutes to then succumb to an equaliser in stoppage time; surely not again?

Kentley seemed convinced it was going to go pear-shaped any second as he texted: *"I'm afraid to say... it's coming"*. The BBC was now reporting that Gary Madine had hit the post and Silvestri had defied Pratley with a fine save as the Trotters threw the kitchen sink at us. But this time we held on and we'd join the likes of Manchester City, Man United, Liverpool, Chelsea and Spurs in the last 16; only the second time we'd got this far in 13 seasons. The only shock result in the 4th Round was at Shrewsbury, where the home side pitched Sheffield Wednesday out 3 – 2 with a 97th minute winner. The other ties went with the form book although Peterborough would take WBA back to London Road for a replay.

For the record, both Leeds goals were well worked moves, although the Douk's opener did owe a debt of gratitude to Bolton keeper, Ben Amos. Sol Bamba intercepted the ball on half way and then laid it forward to Stuart Dallas; the Irishman in turn pushed it through to Doukara. The Douk took a couple of touches to get the ball from under his feet and then lashed at it with his left foot. Somehow, Amos was wrong-footed and as he dived to his right the ball was heading more to his left. It struck him on the knees and ballooned over his body into the corner of the net. As I watched the BBC video of the highlights the following week, it struck me that once again we'd got a bit of luck there, as we seemed to be doing far more often these days. There was nothing lucky about our second though. Started by Lewis Cook, out on the right wing, he slotted the ball through for Antenucci who dashed to the by-line before cutting the ball back to Toumani Diagouraga. 'Dave' clipped it first time with his right foot past Amos.

The Bolton goal, ten minutes from time, was another in the ever growing portfolio of Leeds United defensive horror movies. A right wing corner was won in the air by Bolton and it got through to Darren Pratley who smashed the ball into the roof of the net from two yards at the back post.

After the game, Steve Evans was full of praise for Sully Doukara. He told the BBC:

"When I arrived Souleymane Doukara felt discarded, didn't feel loved. And that's harsh. I told him he was going to get the biggest opportunity of his life and he is enjoying every minute of it.

"He is going to get fitter and sharper and I don't think there will be many teams who will look forward to playing against the big fella.

"His power and purpose all afternoon was great. He has got a heart the size of Big Ben and I am pleased he is getting these rewards."[1]

Bolton Wanderers 1 **Leeds United 2 (Doukara (8), Diagouraga (39)**, Pratley (80))
17,336 (**Leeds 6,630**)

---

[1] *http://www.bbc.co.uk/sport/football/35389175*

17!

The winter transfer window closed gently at 11pm on the Monday after the Bolton cup tie and there were no more deals at LS11. In terms of senior player movements therefore, it was three in and three out. Diagouraga was bought for a rumoured £575,000 while Bridcutt and Carayol signed loan deals until the end of the season. Going out, were Sam Byram to West Ham for £3.7m, Tommaso Bianchi on loan to Ascoli and young Chris Dawson, who was released from his contract at Leeds and was immediately snapped up by Neil Redfearn at Rotherham. Bianchi's career at Ascoli didn't get off to much of a start as news filtered through during our game at Bolton that he'd been sent off in his debut against Cesena in Serie B. In an interview with the YEP[1] following the close of the transfer window, Steve Evans claimed that beyond the offer for Diagouraga, Leeds had made four other bids, all of them for strikers. The YEP reckoned Leeds offered £300,000 for Barnsley's Sam Winnall, a fee Barnsley saw as derisory and then failed with attempts to bring Fraizer Campbell from Crystal Palace or Kike from Boro. Kyle Lafferty had been chased by Evans throughout the window and was now said to be his preferred option if a loan move could be arranged. Boro had managed to pull off the

---

[1]   *http://www.yorkshireeveningpost.co.uk/sport/leeds-united/latest-lufc-news/leeds-united-evans-looking-long-term-after-falling-short-in-january-transfer-window-1-7714021*

deal of the century by signing Jordan Rhodes for a rumoured £11 million from Blackburn. In the same YEP article Evans concluded: *"People will roll their eyes when they hear me say this but if we'd been in Middlesbrough's position in the league, do I think we'd have signed Jordan Rhodes? I believe we would have done."*

The latest eyebrow-raising moment in the recent history of Leeds was publicised on the OS in the run up to the home game with Forest. A picture of the front cover of the match-day magazine showed clearly that despite it being the 17th home game of the season, the programme was numbered '16b'. This had all the hallmarks of Massimo Cellino of course, he who has the irrational fear of the number 17 for reasons well documented in last year's book. When at Cagliari, he famously had all seats with the number 17 on them renumbered 16b and of course he 'retired' the number 17 shirt at Leeds soon after he arrived. The anti-Cellino brigade on Twitter grasped the opportunity to ridicule this latest move and they posted comments such as: *"Looking forward to next season now, the 2016/16b season!"*

For many, looking forward to next season was about all that was left to be positive about, although there lingered the hope that we might win that FA Cup tie at Watford in a couple of weeks to progress into the quarter-finals. The game had been confirmed for Saturday 20th February and it left me in a quandary as to whether I'd be doing that or whether I'd be at Crawley Town to knock off the last but one of the 92 grounds. I had a few friends booked to join me at Southend on March 1st which was supposed to be the last of my 92 but Feb 20th was the only home game Crawley had that worked for me. I started to research whether Crawley had a reserve side or even a ladies team that played at their Broadfield Stadium as either would still count under the normal rules of 'doing the 92' but I drew a blank on both counts. Maybe we'd have to be celebrating just 91 at Roots Hall in Southend after all. Ground 90 was to be AFC Wimbledon on 13th February, a date opened up for me by Sky TV who'd picked our home game with Boro as another live game and moved it to the Monday night. I would ponder my options a little longer...

I'd already started to think about the number 17 as I sat on the M6, in miles of stationary traffic on the morning of the Forest game. As I'd pulled out of the drive at home, I heard there had been an accident that had closed the motorway near junction 17 (see what I mean?). That was OK; I had loads of time, so I planned to skirt the trouble and head up to junction 18. But as I arrived at the point of no return, another traffic announcement on 5 Live reported that the road had been reopened. I breathed a sigh of relief and got on the M6 at junction 15 as usual. And then I came to a halt within about a mile. Eventually, the BBC traffic news reported that earlier reports that the motorway had reopened were incorrect and it was in fact still closed. Thanks BBC, thanks a lot. My journey to Elland Road took me over three hours with more than an hour just sat there not moving at all and then, when we did get going again, the heavens opened and the roads were completely awash. The car was constantly doing that thing where one wheel appears to suddenly go out of synch with the rest. It was still chucking it down when I got to the ground so I decided to abandon my economy drive and spend £6 in the car park so I only had a short walk down to the Pavilion.

As I walked into the Pavilion to join the crew around our usual table, Peter Lorimer, Terry Yorath and Andy Couzens were giving their thoughts on the upcoming game. I'd missed Yorath's comments but was told he once again dismissed the current squad as, *"crap"*! I met @DebsHLUFC aka Debbington or Debs for the first time today, she is a name I'd often seen on Twitter but never met until now. She introduced herself by tweeting: *"I'm sat next to you!"* I'd been chatting with Kev and Zack and Shirley and Derek who were all offering me advice as to which game to go to on Feb 20th. No one thought I should be choosing Crawley Town! Mind you, young Zack was saying he was not going to the Watford game as he was due at a party with his girlfriend. Needless to say he didn't get much support for that attitude…and he later changed his mind!

When the team came through, it was just the one change; Liam Cooper was fit again and was straight back into the side pushing Sol Bamba back onto the bench.

Silvestri
Wootton Bellusci Cooper Taylor
Bridcutt Diagouraga
Dallas Cook Doukara
Antenucci

Subs: Peacock-Farrell, Coyle, Bamba, Adeyemi, Murphy, Erwin, Carayol.

To be honest, with Chris Wood still injured no one expected anything different to this although a few folk were disappointed that Botaka seemed to be no longer in the reckoning. Just before we left the Pavilion, Leicester City had thrown down a marker for the rest of the Premier League clubs with an astounding 3 – 1 win at the Etihad. Many of us watching their game on the screens in the Pavilion could only wonder how Leicester had reached these dizzy heights at the top of the Premier League while we still languished in the Championship; the Foxes had shared a season in League One with us not so long ago.

I made my way over to the ground at the usual time of 2:40pm…well, to be honest I was a bit late and I shuddered as I saw it was actually 17 minutes to the hour. The weather was still filthy and as I took my place in row GG it was with no great expectation that I scanned the skies above Elland Road. There had been talk that a number of Leeds fans had paid £500 to hire a small plane to fly over the ground with a *"Cellino Out"* banner flying in its wake. I guessed the weather was too murky for such a flight and we certainly didn't see or hear anything flying over the stands other than the usual wayward Bellusci free kicks.

Our little band of fans in the immediate area of rows GG and HH in the Kop was nodding in appreciation of the start we made in this game. Stuart Dallas in particular was having some joy on the right wing and we saw more crosses come in than we'd seen in the previous 16 games at Elland Road put together. After just three minutes a sweet right wing cross from Dallas was met perfectly by the forehead of Sully Doukara at the back post but agonizingly it went a foot wide. Leeds had lost the toss and were kicking towards us in the first-half, so we got a great view as several similar crosses bombarded the Forest box. It wasn't all one way traffic though, at the other end, in front of the South Stand, the lively Nelson Oliveira had a couple of shots and his strike partner, Gary Gardner smacked a shot against the crossbar. It was a good match with Forest playing a counter attacking game and Leeds dominating most of the possession. At half-time, all sides of Elland Road rose to applaud, including over 2,000 Forest fans who packed the away section over in the far end of the West Stand.

It was one of those typical Championship games which ought to end in a draw – a third of all Championship games this season did – but there was always a chance that either side could come up with a moment of brilliance or, more likely, Forest would win a header in our six-yard box...

Exactly on the hour, Forest effectively won the game as Leeds' super porous defence once again offered the opposition a chance they were unlikely to refuse. This was just one more example that proved that Terry Yorath and I were both right. I was angry; had we been able to win this game we'd have been level on points with Forest and their fans were still harbouring hopes of a late challenge for a play-off spot. This was as big a blow as we'd suffered all season.

Ex-Leeds full back, Eric Lichaj had the ball on the Forest right wing, in the north east corner and he was loosely being marshalled by Sully Doukara. Lichaj poked the ball back to Gary Gardner and Sully didn't react, he just watched as Gardner whipped the ball across first time into that darkest of places, the Leeds United six-yard area. Peppe Bellusci and Liam Cooper were doing the 'arms in the air' thing, appealing for an offside decision, while Oliveira stole in and stooped to head wide of Silvestri. Even at this stage we all thought Silvestri would stop the header, it wasn't the best I've ever seen and Silvestri got a good left hand to it. Unfortunately, his wrist wasn't up to the challenge and he merely shovelled the ball into the corner of the net. Referee Scott Duncan had a good long look towards the liner on the east touchline but he was motionless, albeit not looking too confident. Subsequent viewings of countless replays would suggest Oliveira was a few inches offside and Steve Evans certainly felt the goal shouldn't have stood but accepted it was the way things often go for Leeds. As I watched the Forest players walking back to their half to line up for the restart it was hard not to focus on the goal scorer and the big white '17' on his back.

Leeds huffed and puffed for the final half hour and threw on Lee Erwin and Muzzy Carayol to try to unlock the resolute Forest backline but we never looked like scoring. In the final minutes of the game, Evans took Scott Wootton off and replaced him with Tom Adeyemi in a strange move albeit one roundly cheered by many Leeds fans who still had Wootton down as a waste of a shirt. I had to admit that this game had shown how poor he was as an attacking full back as time and time again he failed to turn possession out on the right wing into a useful cross. But in recent games he'd more than played his part at the back in the absence of Berardi and more recently with Sam Byram no longer an option. Our best player on the day by far had once again been Liam Bridcutt and his statistics after the game backed up my view. He completed more passes than any other Leeds player - 78 in all - and he was dominant all over the pitch even in the final third. If only his mates could match his performances we'd be flying. Forest had done a job on us though and in particular David Vaughan man-marked Lewis Cook out of the game. Afterwards, Steve Evans told us: *"If Cook had gone for a shower at half-time, he'd have passed him the shower gel. That's how tight he is to him all afternoon!"*

As I trudged back up to the car park, I was as down as I'd been all season, more so really. Much as I didn't want to, I knew I had to let go of any hope we could still make something of this season. There were still 16 games to go but with no further strengthening in the transfer window I had to finally accept we were not good enough to go on a run of several wins on the bounce. I had to let it go. There would be no positive end to this particular Mission: Impossible.

Leeds United 0 Nottingham Forest 1 (Oliveira (60))
24,079 (Forest 2,266)

Fantastic Light Show

Britain was still in the grip of a series of violent storms bringing high winds and torrential rain causing appalling flooding in parts of the North; Imogen was the eighth to batter us this winter and we were all playing the same game trying to guess the name of the next one. They are named in alphabetical order and alternately male and female. Thus, Desmond was followed by Eva and then Frank, Gertrude, Henry and now Imogen.

At Leeds it was eerily quiet, almost becalmed. There appeared to be little or no direction for the club with Cellino still awaiting the outcome of his rule K arbitration by the FA which in turn seemed to be preventing the FL ruling on his appeal against his latest ban which had been imposed as long ago as last October. The YEP informed us that part of the reason no major transfers were achieved in the recent window was that the Cellino family had decided not to inject any further funds into the club via the family trust until the outcome of the various appeals was known.[1] Rumours continued to circulate about the possible involvement in the club of Steve Parkin,

---

[1] http://www.yorkshireeveningpost.co.uk/sport/leeds-united/latest-lufc-news/leeds-united-no-answers-yet-to-trying-questions-1-7723019

who'd been seen with Cellino at recent games, while Cellino himself dismissed rumours of investment from a Qatari consortium as mere *"fairy tales"*.

This seemingly enforced moratorium was making life difficult for Steve Evans, who was constantly being quizzed as to why Leeds had not invested in the *"quality"* players he'd openly stated we needed. He tried to imply that a few deals had fallen through as the demands of the selling clubs were too high or the wage demands of the players concerned were excessive but it now seemed as though maybe it was all down to Cellino not having access to funds. Whatever the cause, Leeds were left with a side still well short of the quality we all knew we needed.

Elsewhere in the Championship this week, two more clubs pressed the panic button and sacked their managers, news that must have made Big Steve squirm a bit. Rotherham predictably decided Redfearn was not the man to keep them in the Championship and he was on his way after just 21 games in charge. They were fresh off the back of defeats to Bolton and Charlton who were themselves in dire trouble at the bottom of the table. At the other end of the Championship, Derby surprisingly decided that Paul Clement was not developing their side as the board wished and he was gone after eight months in the job and with Derby sat in 5th. Derby told the press that promotion had never been their prime target this season but it was hard to get beyond the thought that a recent run of seven games without a win had caused them to think a new man might just keep them in the hunt. For both Rotherham and Derby it looked like a last throw of the dice, albeit with totally different ambitions. If promotion for Leeds looked like a Mission: Impossible then the chances of Rotherham avoiding the drop looked to depend on a miracle.

At Charlton, discontent with their Belgian management had reached such a level that one enterprising fan had forged a Director's Resignation notice and submitted it to Companies House. The club issued a statement saying the resignation of Chief Executive, Louis Mendez, had been falsely submitted and they were investigating. Now this ruse was public, I fully expected to see a similar prank from Leeds fans; I expected to see a thousand Cellino resignation documents flood into Companies House.

That wasn't the latest action taken by the 'Cellino out' campaigners though; instead they had a whip round for an advertising campaign under the slogan: *"TIME TO GO MASSIMO"*. The first poster appeared right outside the main entrance in Lowfields Road, exactly where a similar one appeared some four years earlier in a campaign aimed to oust Ken Bates. That one, sponsored by Leeds United Supporters Trust (LUST) had been titled, *"TIME FOR CHANGE"*. I couldn't help thinking that one hadn't done us much good in hindsight. When told about the *"Time to go Massimo"* poster, Cellino allegedly replied to Adam Pope of Radio Leeds, *"I agree!"* Mind you, the next thing he did was to commence legal action to get the poster removed, which it was, very quickly.

Meanwhile, Rotherham hadn't let the grass grow under their feet as they announced that Neil Warnock was the Red Adair figure they'd turned to in order to try and find that miracle. Colin doesn't half get around doesn't he? Once again it looked like he'd be in the opposition dugout for another Leeds game together with his regular sidekick, Kevin Blackwell. We were due at Rotherham on 2nd April.

With no Leeds game on Saturday, I was on the '92' trail again watching AFC Wimbledon v Luton Town at Kingsmeadow; ground number 90 of 92. I travelled down to Euston on my usual and very familiar 06:48 London Midland train from Stafford and arrived bang on time at 08:45. I took the tube to Waterloo and then the 09:12 train to Norbiton and arrived there around 09:45. OK, it was a tad early for a 15:00 kick-off I admit. It's about a twenty minute walk from the little Norbiton station to Kingsmeadow, which is approached under a metal-work arch on a little lane leading off the Cambridge Road. There was no one at all at the ground yet, but I had a good look round and took a few photos by standing on tip-toe and leaning over a security gate. By this time it had started to rain quite hard so I decided to walk back up Cambridge Road to Kingston where I was due to meet up with a couple of Leeds fans who lived not far from there.

Predictably, I got soaked but arrived in the 'Kings Tun' in the town centre about 10:30am. By the time Ricky and Mike arrived around midday, I'd already enjoyed a Wetherspoon 'Large Breakfast' and several pints of Doombar.

I've met Ricky and Mike many times at Leeds games over the years but I'd never before realised quite how much they enjoy a beer. In the hour or so we had in the pub we threw down another few pints of Doombar before walking to Kingston station to get a taxi to the ground. I was already feeling pretty much at peace with the world. Ricky was clearly on a mission though and as soon as he'd collected the tickets he was off into the bar, with Mike and me trailing in his wake. On the big screen in the bar we caught the tail end of the Sunderland v Man U game and of course the 2 – 1 result was a great reason for a further celebratory pint!

By the time we left the bar to make our way to the Chemflow End terracing, there was hardly a spare inch to stand in but the three of us eventually squeezed in right at the far end near the front. There was a great atmosphere in the little ground and it looked almost full. It's only tiny of course, the Cherry Red Records Stadium, as Kingsmeadow is also known these days, is listed on www.footballgroundguide.com with a capacity of 4,850. The attendance would later be reported as 4,439. In the match-day programme, Wimbledon Chief Executive, Erik Samuelson, explained the current status of plans to build a brand new stadium at the Wombles' traditional home, Plough Lane, where they want a 20,000 capacity arena.

The game was a helter-skelter affair with the most recognisable player being Craig Mackail-Smith in the orange of the Hatters. Predictably he came in for plenty of banter from the home fans. The Wombles took control of the game when Ryan Sweeney scored when his header cannoned off a defender to loop into the top corner. Two minutes later it was 2 – 0 as Lyle Taylor stooped to head a bouncing ball firmly into the corner of the net. As half-time approached, Ricky disappeared. Then, just as the whistle went, Mike got the call on his mobile explaining that Ricky was already in the bar and he'd *"got them in."*

We all demolished our latest pints in good time for the second-half but then Mike and I headed for the bogs...and the queue there was a mile long. By the time I got within peeing distance of a urinal the news filtered through that Wimbledon had scored a third and then by the time I was washing my hands someone shouted it was now, *"four fackin nil!"*. Oh tremendous, I'd now missed two more goals this season.

Luton got a consolation goal in the 59th minute and we did see this one, albeit of course it was at the other end of the pitch.

At the final whistle, Ricky went missing again...you guessed it, he was already in the bar and he'd *"got them in"* again! By this time, I'd had so much ale today I was pretty relaxed; relaxed to the extent that I wasn't really keeping track of time and particularly the fact that I needed about an hour and a quarter to walk back to Norbiton station, get a train to Waterloo, a tube from there to Euston, and then make my way up to the concourse for the 18:46 for Stafford. I left the other lads at 5:30pm. You do the maths!

Predictably, I arrived two minutes too late. A chat with the bloke on the information desk told me I could try the 19:07 Virgin train but they wanted £61-50 for me to ride on that one. Back at the concourse, I spotted a London Midland train was leaving for Birmingham at 19:13 and the memory of one previous predicament similar to this reminded me I could get a connection for Stafford from there, as long as I got in before 11 o'clock which I ought to do...

Sadly, the train I got on suddenly came to a grinding halt not far outside Euston and we sat, without moving, for an hour or so while the fire brigade debated whether or not it was safe for our train to pass a building that was on fire further up the line. This accumulation of problems could only happen to me. To prove I was destined not to make that Stafford connection, we then got going again only to stop once more at Bletchley. After another delay of twenty minutes or so, the guard informed us over the PA that the driver had now run over his legal hours and we'd have to wait for another train to hook up with us and then the driver of that one would take charge of the new elongated train. Time was ebbing away of course. Eventually, the train began to move and the guard informed us that plan B had been scrapped and the existing driver would continue. Unfortunately, when we reached Northampton they'd changed their minds again and we were told our train was going no further and we were instructed to board another one that was waiting over at platform 1. Another age went by and I calculated that I then had no chance of getting to Birmingham New Street until around 11:35pm. I only had one option left; I called Mrs W.

Mrs W *"reluctantly"* agreed to drive the 65 miles to Birmingham to meet me outside the station and I joined her in the car at midnight. My cheery *"Happy Valentine's Day!"* greeting didn't go down too well! I'd had to confess that this whole fiasco had begun with that extra pint in the bar after the game. Obviously I blamed Ricky for that but then had to confess that my plan to buy a Valentine's Day card had also fallen by the wayside due to my lack of time at Euston. We arrived home at 1am and then I was up early Sunday morning designing and printing a home-made Valentine's card on the computer...

On Valentine's Day 2016, the Mail on Sunday carried an exclusive article claiming that Cellino was seeking to destroy the current TV deal Sky had with the FL.[1] The article claimed Leeds had started legal action against the FL to attempt to dismantle the collective selling of TV rights and win the right to sell their own games. Other clubs, many of whom had lots to lose if the bigger clubs got an increased slice of the cake of course, were said to be livid and vented their fury at Leeds' new Executive Director, Paul Bell, at a meeting of the 72 FL clubs. In a YEP article later on Sunday, Bell denied this was an attempt by Leeds to go it alone although he stated: *"The club has, however, made it clear to both Sky and the League that it opposes the degree of control exercised by Sky over the league fixture list, and seeks transparency as to how these*

---

[1] *http://www.dailymail.co.uk/sport/football/article-3445896/Massimo-Cellino-new-fury-Leeds-United-owner-launches-bid-break-clubs-100m-television-deal.html*

rights have been sold."[1] Most took that to mean Cellino wanted to *see* the TV contract he claimed never to have had sight off. To the cynics amongst us, The Mail on Sunday article looked like an attempt to further whip up the anti-Cellino feeling growing amongst the Leeds support.

And growing it was; it was rumoured that something like £4,000 had been raised now for the 'Time to go Massimo' advertising campaign and they promised a spectacular light show beaming messages onto the stadium prior to the Boro game, a Monday night, live on Sky fixture, where there were bound to be plenty of cameras to pick up even more publicity for the cause. As I wandered up to the club shop to pick up my match-day programme the only hint of what was to come was a few extra police on duty. The protesters had informed the police of their plans and were determined to keep the protest peaceful.

By the time Jed Stone, Lorimer and Yorath appeared in the Pavilion around 6:30pm, latecomers had brought news that anti Cellino messages were being projected onto the south end of the East Stand from the back of a van parked near the Peacock. Si managed to capture the various messages on his iPhone and I scrolled through them whilst Yorath reminded us how crap we were but that we'd probably beat Boro 2 – 1!

"17 reasons why it's time to go", one message read in giant yellow lettering on a purple background. The reasons scattered on the projected message included: *"The sick-note six"*, *"Sam Byram"*, *"Hockaday"*, *"Not buying Elland Road"* and even *"16b"*. It was a catalogue of all the mad events of the Italian's reign. Another message said simply: *"12 years of false promises, we've had enough"*, with the faces of both Cellino and Ken Bates staring down from the top of the East Stand. The stunt had clearly been well thought out, right down to the location, right above the statue of Billy Bremner. Another

---

[1]   http://www.yorkshireeveningpost.co.uk/sport/leeds-united/latest-lufc-news/leeds-united-and-cellino-deny-seeking-individual-tv-rights-1-7731536

message read: *"Billy wouldn't accept this...so why should we? Sell the club!"*

We'd later learn that the impressive projection cost £2,600. We knew this because one of the organisers posted a picture of the invoice on Twitter, apparently to ensure full transparency of the use of the cash raised from donations. The invoice was from EMF Technology Limited, the firm behind the projection of a nude image of Gail Porter onto the Palace of Westminster back in 1999. That was part of a publicity campaign for FHM magazine and its poll to find the world's 100 sexiest women. I've enjoyed doing the research into that...

As we sat in the Pavilion debating the merits of the campaign (the 'Massimo time to go' one, not the 'sexiest women' one) and what it might mean for the club if Cellino was indeed hounded out, everyone suddenly fell silent as the live feed from Sky being broadcast on the big screens suddenly showed pictures of the projections. They'd been tweeted by fans and if that was part of the plan too, to get the messages out on live TV, it worked a treat. I have to say though, that most fans were more bemused by it all than anything else. If you'd spent an hour or two on Twitter following the #lufc hashtag today you could be forgiven for thinking that all Leeds fans were against Cellino and were ready to take up arms against him. But the vast majority of Leeds fans are not actually on Twitter all day and many have no idea what a small number of fans get up to on social media. All they are interested in is meeting up with mates, having a few beers and watching the game. Hence, as Nigel, Kentley, Jo, Mike and I took up our positions on the Kop; most folks' focus was purely on the pitch.

Evans named an unchanged side; the one that performed so dismally against Forest. The only change in the squad was Alex Mowatt on the bench; he replaced Carayol who was not allowed to play against Boro, his parent club, under the terms of his loan.

Silvestri
Wootton Bellusci Cooper Taylor
Bridcutt Diagouraga
Dallas Cook
Antenucci Doukara

Subs: Peacock-Farrell, Coyle, Adeyemi, Murphy, Mowatt, Erwin, Bamba.

It was bitterly cold, the temperature would drop to minus 2 before the end of the game and we all needed something to warm us up, especially since my pie and peas in the Pavilion had only been luke warm. For once, Leeds came out of the traps like whippets with their tails on fire as they clearly tried to put that limp performance against Forest behind them. Leeds had a couple of shots and won a corner inside the first five minutes as the Leeds crowd urged them on while the 3,000 Boro fans over at the far end of the West Stand were temporarily silenced. You got the impression Boro felt this was going to be an easy three points and now they weren't so sure.

We were looking very sharp and Lewis Cook in particular was at his Duracell bunny best. Boro are a decent side though, a more than decent side and gradually they played themselves into the game. We watched in horror as Liam Cooper pushed his hand into the face of the £11 million man, Jordan Rhodes and the Boro striker went down as if shot by a sniper lurking on the Kop. Referee Craig Pawson was oblivious thankfully but it was a sign as to how Rhodes was getting under the skin of our captain. Rhodes' movement was a lesson to any young striker watching, as he went like lightning back and forth at any set piece with both Bellusci and Cooper doing pirouettes trying to stay with him. They then both failed miserably as Rhodes rose to head a right wing cross into the net but we all breathed a sigh of relief as the linesman in front of the East Stand raised his flag to signal the ball had already crossed the by-line. Within seconds, messages were fed through mobile phones from fans watching on the TV at home that the liner got it wrong; the 'goal' should have stood. It was a let off. When the half-time whistle blew, the whole of Elland Road was on its feet to applaud a fine first-half.

Nigel was on half-time coffee duty today and he duly returned with three coffees, for himself, Kentley and Jo, only for each in turn to spit out their first gulps and then pour the rest away as they found great clumps of some unidentified 'matter' floating in them! The general consensus was that Nigel had 'found' several old milk mini pots in his jacket pocket and offered those instead of picking up fresh ones! There were other suggestions as to what the contamination was but you may be eating as you read...

The second-half began as the first ended, with both sides neither asking nor giving any quarter. The fans were doing their part too and then, on 56 minutes, there was a break in hostilities as Boro fans held aloft their mobile phones in torch mode en masse. It was a tribute to Boro football broadcaster, Ali Brownlee who passed away recently after losing his battle with cancer; he was just 56 years young. Leeds fans around the ground followed suit and soon thousands of star-like silver lights lit up all sides of the ground as the face of Ali Brownlee looked down from the big screen. It was an emotional scene.

When the screen changed back to show the score and the time again, both sets of fans renewed their vows of support and off we all went again. Rhodes missed a couple of gilt-edged chances while for Leeds Sully Doukara had a decent header miraculously saved by Dimi Konstantopoulos, down to his left in front of the Kop. Leeds brought Alex Mowatt on for Stuart Dallas and later Erwin for Antenucci and Murphy for Diagouraga while Boro introduced David Nugent and the dangerous Albert Adomah. But it was Leeds who piled on the pressure in the final minutes, with wave after wave of attacks and several more corners and the noise from the Kop was as good as I could remember; it always is when we get on top and really press-on. But it was not to be and the closest we got was a bullet of a half-volley that Erwin thrashed just over the bar.

Once again Elland Road rose as one to salute a valiant effort and I'm sure most Leeds fans went home satisfied with their night's entertainment. It had been well worth braving the cold tonight, not only for the action we saw on the pitch but also for the two excellent light shows. Leeds would end this round of games in 16th in the table after a run of 9 games with just one win, against Bristol City. We were still in the FA Cup though! That was our next game, the 5th round tie at Vicarage Road...but I wouldn't be there.

Leeds United 0 Middlesbrough 0
20,424 (Boro 2,782)

Not Great Scott!

I was stood on the south terracing in the Checkatrade.com Stadium in the little neighbourhood of Broadfield, home of Crawley Town. It was 2:50pm when I got my latest text from Kentley; he was supposed to be in Vicarage Road to provide me with regular updates on our FA Cup 5th round tie with the Hornets. It read: *"In a right mess here! To move 20 ft takes ages! Nightmare!"* He'd arrived at the usual parking spot, the Girls Grammar School in Watford, to find it already full and he was now stuck in traffic looking for an alternative. I wasn't surprised he was having trouble as he'd first texted me as late as 12:19 to say he was not even on the M6 at that point... while I was already in Crawley, 60 miles further south than he was heading! He always, always leaves it too late before setting off.

Kentley had missed out on getting a ticket for the Watford game – it was sold out in a couple of hours and many regulars had failed to secure tickets – so I sold him mine. I was guaranteed one with my away season ticket and I also subscribe to the auto cup scheme whereby I automatically get cup tickets. I was originally going to go to Watford but when

Kentley missed out it gave me an excuse to miss it and instead do the Crawley game which would then ensure that the little gathering I'd arranged at Southend the following week would be a celebration of the full 92 and not the far less significant 91. So, here I was, stood in the Broadfield Stadium or Checkatrade Stadium to give it its current sponsor backed title, while Kentley was *nearly* at Vicarage Road.

Steve Evans had been forced to make just one change to the starting eleven to face Premier League Watford; Liam Cooper had picked up an injury and so Sol Bamba returned in his place as centre back and skipper. An unspecified injury kept Muzzy Carayol out altogether and that left space for Jordan Botaka.

Silvestri
Wootton Bellusci Bamba Taylor
Bridcutt Diagouraga
Dallas Cook Doukara
Antenucci

Subs: Peacock-Farrell, Coyle, Adeyemi, Murphy, Erwin, Mowatt, Botaka.

Watford had a decent team out for this one, although the free scoring Odion Ighalo was left on the bench. Troy Deeney started though and he'd scored in his previous five outings against Leeds. Watford sat comfortably in 9th spot in the Premier League with 36 points, only 5 behind 5th placed Man Utd. It was never going to be an easy game for Leeds but I reckoned we could get a draw if we could just keep Deeney quiet and, more to the point, if our perpetually error prone defence could for once keep a clean sheet, something we'd managed only eight times this season in 34 attempts.

By half-time all was looking good. Kentley made it to the ground about ten minutes into the match and he reported: *"Leeds into the game now. No chances but well into it. 50-50 now. 0 – 0"* At Broadfield, it was also nil-nil although to be honest Plymouth were battering the home side. As I looked around the little ground I marvelled at the support Plymouth had brought; some 1,500 fans from the South Coast filled the far end of the ground, whereas Crawley only had 500 more than that in all of their sections. Up in Watford, Leeds had more fans than Crawley and Plymouth had mustered between them.

At 16:11 my phone vibrated in my pocket again and when I looked at the screen it was bad news. *"1-0 Watford. Scott Wooton* [sic] *own goal. Comedy goal"*.

No one was particularly laughing though, not even at Broadfield. Seconds after Kentley's latest text message, the home side fell behind to a fine header in the six-yard box at the far end of the ground from where I was now stuffing the phone back in my pocket and wondering what, *"comedy goal"* meant.

I've since had chance to view many replays of the 'comedy goal' but it still doesn't make me laugh. Cry, yes, but not laugh. The ball was pushed out to the Watford right wing to Ben Watson who had far too much space. It was a simple task for him to loft the ball over to the back post where initially Marco Silvestri started to come for the ball. Then he stopped, obviously thinking he couldn't reach it and he started to retreat. In the meantime, he'd clearly put a seed of doubt in the mind of Scott Wootton or at the very least his movement had taken Scott's eye off the ball for a split second. Wootton shaped to scoop the ball on past the back post with his right boot but got it all wrong and instead sliced it inside the post off his knee. If you were a Watford fan I'm sure it had some comedic value but for Leeds fans it was sure to bring the anti-Wootton sentiments back to the surface. As a former Man U academy star, Wootton had never been very popular with some and for much of this season many had complained that in Berardi's absence he was wrongly played at right back in preference to Byram, or Coyle. I'd certainly concluded in recent games that he was useless as an attacking full back and was most probably far more suited to a centre back berth where he'd played at Man U.

The next text was therefore not surprising: *"booing in away end sparks fighting amongst Leeds fans"*...

At Broadfield, the home side came more into the game as the minutes ticked away and in the 83rd minute Shamir Fenelon poked the ball home from close range to equalise. The game would end all square, a great result for mid-table Crawley against a Plymouth side looking likely to grab one of the automatic promotion places. That was 91 done for me, just one more to go.

As the final whistle blew at the Checkatrade, I remained on the South Stand terracing waiting for any more news from Vicarage Road, I was still hoping for a positive text, maybe even a phone call with good news. But all I got was more bad news in a series of downbeat texts:

"I'd love Wooton [sic] *to score and stick his fingers up to the away end*

"Ante is not good enough for our team. Pace seems the main problem.

"Zero creativity in the last third. Botaka on for me

"Atmosphere gone. Season is gone if we don't score...

"The booing of Scott Wooton [sic]*has soured it all.*

"Bellusci shoots from half way line, sparks louder Massimo time to go" chants"

I sent a text of my own, asking: *"Is Erwin on yet?"* Kentley responded: *"No. 'Evans give us a sub' is the song now."*

Finally, with the terracing now completely empty around me and a few stewards urging me to move on, the confirmation arrived with a simple, *"That's it. 1 – 0. Shame that."*

Back in the car, I was heading for Reigate, half an hour up the M23 from Crawley, where I'd arranged to meet my lad Adam for a pub meal before wending my way back to Shropshire. During the short trip to Reigate, I listened as Steve Evans gave his downbeat summary of the game on 5Live.

"I think the performance was good. It was the cruellest way ever to go out of the FA Cup - it was a terrible goal to concede. We dominated the quality of the play until half-time. If you came here in the first-half, you'd have thought Leeds United were the Premier League team.

"Scott Wootton's in tears, he's apologised to every member of staff and he'll not sleep for days."

Indeed, not great Scott, not great at all.

Watford 1 **Leeds United 0** (Wootton og (53))

18,336 (**Leeds 4,065**)

Rocket on Cook's menu!

O n the eve of the home game with Fulham, the Mail ran a story claiming that a Leeds fan had been paid £500 a month by the club to post tweets on Twitter in favour of Cellino as a propaganda exercise to counter the many anti Cellino posts appearing on social media.[1] Quite why the club would do that when they could just as easily have one of their own employees do it for free is beyond me and I had to conclude it was yet another ruse to discredit Cellino and when asked to prove the payments had been made no one seemed able to find any evidence. Scott Gutteridge would eventually post a statement to the effect that he made the whole thing up to rile the anti-Cellino protesters.

Tuesday, 23rd March was designated 'National Toast Day' (NTD)… who the hell comes up with these things and how do they get them to be officially recognised? The Tiptree World

---

[1]   http://www.dailymail.co.uk/sport/football/article-3459201/Leeds-fan-says-paid-praise-owner-Massimo-Cellino-online-club-hoped-supporters-onside.html?ITO=1490&ns_mchannel=rss&ns_campaign=1490

Bread Awards[1] celebrated its first NTD in 2014 and when asked the purpose, Caroline Kenyon, director of the awards said: *"...the political scene is filled with anxiety in the UK and US, while there is conflict and uncertainty in the Middle East."* A few pieces of toast ought to sort that then.

I was just hoping that we weren't 'toast' once Fulham had finished with us and while still on the cooking theme; Steve Evans was trying to boost Lewis Cook's confidence after his disappointing recent displays. He'd been moved to a 'number 10' role in the Forest and Watford games with varying degrees of success and the hope was that freeing him up a bit more might lead to a few goals.

Despite a campaign to raise more funds for protests by the 'Massimo Time To Go' group, there was no sign of any new campaign at Elland Road as I wandered into the Pavilion around 5:30pm. All the talk around our table was about Scott Gutteridge and whether he really had been paid £500 a month to post pro-Cellino propaganda; Leeds fans are nothing if not opportunist and there were plenty of lads ready to sing Cellino's praises if they could get on the payroll!

On the big screens we watched as the latest details of the trial of ex-Sunderland footballer Adam Johnson were broadcast; he was accused of sexual activity with a 15 year-old girl. Most of us couldn't understand what in the world would possess him to stray from his girlfriend and mother of his daughter, Stacey Flounders, who looked stunning in the press photos. Our attention to the big screen soon faded as they switched to discussion of the recently announced referendum on the UK's membership of the European Union...

Despite Evans' support of Scott Wootton after his gaffe at Watford, he was left out of the side to face Fulham. Lewie Coyle instead got his second start of the season and his full league debut. There were other changes too; Liam Bridcutt was missing as he took time out for 'personal reasons' (later

---

[1]   *http://www.express.co.uk/life-style/food/646821/National-Toast-Day-Breakfast-Jam-Tiptree-World-Bread-Awards-Trending-Twitter-bread*

said to be a funeral) while Peppe Bellusci was suspended for picking up his tenth yellow card of the season at Vicarage Road. Stuart Dallas also stepped down with Alex Mowatt taking his place. Sol Bamba and Tom Adeyemi started.

Silvestri
Coyle Bamba Cooper Taylor
Adeyemi Diagouraga
Doukara Cook Mowatt
Antenucci

Subs: Peacock-Farrell, Wootton, Berardi, Dallas, Murphy, Botaka, Erwin.

Muzzy Carayol was still missing with a groin strain while Chris Wood was also still out as he continued to struggle with a hamstring problem; hamstrung by a total lack of quality if you ask Terry Yorath!

Our usual little gang settled down in the Kop and we all tried to work around the fact that Ryan and Jack, in the row in front of us, were clearly the worse for wear with drink. The brothers swayed and gabbled away to us and none of us had the faintest idea what they were going on about! We've all been there of course.

It was a lively start to the game on a cold night in front of only 17,000 fans under an almost full moon; it looked huge as it hung over the massive East Stand roof over to our left. Fulham had the best of the opening minutes as Lewie Coyle made his first significant intervention of the night by blocking a goal bound effort from Luke Garbutt, one of several Fulham players with Elland Road experience. Garbutt, like team mate Tom Cairney, was also trained in the United academy and was now on loan to the Cottagers from Premier League Everton. As the Fulham pressure continued, Sol Bamba somehow managed to head a mishit volley from Ross McCormack onto his own crossbar and away to safety. Quite why 'McContract' was free at the back post we were at a loss to know; Kentley was screaming at our defence to mark him several seconds before he got the ball; 'McContract' that is, not Kentley.

The superstitious amongst us were then eyeing the clock as *"17:00"* ticked up onto the screen at the far end of the ground. Fulham were the most entertaining side to watch in the

Championship this season in terms of goals scored in their games. 103 goals in their 32 league games was the highest number in the Championship, so it was always unlikely this game would be goalless. By contrast we had only seen 63 goals in our 31 league games and our total of just 12 goals scored in home games this season was the second worse in the whole of English football. Only Dagenham and Redbridge, rock bottom of the football league, had scored fewer at home. So the last thing we needed was for Fulham to take the lead…

Luke Garbutt received the ball out wide on the Fulham left wing and, for once, the electric Coyle wasn't close enough. Garbutt had time to take a touch and then as Coyle sprang towards him he was able to curl a left-footed cross towards that no man's land that's also known as our six-yard box. Amazingly, this time Liam Cooper was up to the challenge and he rose above Moussa Dembele to head clear. Sadly, his header wasn't strong enough though and it bounced up perfectly in front of that other ex-Leeds academy man, Tom Crainey, he that was deemed too small by Leeds many moons ago. He looked anything but too small now and as the ball lifted in front of him he cushioned it on his chest and then hit a left-foot volley straight past a statue-like Silvestri. The ball wasn't travelling that fast although it was well-placed, just inside Silvestri's left hand post. The issue I had was that Silvestri was stood only two yards from that post and had he been on his toes he really ought to have stopped it. It was the 17th minute though and Monsignor Philip Moger clearly wasn't in the ground with his holy water so I guess we just assume Silvestri was turned to a column of Italian marble for an instant.

Elland Road was surprisingly accepting of this situation, it sort of shrugged its collective shoulders and adopted a *"qué será, será"* attitude; no one expects any better these days. On the pitch, Leeds continued to work hard against a crisp passing Fulham side and a few half chances were created and spurned as we showed yet again that, for whatever reason, we are incapable of shooting straight. Sol Bamba hammered a close range effort over the bar and then Tom Adeyemi did the same and we were just beginning to think it would turn into another one of those – 'should've been a draw' games. At the other end Lewie Coyle was already making a name for himself as he got better and better with each passing minute while Sol Bamba was also having a great game if you count doing sterling work to correct your own errors as being a good contribution. Then, in the 38th minute we had one of those moments that no one in the ground will ever forget; one of those moments that remind us why we go to games week in, week out. A Bradley Johnson v Arsenal moment, A Luke Murphy v Brighton moment, A Billy Sharp v Boro moment, even an Aidy White v Everton moment.

Alex Mowatt had the ball on the Leeds left wing, in front of the East Stand about ten yards into the Fulham half. He rolled the ball infield a few yards to Lewis Cook who took two touches and then had a quick look up at goal. He was fully 40 yards out if you included for the angle, as he was still only 5 yards from that left touchline. We watched almost in slow motion as he focussed back on the ball and pulled the trigger with his right foot. He gave it everything he had and the effort lifted both feet off the ground while the ball flew as if guided by some unseen technology right into the very top right hand corner of the net with another former Leeds man, Andy Lonergan, stretching every sinew to try to get a hand to it. He failed and the tell-tale ripple of the netting was met with one of those famous Elland Road roars. Steve Evans would later state it was the best goal he had ever seen and I have to say I have never seen one better, albeit maybe a few equally as good. It just showed that it's always worth having a pop, from whatever distance.

Coming so late in the half, it was still fresh in our memories as the half-time whistle blew and so another cheer and generous applause was ringing in the ears of the Leeds players as they trooped off for a half-time cuppa and Nigel went off on the now routine half-time coffee run.

The second-half was not a memorable affair and consisted mostly of Fulham continuing to shift the ball around sharply and accurately while Leeds huffed and puffed to win it back. Neither side created much, although towards the end, Leeds could and probably should have nicked all three points. Lee

Erwin and Stuart Dallas had replaced Antenucci and Mowatt in the 68th and 78th minute respectively and for those final few minutes Leeds came alive. Fulham suddenly had their hands full and the fans began to ramp up their support as we sensed a winner was possible. The chance we felt would come arrived at the feet of Stuart Dallas. Lewie Coyle, who we were now no longer studying closely as we just accepted he was doing his job well, swung over a long right wing cross that found Dallas unmarked on the penalty spot. With the whole eight yards of the goal yawning open in front of him Dallas hit the ball on the half volley with his right instep just outside the right hand post, to our left as we looked through the netting to see where it went. It was the chance we all knew we'd get and we fluffed our lines and the game ended 1 – 1 as 16% of all Championship games had, so far this season. Indeed, so closely fought are the majority of games in the division that a massive 27%, more than a quarter, end either 1 – 1 or 0 – 0. This is why teams can progress up the table so quickly if they can just string together three or four wins on the trot. Sadly, we seldom manage it. In the final few minutes, Leeds fans had one more thing to cheer on this cold night as Fulham's Fernando Amorebieta was sent off for a second yellow card as he blatantly handled the ball to prevent another Leeds attack; if we couldn't grab a winner this was the next best thing! Doukara and Amorebieta had been engaged in 'manbags' throughout the game and as the Fulham man walked off he appeared to pull the neck of his shirt down to show the referee one of his wounds. That particular incident would come back to bite us later in the season...

We'd end this round of games in Massimo Cellino's favourite spot, 17th in the table, with 38 points. The bottom three, Charlton, Bolton and Rotherham all lost this evening, to leave Leeds now 12 points clear of the best of them, Rotherham United. At the top it was Hull with 63 points, Burnley 62, Boro 61, Brighton 60, Derby 57 and Sheffield Wednesday on 54 in the top six. Our next challenge was an away trip to fourth placed Brighton and Hove Albion.

Leeds United 1 Fulham 1 (Cairney (17), **Cook (38)**)
17,103 (Fulham 364)

Seagulls, Shrimpers and Leeds all at sea!

Mrs W and I set off for the South on Sunday morning. It had been a traumatic week but we'd decided we were just about fit enough to make the trip. Mrs W was recovering from an emergency tooth extraction that had left her in hospital for two days this week while I was convinced I'd picked up some sort of bug while visiting that had left me not knowing which way to turn... literally! Our first stop was to see younger son, Adam, in Reigate, Surrey which we accomplished without drama seeing him for a meal on Sunday afternoon and then again for breakfast on the Monday morning. We then set off for Brighton.

We arrived at the seaside around midday, dropped the car at the hotel (The Brighton Hotel on the seafront) and went for a walk along the pier. It was cold; very cold, but there were patches of blue sky and if you *could* get out of the way of the wind it was quite pleasant. The skyline on the front had changed significantly since our visit 12 months ago with the addition of the 450 foot British Airways i360 tower that now, er, towered over everything else for miles around. The project is due for completion this summer when for £15 a time you can board the 360 degree viewing platform and then slowly rise up into the sky. It's described as the world's first vertical cable car and was conceived and designed by Marks Barfield Architects, the creators of the London Eye. It will be some feature when it's finished. We stopped for a coffee and cake at Alfresco which is near the new tower and looked out upon the mangled metal remains of the old West Pier. The new tower has been purposely placed at the site of the old pier as a sort of vertical alternative.

Our pre-match drinks venue was the Fiddler's Elbow in Boyces Street where I have now been for the last few years before games in Brighton. Si, Nigel and Kentley eventually turned up and we made our way from there to the station for the short trip to Falmer. We'd spotted Jo E and Simon leaving the pub as Mrs W and I arrived and Jo proudly showed us she was the custodian of the big purple Massimo Time To Go banner that was destined to go on display inside the ground. It was uncannily the same colour purple as Mrs W's new jacket she was wearing!

The usual chaotic scenes met us at Brighton station as we were forced to queue in a Disneyland zig-zag fashion while we waited for a train. It took ages and then when it did arrive there were hoots of derision as it was just a tiny three carriage effort that was nowhere near big enough. We assumed there would be others but we all pushed and shoved to make sure we got on just in case. The situation wasn't helped by the railway staff then releasing fans from the back of the line who all came steaming along the platform to queue jump! The police, trying their best to restore order, were clearly not best pleased. We lost Si sometime during the walk into the ground so Nigel, Kentley and I took up our places in row Q, to the right of the goal posts and about midway up the stand. There are no bad spots at the Amex of course which looked just as good as I remembered from previous years. I sampled the soft cushiony fabric of the well-padded seats for a few minutes before the game kicked off. Looking around, I spotted that Jo's 'Massimo Time To Go' banner wasn't the only focus of Leeds fans protests; this was yet another Sky TV live broadcast of course and many fans were carrying posters with anti-Sky legends.

"Money and Sky TV is killing the game" was one of many similar examples.

Steve Evans made two changes to the side that started against Fulham on Tuesday night as, finally, Mirco Antenucci was left out (he'd been looking really uninspiring for several weeks... since that latest baby of his was born actually) together with Tom Adeyemi. Back came Liam Bridcutt after he missed Fulham due to personal reasons and Scott Wootton for his first game since his own goal at Watford.

Silvestri
Wootton Bamba Cooper Taylor
Bridcutt Diagouraga
Coyle Mowatt
Cook
Doukara

Subs: Peacock-Farrell, Berardi, Adeyemi, Murphy, Antenucci, Carayol, Erwin.

Although the team hadn't exactly been firing on all cylinders lately, I accepted that Evans didn't have much wiggle room in his player selection. Chris Wood was clearly still not fit; Bellusci was still suspended; and now Stuart Dallas had a knock. I was pleased to see Antenucci rested and my only annoyance was that there had been no attempt to bring in young Eoghan Stokes who'd been scoring freely for the development squad; surely he was worth a try? At least this side looked strong defensively, in numbers if not quality with both Wootton and Coyle shoring up the right hand side...

The attendance was later reported as 25,150, including 1,522 Leeds fans in the South Stand. Mind you, after the game we'd be stood in the mammoth queue for the trains back to Brighton Station and talking with some of the Seagulls' fans they reminded us that Brighton, like many clubs these days, include season ticket holders regardless of whether they are actually in their seats. Hence these lads reckoned there were probably only around 20,000 in the ground. That at least explained why so many of the nice cushioned blue seats were visible.

For 17 minutes (you know what's coming don't you?) Leeds matched Brighton and it looked like it would be another of those typically tight fought Championship affairs with few clear cut chances. Brighton won a couple of corners as first Wootton and then Coyle cleared their lines and Liam Rosenior was booked for pulling back Coyle. Alex Mowatt had a shot blocked away for a Leeds corner too and it was all looking OK. And then the clock ticked over to 17 minutes...

That man Rosenior was waltzing his way down the Brighton left wing but he was being closely watched by both Coyle and Wootton who seemed to be working well together. But somehow, the Seagull then cut inside and darted between both Leeds players as he made a dash into the penalty area. There was an audible, *"Oh Shit"*, from 1,500 Yorkshire mouths as we realised the danger straight away. Coyle had stepped away to ensure he didn't bring Rosenior down so Scott Wootton was left to deal with the danger but he was already a yard behind his man. He leant on him with his shoulder and then there was a tangle of legs and the Brighton man went sprawling. There was no protest from Wootton but it was the softest of penalties and already our latest away day was turning sour.

Tomer Hemed took the kick and the p*ss as he dinked it straight down the middle while Silvestri dived away for an imaginary ball he saw heading inside the post. *"Boll***s!"*

The penalty sort of set the mood for the rest of the night. The way it panned out we never had any hope from that moment on. The game unfolded in front of our eyes like a nightmare, almost in slow motion and silence. It was 2 – 0 to the home side four minutes later and it was another defensive cock-up of gargantuan proportions. There was no danger at all as Liam Cooper looked for options with the ball at his feet midway inside the Leeds half. He chose to play a sideways ball to Sol Bamba. Sol controlled the ball and then had one of his now infamous 'moments' as he passed the ball forwards towards Liam Bridcutt while looking towards the touchline. The Bridcutt pass may well have been on a second earlier when he last looked in that direction... but now Brighton's Sam Baldock was in the way. Baldock duly collected the ball, played a neat one-two with Dale Stephens and then stabbed

- 303 -

the ball across the box towards the unmarked Hemed. Hemed would have scored anyway had the ball reached him but Cooper stuck out a leg and diverted it past Silvestri just for added embarrassment. I'd been reading on social media people actually saying how our defence had improved so much this season and they used as evidence the fact that we'd conceded only 35 league goals before this game, fewer than about a dozen other Championship sides. For me, I still maintained that, had we addressed the issue of this defence two years ago, we'd be in the bloody play-off positions, so many goals had we gifted away this season. A team can be successful scoring as few as we score but only if they don't give goals away at the other end. As I stood shivering, looking down on Silvestri doing that, *'Damn that was unlucky'*, gesture he does, smacking one hand against the other, I started to think this might be a very bad night indeed for Leeds United. Massimo Cellino was in the stands here somewhere and I just felt in my Guinness filled bladder that he might be about to explode.

The Leeds fans were already resigned to another defeat but were still in surprisingly good mood and, for the most part, kept up a good level of support for the team with the usual array of songs. Our support was tested a bit more though just six minutes later as we went three down. This cotton wool defence of ours had already shown it couldn't deal with wingers cutting inside and couldn't guarantee not to pass the ball straight to the opposition in a dangerous place, now we showed we couldn't work an offside trap either.

A long ball was lobbed over the Leeds back line for Anthony Knockaert to chase and momentarily a few Leeds hands were raised in appeal; it was another cameo of our poor judgement that we'd seen many times, this season and last. There was no flag and initially at least no danger as Sol Bamba was alert enough to get one of his ten foot telescopic legs to the ball to nick it off the toes of Knockaert. But sadly for us, Sol's clearance only found Hemed and the Brighton man was far too quick of thought and action for a static Liam Cooper. Hemed pushed the ball past his man and then clipped it neatly through Silvestri whose own reactions again looked very suspect. Three-nil and very quickly the mood in the Leeds end went from resigned acceptance to downright anger at how easy we were giving this game away. A few voices up behind us began a, *"Massimo time to go"*, chant and then, more angrily, sent a message direct to our Italian owner with a, *"sell the club and f*ck off home"* suggestion. That got quite a bit of momentum at first but then a huge bloke in front of us turned around and angrily raised two fingers at the main group singing the anti-Cellino songs. *"Why don't you f*ck off you w**kers?"* he shouted at them, over and over again, his voice booming out as loud if not louder than the protestors. Gradually, others took his lead and soon there was a full blown descant being sung from the Leeds supporters. While the protestors sang, *"Sell the club and f*ck of home"*, another group chanted, *"Support the team or f*ck off home"*, it wasn't exactly your usual Sunday morning church descant but it was a vocal masterpiece none the less! I turned to Kentley at one point and whispered… *"If this all kicks off, I'm with the big lad!"* The lad clearly had balls of steel (the bloke in front of us not Kentley!) and on balance I was with him. If ever our lads needed some support it was now or we may collapse even more.

Things did get a little worse before the break as we succumbed for a fourth time. The final failing of this defence of ours is an inability to deal with a ball into our six-yard box, and to be fair we've struggled with that skill for years. No one had commanded our box for as long as I could remember so it was probably fitting that the fourth goal was a powerful back post header from a Brighton left wing corner. Lewis Dunk showed far more determination to get to the ball than any Leeds defender while Silvestri basically performed the role of spectator; he may as well have been up in the stands with us.

As the half-time whistle blew, there were a few muffled *"boos"* but by this time many of the more vocal Leeds fans had adjourned to the concourse and most would stay down there for the rest of the game. I slumped down in my seat and the soft cushion was at least a minor comfort.

As so often happens when one side races into an unassailable half-time lead, the game petered out in the second-half. Brighton were content to knock the ball about or contain Leeds when we had it but were not going to bust a gut risking injury or undue effort when the job was already done. There was the temptation to think that we played well in the second-half as we did get more ball but I'm sure Brighton had several more gears had they been needed. Apart from our woeful defence, that other fact of life with this side of ours was clear throughout this game. We can't shoot. We amassed 17 (I know, I know) attempts on the target but only one of them hit it! That compares with the Seagulls' meagre 11 attempts of which they got six of theirs in the right area. We had more possession and won more corners too but critically, Brighton made no defensive errors; we made four.

After the game, Si, Kentley, Nigel and I wended our slow way to the station and then, with thousands of others we queued as we waited for a train back to Brighton. Surprisingly, many of the Brighton fans were complimentary about the way Leeds played. I know it's always easy when you've won to praise the opposition but remembering those stats, most Seagulls felt that other than those four defensive calamities, there was not actually much else between the two sides. It reminded me of our trip to Middlesbrough when we lost 3 – 0 with three howlers from our boys but in my assessment we outplayed a very good Boro side that day. Football is a game that demands you get all the bits right though, not just one or two.

Back in Brighton and two of the lads decided they wanted food so we stopped off at a pizza place before continuing on to our hotel for a nightcap or three.

It was 3am before we called it a day and there was still, amazingly, no news coming through that Cellino had sacked Steve Evans. The Italian had apparently left the ground at half-time, unable to take the embarrassment any longer, and his only stipulation to the management was that they were to give no post-match interviews to the media. Paul Raynor did a brief Sky interview to comply with the TV contract. He told them:

"The first-half performance was shambolic. Our defending was atrocious and the manager is going to dissect it with the players.

"We only had 15 minutes at half-time to try to put a shape together and to show a bit of pride and commitment and heart out there and I felt we did that in the second-half.

"But the first-half was absolutely shambolic and it simply was not good enough.

"We can't worry about the chairman. If I was him I would have gone as well to be fair, because he doesn't want to see his football club playing like that and I don't blame him for that."

In the bar at the hotel we were joined by a lad who had just accepted his girlfriend's proposal of marriage. She had organised the little break in Brighton, bought him an expensive watch and on the back had inscribed: *"Will you marry me?"* It was the 29th of February of course. The lad appeared a bit shell-shocked and explained that he'd had no inkling this was going to happen. In fact he told us he'd never heard of this concept of women proposing on 29th February. What we couldn't understand was why he preferred to be in the bar supping with us into the small hours and not upstairs "celebrating" with his very attractive fiancée who we'd spotted briefly when we first arrived back at the hotel. Kentley assured us that's where he'd have been!

The following morning, Mrs W and I had breakfast with Kentley and we were able to regale her with the story of the previous night; Mrs W had preferred to go to the nearby cinema where she watched the new movie, 'Room', starring Brie Larson and she was tucked up in bed (Mrs W not Brie) while we lads were drowning our sorrows at the bar. After breakfast we set off on the next leg of this mini tour of Britain's seaside towns as we all headed for Southend. It was the day I completed my '92'.

Apart from a nightmare journey trying to avoid the usual chaos of the M25, we had a fabulous time in the land of the Shrimpers. My good friend Andy, a Shrimper himself of more years than he cares to recall, had organised a table in the Blue Lounge at Roots Hall where a group of my fellow Leeds mates celebrated my achievement. Keith and Gill who live near Southend, together with Nigel, Kentley, Mrs W, myself and Andy the Shrimper, were all wined and dined and entertained by former Shrimpers striker, David Crown. I was presented with a signed match ball and Andy had organised a fantastic '92' themed cake. We all enjoyed a brilliant evening. Southend drew the game 1 – 1 with Crewe with both goals coming in a frantic final few minutes. Referee Dean Whitestone played a not insignificant part in the proceedings. He awarded a soft first-half penalty to Southend which was brilliantly saved by young Crewe keeper, Ben Garratt. Then, in the 86th minute he awarded a free kick to Crewe, some 35 yards out and proceeded to pace out about 15 yards before allowing the wall to form. Not surprisingly, with all that room to work with, Crewe's George Cooper curled the ball into the net over the distant wall! Then, maybe to make amends, Southend won a second penalty and this time despatched it without drama. It was a great night that I will long remember and a fitting way, in the company of several very good friends and fellow Leeds fans, to complete that particular journey. Si even put in an appearance without telling me he was going to be there! That was a shock just bumping into him there!

By the time I'd got back home on the Wednesday afternoon, Steve Evans was still, surprisingly, in a job. Moreover, Cellino had come out and stated that he would not be sacking Evans as that wasn't the main problem. He told Sky Sports News:

"That is not the problem. I wish it was just this problem.

"We have a problem because we are in an emergency moment. We have five players out and I didn't speak with him after the game because we are both very disappointed and very embarrassed about what happened, but it is not just because of the coach."[1] We are not used to such logical analysis from Massimo, we were all nervous!

Our next game was now almost a proverbial six-pointer against relegation threatened Bolton Wanderers, at Elland Road on Saturday. Defeat in that one and I was totally convinced Cellino would press the panic button. Steve Evans was now battling to achieve a new Mission: Impossible; avoid relegation.

Brighton 4 **Leeds United 0** (Hemed (18 pen, 28), Cooper (22 og), Dunk (38))

25,150 (**Leeds 1,522**)

---

[1]   http://www.skysports.com/football/news/11715/10187569/steve-evans-safe-as-leeds-boss-says-chairman-massimo-cellino

Coffin and Splutterin

In the aftermath of the first-half humiliation at the Amex, Leeds were easy prey on social media and in the press. Steve Evans was inevitably the main focus of the fans ire and with Cellino having demanded he focus on the pitch and stop talking to the press, he couldn't easily defend himself. A few weeks earlier, Evans had stated that contract talks in respect of the likes of Lewis Cook, Alex Mowatt and Charlie Taylor were *"ongoing"* and the club was determined to keep them. Unfortunately, these days, everything said at Leeds is scrutinized under a very powerful microscope and when Adam Pope and Phil Hay got on the case they were informed by the relevant agents that there had, in fact, been no talks whatsoever in recent weeks. In his brief Bolton pre-match press conference on Friday, Evans had to admit as much and replied meekly: *"Maybe that's what I would have liked to have been true."*

The 2014/2015 accounts were filed at Companies House this week and became available to download on Thursday. The main highlights had been published by the club the previous week but this was an opportunity for the finer detail to be put under the magnifying glass. As I well know from my own career in accountancy, you can't really establish much of what things are really like from the top line accounts; it's too easy to 'lose' detail hidden behind the big numbers. Financial accounts packs are like bikinis, they hide the bits you really want to see! The accounts looked to be in a vastly better shape than under GFH though and it didn't look to me as if the Cellino family was anything like the burden Bates and GFH had been. The bottom line was that Leeds lost £2 million in the year compared with £23 million the previous year, on a turnover marginally down to £24 million. We had to remember that there was a one-off profit on the sale of Ross McCormack in there though without which the loss could have been £10 million or more.

I pulled up in my now usual parking spot at the north end of Lowfields Road at around 12:30 and as I stepped out of the car two lads passing by stopped and called over. *"You're the bloke who's just completed the 92 aren't you?"* the one said, offering his hand in a firm Yorkshire handshake. It was @sirwev aka Richard who'd apparently been following my 92 progress on Twitter. It was the first of many congratulations I'd receive during the day.

Inside the Pavilion, most of the talk was about the latest round of protests from the #MassimoTimeToGo.com group which had raised yet more funds for yet more inventive ways to put their case. Today they were holding a mock funeral outside the ground. Four coffin bearers carried a white coffin emblazoned with a blue and yellow stripe and the legend: *"1919 – 2016"*. I didn't witness any of this of course but it was all recorded and various videos were posted online.

There was also a trailer-ad doing the rounds carrying one of Massimo's famous quotations: *"If I'm not welcome, I'm not welcome. I go away and you never see me again..."* Underneath in white capital letters the protesters had written: *"YOU'RE NOT WELCOME"*. Finally, as we gathered inside the stadium prior to kick-off, a small plane circled overhead pulling a streamer banner with, *"MASSIMO TIME TO GO"*, picked out in red letters against the brilliant blue sky. You had to give it to these folk; they were nothing if not inventive and were not shy of putting their hands in their pockets.

In the Pavilion, our mood was one of nervous expectation, a win against fellow strugglers Bolton Wanderers was vital and even Terry Yorath, the perpetual pessimist, told us he thought we'd win 2 – 0. That was only after he cut Andy Couzens short with: *"Andy, you can talk all you like, but when you're crap, you're crap and we're really crap!"*

On the big screen, we watched as Arsenal grabbed a 2 – 2 draw at Spurs as both sides continued to trail in the wake of Leicester City. The Foxes would go 5 points clear at the top of the Premier League later in the day with a 1 – 0 win at Watford, with just nine games to go. Once again all Leeds fans couldn't but help think back just two years to when Leicester were playing us in the Championship...

Steve Evans made three changes to the side that crumbled at the Amex. Back came Peppe Bellusci; available again following his two match suspension and it was no surprise to see him replacing the hapless Sol Bamba after his miserable night in West Sussex. Lewie Coyle moved to right back to oust Scott Wootton and leave room to bring in Muzzy Carayol and Mirco Antenucci was back in place of Alex Mowatt. It was a balanced looking side.

Silvestri

Coyle Bellusci Cooper Taylor

Bridcutt Diagouraga

Carayol Cook Antenucci

Doukara

Subs: Peacock-Farrell, Berardi, Murphy, Dallas, Bamba, Adeyemi, Mowatt.

As the game kicked-off, many of us were still craning our necks looking to the sky as the little aeroplane continued to circle around the stadium. It was a shame really that it was in such circumstances we got this sideshow, it would be almost as good as cheerleaders to have it up there every week!

Both sides had early sights of goal with former Leeds keeper, Paul Rachubka and our own Marco Silvestri both needing to be on their toes to keep out stinging shots. It was Rachubka who was once taken off at half-time after three appalling mistakes that left us 3 – 0 down at home to Blackpool as I mentioned earlier. He would never play for Leeds again. Now here he was four years later looking rock solid!

Someone else would be taken off today, young Lewie Coyle. He went in for a 50-50 ball and came off worse and his game ended on a stretcher in the 21st minute. It's an ill wind that blows nobody any good though and Gaetano Berardi got the call for his first appearance since his injury back in December. Memories of Gaetano's debut came flooding back as within ten minutes he mistimed a tackle and found himself in the ref's book. He was sent off in his debut against Accrington Stanley in the League Cup at the start of last season.

Rachubka was starting to annoy us by this time as he next turned away a fierce drive from Muzzy Carayol. The bloke was looking almost unbeatable! Almost, but not quite!

In the 37th minute Leeds won three corners in quick succession in our first period of sustained pressure on the Rachubka goal. From the third of them we broke the deadlock. That's Leeds United scoring from a corner kick for the first time in living memory!

Carayol took the kick from the right wing, down in the south-west corner in front of the 725 Trotters fans and Liam Cooper flicked it on from around the penalty spot. It dropped behind Mirco Antenucci, about three yards out but he somehow twisted around to hook the ball home with his right foot over his left shoulder. Off he went to celebrate with his thumb in his mouth. He'd have the ball in the net again not long afterwards but this time the liner's flag thwarted him. At the other end Silvestri was looking more like Rachubka at his worst as he flapped at a cross ball from the Bolton left wing to be rescued only by an alert Liam Cooper sliding in to hook the ball away to safety, just inches from the goal-line. Just as so often this season, the weak spot in our armoury was quite clearly our powder puff defence. Would it hold out this time?

When the teams came out for the second-half we could see there was no Liam Cooper and instead big Sol Bamba was out there in his orange boots and captain's armband. I'm sure there were a few in the crowd who'd seen Sol's capers at the Amex and like me they were probably nervous but within a few minutes Sol had already used those telescopic legs to good effect and for once he looked solid. The game moved on to the hour mark and suddenly Carayol was bringing the ball out of defence. He slotted a perfect pass inside the Bolton full back and Antenucci was off after it as we have seen him do so often. We thought he'd shape to try to curl the ball into the far corner but this time he hit a lame left-foot cross low across the box looking for Doukara. It was intercepted by a back-peddling Rob Holding but he could do no more than side foot the ball out towards left edge of the box; Antenucci was already after it again and he simply wrapped his right foot round it and bent it into the far corner. As Steve Evans would say after the game, *"you're born with the ability to do that with a football"*.

Bolton tried to respond by sending on a couple of substitutes; my heart sank at the sight of number '17', Liam Trotter coming on along with Kaiyne Woolery but then Kentley and I both burst out laughing as Trotter took up position to the right of the strangely and simply named 'Derik'… it looked like we were in an episode of Only Fools and Horses! We weren't laughing a few minutes later though as that Leeds defence went AWOL again, this time allowing Woolery the freedom of Leeds to steam through and hammer the ball home from twelve yards. Cue the usual nerve jangling final fifteen minutes.

Stuart Dallas calmed proceedings down somewhat when he came on for Carayol and then Peppe Bellusci took command with a peerless display as he dragged us across the finishing line almost single-handed. He looked like a Colossus, striding out of defence with the ball time and time again. When the final whistle blew there was a tremendous roar from the Leeds faithful but there was a hefty degree of relief mixed in with the joy. This was a big three points and no mistake. It was only our 3rd win in 11 games and the previous one had also been against Bolton, in that FA Cup triumph at The Macron. We'd end the day in 16th position in the table with 41 points, nine clear of the best of the bottom three; Rotherham. Bolton were now bottom with 25 and between them was Charlton with 28. As a warning to us all though, Rotherham, now under Neil 'the miracle worker' Warnock of course, Charlton and fourth from bottom MK Dons all won. We weren't safe yet.

Leeds United 2 Bolton Wanderers 1 (**Antenucci (39, 62)**, Woolery (74))
21,070 (Bolton 725)

Schoolboy error!

Leeds hadn't won in Cardiff since 1984 and never at the Cardiff City Stadium. It was also '84 that last saw us complete the double over our Welsh adversaries. I got married in 1984; I know how long it's been...

I was driving this time and I picked up Kentley around 1pm. It was a damp day but the temperature was rising after the recent cold snap; it was a respectable nine degrees. We had a trouble free run down the M6, M5 and M4 and our only surprise was having to shell out £6.60 to cross the inventively named Second Severn Crossing into the principality. To our right we could see the original Severn Bridge and it looked just the same as the model I'd built as part of a school project back in the 1960's. I was a scholar of suspension bridges all over the world in those days and they still hold a fascination for me.

We were the first car to arrive at the away parking area at the stadium and we swallowed hard as we parted with another £8 for that privilege. It was now raining with that Peter Kay stuff that *"soaks yer through"* so we didn't hang about as we walked back into the city centre, just stopping briefly to admire the magnificent looking Millennium Stadium as we crossed the River Taff. We were heading for The Prince of Wales, a Wetherspoon pub on St. Mary Street, not far from the station. It's a former theatre and cinema and inside retains many of the features and layout from its former life. We sat upstairs overlooking the huge bar and marvelled at the sheer size and grandeur of the place. We ordered food and some beers and then eventually Nigel and Si joined us and we whiled away the time waiting for and then discussing the team selection and our chances of ending that Welsh hoodoo.

We'd become used to Steve Evans switching the team around and when the details came through on Twitter just after 6:45pm there were four changes from the side that started against Bolton.

Silvestri
Berardi Bellusci Bamba Taylor
Bridcutt
Murphy Cook Mowatt
Antenucci Doukara

Subs: Peacock-Farrell, Wootton, Carayol, Botaka, Erwin, Dallas, Diagouraga.

I wasn't sure about it at all. Coyle and Cooper were both said to be carrying knocks but for me, this side had too much Murphy in it and I felt we'd need the reassurance of having both 'Dave' and Bridcutt helping out the defence as I felt we'd have plenty of work in an arena where the home side had lost just one game in 14. A win would more than likely see the Bluebirds fly into a play-off spot. There were a few likely spoilsports in the Cardiff squad including the ageless Peter Whittingham and Craig Noone who'd both hurt us in previous encounters. They didn't have anyone wearing '17' though!

We'd decided that due to the rain and the fact it was a twenty five minute hike back to the ground, we'd grab a taxi from the station just around the corner but Nigel for some reason decided he was getting a train. Thinking he knew what he was doing, Si, Kentley and I popped into the station to see how much the train would cost and when Kentley tapped in 3x 'single fare to Ninian Park' it came up trumps at only £5.70! *"That's a result"*, we all thought. Kentley had obviously raided his piggy bank again before this trip and he began piling a handful of shrapnel into the machine. Sadly, it took so long due to all the coins being such small value that each time we got near to £5.70 the bloody machine timed out. Eventually, I stuck my debit card in the slot and within

seconds we had three single tickets to Ninian Park Halt. It was then that we turned our attention to the departures board...
"Now then, when is that next train to Ninian Park Halt?"
19:35 was the answer. The game kicked off at 19:45... *"Sh*t"* we all said in unison. We'd committed a schoolboy error here; so wrapped up in the process of getting a ticket, no one had thought to check if there was actually a suitable train! A cheap £5.70 was now going to have to become a more expensive taxi fare plus a set of three useless rail tickets!

In the queue for a taxi we were joined by another Leeds fan who offered to share the ride and the cost. We had no idea what Nigel was doing but he'd disappeared. We'd later learn that his knowledge was way better than ours and he'd managed to get a train out to Grangetown, another little station only a bit further away from the stadium than Ninian Park Halt. Research, research, research! No matter, a taxi duly arrived and it cost us only £5.60, cheaper than the bloody train would have been! The lad travelling in the taxi with us then pulled off that great taxi trick... *"I've only got a twenty quid note lads..."* he told us and of course Si responded in time honoured fashion... *"No worries mate, have it on me!"* We'd all learned a lot this evening.

Leeds hadn't sold all their ticket allocation for this one and when we climbed up to the seats in the corner between the Grange Stand to our left and the Ninian Stand to our right, there was plenty of room to spread out. In fact the stewards told us we could stand anywhere we wanted, except ironically, in our actual seats which were on the very back row. We had a laugh about that with a steward who explained it was, *"more than my job's worth"*, to let us sit in the back row!

We took up station just in front of Big Clive of the Surrey Whites who was brim full of confidence. He explained how he'd just had news of a new baby grandson; he'd had an offer accepted on a new flat in Leeds; and he'd stuck a tenner on Leeds to win. What could possibly go wrong I wondered!

Leeds had the odd sight of goal during the first-half hour but it was mainly the home side that controlled the game and Marco Silvestri was called into action three or four times to deny them. One was a superb full stretch dive to prevent a

Whittingham free kick breaking the deadlock. The Leeds fans had plenty of sharp intakes of breath as chances came and went for the Bluebirds and in between times we amused ourselves with a number of witty little ditties such as, *"You're just a bus stop in Newport"*, which tickled me. In the 15th minute, the stadium applauded as a picture of fifteen year old Mark Butterfield was beamed onto the big screen. Mark was the son of Leeds United steward Ian Butterfield and he should have been at this game with his Dad but had succumbed to cancer a few days earlier. The Cardiff supporters joined with us as we remembered one of our own in another moving tribute.

Despite the pressure Cardiff were applying, Leeds did look dangerous on the break and in the 37th minute something unusual for this season occurred: we took the lead!

It started with a left wing Cardiff corner that was initially headed away by Sol Bamba. The ball was eventually won by a combination of Bellusci and Mowatt, deep in Leeds territory and then Mowatt slotted the ball through for Antenucci. He was one on one with Scott Malone as he neared the Cardiff area but he then spotted Sully Doukara steaming in to his right, unmarked. Sully took one touch and then stabbed the ball towards goal. He didn't hit it that well but Fabio Da Silva, sliding in to try to block the shot, could only deflect it away from keeper David Marshall and into the opposite corner of the net. That was a great moment and we all went berserk as Sully went across to do his punch ball thing with the corner flag before Antenucci launched himself into his arms.

The Cardiff players seemed to metaphorically shake themselves down very quickly and in the remaining few minutes of the half won three corners in quick succession. There was much gnashing of teeth among Leeds fans as our defence scrambled and fumbled the ball away each time without ever seeming confident about it.

There were no changes at half-time and Leeds were on the attack from the kick off. We should have scored as a ball rebounded to Antenucci with the keeper stranded to the left of goal but Ant's shot was weak and a defender scrambled it away. Moments later, both Bridcutt and Antenucci had good chances that we spurned. As if reprieved, Cardiff then got into their stride and began to dominate long spells of the game. Both sides were resorting to some agricultural tackling by this time and Bridcutt was booked for a cynical foul. Cardiff's Fabio Da Silva followed shortly after and then Mowatt for another clumsy tackle. Most chances were going the way of Cardiff and each one they missed was followed by 1,500 Leeds fans blowing out their cheeks and shaking their heads in disbelief. Leeds were showing once again that we just do not know how to play in this situation; it's a time that needs someone to put their foot on the ball, have a look up, find a safe pass but too often our passing was hurried and most Leeds attacks fizzled out with someone giving the ball away. Cook was as guilty as anyone in this respect, often undoing great work having won the ball in the first place. We were all thinking there was no way we'd survive another half an hour when suddenly Da Silva slid in and took out Charlie Taylor, wide on the Leeds left wing. A murmur went round the Leeds fans: *"He's just been booked hasn't he?"* someone called out and then a chant of, *"Off! Off! Off!"* broke out all around me. The ref, Darren Deadman, was walking ever so slowly towards the retreating Fabio. Then he began fiddling in his pockets and first out came the yellow card… and then the red one. Fabio was off, City would see out the final half-hour with ten men.

The one man deficit made no difference whatsoever to the game and Cardiff just got more and more on top. Time and again we'd give the ball away and invite Cardiff to attack and suddenly Silvestri was on overtime. The ball was hammering in towards him from all angles. One shot cannoned back off a post and another struck the bar while several times Silvestri launched himself to push the ball away for corner after corner. It was the Alamo out there! For the fans it was a nightmare as we got closer and closer to a famous victory but we all still felt we'd crumble at some point. Cardiff replaced Whittingham with Noone and he was causing havoc. Berardi had got himself in the book by now as well and we all wondered if he'd be following Fabio off in the coming minutes.

We winced as Liam Bridcutt made another last ditch tackle that he badly mistimed and Steve Evans was obviously thinking the same as us. 'Dave' Diagouraga replaced him seconds later. Then Dallas replaced Mowatt while Cardiff sent on another former assassin of Leeds hopes, Sammy Ameobi. It was all Cardiff now and it was starting to become almost funny, hilarious even, as the ball continually cannoned back away from our goal off the woodwork or Silvestri's fists. We were starting to suffer a bit of delirium as we hollered and howled at our players to, *"Get yer foot on the bloody ball for f*ck's sake!"* We were so close, we all knew it would feel terrible if we collapsed at this late stage; it would feel like a defeat.

Lee Erwin was Evans' final throw of the dice and Sully Doukara took about an hour to make his way across the pitch to the rapturous applause of the Leeds fans. There were now only four minutes to go but we knew Darren Deadman would be adding on plenty more.

"SIX BLOODY MINUTES!" we all exclaim in anguish as the PA booms out around the stadium. We thought the job was done but now we had another six minutes to survive. Stuart Dallas goes in the book for another rash tackle as he takes up the theme and on we go.

We really were close now, four minutes of the six were up and we were starting to think the impossible was on; a double over Cardiff City... not done since Eddie Gray was our manager! Not done since before I got married! Leeds messed up again as a poor pass eluded Lewis Cook over on the far touchline in front of the dugouts; Steve Evans went ballistic. Cardiff take a quick throw and then launch the ball forward and a very tired Charlie Taylor mistimes his clearance straight to a Bluebird and Evans goes ballistic again. But Cardiff are tired too and Craig Noone fails to control the ball, allowing Dallas to nip in and collect it. Both sides are now like heavy weight boxers in the twelfth round of a bloody battle and every touch is an effort. Dallas hammers the ball down the Leeds left wing with everything he has and suddenly Antenucci is in the clear behind the home defence. Three Cardiff players are in his wake but they are all totally shot and they can't catch him. Mirco takes one, two, three touches and he's still running towards goal. He's in the area, a fourth touch, Lee Erwin is inside him unmarked. And then, calm as you like, Antenucci steers the ball past Marshall into the far corner of the net and we all knew we'd done it!

Everyone was jumping up and down and hugging anyone within hugging reach. The bloke stood next to me wouldn't let go as he grabbed me and squeezed the remaining breath from me. Even Nigel was whirling around like a one man helicopter as we broke into a rendition of, *"All Leeds aren't we"*; what a moment that was. It's why we do it and we all know that if we watch enough games sooner or later we'll get a moment like this, even watching Leeds!

At the final whistle, we were all exhausted, the tension had drained us and, down on the pitch, the players looked shattered too; shattered, but very, very happy. They all came wandering over to our corner and they began stripping off, shirts, socks, shorts; the lot. Predictably, Peppe Bellusci was first and he was soon parading around in his now familiar black speedos as fans down at the front waved their new trophies around their heads. Gaetano Berardi looked a bit embarrassed by it all but, with a little encouragement from Peppe; he too stripped off his shorts to reveal what looked for all the world like a pair of my old grandads white cotton Long-Johns! The players were all hugging each other and it was another very special moment with fans and team at one for a change. I'd not shed a tear at a game all season but this was as close as I'd been. I just kept thinking how this was the reason I do this every week, for moments like this.

After the game, Cardiff's manager, Russell Slade told the BBC: *"Sometimes the game is cruel. We were knocking on the door all evening and even dominated with 10 men."* I couldn't argue with that, Cardiff had 25 attempts at goal of which 10 hit the target but Silvestri kept them all out. But Leeds had two half chances and we snaffled them up and more importantly made no schoolboy errors at the back. When we do that, we can actually beat any side in this Championship. We just do it too rarely.

Cardiff City 0 **Leeds United 2 (Doukara (37), Antenucci (90+4))** 15, 273 (**Leeds 950**)

3 point Rovers Return

Things were very quiet at Elland Road, surprisingly quiet. It was almost as if we were in limbo as we continued to await that decision of the FL on whether or not Cellino would be banned again or whether his lawyers had successfully argued his case under the so called 'rule K' arbitration. Steve Evans appeared to be adhering to Cellino's instruction to keep a low profile too and his comments were kept specifically to matters on the pitch.

The Leeds fans were unsure whether the back to back wins over Bolton and Cardiff were flashes in the pan or the beginning of a major change in our fortunes. We were all aware that either of those games could, on other days, have gone against us, particularly the one at Cardiff where we undoubtedly rode our luck. So, a lunch-time game at Blackburn's Ewood Park was still being approached with care as it was a long time since we'd got a positive result in that neck of the woods and they were just running into some form having won four on the bounce in the Championship on their own turf. On the eve of the game, Scotland manager and former Leeds hero Gordon Strachan called up Liam's Bridcutt and Cooper for the forthcoming international against Denmark; Coops qualification criteria was apparently that he'd once stopped for a sandwich at a service area north of the border... or something like that!

I had a very pleasant and unhindered drive up the M6 and the M65 and headed straight for the usual pub of choice in Blackburn, the Golden Cup in Darwen, at the top of Bolton Road, where a very nice young lady took five quid off me for the privilege of using their car park.

It was about ten past eleven by the time I got in the pub and predictably it was already rammed full of thirsty Leeds fans eager to empty the pub's stocks of Thwaites Original and Wainwright Bitter. Armed with my pint of Original I sat down for a natter with Andrew L and his mate Lee who wanted to know all about my '92' travels. We passed half an hour chatting about that and the Leeds team when it was announced and then we set off on the long walk down to the ground at the bottom of the hill. On the way out I spotted @MOTForever aka Andrew B whose excellent 'Travels of a Leeds Fan' blog is still the best match summary you will find and then I had a quick word with Chris, Phil, Wayne and Simon. Phil still ribs me every time we meet about how I called him 'Sean' for twelve months or more having been convinced that was his name!

As I got near the Fernhurst, a pub just opposite the ground on Bolton Road, I spotted Nigel and Si and joined them for the final few yards to the away turnstiles. Kentley, the fourth member of our regular little group, had messaged to say he was late again and he'd see us in the ground. Some things never change!

Silvestri
Berardi Bellusci Bamba Taylor
Bridcutt
Diagouraga Cook Mowatt
Antenucci Doukara

Subs: Grimes, Wootton, Carayol, Botaka, Murphy, Dallas, Wood.

There was just the one change to the starting line-up from Cardiff; Luke Murphy must have considered himself very unlucky to make way for Toumani Diagouraga after most Leeds fans thought he did well in the Principality. Young keeper Eric Grimes got a seat on the bench with our other keeper, Bailey Peacock-Farrell (all three of him), poorly, while Lee Erwin slipped off the end of the bench altogether to accommodate a fit again Chris Wood.

As I took up my place high up behind the goal in the Bryan Douglas Darwen End the first thing that struck me was the state of the Ewood Park pitch; it was very bare in places and was sure to make accurate passing a difficult task. The second thing that struck me, as I tried to avoid choking on the fumes from a flare thrown from somewhere among the Leeds fans over to my right, was the amount of empty seats on the other three sides of the ground. A crowd of just 16, 071, barely half the capacity of this fine old stadium, would be reported later of which 3,344 were in the away end. I spotted Sofia Jamel, Marco Silvestri's partner, a couple of rows behind and I then couldn't stop myself having a quick look at the Italian fashion model every few minutes. I just hoped no one spotted me looking!

Rovers started well and gave the recently invigorated Leeds back four plenty to think about for the first fifteen minutes but they stood firm and resolute... not something I thought I'd ever be writing about this particular Leeds defence but fair do's, they were improving. Then, in the 15th minute, Sully Doukara was hauled down on the edge of the Rovers' box. Up stepped Alex Mowatt and his inch perfect free kick was matched only by an inch perfect outstretched glove from Rovers' keeper, Jason Steele, knocking the shot away for a corner. From that point on, Leeds took absolute control of this game and despite the dubious pitch, our passing and movement was as good as I've seen all season. Leeds peppered the home goal with shots, albeit without getting past Steele but it was a performance that had the Leeds fans roaring their side on and thoroughly enjoying the whole occasion. We even dared to think we might be on the verge of three wins in a row for the first time since February the previous year. In the 34th minute that thought got very much stronger in our minds.

Another Leeds attack ended with the ball flying away for a corner and Alex Mowatt trotted over to the right hand side at the far end of the ground from where we watched. Then, seconds later we were all dancing up and down as Mowatt's corner eluded a gaggle of players at the near post to find its way through to Sol Bamba, all legs and arms akimbo and he acrobatically volleyed the ball into the roof of the net with his big right boot. Leeds don't score from corners as a rule, but now we'd done it twice in three games following Antenucci's similarly acrobatic back post effort against Bolton. Slowly but surely this Leeds squad was breaking down the hoodoos; winning at Cardiff, scoring from corners and who knows, maybe winning three in a row and winning at Ewood Park! My mind floated back to that conversation with Big Clive at Cardiff when he was adamant we'd go on a run of ten wins on the trot to make the play-offs! Surely we couldn't do that could we?

It was like the old days now, Leeds fans belting out their anthems while choking on the smoke of yet more flares – one landed on the pitch and held up play for a while – and the team was ripping into Rovers like there was no tomorrow. Half-time came and things settled down bit. We got a message from Kentley to assure us he was in the ground but the stewards wouldn't let him cross into our section so he'd see us after the game.

The second-half saw more of the same from Leeds and Rovers were finding it hard to get a foothold and not just because of the state of the pitch. Blackburn made their first substitution in the 63rd minute but still it was all Leeds; we just needed a second goal to rid ourselves of that irksome little thought that Blackburn would sneak an equaliser and ruin the day. In the 69th minute we got it.

A Blackburn corner was cleared away as far as Alex Mowatt who strode out of defence purposely. He spotted Antenucci in his favourite spot out on the left wing, just inside his own half and Alex found him with a perfectly weighted through ball. Mirco set off as fast as his legs could motor with two Rovers players in his wake, he was running straight towards us in the Darwen End. We were all roaring him on and then as he got to the edge of the box he took a heavy touch and the ball seemed to get away from him; he was too wide now and the keeper had narrowed the angle. We groaned. Amazingly though, Mirco still got to the ball first and he just dinked it with his left foot over the onrushing keeper and the ball rippled the netting inside the right hand post, just down to our left as we looked at the action. Antenucci was as cool as you like and he merely stepped over the advertising hoarding and hugged a Leeds fan in the front row before the rest of the Leeds players piled in behind. Mirco got the inevitable yellow card for, 'leaving the field of play'.

Now we could relax. There was still twenty minutes plus added time to go of course but Rovers thus far had showed no signs of getting in the game and even this early there was a steady stream of Rovers' fans leaving the ground; they thought it was all over. Both sides made two substitutions and gradually the clock ticked over to the 89th minute; we knew there would be a boatload of added time due to the various stoppages but no one thought we were in any danger now. There was that Bristol comeback of course, that was circulating somewhere in the back of my mind but that would only come into play if Rovers got a goal back. Bugger me, in the 89th minute they did just that.

Blackburn took a short corner out on their right wing and Craig Conway swung a long cross to the back post. Two Leeds players launched themselves at the ball but both had misjudged its flight and it bounced off Rovers' Danny Graham at the back post towards the goal line. Simeon Jackson was in there swinging a leg at the ball as was Sol Bamba, while Sofia's old man was scrabbling about on the floor not quite knowing where the ball was. Suddenly it popped up and Jackson this time hooked his boot round it to thrash it high into the net. I have to say, this was far more like the usual fayre this Leeds defence had served up this season. *"Oh here we f*cking go"*, someone moaned just in front of me. On the pitch, the Blackburn players had rescued the ball from our net and were now haring back to take up their positions for the restart. Suddenly they had hope, their supporters, (those that hadn't already left at least), had suddenly found their voices. We'd been in this position so many times and more often than not we screwed it up.

Blackburn poured forward and now they looked the dominant side; Leeds resorted to lumping the ball up to Chris Wood, one of the two subs we'd brought on, Stuart Dallas being the other. To be fair, he did manage to control it a few times but the rest of the Leeds players were now so deep that eventually he was overrun and would lose it. The noise inside the stadium was already deafening but then the announcement went out over the PA that there would be six minutes of added time and a new, ear splitting, decibel level was reached. The Leeds fans were beside themselves and all I could hear around me was, *"Six f*cking minutes! Where the f*ck has he got that from? The cheating b*stard!"*

With more stoppages during the added time and a final, very slow substitution by Leeds who sent on Luke Murphy for Diagouraga, referee Keith Stroud added on almost nine minutes of additional time! It was without doubt the longest nine minutes of my life but somehow we survived and at the final whistle the players all trooped over towards us and for the second time in a few days, players and fans were able to jointly celebrate a fine away win. Steve Evans was in deep conversation with Peppe Bellusci initially but eventually, when the rest of the players had begun to move away towards the tunnel, Evans came right over to us and did his cheerleading thing again. *"Woooooooooooooaaaaaaaah"*, we'd holler, until Evans swept his right fist in an exaggerated upper cut to some imaginary chin. Three times he did it before applauding us and then he strolled off himself, job done.

Three games in a week, three wins and Leeds were in danger of getting a nose bleed as they sat 12th in the table after the rest of the day's games ended later that afternoon.

As I drove home, I listened as England dominated the first-half of their crucial Six Nations game with Wales at Twickenham; they would go on to win the game and the Six Nations title. In the Premier League news came through that Max Gradel had scored in Bournemouth's game with Swansea and I thought back to the first day of the season when I was driving home after the Burnley game at Elland Road. Max made his debut for the Cherries that day but then got a serious knee injury that kept him out for six months; it was good to hear he was back. Someone else who was back was Neil Warnock; he was performing miracles for Rotherham in his Red Adair role to try to keep them in the Championship. They'd won three on the trot before today but news came through that they were currently three – nil down at home to Derby with only a few minutes to go. By the time I'd put the car away in the garage and settled down in front of the TV they'd got it back to three-three! We'd end the day 11 points ahead of them and they still occupied the last of the three relegation spots. We were almost safe… but not quite. While no doubt big Clive was still thinking we might make those play-offs with ten on the spin, some of us were still cautiously looking over our shoulders monitoring the progress of teams like Rotherham, Charlton and Bolton. It was going to be a fascinating end to the season right from top to bottom. The pressure was on throughout the Championship and nowhere more so than at Forest where Dougie Freedman was sacked; they were just two points below Leeds. Meanwhile at Boro, there were rumours that manager Aitor Karanka had walked out, even though they sat second in the table.

… I opened up the lap top once the England v Wales game finished on TV and dialled into my Twitter account. @AllHailMassimo had tweeted: *"Sat behind @Sofiajamaled today – felt sorry for her as @DaveLUFCWatkins spent most of the 1st half with back to play perving on her"*…

Blackburn Rovers 1 **Leeds United 2 (Bamba (39), Antenucci (69),** Jackson (90+4))
16,071 **(Leeds 3,344)**

Predictable!

It was another week that reminded me I wasn't getting any younger. There were more deaths in the world of TV celebrities; Paul Daniels the magician died aged just 77. He and his wife and stage assistant, Debbie McGee, had entertained us on his TV show for 15 years from 1979 to 1994. I also learned this week of the death of Keith Emerson, arguably one of the all-time great keyboard players of the progressive rock era that I grew up with. News of Emerson's passing on 10th March had somehow eluded me until now so driving to the home game with Huddersfield was an opportunity for me to listen to ELP's 'Pictures at an Exhibition', one of my all-time favourite albums.

There was another 'Massimo Time To Go' protest going on outside Elland Road; another sophisticated affair involving an expensive and professional looking advertising trailer parked up outside the Old Peacock pub. There was also a slightly less sophisticated 'In Massimo We Trust' protest, involving an old bedsheet. These were the two polar opposite groups involved in the Cellino debate but as far as I could make out neither spoke for more than a couple of thousand Leeds fans. The vast majority wandered past the protests showing only mild interest. Of more concern to many, was news that Steve Parkin had finally dipped into his pocket to support the club in the form of a major sponsorship deal. His Clipper Logistics business would have its logos adorn the East Stand in the weeks to come although the hoardings hadn't been erected in time for the Huddersfield game. As I took my place on the Kop and looked up at the East Stand it was still boringly grey. It would have been a great day to launch the new livery as

Elland Road was as full as it had been all season; more full in fact, with a season best crowd of 29,311 that outstripped even the opening day figure against Burnley. It was an impressive sight with even the bright yellow 'Cheese Wedge' seats almost completely hidden under Leeds fans' bums. It crossed my mind how it would be like this and better, if we could just start to win on a regular basis. I was sure that many of the 'extra' fans in today were there because of the recent optimism, albeit probably unfounded, that we could still scrape a play-off spot.

There was a problem with all this optimism though; Peter Lorimer summed it up before the game when he spoke of how it would be so typically Leeds to come up short in front of the big crowd. He knew full well that we'd done it so many times before; Leeds have a habit of teasing us and then for it to all explode in our faces. Around our table in the Pavilion we'd also noted that the betting slips were actually giving slightly longer odds on a Leeds win than for Huddersfield; they're usually pretty good these bookies. Undeterred, I put a quid on two possible Leeds wins of 3 – 0 and 4 – 0, the latter a very interesting 66/1.

There was another talking point around the table too; Evans made two changes from the starting eleven that did so well up at Blackburn. He'd made at least one change after the Bolton and Cardiff encounters of course and we'd won the subsequent game but today he shocked us; he left out Lewis Cook.

It was announced this week that Cook was in the England U19 squad that was due to play three games during the coming international break; Cook was due to fly out to Spain after the game. That was the only reason I could think that Evans decided to rest him. Stuart Dallas came in to replace the youngster. The second change saw the return of Luke Murphy for Diagouraga who was rumoured to be carrying a slight injury but like Cook was still listed on the bench.

Silvestri
Berardi Bellusci Bamba Taylor
Bridcutt
Dallas Murphy Mowatt
Doukara Antenucci

Subs: Peacock-Farrell, Coyle, Cook, Wood, Cooper, Diagouraga, Carayol.

Huddersfield were in mixed form, having won three, lost three and drawn one of their previous seven games. Scanning their line up I was at least pleased to spot that their number '17', the nuisance that goes by the name of Harry Bunn, was only on the bench. We all settled down as best we could in what seemed an unusually cramped North Stand while Nigel got chatting with a large lady who announced she was *"from f*cking Castleford"* who'd squeezed into the seat next to him. 2,082 Terriers fans were strangely quiet as the game kicked-off, no doubt nervous after the two 3 – 0 wins we'd achieved in our most recent battles with them. It was either that or they could hear Miss Castleford shouting, *"F*ck off back to dog land you f*cking w*nkers"*! Then, after just ten minutes of play, the Terriers' fans exploded into life.

Town moved the ball down their right wing to Jamie Paterson who for some bizarre reason had Peppe Bellusci marking him... but not very well. Paterson shifted the ball inside to Joe Lolley who had Taylor licked and then as he tried the same shuffle past Sol Bamba he was caught by big Sol's trailing right leg. Even from a hundred yards away we could all see it was a clear penalty, well everyone apart from Miss Castleford who thought the referee was a, *"f*cking cheating bastard!"*.

Nahki Wells stepped up to take the kick and hit it well but Marco Silvestri surprised everyone by guessing correctly and getting a strong right hand to it. The ball ricocheted up in the air but Marco was up in an instant to clutch it safely to his chest. 27,000 Leeds fans roared their approval before the South Stand began a chant of, *"Nahki Wells is f*cking sh*t"*, that soon reverberated all around the ground.

For the next ten minutes it really looked like Leeds would make Huddersfield pay for their profligacy as we turned the screw and Sol Bamba should probably have done better than head the ball over from a Dallas left wing free kick. But in the 22nd minute we were ahead. Doukara battled his way into a crowd of Huddersfield players before being dispossessed through sheer weight of numbers but Liam Bridcutt nipped in from behind to win it back. He took a couple of touches as he moved out towards the Leeds right and then clipped a high ball in towards the back post. Stuart Dallas steamed in unmarked to power a header into the roof of the net over the helpless Town keeper. Dallas stepped over the advertising boards just down in front of us to be buried under a pile of fans before the rest of the players arrived to extract him. Dallas, predictably, was booked for 'excessive celebration' of the goal. Everything looked good at that moment and I was even wondering if I was on for a winning bet.

But there was something not quite right with the Leeds demeanour out on the pitch. I guess it was that the players Evans had sent out there were not comfortable in the formation he'd chosen, at least that was how it looked to me. Despite going a goal down, Town were now bossing the game and Silvestri did well to keep out a stinging 25 yarder from Phillip Billing before Dean Whitehead blasted a shot over the bar from the resulting corner. You could sense the crowd was getting nervous. Five minutes before the break, Huddersfield won a corner out on their left in front of the 'Cheese Wedge'. Despite eight Leeds players packing our six-yard area no one spotted Mark Hudson wandering in at the near post and Silvestri seemed totally uninterested in claiming the ball. Hudson merely had to stoop to nod home with Bamba the wrong side of him. It was yet more proof, as if proof were needed, that our defence ain't good enough. I was thinking of reporting them under the Trades Descriptions Act. When the half-time whistle blew it was the Terriers fans who were cheering wildly and the Leeds fans who were wondering if this was going to be another example of Leeds doing their 'so near but so far' routine. They'd teased us with those three wins and many of us had begun to believe we had a decent side after all; now we were not so sure. Miss Castleford gave a final, *"F*ck off you w*nkers"*, towards the Town fans as she disappeared off to the concourse.

As the teams reappeared I shuddered. Harry Bunn was coming on for Huddersfield, a big black '17' emblazoned on the back of his lime green shirt; I temporarily forgot about that though as both teams got stuck into an exciting opening to the new half. Billing had a decent effort saved by Silvestri while

Antenucci saw one of his trade mark curling shots fly just wide. On the hour there was a flurry of activity as Bellusci picked up his regulation booking and then Huddersfield brought on Matmour to replace Paterson. Lewis Cook then replaced Murphy and then minutes after that, Leeds self-destructed again.

Alex Mowatt sold Silvestri short with a hospital back pass that our keeper did well to hack into the Kop for a corner, risking life and limb as a Huddersfield striker bore down. Our defence isn't very good at defending corners though… This one floated over from the Town right wing, our left as we looked on from the Kop. Another in-swinger, this one was again not considered worth going for by Silvestri who allowed it to float to the back post. Charlie Taylor seemed to see it late and he could only scuff it out to the edge of the box where Harry Bunn was waiting all alone. I think our players are so afraid of the number '17' that they all pretend not to see any opposition player wearing it. The ball looped out ominously towards Bunn who was able to watch it all the way onto his right boot and he met it perfectly on the volley to smash it past Silvestri. Bunn and his mates celebrated wildly on the by-line just yards in front of the Kop, much to our annoyance. Miss Castleford was beside herself and the air was blue.

The next eight minutes were a blur; it was Brighton all over again, as each time Huddersfield attacked they seemed to score. Just four minutes later it was 1 – 3 and the game was over. Bellusci was once again well out of position as he hacked the ball up-field from a spot out on the Leeds right wing and just inside his own half. A Town centre back returned it on the full to perfectly dissect the now retreating Bellusci and his hapless partner, Sol Bamba; the *"f*cking sh*t"* Nahki Wells was after it in a flash. Bamba managed to get to Wells but was then cleverly side stepped by the dogged Terrier and then he simply rolled the ball across the six-yard box to substitute Karim Matmour who tapped it into the net. Cue more Huddersfield celebrations and more profanities from our new friend from Castleford. Another four minutes passed and it was 4 - 1 and Elland Road was emptying faster than a sprinters training camp during a fire drill. Joe Lolley was aimlessly carrying the ball out wide on the left when he spotted Nahki Wells in a couple of yards of space, right on the corner of our six-yard box. Lolley poked the ball through and Wells simply lashed it at goal; it was too powerful for Silvestri from point blank range and Marco could only divert it into the corner of his own net. If your six year-old was part of a defence that allowed the opposition that much space you'd ground him for a week and buy him a hockey stick.

As soon as the game ended, I was on my way. I didn't stop to see the players off the pitch or for the usual post-match chin-wag with Nigel. I jogged up Lowfields Road to the car, set off and was on the M621 before 5pm. I listened to Katherine Hannah and Noel Whelan as they chewed the fat on Radio Leeds and then to Evans as Popey interviewed him in the players' tunnel.

"If you defend individually, badly, you're going to concede goals in the Championship and it doesn't matter if it's Huddersfield or anyone" he told the listeners and he was obviously fed up of his team making defensive errors. Answering Pope's query as to why he changed a winning side Evans reiterated that he'd changed his side after Bolton and Cardiff too and no one queried those changes because we won the following games. He stressed again how he felt, *"had we defended individually, properly, it would have been as successful as the other games but we haven't defended like that in the previous games."* He admitted that, with the benefit of hindsight, he might have changed his subs but reiterated that Diagouraga had picked up a minor knock at Ewood Park and that Cook had told him he was, *"exhausted"* at the end of that game. *"We didn't have that defensive quality today and we didn't have that defensive desire for me individually and if it goes like that individually then it ends up the same collectively."* I switched off the radio and shook my head. At the end of the day this was typical Leeds United; it was all too predictable.

Leeds United 1 Huddersfield 4 (**Dallas (22)**, Hudson (41), Bunn (69), Matmour (73), Wells (77)) **29, 311** (Huddersfield 2,082)

They Shoot Horses Don't They?

I hate international breaks! I especially hate international breaks that mean there's no Championship or Premier League football on over Easter. This break was all in the name of giving the national squads time to prepare for the forthcoming Euros but I'd rather have been watching Leeds. Many people were convinced the season for us was over; that we'd be going neither up nor down, a bit like the Grand Old Duke of York. I was still fascinated though by the prospect of seeing whether Steve Evans was going to be allowed by Cellino to have a go at next season and that seemed to me to depend on the next few games. Was Huddersfield just a blip or was it a reminder that we'd just been lucky during that three game winning streak?

Sadly, this international break will forever be remembered not for football at all but for yet more terror attacks. On Tuesday 22nd March 2016, at around 8am local time, two suicide bombers blew themselves up near the British Airways check-in area at Brussels' Zaventem Airport, killing 14 and injuring hundreds more. A third bomb was later safely detonated by police. Just over an hour later, another bomb exploded in the middle car of a three carriage train at Maalbeek metro station, near the centre of Brussels. A further 18 people were killed there. The so-called Islamic State of Iraq and the Levant

(ISIL) were said to be behind the attacks. On Easter Sunday, 27th March, 70 people were killed in another suicide bombing, in Lahore in Pakistan and this time a Taliban group supporting ISIL claimed responsibility.

On planet Leeds this week, the only news being aired was in the Daily Mail. It published an article claiming Cellino had already made his decision to sack Steve Evans but that he may wait until the end of the season to announce it. Evans's current contract was due to run out at the end of June anyway. It was alleged that some of the players had confided in Cellino behind Evans' back that they'd lost confidence in the manager. It was said a *"foreign coach"* was lined up to replace Big Steve as soon as Cellino pulled the trigger.[1] The article sowed the seed once again that the players were going off telling tales to Cellino and undermining the coach. The very idea left a nasty taste in the mouth and if the players really were running the show then that was another reason why promotion for Leeds would always remain a Mission: Impossible.

More bad news, this time in the world of football, arrived on my birthday, 24th March; Johan Cruyff had died. The great Dutch footballer who gave his name to the little show-boat moves he often used to get around defenders, died from lung cancer, aged just 68.

Amidst all this death and destruction, I was only too pleased to find some football to get to and this week I added another new ground to my portfolio; The Weaver Stadium in Nantwich. It was not in the '92' or even the '116' that I'd now decided to complete (the 116 includes the National League, step 5 of the football pyramid) but they were playing host to Darlington 1883 who looked set to win promotion this season to Level 6. One of their most ardent supporters is my friend Brian who lives up in Darlington and so I'd decided to pop along and give him my assessment. They looked good! Nantwich had been involved in a tough FA Trophy semi-final with F.C.

---

[1]   *http://www.dailymail.co.uk/sport/football/article-3504750/Massimo-Cellino-set-sack-Steve-Evans-Leeds-United-head-coach-lines-foreign-alternative-replace-Scot.html*

Halifax Town at the weekend and that may well have knocked the stuffing out of them as they lost over two legs to the Yorkshire outfit and thus missed out on a Wembley final. Darlo looked every bit the part of promotion favourites though as they ran out comfortable 5 – 0 winners. The funniest moment came at half-time when three Darlo subs came out for a bit of a warm up. Both ends at the 'Weaver' are open with just a standing area in front of a six foot fence and it wasn't long before one of the Darlo subs lashed the ball over the fence behind me. After a cursory inspection that found the only gate to be locked, the three lads shrugged and had to resort to doing a few stretches as they'd clearly only brought out one football! It was a classic Peter Kay *"Av it!"* moment.

England got us all excited with a fine display against Germany in Berlin where they won 3 – 2, including a goal from Harry Kane who fittingly performed a perfect Cruyff turn before rifling home from six-yards. Then we despaired as they lost 2 – 1 at Wembley to a Dutch side that had missed out on going to the Euros. Every Dutch player wore Cruyff's number '14' on the front of his shirt in memory of the great man and a sell-out crowd applauded his memory in the 14th minute. Elsewhere, Scotland included Liams Bridcutt and Cooper in their squad for the friendly with Denmark (won 1 – 0). Bridcutt got half an hour at the end of the game while Cooper watched from the bench. He ought to have known he wouldn't get a game as he'd been allocated the number '17' shirt. Lewis Cook had a successful time with the England U19s, playing a part in all three of their games in Spain that saw them safely through to the U19 Championship Finals in France this July. Finally, news came through this week that Souleymane Doukara had been banned for eight games as a result of those scuffles he had with Fernando Amorebieta in the Fulham game that ended with the Fulham man sent off. It was alleged that Doukara bit the Venezuelan defender on the chest, finally explaining why he was so aggrieved at his sending off that day. I found it slightly ironic that a rough translation of Amorebieta could be, *"love bite"*.

As our thoughts began to turn back to Leeds United and the upcoming game at Rotherham, news came of yet another death of an iconic name from my youth. Comedian Ronnie Corbett had died aged 85. I was convinced that should we lose at the New York Stadium on Saturday, then, as far as Steve Evans was concerned, it may well be. *"Goodnight from him."*

It was already goodnight from Paul Hart, the head of the Leeds United academy who announced he was leaving to deal with 'personal matters' after less than a season in the role. Yet again this season we were in danger of racking up more departures than Heathrow Airport and inevitably some fans concluded it was another example of a decent bloke not being able to work with Cellino. Hart would eventually take up the assistant manager's role at Luton. I suppose getting yourself a new job is a 'personal matter'!

The pre-match meet-up was in the Bridge Inn next to the Chantry Bridge (also known as Rotherham Bridge) over the River Don. The Bridge itself dates back to the 15th Century and still to this day is one of the few remaining in England with a well preserved chapel built on it. I should probably have called in to ask the Good Lord for some help later in the afternoon but instead I pushed my way through the crowds packing the pub to meet up with Nigel, Si and Keith. As I slowly eased my way through, I spotted almost everyone and anyone I know from the usual travelling army of Leeds fans. As the only designated pub for away fans it was hardly surprising they were all in here and some decent beer was on tap too; the pub is part of the small empire belonging to the Old Mill Brewery from Snaith in the East Riding. I was just enjoying the last dregs of my third pint of the excellent Old Mill bitter when a blue flare was let off just yards away and with the pub's smoke alarm ringing in our ears we were evacuated to the pavement outside. Quite what is in the minds of lads that do this sort of thing (let flares off, not drink beer) God only knows. Not only was inhaling the acrid smoke most unpleasant but it was a stupid thoughtless act that could well mean we will be given no pub at all in future visits to the town as is already the case in many places around the country. And worse than that we met Andy and Jayne outside the pub and Jayne was going absolutely mental about it all…

...she'd washed her hair that morning and now it was full of smoke! The good news was that the police were soon marching a lad off to an awaiting van; I confess I'd never seen him at any games before.

Due to the unforeseen interruption, we still had more than half an hour to kill before the game so Si and I decided to make a short detour to have a look at Rotherham's old Millmoor ground that still stands within a flare's throw of the much newer New York Stadium. Millmoor was built on the site of an old flour mill in 1907, hence the club's nickname of 'The Millers'; it's still just about serviceable today albeit parts are overgrown. Its four massive floodlight pylons are still in place, one at each corner of the ground and they look not dissimilar to the ones we had at Elland Road in the 70s and 80s. Ours were the tallest in Europe at the time they were erected in 1973 but looking up at the Millmoor towers, they looked pretty similar.

Having soaked up the character of Millmoor, Si and I made our way to the altogether more modern Aesseal New York Stadium, built at a cost of £20 million and opened in 2012. It looks huge from the outside yet has a current capacity of only 12,000; 11,418, including 2,311 Leeds fans were making their way in today.

I took my place up behind the goal at the South Stand end with Nigel and Kentley (who'd arrived just minutes before kick-off as usual) and surveyed the names on the backs of the yellow shirts lined up around the centre circle. The tribute of one minute's applause was in honour of former Millers boss Jack Mansell who died the previous week. There were three changes from the side that started a fortnight ago against the Terriers. Chris Wood replaced the banned Doukara while Cook and Diagouraga were recalled at the expense of Murphy and Dallas. It was a strange line-up in that it looked very narrow and unlikely to give Chris Wood much to attack; Dallas and Carayol being the wide options on the bench.

Silvestri
Berardi Bellusci Bamba Taylor
Bridcutt
Diagouraga Cook Mowatt

Wood Antenucci

Subs: Peacock-Farrell, Coyle, Cooper, Adeyemi, Dallas, Carayol, Murphy.

The early morning rain had given way to sunshine as the game kicked off and another good sized Leeds crowd was in great voice. Over in the stand to our left, in amongst the Rotherham fans, we could see a few lads joining in with our songs and soon a steward was questioning them about their allegiance! Leeds were dominating possession but as we'd seen so often we were not creating that much. It was therefore no surprise when around the half hour mark we fell behind to a sucker punch. As with most goals we concede there was an element of chance about it. Charlie Taylor took a hefty blow from the ball as he dived to block a goal bound shot and he was clearly still struggling as he then raced to try to cut out a simple left wing cross. Lee Frecklington was able to throw himself feet first at the low ball and got there a split second before Taylor to shovel it past the wrong-footed Silvestri. That was the tale of the first-half and the second started in much the same vein with Leeds the better side, having more of the ball and a mounting number of attempts but Lee Camp in the home goal was having his usual efficient game and nothing was getting past him.

As the hour mark approached, Evans made his first changes – Dallas and Carayol for Mowatt and Cook; it was not a popular move with the Leeds fans. There were a few muted boos and a brief chant of, *"You don't know what you're doing"*, before we settled down again to see how things progressed. In fact, a few minutes later the fans anger was deflected away from Steve Evans and onto Rotherham's Matt Derbyshire. Back in November, Berardi received an elbow to the face from Rotherham striker Leon Best; now he'd suffered the same fate at the elbow of Derbyshire. Last time Berardi reacted so violently that he and Best both got red cards but this time he took out his frustration on the turf as he smashed his fist into the grass time after time before jumping up to speak with referee Kevin Friend. A red card for Derbyshire seemed to placate the Swiss defender and shortly after, Leon Best, who'd been in and around the incident, was substituted. Berardi was patched up with the traditional Kisnorbo and given a clean shirt before he resumed after a few minutes.

Leeds' fans were incensed by this treatment of Berardi and so too seemed the players and Leeds were now pounding the Millers' defence. Shots rained in from Wood, Dallas, Carayol and a couple from Antenucci but that man Lee Camp looked unbeatable. We held our breath as Bellusci made a rash tackle and then relaxed as his card was only yellow and off we went again. Berardi's last action was to try his luck with a wild shot that sailed wide before he was substituted by Luke Murphy and then, five minutes later, it was Murphy who finally got the break we needed.

A deep cross from the Leeds left by Charlie Taylor was headed clear but Murphy collected it about 25 yards out and after one touch tried his luck. His luck was in, as this time the ball struck Kirk Broadfoot, trying to block the shot and then sailed past the wrong-footed Lee Camp. It was no more than we deserved and I sensed we might now go on to win the game with ten minutes left to play. Against ten men we certainly wouldn't lose it I thought...

It was all Leeds now but as the 90th minute approached it looked as though we were destined not to breach Lee Camp's defences again and I'm sure most Leeds fans were ready to accept the point. But Leeds United has, in recent years, become a master of finding new and inventive ways of losing football matches. We seem cursed with the need to conjure up defeat from even the best of positions and we specialise in collapsing against ten men. The game was in the 89th minute when Mirco Antenucci broke away down the inside left channel and for one moment we thought maybe we'd actually snatch victory but then the curse struck. Mirco lost the ball but then had the presence of mind to foul his marker to make sure the Millers didn't break away. But Mirco has never struck me as having the most fertile brain in our camp and before the referee had blown his whistle he let his man go again and began to protest his innocence to try to avoid what he saw as an inevitable yellow card. What are we told in our first football training session? *"Play to the whistle"* is one of the first incontrovertible rules. Perhaps it's different in Italy.

Kevin Friend waved play on as the Rotherham player streaked towards goal; he played it forward to Danny Ward on the right edge of our penalty area at the far end of the pitch from where we were looking on in horror. Ward had both Sol Bamba and Charlie Taylor in close attendance but not close enough; not, *"I'm not letting you get that ball into our box"* close anyway. We were still fine though as Peppe Bellusci was in the middle marking Frecklington...

Peppe Bellusci is a conundrum; we've seen him do so many stupid things on a football field and yet we constantly forgive him and forget his shortcomings when he plays well for a few games. Fundamentally though, the man is unstable; an accident waiting to happen, a sort of footballing Cellino. He is not what you need in your Championship defence. As the ball sailed over towards him he was well placed to head the ball out for a corner, as we've seen defenders do for time immemorial when they have an opposition player at their backs. But not Peppe, oh no, Peppe is a showman; we may have just fought back from a goal down, be seconds away from a point away from home in a Yorkshire derby and still be needing a few valuable points to ensure Championship survival, but Peppe is Peppe. Facing his own goal he launched himself into a preposterous bicycle kick, attempting to hack the ball over his left shoulder; he missed it. Frecklington must have thought all his Christmases had come at once as the ball fell neatly at his feet but then as he nudged the ball wide of Silvestri he was just clipped by one of our keeper's gloves and of course he went down as if shot by a sniper's bullet. Toumani Diagouraga cleared the ball away but Kevin Friend had already pointed to the spot and was now holding up a red card to Silvestri. We might just as well have pointed a loaded gun at our collective feet and pulled the trigger. Bellusci was anything but contrite though, it looked as if the instruction from the bench was for Chris Wood to don the keeper's jersey - he was the biggest unit in the side so it made some sense – but Bellusci grabbed it and pulled it on despite Wood's protestations. Could Peppe rescue the situation? Was he a brilliant goalkeeper in another life? Was he buggery! With Bertie Big Bollox dancing on the line and then moving to his left, Greg Halford fired the ball into the opposite corner. There was no real sign of any humility on the part of Bellusci and indeed looking at him it would have been easy at that moment to think all the talk of players like Bellusci calling the shots in the dressing room, was actually not far from the truth. If he has the ear of Cellino, what chance does Evans have?

If you get beat by a better side you have to shrug your shoulders and accept it but with us, we seem to be the architects of our downfall far more often than sides outwit us through their own efforts. Of all the problems our club has, it's been this self-destruction on the pitch that has been so difficult to accept for several years now. Our players just don't seem to think; they constantly make the wrong calls and it really is depressing. If you had a horse that was as bad as this you'd shoot it; put it out of its misery, cut and run. Sadly, many fans are on the point of doing just that; cutting and running.

Rotherham, under Neil Warnock, had now won five of their last six games and were, incredibly, out of the bottom three. Those places were filled by Bolton, Charlton and MK Dons, with Leeds safe in 14th, ten points clear of the drop zone. At the top, Burnley and Boro led the way followed by Brighton, Hull, Wednesday and Derby, who looked the most likely quartet to contest the play-offs.

After the game, amidst rumours that an un-named Championship club was interested in Evans' signature, he himself was clearly not ready to throw the towel in although he was just as clearly dumbfounded and dejected at how his team had lost this game

"I have just lost in a derby at a club that is very close to my heart and it's hard to take.

"I have not had any phone calls, the people that look after me, what they have had is not for me to be talking about because I want to be Leeds United head coach. All I have to think about now is QPR on Tuesday."[1]

Rotherham United 2 **Leeds United 1** (Frecklington (27), **Murphy (79),** Halford (90, pen)) 11, 418, (**Leeds 2,311**)

---

[1] *http://www.bbc.co.uk/sport/football/35902169*

Bellusci Big Bollox

Peppe Bellusci had become the most unpopular man in Leeds following his unsuccessful Kung Fu clearance attempt at Rotherham on Saturday. No one wanted him in the side for the Tuesday night home game against QPR; no one that is, apart from me. I was in the Terry Yorath camp in general in that I too was convinced that none of our centre backs were any good. *"Get rid of the lot of them"* Tel told us again in the Pavilion. Tel also complained that he was convinced Leeds had no defensive coaches at all judging by the way our defence regularly collapses. But for now, I still felt Peppe was the best of a bad bunch. After all, it wasn't like Cooper or Bamba had been exactly faultless this season; they all had a mistake in them. Jed Stone did suggest to Yorath that Sully Doukara had probably played his last game for Leeds and Yorath perked up at that point as he quipped, *"Well that wouldn't be a bad thing would it?"* Andy Couzens and Pete Lorimer were also in the Pavilion and when it came to the match predictions both Couzens and Yorath went for a draw; Couzens 1-1 and Tel 2 – 2. Lorimer went for his usual 2 – 1 Leeds win. So, two Leeds legends went for a pair of draws…I just hoped our performance wasn't pants…

At that stage we had no idea if Evans would stick with Peppe or not. We knew Doukara was out and of course we knew

Silvestri was suspended for this game after his Rotherham red. Evans had confirmed before the game that Bailey Peacock-Farrell (now affectionately known as BPF) would get his competitive debut in goal; *"As I sit here tonight it's either Bailey or Me and I don't fill the goal as much as I used to so that may be an issue"* Evans told reporters, referring to the vast amount of weight he'd lost in recent weeks. When Kev and Zack spotted the team on Phil Hay's Twitter account, it was confirmed that BPF was in but so was Peppe.

Peacock-Farrell
Berardi Bellusci Cooper Taylor
Bridcutt
Dallas Cook Murphy Carayol
Wood

Subs: Grimes, Coyle, Bamba, Diagouraga, Mowatt, Adeyemi, Antenucci.

It would emerge later that Evans' dilemma over Bellusci was made easier when Sol Bamba reported to the ground not feeling on top form.

Before the game, there was another immaculately observed one minute's silence, in honour of Chris Loftus and Kevin Speight, the two Leeds United fans murdered in Istanbul on the eve of our UEFA Cup semi-final with Galatasaray exactly 16 years earlier...

The first-half passed with little in the way of goal-mouth action as two evenly matched teams slogged it out in midfield. QPR boss Jimmy Floyd Hasselbaink would mention his surprise after the game that Evans had chosen to go with a 5-man midfield in a home game and it was this that largely contributed to the stalemate. BPF looked calm enough in the Leeds goal and the Kop applauded and cheered every touch the lad got. At half-time we had the spectacle of Si doing the penalty competition in front of the Kop, thus realising a dream of his although it wasn't BPF he faced in the goal in front of the Kop, it was Lucas Kop Cat! We all fell about laughing our heads off as he completed his first ten revolutions around the ball and then, totally disoriented, blasted his shot over the bar! Fair play though, he managed all three attempts without throwing up and he got his goody bag reward containing a scarf, a mug and various other bits from the Leeds store.

The game turned on two specific moments late in the second-half, the first in the 70th minute. Luke Murphy collected the ball wide on the Leeds left, in front of the West Stand and then side-stepped a tackle and moved infield. Ahead of him, Chris Wood was pointing where he wanted the ball and Murphy clipped it perfectly into his path just a couple of yards in front of goal. Wood slid in ahead of a sluggish looking Alex Smithies in the Rangers' goal and the ball trickled over the line. That should have been the three points wrapped up for Leeds but as we'd seen so many times this season we don't manage the latter stages of a game very well and this game would underline the problem.

As we got to the last ten minutes, Evans made a couple of substitutions, presumably to break up the game and maybe get fresh legs on to protect the lead; Diagouraga and Coyle came on for Murphy and Dallas respectively. QPR had all three of their subs on by now including Sebastian Polter, who'd replaced Jamie Mackie in the first-half and Tjaronn Chery. There was another peculiar trait Leeds had shown this season; more often than not opposition substitutes had proved to be a problem for us. There was that disastrous moment down at QPR when Charlie Austin was brought on in the 58th minute and scored with his first touch, but there had been many more examples throughout the season. Thankfully, Charlie Austin has since moved on to Southampton.

We were into the last few minutes, just as we'd been on Saturday at Rotherham when we'd felt similarly confident that we were going to get a decent result, when Sebastian Polter broke away down the inside left channel with Peppe Bellusci and Berardi in pursuit. Watching from the Kop, I was a good 100 yards from the action, so it was hard to tell what happened next but it was clear to see that Polter had gone down and now I could see referee James Adcock pointing at the spot…

Having since watched replays of the incident we now know it was another rush of blood to the head by Billy Big Bollox; Peppe Bellusci. Polter was going nowhere, well to the left of goal and heading towards the by-line; Bellusci was behind him and Berardi was covering inside. There was absolutely no danger. But then Bellusci appeared to stumble and get his legs tangled up with Polter and the QPR man obviously went down. It was as clear a penalty as you will get. The other substitute, Tjaronn Chery, stepped up and lashed the ball high into the top corner of the net giving BPF no chance, although he guessed the right way. Kentley searched through Twitter on his iPhone and soon confirmed for us that it was indeed Bellusci's error; his second catastrophic error in four days. Even if we hadn't had Twitter though we'd have soon understood who the miscreant was as the South Stand began to boo Bellusci every time he touched the ball and a section of the Kop, up at the back somewhere, picked up on it and joined in.

Steve Evans immediately made his final change, bringing on Mowatt for Carayol, presumably in case we won a late free kick but the one good chance we did get was missed by Chris Wood when he failed to put away a rebound off Smithies. His blushes were spared by a liner's flag but subsequent replays showed he was very much onside.

When the penalty was awarded I'd sunk down into my seat and at the final whistle I was still there. For a moment I was drained and the quiet manner in which the majority of Leeds fans made for the exits told me most of them felt the same. There were a few boos when the final whistle went but it was all very half-hearted; we Leeds fans were by this time punch drunk, we'd had so much thrown at us this season that even an 87th minute penalty needlessly given away by a defender who'd done almost the same just a few days ago just didn't seem that bad in the context of the nightmare we were living as Leeds fans. We seemed to be stuck on a sort of mad carousel of despair which keeps turning just fast enough to prevent anyone getting off.

I said cheerio to Jo and Mike and then Nigel and Kentley and then walked as far as my car with Si who was stopping over in Leeds for the night. As I set off home I switched on BBC Radio Leeds. There was a lot of talk about Bellusci's error of course but surprisingly it was also said that apart from that mistake he'd had a good game! A few of the statistics sites I looked at when I got home confirmed they thought the same. It was somehow another typical Leeds United facet that our best player had cost us two points just as he cost us one on Saturday. Evans was going to have another difficult decision to make as he pondered the biggest question of the moment; what to do about a problem like Bellusci Big Bollox? I thought he was particularly honest after the game when he said:

"Giuseppe Bellusci is a very good player and has had a couple of games where he's done things you would expect better of him. I tell you what he is, he's a man. He walked into the dressing room and was very humble to everyone. He did the same at Rotherham. He's an honest man who doesn't take things lightly. We have a tight-knit dressing room where we support all our players. I would (pick him with confidence) on Saturday. There are other good centre-halves who have cost me more."[1]

The coming days would show that Leeds fans, on Twitter at least, didn't share Evans' view and for them nothing short of a public hanging would assuage their anger.

There were a few distractions doing the rounds this week that meant that it wasn't just Bellusci occupying the minds of Leeds fans though. Former MD David Haigh had finally been released from a Dubai jail and was expected to start publishing his story about what went on at Leeds under GFH; that was expected to be tasty. The FA announced it was charging Massimo Cellino's son Edoardo over comments he'd made on social media. Phil Hay tweeted: *"In one of the social media posts Edoardo Cellino called a Leeds supporter a "spastic". He has until April 11 to respond to the charge. #lufc"* And of course there was Doukara's ban for biting an opponent to chew over as well. As always at Leeds, there was plenty of food for thought and some interesting debates to be had over the team selection for the next game, against table topping Burnley at Turf Moor.

Leeds United 1 QPR 1 (**Wood (70)**, Chery (87, pen))
17,388 (QPR 342)

---

[1] *http://www.bbc.co.uk/sport/football/35914347*

Rotten Wood

It was an idyllic sight; Si, Nigel and I stood in the sunshine on the steps leading up to the pavilion looking out on the green sward of the Burnley Cricket Club pitch. We each had a pint in hand and we watched the groundsman lovingly roll the square in preparation for the first game of the season; a 40 over aside game with Enfield Cricket Club the following day. That's Enfield near Accrington, East Lancs by the way not Enfield, North London. Cricket has been played on this ground since 1843, 40 years before their footballing neighbours set up stall next door and parts of the pavilion looked like it could well date from around then! There was plenty of rotten wood and flaking paint.

As always, there were lots of familiar folk around, either up on the balcony, sat on the seats around us, or just milling about on the edge of the outfield in front of the pavilion. I'd managed to grab a few words with Simon and 'Muddy Andy'. Heidi Haigh was there taking photos of anything that moved and we chatted with Andy J for a while; he was trying to decide whether to invest in a season ticket again for next season. At one point a voice hailed me and I turned to see a bearded lad making his way over the seats towards me with his hand outstretched. Karl had spotted me and just wanted to say 'hello' as we'd not been introduced before. We shook hands and exchanged pleasantries before he returned to his mates and

I resumed a conversation with Nigel. As we chatted away I suddenly became aware of a cold damp feeling in my left shoe and then I remembered I had another pint underneath a nearby seat. Well, I did have, Si had bought me a pint which I'd put down there before saying hello to Karl but the plastic pint pot was now on its side and my Thwaites Original was making its way down the pavilion steps faster that Jimmy Anderson with a new ball! I must have kicked it over as I stretched to shake hands with Karl. Jimmy Anderson, 'The Burnley Express' played here as a junior.

Kentley joined us around noon, just as we were heading off towards Turf Moor; he'd texted me the previous night to say: *"Time you leaving tomorrow Dave? Thinking I'll jump in with you"* but then when I informed him, *"I was going to leave at 8am"*, he changed his mind and texted me back: *"Hahahahahahaha, I'll leave it then!"* Kentley doesn't know there are two eight o clocks every day! We were eager to see what improvements had been made to the David Fishwick Stand where we'd be spending the afternoon as we knew it had supposedly been given a bit of a facelift. It certainly needed it too, as the last time we were here it was a bit like stepping back in time, perhaps not quite as far back as that cricket pavilion but certainly into the 1950s. The initial impression was good; the turnstiles were now fully automatic, operated by reading a bar code on the tickets and then as we wandered into the concourse it had clearly had a lick of paint. But the layout was exactly the same as it was two seasons ago and to be honest the place just isn't big enough to house the numbers the stand can hold. We were only given one half of the Fishwick Stand this time but that also meant we only had the one toilet block. Predictably there would be enormous queues all day long and it took an age to get through the crowds crammed in the concourse. The place is unfit for purpose.

Evans apparently made a late change to his starting line up by not playing Peppe Bellusci after having a chat with him during the morning and deciding his mind wasn't right. Thousands of Leeds fans could have told you that Steve! Sol Bamba therefore returned to the fold as did Silvestri after his one

match ban and Toumani Diagouraga who replaced the injured
Liam Bridcutt.

Silvestri

Berardi Bamba Cooper Taylor

Diagouraga

Dallas Murphy Carayol

Cook

Wood

Subs: Peacock-Farrell, Coyle, Bellusci, Adeyemi, Antenucci,
Mowatt, Phillips.

I've shown the line-up as a 4 – 1 – 3 – 1 – 1 formation just as
Evans explained it on LUTV before the game. Many Leeds
fans expected us to be soundly beaten by Burnley who were
unbeaten in 17 league games going back to Boxing Day when
they got thumped 3 – 0 at Hull. I thought we had a chance;
we'd actually been playing quite well recently without getting
decent results due to those persistent individual errors. Burnley
had also only shared the points in their previous three games
including two draws at Turf Moor against Cardiff and Wolves.
Leeds had another big following of well over 2,000 fans, with
the most vocal section of the Burnley fans also now housed in
the Fishwick Stand on our left hand side. As Leeds kicked-off,
and sent a long ball forward we began a rousing rendition of
MOT; it was still going as Burnley keeper Tom Heaton
cleared the ball back up towards us. Sol Bamba challenged for
the ball in the air but it broke behind him and was collected by
Andre Gray who shielded it well from Liam Cooper before
passing it out to Scott Arfield on the Burnley left. Stuart
Dallas was watching with interest but showing no sign of
helping Berardi who was trying to marshal Arfield out wide on
his own. But Berardi wasn't close enough; the perennial
'Leeds defender not close enough' and Arfield suddenly
moved the ball onto his dangerous left foot and lashed it across
Silvestri into the far corner of the net. 2,000 voices stopped
singing MOT and most spluttered something akin to, *"Oh for
f*** sake."* It was the worst possible start and it would prove
to be one of three decisive moments in the game. Bamba ought
to have won the header; Dallas ought to have tracked the run

of Arfield; Berardi ought to have been tighter and Flappy McFlappyhands ought to have stopped the shot. Does no bugger do their job in this side of ours? Do we never learn? Well, no we don't because minutes later George Boyd got himself in exactly the same position as Arfield and once again his cross shot beat Silvestri. Thankfully, this time it scraped past the outside of the post.

Daft as it sounds, from that point on, Leeds were the better team; we had more of the ball, created numerous corners and more attempts at goal and when Lee Mason blew the half-time whistle, Leeds trooped off with heads high, a spring in their step and our applause ringing in their ears. Some fans were even muttering, *"Why the f*** can't we play like this every week?"* I made my way down the steps to the concourse to shed some more of that Thwaites' Original. Big mistake!

Once again it was absolutely rammed with folk queuing up to buy more beer while just as many were slowly trying to push their way through to the toilets. It was total chaos and was being made even worse by a huge crowd of young Leeds lads bouncing up and down in the middle chanting, *"Let's go fu***** mental!"* Every now and again one of them would launch a half full beaker of lager up into the air and it would soak anyone in the firing line. I could see Jo E trying desperately not to spill a full pint she was handing over her head to Martin while there were several lads pushing through the crowd with a pint in each hand sloshing it all over anyone they brushed past. I was nearly through, I could see the Gents and there was an oasis of space before I got to the bog's entrance where another queue began and then it happened, splat! The back of my head was dripping with beer and it was running down my neck inside the collar of my shirt. I was angry! Another chap behind me was drenched as well, incredulous that these lads could be as stupid as to, *"spend £4 on a pint of sh*te lager and then throw most of it away!"* I was half of a mind to wade into the crowd of lads causing the bother but a) I was still desperate to get to the bogs and b) I remembered a rule my old man once told me: *"Never reason with a drunk."* I joined the queue for the bogs shaking the lager out of my hair.

Leeds bossed the second-half even more than they bossed the first, but those two other decisive moments came and went. They were both Chris Wood headers at the back post, just yards in front of where we stood in the David Fishwick Stand. The first came from a pin-point left wing cross from Muzzy Carayol finding Wood with a yard of space from his marker, Ben Mee, at the back post. As Wood rose all of an inch off the ground, we all had our hands in the air shouting *"goal!"* Then we slowly brought our hands down to cover our faces as the ball went a foot wide. It was a shocking miss. The second was even worse. A first time left foot cross from Charlie Taylor picked out Wood at the back post. Once again he rose to meet the ball with no one within an arms' length of him but yet again he was both high and wide with the header and he immediately mimicked us with his head in his hands. It was the second example of rotten wood I'd seen today; you could probably paint that old pavilion and make it decent but this Wood seemed beyond repair; at that moment I decided he was no use to Leeds whatsoever and I didn't want to see him in a Leeds shirt again.

The game ended 1 – 0 to the Clarets while we could only whine about those two Wood chances... After the game Steve Evans told the BBC: *"With the two Chris Wood chances, they're bread and butter to him, he would normally put them in the net. His performance all-round, other than that, was very good. The whole team, we've bossed it with some real quality of passing and movement. The only disappointing thing, and the mystery to all of us, is that we've lost the game."* It was no fu**ing mystery Steve; Chris Wood is just f***ing crap.

Fortunately for Leeds, the bottom three, Bolton, Charlton and MK Dons all lost and Leeds finished the weekend 15th in the table, 11 points ahead of MK Dons and thus still relatively safe. Amazingly though, only two points now separated Leeds in 15th from a resurgent Rotherham in 21st. They were on an amazing unbeaten run under Red Adair; six wins from eight and against all the odds looked likely to escape the drop. Bolton's defeat at Derby meant they were already relegated.

Burnley 1 **Leeds United 0** (Arfield (1))

18,229 (**Leeds 2,188**)

Blues and Poos

K entley had just arrived. *"I'll have stop get fuel Dave"*, Kentley informs me as I slide into the passenger seat of the BMW. I think I've mentioned before how these Stokies miss out words the rest of us consider essential. He was already half an hour behind schedule when he picked me up at 15:45 and now we were going to, *"have fill up on way"*. I leaned across to have a look at the dashboard. The little figures shining back suggested we had only eight miles of fuel left! I reckoned it was about, well, roughly eight miles to the BP filling station near junction 15 of the M6; the nearest one by some distance. I was just about to exclaim that it was going to be, *"a bit tight"*, when the little digit changed again. '7' was now showing on the dashboard and we'd only gone about fifty metres down the road. Ten minutes later, as we waited in traffic to go across the roundabout and then up the hill to the filling station, the number '1' popped up! I swear we coasted 'sans engine' into the forecourt and up to the first diesel pump in the line. It looked as though this was going to be our lucky day!

We made good progress down the M6 and arrived in my usual parking spot behind McDonald's on the Bordesley Circus roundabout, a little after 5:30pm. We'd just set off walking, heading for the Cricketer's Arms in Little Green Lane, behind Morrisons opposite the ground. We'd probably gone about fifty yards when suddenly I hear Kentley scream, *"Oh Sh*t!"* I turn round and he's holding out one arm and looking up at the sky. On the sleeve of his favourite Liam Gallagher lookalike, very expensive blue jacket is the biggest dollop of bird poo I've ever seen! It was dripping off him, all gooey and green and Kentley was retching as he gingerly held it away from his face! The only thing I could think to say was: *"Bloody hell mate, that's a lucky omen!"* I was actually thinking it was tremendous luck that the bird had chosen to unload over him and not me.

We retraced our steps back to McDonald's and Kentley spent fifteen minutes cleaning up his jacket and then we were on our way again, this time careful not to walk under any lamp posts which we surmised were the toilets of choice for the local Albatross population.

Armed with a pint of Carling for me and a couple of cans of Coke for Kentley (The Cricketer's is a bit behind the times and doesn't have Coke on tap) we went outside to chat with Chris and Tom who'd driven up from London. They were doubled up with Kentley's bird poo tale but the insistence I had that it was a good luck omen persuaded them each to place a ten pound bet on a 4 – 0 Leeds score line with BetFred. Tom got odds of 225/1 while Chris, after searching around on his phone for a bit, came up with a 275/1 offer! We also chatted with a couple of lads from Milton Keynes – Dave and John – neither of whom was impressed by my bird poo joke; *What do you do if a bird sh*ts on your car? Don't ask her out again...*

As we queued to get in the ground, everyone was in good spirits; some of our lads had armfuls of Peperami snack bars that were being handed out for free; I took one and stuffed it in a pocket having never tried one before. Even the police were having a laugh with us as we teased one lady copper at the turnstiles. I'm not sure I've ever noticed before but are women officers allowed to wear so much make-up on duty? It was a bit embarrassing as shouts of, *"Go on Dave, you're in there mate"*, came from somewhere in the queue behind me. A cheerful programme seller spotted my Peperami sticking out and we had the inevitable double entendre comments. He also warned me that he reckoned the Peperami bar he'd been given was stale but I've since been told that's how they all taste!

Nothing stale about Steve Evans' team for the game though as he brought back Antenucci in place of Carayol. With Liam Bridcutt still out injured Evans went with a 4 - 1 - 3 - 2 sort of formation. Bellusci remained on the bench.

Silvestri
Berardi Bamba Cooper Taylor
Diagouraga
Cook Murphy Dallas
Antenucci Wood

Subs: Peacock-Farrell, Adeyemi, Coyle, Phillips, Mowatt, Bellusci, Carayol.

Leeds picked up where they left off up at Burnley and looked really sharp in front of another noisy Leeds contingent of almost 1,400 in the Gil Merrick Stand. The Birmingham support was meagre and we told them as much as we chanted, *"Your support is f***ing sh*t"*. The only vocal section appeared to be a couple of rows of lads high up to our right in the adjoining stand. The funniest chant of the night was probably, *"You've got six fingers, we've only got five"*, which we did holding up one hand with fingers outstretched. Quite why that came out here, I have no idea.

Leeds had scored just three goals in the first fifteen minutes of games this season so it was a bit of a shock when we made that four. Leeds knocked the ball back and forth out on the right wing at the far end of the ground from us and then Antenucci rolled it into the path of Stuart Dallas. He had a couple of Blues' defenders shadowing him but he did a little jink to the right and got himself half a yard of space before hitting a shot all along the turf into the opposite corner of the net. It was not dissimilar to Scott Arfield's first minute effort up at Burnley and once again I felt the keeper should have got to this one. There were just eleven minutes on the clock.

Leeds continued to dominate and Birmingham looked a very poor and disinterested side; surprising since they still had half a chance of grabbing a play-off place with eight points more than we currently had. As the Leeds players left the pitch at half-time it was to the sound of generally positive noises from our supporters and the rustle of Peperami wrappers.

We were joined by Jo E at half-time, she'd come down on *"the fun bus"* as she called it but most of her mates were among those I'd seen down in the concourse swilling ale when I nipped down there for a pee. She also had a surprise for me; another one of her special chocolate brownies! You should have seen Kentley and Nigel's faces! Talk about Pavlov's dogs. I let Kentley have one small piece to try but I scoffed the rest. It finally took away the taste of that stale Peperami I'd eaten!

Jo stopped with us for the second-half and Si had joined us by now as well. Within minutes of the restart we were all bouncing, as Stuart Dallas popped up to score a second. It was another simple goal but one executed to perfection. Silvestri launched a kick downfield and for once, Chris Wood won his aerial challenge, knocking the ball behind him off the top of his head. Dallas was right there, about twenty yards out and he took one touch before volleying precisely into the corner of the net with the Blues' keeper once again looking like he was pondering his summer holidays. 2 – 0 up but 40 minutes to go, still, the way we were playing I was wondering if Chris and Tom would be collecting big time come the end of the game. Then we got a timely reminder that Leeds don't do easy.

2 – 0 is a great score, as long as it stays 2 – 0. After all, if the opposition scores, you are still a goal to the good. The problem is, if the opposition does score, then you start worrying they'll get another and that next goal is then very expensive; it costs two points. We'd enjoyed our 2 – 0 lead for about three minutes when Birmingham won a free kick, just to the right of goal, a few yards outside our box. We watched nervously as David Cotterill fired in the free kick and then we were up celebrating as Marco Silvestri flew across his line to parry the ball away. Sadly, it bounced up perfectly in front of Clayton Donaldson and he hooked it into the net from about eight yards. Bollox! Now we had that nervous, 'we're going to f*ck this up' feeling and we'd have to suffer it for the best part of forty minutes.

It was totally nerve shredding. The big screen over to our left was ticking the minutes off in big yellow lights but each minute seemed to go on for ever. Out on the pitch it was crystal clear that the players were besieged with nerves too as they began that infuriating thing of giving the ball away far too quickly after having won it back. We seemed to just focus on getting the ball away from goal rather than holding it and running the clock down with a few passes. Birmingham were suddenly interested, sensing there was something to be gained and even their few fans were now making a lot of noise. Both sides began to make their substitutions; Birmingham first, then Evans responded by bringing on Mowatt for Antenucci, not a change I'd have made. Mowatt is no longer a crowd favourite, having had a mediocre season and there were a few boos. Suddenly Clayton Donaldson rifled the ball into the net but I'd spotted the liner's flag a split second before the Birmingham fans erupted in celebration. That was a moment of joyous relief as we waved at them mocking their short lived euphoria. A few lads were waving half-eaten Peperami bars at them.

Birmingham then made a second change, bringing on Diego Fabbrini who we all thought we remembered scoring against us in the past; he has one of those names that suggests he scores every week. We eventually remembered it was he who profited from Sol Bamba's slip up at the Riverside while he was on loan up there. We looked at the scoreboard again and it had only nudged on to 76 minutes. *"It's bloody stopped"*, Jo moaned. I stared at it for what I thought must have been a full minute or more and it didn't change. It was about this time someone mentioned the name of Kyle Lafferty, the player it had been rumoured Steve Evans was keen to sign; I hadn't even noticed him until then but now felt he was sure to score against us to punish us for not signing him. Right on cue Lafferty blasted a shot at goal and then had another go at the rebound but Silvestri clutched it like a long lost child and collapsed to the ground to waste more time.

That clock had finally ticked over to '80' but our attention was now totally focussed on the far end of the ground where all the action was taking place. Lafferty set up the man with the exciting sounding name but Fabbrini's shot flew miles over the bar. Evans made two more changes, presumably to waste more time; Carayol replaced Dallas and then, to the sound of a few more boos, Bellusci took to the field in place of Luke

Murphy. Bertie Big Bollox immediately took control of the Leeds midfield and his first action was a scything tackle that had us all gasping, *"Ooooh"* and scrunching up our faces. Jo did her clock impression again as she confirmed 90 minutes were now up, *"Tick-Tock, Tick-Tock"*, she mimicked suggesting this was the slowest clock in the world as we tick-tocked away the 4 minutes of added time. On the pitch it was now getting tetchy with numerous poor tackles and Lafferty and Sol Bamba picking up bookings. We were bloody close now though; we could almost see the finishing line. Alex Mowatt could clearly see his as he went sliding in on Ryan Shotton, out near the Blues' right wing. Up went a red card and Alex was off. That ought not to matter much for the one minute or so we reckoned was now left. The ball was then swung in towards Silvestri and we all started to cheer as we assumed it would be a simple catch for him... but the silly bugger opted to punch it away with both hands and the Leeds supporters all groaned again and a few, *"What the f*ck's he doing"*, were heard. Then the final whistle went.

For a match that, in the scheme of things mattered little, the final 40 minutes of this game were as intense as I can remember. I think it was because we'd played so well in that first-half that it would have been really cruel had we given up any points. We'd done that too often and we all needed to see us break the trend, prove to ourselves if you like, that we don't always bugger it up. The players all trooped towards us and there was genuine joy being shared by everyone left in the ground. They all looked like it was important to them too which was great to see. Steve Evans had almost left the pitch when the Leeds fans started the crescendo that usually ends with a swift uppercut from the enthusiastic Scotsman and he didn't disappoint as he stopped and performed the manoeuvre three times before disappearing out of sight. It had been a great day out and as we sped back up the M6, I thought again about that bird poo; it is only coincidence... isn't it?

It may have been a good day on the pitch for Leeds but off it things continued to look shambolic. This was the week that Lucy Ward took the club to court in her unfair dismissal and sexual discrimination case and the outcome became public the day after the Birmingham game. The likes of Adam Pearson and current Club Secretary Stuart Hayton gave evidence in defence of the club but the tribunal concluded that the club was entirely in the wrong and Ward won her case and substantial compensation. Worse though were the quotes that came out during the three day hearing, many attributed to Cellino. The tribunal panel said that they were convinced of the truth of evidence that Cellino had made sexist comments to another club employee saying women had no place in football and belonged *"in the bedroom or at the beauticians"*. The documenting of such comments would lead to Ward's legal team asking the FA to investigate Cellino's part in the sorry episode. Pearson's reputation took a bashing too as the panel described him as, *"evasive and inconsistent"*. No one at the club came out of this smelling very good. [1]

On Friday, the day before the Reading game, Cellino hit back with a statement appearing on the OS denying the sexist comments were ever made by him. The statement read:

"At an employment tribunal this week regarding a former Leeds United employee, the tribunal chairman wilfully chose to publish to the attending press hearsay evidence of an alleged conversation between Mr Cellino and a third party, in which sexist remarks were alleged to have been made by Mr Cellino. Mr Cellino was not in court, nor was he a party in the case. However, Mr Cellino categorically denies making the statement, which has since dominated the media coverage of the hearing, and would like to make it clear that such a statement does not represent his views of women in football whatsoever."

Meanwhile, the 'Massimo Time To Go' group were ploughing ahead with their next protest, a march from the City centre to the ground ahead of the Reading game on Saturday, 16th April. Birmingham City 1 **Leeds United 2 (Dallas (11, 50)**, Donaldson (53)) 16,081 **(Leeds 1,365)**

---

[1]   http://www.yorkshireeveningpost.co.uk/news/cellino-did-make-those-sexist-comments-says-judge-as-leeds-united-employee-wins-unfair-dismissal-case-against-the-club-1-7850172

Wood floors Royals

I walked down to the Pavilion with a lad who parked behind me on Lowfields Road and for the sake of conversation asked him if he was doing the Massimo Time To Go (MTTG) march. He told me in no uncertain terms he wasn't and he thought it was a complete waste of time. *"...and who the f*** do they think is waiting to take over from Cellino anyway?"* he asked rhetorically. *"No fu**** is going to shell out what he wants for it, not unless someone like Red Bull gets interested again. I wish they'd have bought us, get rid of all the greedy bas***** and hangers-on and put some serious money into the club. But then the protesters would be out again saying they'd have us playing in red and changing the badge and everything; would they fu** as like"*. He spoke very much like I thought; I too saw a huge organisation like Red Bull as our most likely salvation, an opportunity to buy out all of the other interests in the club and wipe the slate clean; an organisation that had to 'do the right thing' by the club for the good of its worldwide reputation. Get rid of all the sleaze, controversy, knee-jerk management and put in place a thought out plan and money, lots of money. The problem was though that Cellino seemed 'locked in' to Leeds now with no immediate prospect of extracting himself without suffering a huge capital loss. More of the same seemed to be in store for the foreseeable future and moving Leeds to the Premier League looked likely to continue to be Mission: Impossible.

In the Pavilion there was some optimism, at least about the prospect of beating Reading anyway. They had an almost identical record to Leeds and sat one place above us in the table as they continued to rebuild under the stewardship of Brian McDermott. They came into this game on the back of two defeats though, to Middlesbrough and Birmingham and, again like us, had a very young squad. Lorimer and Yorath were in the Pavilion as always and they were not quite as optimistic as they debated the lack of quality in our squad; a favourite discussion point for Yorath. He put it brilliantly when he said that Peter Shreeves, his assistant while he was in charge of the Welsh national side, reckoned every good side needed 7 'piano pushers' and 4 'piano players' to succeed. There was no doubt that our current side had plenty of hard working piano pushers but Yorath doubted we had many piano players; that is players of genuine skill and quality.

On the big TVs we watched as bottom club Bolton took on top club Middlesbrough (Boro would win 2 – 1 after going a goal behind) on two of the screens while the Scottish FA Cup semi-final between Hibernian and Dundee United (4 – 2 to Hibs on penalties after a goalless game) was played out on the other two. The Hibs game was on thanks to Tony's special request to the lady who manages the Pavilion. *"She's got lovely eyes hasn't she?"* Tony tried to persuade us as the lady in question wandered past us again. All I can say is that she must have her eyes in her arse because that's where Tony's gaze was fixed.

Silvestri
Berardi Bellusci Cooper Taylor
Diagouaga
Cook Murphy Dallas
Antenucci Wood

Subs: Peacock-Farrell, Coyle, Wootton, Sloth, Botaka, Phillips, Erwin.

Steve Evans was forced into making one change as Sol Bamba had succumbed to the virus that was sweeping through the camp. We'd be told later that several other players turned out despite feeling under the weather.

Elland Road looked surprisingly busy with over 20,000 inside including 480 hardy followers of the Royals. No one knew exactly how many had partaken of the protest march or how many of them had diverted to the pub instead of the ground when they got to Elland Road. Pete was with us in the Kop for this one and our little band even included Lynn who was very, very pregnant. She informed us she was now, *"full term"*, and on hearing that, Pete was rehearsing his, *"Get some hot water and some towels"*, and, *"Don't panic Mr Mainwaring"* speeches... There was no danger of the first-half excitement sending Lynn in to early childbirth though; it was more likely to induce a widespread coma. Antenucci had one of his trademark curling shots beat the keeper only to see his effort hacked off the goal-line while Chris Wood did what Chris Wood seems best at... lofting shots and crosses into the Kop. Reading, wearing a shocking violet strip that invoked memories of an old white Leeds kit your mum had washed with a new red towel, looked like the young and inexperienced side they are but somehow, just before half-time, Leeds contrived to give them the lead.

It was that same old formula that had undone us a thousand times before; a free kick from the Reading left met by Michael Hector, unmarked at the back post, six-yards out. The ball fell perfectly at his feet to enable him to half-volley it past Silvestri. Before he wheeled away towards the Reading fans he made some sort of a gesture to the Leeds contingent in the South Stand that got them agitated and singing, *"Who the fu***** hell are you"*, either to Hector or the Reading fans. There was a very resigned air inside Elland Road as the players trooped off at half-time.

The second-half started much better for Leeds and Evans had shuffled his midfield trio around so that Cook was now operating much more centrally. He'd hardly been in the game first-half but now he was much more visible. With three minutes of the second-half gone, Leeds were level. It was the sort of goal Leeds more usually concede rather than score as a routine cross by Berardi found Diagouraga ghosting in unseen at the back post to nod the ball down past Al-Habsi in the Reading goal.

With an hour or more gone, Kalvin Phillips replaced 'Dave' who went off to rapturous applause but not a few frowns as we once again wondered why one of our best players was being taken off. The revelation about the virus would later clear that one up. Phillips took up where 'Dave' left off and was soon powering through the visitor's defence. Then, in the 69th minute of the game, we got a glossy Wood finish.

It was another case of the Reading defence going missing, as this time Charlie Taylor whipped the ball across from the left. Wood came from nowhere to appear at the front post and nod the ball home. From where we stood, a hundred yards or so away, we first of all thought Wood had missed the chance as we saw it cannon off the post and then Al-Habsi seemed to scoop it away. But Wood was already celebrating in the south west corner and the liner was scooting down the touchline. It was that 2 – 1 score line again, the one we defended nervously down at St Andrews on Tuesday night when we thought the clock had stopped. The feeling was exactly the same this time around and the clock on the big screen in front of the South Stand was now the one taking an age to move from one minute to the next.

This time we would pay the price for playing a form of defending entirely unsuited to holding a one goal lead. You really do need to put your foot on the ball and hold it but, as Yorath rightly pointed out, our ranks are mainly filled with piano pushers not piano players. I sometimes wonder if we have a single brain between us. There was an element of farce about the Royals' equaliser it has to be said. Reading were attacking towards the Kop this half and found themselves hemmed in on their left wing, in front of the West Stand. Suddenly we can see the linesman on that side put his flag up, to signal a throw in to us but referee Simpson, Jeremy not Homer, gives a free kick to Reading for handball. The Leeds players were infuriated and were still complaining as Reading got on with the game. Ola John whipped the ball into our box and Simon Cox was this time the player enjoying yards of space in the Leeds penalty area. He had time to trap the ball before thundering a rising shot that smashed against the underside of the bar. Leeds had plenty of bodies in our box but not many brains, and the ball then fell to Stephen Quinn near the edge of the area, another Reading player left all on his lonesome. It was now getting comical out there as Quinn slipped as he hooked his right boot around the ball but completely mishit it, sending it off at a right angle towards our back post. Incredibly, a third Reading player lurking there, Deniss Rakels, must also have a bad case of halitosis as he too is unmarked. Unlike his mates though, Rakels' aim is deadly and he powers the ball past Silvestri. I've said it all season, this defence of ours is... ah, what's the point?

I think most Leeds fans would then have settled for the point. The game had all the typical Leeds' hallmarks of an impending disaster; a late own goal from Peppe Bellusci maybe or a shot sneaking in at Silvestri's near post to lose the game 2 - 3. I don't think any of us inside Elland Road this particular afternoon expected Reading to fall on their own sword; but they did.

Marco Silvestri looked like he'd settled for the draw as he dallied and dawdled before launching a clearance up-field. Perhaps he should take his time more often as, just like the kick that led to the second Dallas goal on Tuesday, this one also found the centre of the pitch and not one of the stands. What was about to follow could easily be one of those what happened next video clips that they used to show on 'A Question of Sport'. A Reading defender was under the high ball and it looked a simple clearance but somehow it skewed off his boot and flew behind him. There was still no real danger though as another couple of Reading players were marshalling Chris Wood... and in any case when have we ever seen Chris Wood run twenty five yards to beat the keeper in a one on one? But incredibly, one of the Reading players then stumbled over and fell to the ground as if tripped by some unseen force and Chris Wood is indeed left to run at goal with just Al-Habsi between him and glory! We are all agog as we can see the keeper coming out to narrow the angle and then, cool as you like, big Chris slides a left-foot shot past Al-Habsi and into the corner of the net! If you were writing the script of this season at Leeds, you would not put this sort of thing in it! No one would believe it!

The celebrations were fantastic all around the ground and there was not a little head shaking, in utter disbelief. There was still time for Chris Wood to remind us that we were indeed not dreaming as Lewis Cook put him in the clear yet again but this time he reverted to type and blasted his shot way off target. It would have been an amazing hat-trick had he scored and we'd probably have all dashed home to stick a tenner on the lottery. We had pulled off a 3 – 2 home win and we were now up to 12th in the table. Of far more significance though was the fact that with 54 points now on the board and with MK Dons only drawing at Preston, Leeds were finally mathematically safe from relegation… unless the FL came up with a points deduction for any of Cellino's indiscretions. It looked odds on now that MK Dons and Charlton would join Bolton as the three relegated clubs as there was now a 9 point gap between any of those three and a gaggle of clubs on 47 points with only 4 games to play. Leeds were now just 3 points adrift of the team in 10th, Preston, where we go on the final day of the season. Who'd have thought that possible a few weeks ago!

On the journey home on the M62, just near the Huddersfield turn off, I was caught in the most biblical of storms. The sky went as black as night and then in seconds the road was two inches deep in hail. We crawled along for miles until we arrived at the edge of the storm and then we were blinded by the sunshine. Just like at Leeds, we had no idea what was coming next.

The day after the Reading victory, the FL announced that Lewis Cook had won their young player of the year award, an honour previously taken by some pretty special players. David Nugent, Gareth Bale, Fabian Delph, Wilfried Zaha and Dele Alli have all had their names on that trophy in the past. Earlier in the day, the Daily Telegraph published an interview with

Massimo Cellino[1], peppered with the sort of quotes only Massimo can come up with. One statement he made was hard to argue with:

"When the fans call me a bas****, it hurts me a lot, but I understand the fans who are pi**** off. Maybe if I was in their position I'd say the same thing. They're so used to eating sh** that they don't believe something good could happen. So many times they've had the illusion of the right thing coming along so why should they believe Massimo Cellino is the right one?"

That was pretty much how I am sure most Leeds fans felt at this time about him. Just like us not believing Chris Wood would tuck away that winner against Reading, we've seen so much bad from Cellino that it is impossible for us to believe he is the right one. Another quote from Cellino seemed to confirm that Steve Evans wouldn't be with us next season.

"I cannot work with English managers," Cellino said. *"I never want to learn. I give up. When am I going to find a manager in England who is actually a coach? They want to control everything. But it's wrong because when they go you have to start all over again."* It did start to look as if that crazy carousel would continue spinning next season, albeit there may well be new faces riding on it. For now though, I just wanted to enjoy the last few games and then we could think about the future; next up, another winnable game against Wolves at Elland Road on Tuesday night.

Leeds United 3 Reading 2 (Hector (39), **Diagouraga (48), Wood (69, 85)**, Rakels (81))
20,881 (Reading 480)

---

[1] *http://www.telegraph.co.uk/football/2016/04/17/massimo-cellino-one-day-leeds-will-be-the-best-side-in-europe/*

Sol n Dave

For the umpteenth time this season I had an awful journey up to Leeds. I was held up on the M6 with animals on the road (I never saw any), on the M60 with a broken down lorry (I didn't see it) and on the M62 with nothing other to blame than volume of traffic. I had a minor road rage moment too. When you're ambling along with all three lanes chock-a-block the last thing you need is some arsehole sitting on your back bumper; it was a big 4x4 with bull bars, all shiny chrome and filling my mirrors. When I got the chance, I pulled into the middle lane and waited for arsehole to draw level; instinctively I held up the middle finger of my right hand. Isn't it amazing how people can drive like absolute twats but then if you show the least bit of dissent to them they go nuts! Arsehole slams on his brakes as he spots the upraised digit and out of the corner of my eye I can see his front passenger window open; I continue to stare straight ahead, making out I haven't noticed him and then just let my eyes swivel without moving my head to check out what arsehole is doing. He's a little bald bloke, driving this fu***** great 4x4 and he's now leaning across mouthing obscenities at me through the open window and shaking a fist; he's going puce in the face. I continue to ignore him; they don't like that and they can't get their own back if you don't respond. I get the chance to speed up a bit in my lane and I pull ahead of him and all is well for a few miles and then his lane catches up and I can see him drawing level again. Once again I ignore him and keep looking straight ahead but I can just sense him leaning across again trying to get my attention. I can see the cars ahead starting to pull away as whatever was holding us all up must have disappeared. I wait until I can see plenty of clear road ahead and then I floor the throttle... but just before I did I couldn't resist one last gesture and I gave him a little wan*** sign. I swear I could see him bouncing up and down, his face like a beetroot as I stole a quick glance in my mirror and then disappeared up the road. Arsehole!

The whole journey, exactly 100 miles, took me over two and a half hours, so it was 6pm when I finally wandered into the Pavilion. Steve and the other lads from County Durham were already there and it wasn't long before the rest of our usual group joined us and we chewed the cud wondering what team Steve Evans would put out for the visit of Wolves.

Silvestri
Berardi Bamba Cooper Taylor
Diagouraga
Coyle Cook Murphy
Wood Erwin

Subs: Peacock-Farrell, Bellusci, Bridcutt, Phillips, Botaka, Dallas, Antenucci.

There were three changes from the start of the Reading game with Bamba, Coyle and Erwin coming in to replace Bellusci, Dallas and Antenucci. There were rumours that the virus that affected certain players on Saturday was still accumulating victims in the camp but we were not told who. My guess was Dallas was one of them, as I couldn't see Evans leaving him out unless he was poorly as his hard working style had been invaluable recently going forward and helping out at the back. Lewie Coyle was an able deputy though. Maybe Antenucci was another victim of the virus and that was why Lee Erwin was given a chance to show what he could do. I have not been a big fan of Erwin but neither had Antenucci done particularly well against Reading.

The first-half was not a festival of attacking football by any means; it was more about two evenly matched teams trying to work each other out. Chris Wood was lively and had three decent chances but as we've seen so often, the closest he got was a shot that grazed the outside of the post. At the other end there were a couple of lapses by the Leeds defence but the Wolves were even less accurate than we were. The second-half would be a different spectacle altogether; one of the best halves of football we've seen at Elland Road in a long time.

Leeds gradually built up a head of steam from the early stages of the second-half and we started to look a very decent side. We may not have many, but we do have one piano player; Lewis Cook and on this night he looked every bit the Young Player of the Year. So often he's not done himself justice, frequently doing three parts of the job but then messing up with his final pass but there was none of that wastefulness tonight. The only shame was that for this, his best game for a while, he was being watched from the stands by Bournemouth's manager Eddie Howe, a well-known fan of young Lewis who had aspirations to lure him to the South Coast.

Just before the hour mark, Leeds were camped in the final third in front of the Kop as we probed again and again looking for a way through a well organised Wolverhampton back line. Diagouraga was now up supporting the attack and the Kop was roaring the team on with a series of *"oohhs"* and *"aahhs"* as each shot was fired in and then cleared away. Diagouraga tried his luck with a swinging right boot but that was blocked at close range and the ball went spinning away to Stuart Dallas who'd replaced Lewie Coyle a few minutes earlier. Dallas chased the ball out to the north-west corner and hooked it back into the middle where Wolves' defender Iorfa headed it up into the Elland Road night time sky. Chris Wood challenged for the ball in the air on the edge of the area and it broke away for Dallas who'd followed in after his initial cross. This time

Dallas lobbed the ball across to Sol Bamba on the right side of the Wolves area about thirty yards from goal. Sol took the ball on his chest and then took a swing with his right foot on the half volley. My view of Sol was perfect and uninterrupted other than the side netting of the Wolves goal that I was looking straight through. Sol caught the ball perfectly and it arrowed from his boot towards the top corner; if the net hadn't been there it would have struck me full in the face and I have to say I did duck involuntarily just before the net bulged. It was right up there with the finest five or ten goals I have ever seen from a Leeds player. Lewis Cook's equaliser this season against Fulham is in the same category as is Bradley Johnson's rocket against Arsenal a few years ago. A few of Tony Yeboah's would make the list too.

The celebrations in the north-east corner were wild and Nigel was more ecstatic than usual as he reckoned he'd caught the goal on video with his phone. He sent me a Twitter message with it attached the following night and it was brilliant; the ball began as a small dot on Bamba's boot but it rapidly grew as it travelled at the speed of light towards our eye-line before the net rippled and the crowd exploded. Anyone who didn't bother with this game as they considered it a pointless end of season jobbie will regret that decision. That is the beauty of football; you really have no idea when a special moment like that will happen.

Despite only 18,000 being in the ground, the atmosphere was now electric and Leeds continued to pile on the pressure with the Kop baying for more goals. Wolves had brought on the usually dangerous (to Leeds) Adam Le Fondre when Leeds put Dallas on, but for once he was not getting a look in. Shots rained in towards us and those *"oohhs"* and *"aahhs"* followed every shot and block. We were actually still talking about Bamba's rocket when Charlie Taylor burst down the Leeds left and sent the ball over to the back post again just four minutes later. Lewis Cook had time to control the ball, look up, spot Diagouraga on the edge of the box and then roll it perfectly into his path. It was the simplest of tasks for 'Dave' to side-foot the ball past Ikeme in the Wolves goal. Cue more celebrations, this time just a few yards away from us in front of the Kop; Sol and Dave did a little jig with each other, celebrating each other's goals.

Still Leeds were on the rampage, and the crowd could sense that the Leeds players' confidence was now sky high while Wolves looked shell-shocked. Wolves made another substitution and then Evans followed suit sending on Jordan Botaka for a tiring Lee Erwin. It was the perfect situation for a player like 'The Wizard' and he didn't disappoint as he proceeded to add his own brand of bamboozlement to affairs. Sadly, it backfired on us.

Botaka chased down a back pass to Ikeme and appeared to have forced the keeper into an error but then our man turned the wrong way, just giving Ikeme time to lash the ball up field. It was collected by James Henry who managed to evade a Charlie Taylor tackle before squaring the ball to his left to George Saville. Berardi was close but, as so often is the case with our defenders, not close enough. Saville was able to move the ball onto his right foot and steer it into the far corner of the net. For the third game running we would face a nervous final few minutes and for a few moments the fans in our section were very, very annoyed. Annoyed that such a fine second-half performance was now in jeopardy and the prospect of seeing a late Wolves equalizer was in most of our minds.

This time though, we did adopt the 'attack is the best form of defence' philosophy and should really have buried Wolves in the final fifteen minutes. Lewis Cook was now on fire and running the show and in one breath-taking move he weaved around three Wolves players as he took the ball from his own area to deep in Wolves territory before laying the ball off to Chris Wood. Wood played the ball back to Jordan Botaka on the edge of the box and Jordan took aim. He curled the most delightful left foot shot towards that same top left corner but this time it agonizingly clipped the bar and bounced down before a Wolves player headed it away to safety. It would have been another goal of the season contender, along with Sol's and Lewis's.

We did offer Wolves one chance of salvation near the end but Marco Silvestri came to the rescue with a fine block while at the other end Liam Cooper glanced a header wide and Dallas smashed a shot inches over the bar. It was that sort of a match; total entertainment. When the whistle went we celebrated as if we'd moved into the play-offs and not the 11th place we'd actually risen to but it was a fine feeling to have won three on the spin for the second time in a few weeks.

I raced up Lowfields Road to get to the car in time to listen to Steve Evans being interviewed on BBC Radio Leeds and he was saying how the second-half was possibly the best half of football he'd ever seen from any of his teams anywhere. Praise indeed. He was pressed on whether he'd spoken to Cellino but he was purposely circumspect saying only that he dearly wanted the chance to work with Leeds as he was sure he could get them promoted but that, *"only the President can make that decision"*.

The day after the Wolves game, we learned that Edoardo Cellino's indiscretion had meant he was now banned from football for the final three games of the season and received a fine of £5,000. As always with Leeds, the constant off field problems took a little shine off the performances on the pitch but this was hardly going to cause the club much hardship. The fact that the FA confirmed they were now investigating Massimo's quotes that were aired at the Lucy Ward tribunal, was far more worrying.

In the world of entertainment it was another sad week as first the death of Victoria Wood was announced at the age of only 62 and then the following day it was reported that the singer 'Prince' had also died. Ironically enough 'Prince' died on the Queen's 90th birthday, Thursday, 21st April, 2016.

It had so far not been a good year in respect of the passing of celebrities and it was another reminder that none of us is getting any younger.

Leeds United 2 Wolverhampton Wanderers 1 **(Bamba (60), Diagouraga (64),** Saville (77))
17,694 (Wolves 478)

Hull City

In the days leading up to the game at Hull the phrase 'Time To Go Massimo' was to the fore again. One enterprising fellow had managed to get several big name footballers to utter the phrase on selfie videos which were then posted on Twitter. Harry Kane, Dele Alli, Jack Wilshere and Mesut Ozil were all involved. For a few days, the Twitter account @WhiteLeedsSite was lauded as an inventive new advertising medium by the MTTG group. But the big question everyone was asking was how did @WhiteLeedsSite do it? On the eve of the game at Hull, Harry Kane confessed he'd been duped. The individual responsible for requesting the selfies was the same guy who managed to get Massimo Cellino on the phone and record a 25 minute conversation with him last season. This time it all turned sour when reports came out that the players had been told they were sending a message to a dying child. The 'official' TTGM group were quick to distance themselves from the stunt, with the perpetrator considered to be very much a 'Lone Wolf'[1].

I stood outside the players and officials entrance of the KC Stadium with about two dozen other fans of both sides. There

---

[1]   http://www.thetimes.co.uk/edition/sport/kane-slams-disgraceful-video-hoax-6t0smqgn5

was a clear blue sky and the sun was warm on our faces. It was 1:20pm and the Leeds United team coach was making its slow progress through the park towards the stadium. I thought it would be good to get another close up look at the players. Most of the Hull City players had already arrived in their own cars; an assortment of Range Rovers and Discoveries and a couple of Bentleys now parked up just a bit further around the perimeter of the ground. They'd all walked from their cars to the players' entrance, stopping every now and then for autographs and selfies with the Hull fans. Sadly, when the Leeds coach opened its doors, our players left via the door on the far side of the coach, out of sight and we caught only the briefest glimpse of them. Only Stuart Dallas responded to a call from the crowd and jogged over to have a quick selfie. It was another example of how far removed from the fans modern day footballers have become. The recent duping of those four Premier League players for that 'Massimo Time To Go' stunt does nothing to help in this respect; it just makes the players even more wary of interaction with fans.

With nothing more to see I wandered around to 'Pitch Side' a bar at the ground set aside for the visiting fans. Eventually Jo B, Si and Nigel arrived and we enjoyed a few beers whilst watching the lunchtime game on one of the many TV's arranged along the walls. Derby and Sheffield were battling out a 1 – 1 draw that kept them both safely in the play-off places. I have to say that our hosts for the day had gone to great lengths to make us feel welcome; there were 'Welcome Leeds' posters on the walls, the bar staff all wore the latest Leeds home shirts and there was a decent array of alcohol available, albeit only cans and bottles. In fact the whole stadium is a decent place to watch football if maybe a little 'sterile' for my taste. It was built at a cost of £44 million and opened in 2002 and is basically a totally enclosed oval with a two tier West Stand cleverly merged into the remaining three stands with a sweeping uninterrupted roof-line. My issue is more with the outside than the inside though as other than the main entrance it is a very grey looking building and could easily be mistaken for a modern prison.

Simon had Kentley's match-ticket so we had the inevitable delay as we waited for his usual last minute appearance before we all made our way in through the turnstiles and then took our places about level with the edge of the penalty area on the east side of the ground at the north end; Leeds had been given the whole of the North East corner. There was no denying the view of the action was first class.

Silvestri
Berardi Bamba Cooper Taylor
Bridcutt
Dallas Diagouraga Cook
Wood Erwin

Subs: Peacock-Farrell, Wootton, Phillips, Coyle, Murphy, Botaka, Antenucci.

There was no Peppe Bellusci anywhere to be seen in the 18-man squad. Initially, Steve Evans said his exclusion was for *"tactical"* reasons but after the game it emerged that Peppe had thrown his dummy out of the pram again; upset that he was not named in the team for Hull he walked out of training and was subsequently told he would not travel at all[1]. It reminded me of his antics over in Austria when he as good as ignored Matty Pears that day.

So, two changes from the Wolves game – Bridcutt replacing Murphy and Dallas back in place of Coyle. It was a strong looking midfield with both Bridcutt and Diagouraga to help out the defence against what the table suggested was the fourth best side in the Championship. They looked like it too for the first fifteen minutes of the game as they totally dominated both possession and territory with wave after wave of attacks, mostly down the Hull right flank and mostly involving former Leeds favourite Rob Snodgrass. *"You're Leeds and you know you are"*, belting out from the 2,356 Leeds fans each time he

---

[1]   http://www.yorkshireeveningpost.co.uk/sport/football/leeds-united/leeds-united-summer-is-the-time-to-rate-actions-not-words-hay-1-7880132

was on the ball. Hull won two corners inside the first two minutes and numerous shots rained in on Silvestri's goal before Leeds finally had a little spell of possession themselves. Amazingly, from our first real move of any significance, we scored.

Lewis Cook had hardly had a kick but now he touched a short ball to Chris Wood about 35 yards out. Wood knocked a perfect ball out to the Leeds left wing for Charlie Taylor to run onto and then set off at speed towards goal. Taylor met the ball first time on the run and whipped it across goal. Lee Erwin stretched but couldn't get high enough at the front post and we momentarily cursed our luck but a split second later we were celebrating as Chris Wood met it perfectly on the volley at the back post with his right boot. Incredibly, we were ahead.

Hull continued to have the bulk of possession and Rob Snodgrass continued to maraud down the touchline down in front of us but the Leeds defence looked relatively untroubled for the rest of the half; untroubled that is until we entered the four minutes of added time...

The board had just gone up and I was starting to consider whether or not I needed to brave the half-time crush in the bogs when Hull started to ping the ball about down that right wing of theirs again. It was like that one touch exercise you often see teams doing during their pre-match warm up inside a small square of training cones. Suddenly the ball is squirted through the Leeds defence to Snoddy and he taps it across the face of goal bisecting Berardi and Silvestri to find Abel Hernandez sliding in to score. It was a well worked goal and no Leeds player was particularly at fault so we mostly shrugged thinking it was a shame to give up the lead so close to the break but, hey-ho, 1 – 1 at half-time in the KCOM (the stadium is now sponsored by Kingstone Communications under the moniker KCOM) is not a bad situation and we'd all have settled for that at the start. It was probably safe to go for that pee now...

Well, no, actually it wasn't! Within seconds of the restart Hull are back in our final third, pinging the ball about again. I have to say it was not with the same urgency as a few minutes earlier and my guess was they were happy running the final few seconds off the clock. But as the ball was rolled across to Huddlestone, he obviously decided enough was enough and he lazily swung his right boot at the ball. There was little pace on the shot, struck all along the turf, but somehow the accuracy was enough to beat Silvestri and the ball nestled in the bottom left corner. Now that was annoying!

I meandered down to the toilet block and tut-tutted to myself as I fought my way through the smokers who were busy filling the place full of choking cigarette smoke; my eyes were sore by the time I emerged again. When Kentley arrived back at his seat though, he had a tale about how a mass of Leeds fans had found themselves in a bit of a conflab with the police in the concourse. It only ended when a line of police was knocked over by the crowd of fans and the cops resorted to aiming pepper spray at the Leeds lads. That soon brought an end to the fracas and Kentley reported it was not only me sporting sore eyes now.

The second-half began well for Leeds and they showed no sign of any hangover from the late drama in the first-half. In fact, eight minutes into the new half and we ought to have been level. Charlie Taylor went round Snodgrass out wide and then was almost past Moses Odubajo; almost but not quite. Odubajo stuck out a leg and over went Taylor for a stone-wall penalty. As usual we celebrated the award of the penalty like we'd celebrate a goal but then we noticed that Chris Wood had hold of the ball. Wood is no one's preferred penalty taker but looking around the players we had on the pitch there wasn't much choice. Stuart Dallas was showing interest and no doubt was just enquiring of Wood that he was OK about taking it and Wood clearly had no intention of letting go of the ball. We'd seen him send one into orbit up at Donny of course and one of the two he *had* converted, at Fulham in October, had only gone in with a helping hand from their keeper. For me, he should never have taken this one. Yes, he had scored three goals in the previous few games and got another earlier in this one but far more important to me were the bag-full he'd missed. He strode up and seemed to strike the ball pretty well but the keeper had read him and was able to first parry it and then clutch it as he dived away to his left. I have now lost count of the number of times I've seen Chris Wood with his head in his hands.

Leeds had already brought on Jordan Botaka at half-time (he replaced Erwin) and now Steve Evans sent on Luke Murphy, presumably in case we won another penalty. Murphy replaced Diagouraga. The game was still end to end but I got the distinct impression Hull were now playing within themselves and had their eyes more on the play-offs than the end of this game. Leeds were doing OK and Botaka was proving his usual 'difficult to play against' self. At one point he totally wrong-footed the whole of the Hull defence with a piece of trickery that I am still trying to work out to this day. In the 72nd minute Jake Livermore scythed down Gaetano Berardi right in front of where we were stood and it was clear that Berardi was in trouble. Livermore was only booked despite our calls for a red card while a full four minutes passed as Berardi was loaded onto a stretcher and carried off around the corner of the ground in front of the main Hull support. The Leeds fans were incensed at the abuse Berardi was getting as he passed in front of the Cod Heads and we would later learn that bottles and coins were also thrown. In that moment, the reputation of Hull City supporters took a mighty fall and it is a moment that I am sure will be remembered in future encounters with them. Lewie Coyle replaced Berardi at right back.

The game was ebbing away now as we entered the 88th minute but as long as Botaka was on the pitch we had hope; he was worrying Hull every time he had the ball. Lewis Cook had the ball on the right wing, near the corner flag about twenty yards to our right; he rolled it inside to Botaka. 'The Wizard' dropped his shoulder and cut inside one Hull defender and then, with the attentions of four more around him he spotted Stuart Dallas to his left. Botaka pulled back his left foot feigning to shoot and then just touched the ball to Dallas with his right. The Irishman took a touch with his right foot and then struck the ball with his left into the bottom right corner. It was a huge goal in the context of Hull City's season as it meant they could no longer make the automatic promotion places and would have to battle it out in the play-offs, most likely against Derby. For Leeds, the goal and the point didn't mean that much in the context of the season but it was great to secure a point and keep our little run going. It was another point saving goal that might just make Massimo Cellino change his mind about giving Steve Evans another season too. After the game, Evans told the BBC: *"I am ready and waiting to speak to the president when he is ready but I have a couple of Saturdays to go and whether I am staying or not I want to go out with six points. We agreed many months ago that we would have the conversation when he was ready; he is well aware there is (other) interest in me. But when you shake hands as two men and say you'll focus on the football, I am all right with that. Every time we win a match it gives me a better chance of staying - or (finding) another employer."*[1]

As I sat in the usual traffic chaos that grips Hull after any game at the KCOM, I wondered what logic Cellino could possibly have for doing away with Evans but I still believed he would not renew the Scotsman's contract. Meanwhile, most fans had now been won over by Evans and recognised he was a rare being; able to operate successfully under the Cellino regime. Two games to go and then we should have the answer as to which way Cellino would jump.

In the days following the Hull game, the inquest into the deaths of 96 Liverpool fans at Hillsborough, 27 years earlier, was finally brought to an end. At over two years, it was the longest in British legal history. The most important of the 14 questions the jury was asked to answer was the one demanding to know if the behaviour of the Liverpool fans had any bearing on the outcome that fateful day. The jury concluded it had not; it delivered its conclusion that the 96 fans that died that day were unlawfully killed. Criticisms were made of the actions of the police and the ambulance services and the Hillsborough ground and it became clear that the way had now been opened for criminal charges to be considered. We'd not heard the last of the ramifications of this tragedy.

Hull City 2 **Leeds United 2 (Wood (15),** Hernandez (45+1), Huddlestone (45+3), **Dallas(88))**. 20,732 (**Leeds 2,356**)

---

[1] *http://www.bbc.co.uk/sport/football/36060679*

Charlton Athletic

L egal cases against the club were now coming thick and fast and on the Thursday ahead of the penultimate game of the season, Nigel Gibbs won his case for unlawful dismissal. He'd been kept on by Cellino after the sacking of Brian McDermott but then had a frosty relationship with new manager Dave Hockaday and was demoted and asked to have nothing more to do with first team affairs. The tribunal judge revealed that Gibbs was on a £200,000 a year contract and was awarded £331,426 in damages less any bonuses he'd been awarded during his employment with Tottenham Hotspur since joining them.[1] The compensation due to Lucy Ward was not due to be fixed until mid-June.

I was with my lad Mark for the Charlton game – it would be his last before he set off for a two year stint in Australia – and I knew he seldom brought us good luck; the last game he was at with me being that 2 – 0 home debacle to Blackburn. We arrived in my now customary parking spot in Lowfields Road not long after 11am but then had to sit in the car as another almighty hail storm blew over. It had been a feature of the weather in recent days; periods of warm sunshine and blue skies interspersed by storms of biblical proportions.

---

[1]   http://www.yorkshireeveningpost.co.uk/news/leeds-united-nigel-gibbs-wins-six-figure-compensation-for-unlawful-dismissal-1-7881956

In the Pavilion, the tables were all arranged ready for the end of season awards dinner after the game. I wouldn't be going although several of us promised to get together to book a table for next season. Let's hope it's a good one.

So convinced was I that Leeds would turn over the Addicks that I placed a quid on 4 – 1 to Leeds at 22/1 and then Mark doubled it with a quid of his own. He wasn't that convinced though and he 'covered' that bet with another; Charlton to win 2 – 1 at 14/1. Had I stopped to think about it, I should have gone 'all in' on that option. Everyone was expecting Leeds to win and a 25,000 plus crowd was anticipated. Every time this happens, Leeds tend to let themselves down and 2 – 1 is the most frequent score in the Championship with 18% of all games ending in that score. I never learn though and as Mark and I sauntered over to the ground I was super confident...

Silvestri
Coyle Bamba Cooper Taylor
Bridcutt
Botaka Cook Murphy Dallas
Wood

Subs: Peacock-Farrell, Wootton, Antenucci, Mowatt, Diagouraga, Phillips, Erwin.

Evans seemed to be placating a sizeable number of fans who'd been criticising him recently for not starting Botaka, citing his super-sub appearances when he had looked a bit of a 'Wizard'. I wasn't convinced; for me he doesn't do enough when he's not dazzling defenders with the ball at his feet and he doesn't do that for 90 minutes. Compared to the line-up that started at Hull, Evans made three changes; Botaka for Erwin, Coyle for the injured Berardi and Murphy for Diagouraga. I'd have left Botaka as an 'impact' sub but I probably would also have brought Murphy back.

The sun was shining brightly as both teams lined up for the traditional one minute's applause to remember all those who'd departed us during the season. The 96 who died at Hillsborough were also in our thoughts following the recent conclusion of the inquest.

Leeds did well for twenty minutes with a number of half chances falling to Wood, Dallas and even Charlie Taylor who was particularly aggressive down the left wing. It was all looking positive. But then, out of nothing, Charlton broke away and a stinging shot struck Silvestri's left hand post, in front of the Kop. It was a warning. We then had another fifteen minutes of mostly Leeds possession but as we've seen all season, we couldn't find the net. Charlton on the other hand didn't need a Sat Nav to know where ours was…

There were only six minutes or so to go until half-time, the same point at which we switched off against Reading a couple of weeks ago and Hull only last weekend. There didn't seem to be any great danger as Ademola Lookman collected a quick throw in on the Charlton left wing but Lewie Coyle was day dreaming as Lookman slotted the ball through to Morgan Fox. Fox cunningly beat Coyle's lunging challenge to hammer in a low cross but we had plenty of bodies in and around our six-yard area. I'd neglected to remember though that we are about as efficient as a chocolate tea pot in there and we have all the reaction speed of a drugged snail. Somehow, Gudmundsson got in between those pillars of strength that masquerade as our centre backs and stabbed the ball home from five yards. It was another body blow and the breath was knocked out of us as we struggled to understand how we were a goal behind to a relegated side that we'd outplayed for most of the first-half.

As always, the Leeds fans regrouped at half-time and we were ready to go again as Leeds kicked off the second period but within four minutes we'd been undone again. Charlton had the ball in the corner, in front of the 'Cheese Wedge' and then it was rolled back to Lookman. Coyle was again far too far away from his man and bought a dummy hook line and sinker as Lookman shaped to shoot and then shifted the ball onto his right side. Botaka was behind him but made no challenge; Bridcutt was in front but too far away. I swear I could've got a shot away in that much space. Sure enough, Lookman pulled the trigger and his aim was spot on as the ball beat Silvestri at the foot of his right hand post. You see, not only are we a disgrace as a defensive unit, but every other side in the Championship is way more efficient than we are in hitting the target. We'd amass 25 shots in this game but only 5 would hit the spot; the Addicks only had eight attempts but 2 hit the target and both beat our keeper. It looked bleak and it was so disappointing that we'd blown it in front of another big crowd and on the day we were all supposed to give our thanks to the players during the traditional 'lap of appreciation' after the game. I couldn't imagine many would be waiting behind today.

To be fair to our lads, there was no sign of throwing in the towel; in fact if anything we then had our best spell of the game. Evans made his usual substitution introducing Mowatt for Dallas and Charlie Taylor, now working in tandem with Mowatt, began a series of great runs down the left wing. On one occasion he bent in a fabulous ball for Chris Wood but the striker's glancing header smacked against the bar. An inch would have made all the difference as Mrs W constantly reminds me... On 71 minutes, Sol Bamba did get us a goal back with a towering header from a left wing Taylor free kick and Mark was immediately checking he still had his betting slip in a safe place. We huffed and puffed for the remainder of the game but Charlton did their job better than we did ours and the game ended 1 – 2; yet another home defeat; our eighth of the campaign. If we could get at least a point from our final day trip to Deepdale, our away record would end up better than our home tally. You have to wonder why we fail so often at Elland Road, despite the interventions of priests and the lemon trees in reception...

A few minutes after the players disappeared down the tunnel, Steve Evans was first to reappear. The Elland Road pitch announcer interviewed him near the dugouts. With a quivering voice he told the fans:

"I'm only sorry I couldn't give these magnificent supporters a win on the final day. What stands out for me is the opportunity to come to Leeds United and be head coach. You hear from a distance how great this club is, how great the supporters are, so from me, my family, my heart, I'm sorry about today, but thank you. And if I am not here, I still love you wherever I go in life, so thank you very much."

He sounded like a beaten man to me; a man who knew his fate. The South Stand broke into a chant of, *"There's only one Steve Evans"*, and then he gave three little 'uppercuts' as they urged him on. Lots of fans believed Evans was the most likely man to succeed with a promotion push under the impossible conditions the Cellino regime seemed to cultivate but equally most fans were sure he'd not get the chance. I shook my head sadly as Evans disappeared and then I joined in the applause as he and the players reappeared seconds later. During the lap of appreciation I was shocked to see just how many fans had already left the ground, even the Kop was only sparsely occupied. A player missing was Peppe Bellusci and I wondered if we'd seen the last of him as even Berardi was hopping around the pitch on his crutches.

I was already thinking about a title for the book this year and at that precise instant I had *"Mission: Impossible"* in my mind. For one dark moment I really couldn't see how we could possibly progress under Cellino, there was just too much that was just plain wrong and if he wasn't going to let Evans have a go at promotion, someone who was clearly relishing the challenge and really got what Leeds is all about, who could he possibly have in mind who'd do a better job. Who in their right mind would take on this 'Mission: Impossible'?

Another mission proved impossible today too; the spectacular protest promised by the Massimo Time To Go group failed to take place as their bus broke down. The latest stunt was to have involved an open top bus ride to the ground with new banners and free pies for fans but hours before the game the bus company reported that the vehicle earmarked for the stunt was out of action.[1] I did wonder if the bus company had got cold feet for some reason.

At the end of season do, the main awards went to Charlie Taylor (Player of the Season) and Lewis Cook (Young Player of the Season and Goal of the Season). How vital was it going to be to hang on to them this summer if there was to be any chance of Mission: Impossible being achieved next season?

Leeds United 1 Charlton 2 (Gudmundsson (39), Lookman (49), **Bamba (71)**) **25,458** (Charlton 363)

---

[1] *http://the72.co.uk/53238/leeds-united-wheels-on-the-bus-dont-go-round-for-cellino-protest/*

Deepdale sums it all up

L eeds continued to work their way through the long list of legal disputes this week and came to a last gasp out of court settlement with Macron for a rumoured £3.5m plus costs. This was the case whereby Cellino cut short the Macron kit deal in favour of Kappa. The case with former shirt sponsor, Enterprise, was one of the few now outstanding although the club would soon announce that '32Red', the online casino outfit, would be on the shirts for next season.

By far the biggest revelation this week though concerned Peppe Bellusci. Social media was full of copies of what was alleged to be his official club contract, supposedly put out in public by a disgruntled employee of the club. The document showed a base salary for the erratic centre back of £707,200 plus an appearances bonus of £132,500. That amounted to an alleged weekly wage of around £17,000. The Massimo Time To Go group put out a statement condemning Cellino for allowing Bellusci to profit from such a contract while, allegedly, the likes of Cook, Taylor and Mowatt were on far less.[1]

---

[1] https://www.timetogomassimo.com/posts/statement-giuseppe-belluscis-contract/

With the play-off season now started, I couldn't resist adding another new ground to my portfolio this week when I spotted that Grimsby Town had a National League semi-final first leg game with Braintree Town at Blundell Park. Although the travel was a bit of a nightmare with various motorway closures meaning the 300 mile round trip took me three hours both ways, I enjoyed my first visit to the Lincolnshire club. It is a lovely old ground, some of it dating back to 1901 if reports are to be believed and it still has a set of four magnificent, if now very rusty, floodlight towers, one at each corner of the ground in traditional fashion. Over 5,000 were packed inside, including a hardy 82 who travelled up from Essex, to see 'The Iron' take a handy one goal lead back to their Cressing Road ground thanks to a second-half penalty. I have to say I thoroughly enjoyed my night out with the Mariners. In the second leg, Grimsby turned it round to win 2 – 1 on aggregate and go through to the final at Wembley against Forest Green.

Talking of 5,000, there were about that number of Leeds fans at Deepdale, home of Preston North End, for the final game of the season. The atmosphere was fantastic; not dissimilar to the last time we were there when a similarly huge Leeds contingent saw Billy Paynter finally grab his first goal for us back in 2011.

Pre-match drinks were taken in The Sumners in Fulwood, just a few hundred yards from Deepdale and, predictably, it was jam-packed full of Leeds fans. There was a real end of term feeling about the place and outside the sun was shining and the temperature was finally up in the twenties. We soon had a big crowd of folk gathering around a table the lads from Co. Durham had secured early doors and the Old Speckled Hen was going down well. The Durham lads, along with many of today's Leeds contingent, had popped over from Blackpool where they were enjoying a boys' weekend. They looked to have had an excellent Friday night sampling Blackpool's finest ale houses! The big topic of conversation was whether Leeds could get a result that would keep us in the top half of the table, something we'd not achieved in the past four seasons; Kev had a *"sizeable"* bet riding on it and was a tad worried. A win would guarantee 12th spot but anything less opened us up to 13th or 14th depending on how Wolves and QPR fared. When the team was spotted on someone's phone there were no real surprises except for one new name on the bench.

Silvestri
Coyle Bamba Cooper Taylor
Diagouraga Cook Murphy Mowatt Dallas
Wood

Subs: Peacock-Farrell, Wootton, Phillips, Botaka, Antenucci, Doukara, Vieira.

The surprise was the inclusion of young Ronaldo Vieira on the bench just a couple of days after he'd signed his first pro contract with the club. The Guinea-Bissau-born central midfielder joined Leeds from York City's academy at the start of the season and was still only 17. The starting eleven had two changes from the Charlton game with Diagouraga and Mowatt replacing Bridcutt and Botaka. Peppe Bellusci was nowhere to be seen albeit a rumour had gone round that he was ill. Not many believed that.

The first-half was a typical end of season affair fought mainly in midfield with the best chance falling to Chris Wood when he chased a long through ball from Lewie Coyle. With Chris Kirkland in the home goal in two minds Wood lobbed the ball over his head only to see it land on the roof of the net. The only other significant first-half action was a clash of heads between Liam Cooper and Preston's Joe Garner. Both men eventually got to their feet but Cooper would not reappear for the second-half and it would prove to be a significant moment.

A few half chances went begging at both ends but it looked to be heading for a goalless draw as we moved past the hour mark.

Leeds then swapped Antenucci for Mowatt shortly after Jermaine Beckford was substituted. Beckford, like his manager Simon Grayson had been the subject of numerous favourable chants from the Leeds faithful; reminders of better days in the history of Leeds United. When Beckford went off, to more applause and a rousing chant of *"January 1st,* *remember the date...*" he finally turned to us and gave us a little Leeds salute – it was what we'd wanted to see all afternoon! Immediately we followed up with a chant of *"You're Leeds and you know you are"*. We tried the same with Simon Grayson but it took ages before he acknowledged us with a quick little wave. To show him how it should be done, we then sang *"Evans, Evans, give us a wave"* and Big Steve was quick to respond with a generous wave which then sparked an ironic chant of *"Sign him up, sign him up, sign him up!"* The Leeds fans were basically having an end of season party, all 5,464 of us. Over to our left one lad was keeping everyone amused by crowd surfing on a little surfboard from the very top to the very bottom of the stand – some distance in this huge Bill Shankly Kop. He then amazed us by going all the way back to the top, with the police, stewards and nearby Preston fans all joining in to applaud his efforts. There was not much going on down on the pitch at this time, until Antenucci began to get going. His movement seemed to unnerve the Preston defence and then, with 12 minutes remaining, Luke Murphy chased a ball into the home area down below us. Murphy was going nowhere but Chris Kirkland didn't seem to realise and he went down to cover any possible shot from the Leeds man. He got his timing all wrong though, his glove clipped Murphy and down he went. Referee Andy Haines pointed straight to the spot.

It was another magic moment as over 5,000 Leeds fans celebrated like only we know how; it didn't seem to matter that nothing was riding on the game. Maybe it was such a great celebration as we all knew it was likely to be the end of the Steve Evans era and we wanted to see him go, if indeed he was going, with a victory so we could give him an extra good send off. It was certainly something in my mind. It would also send us all off on our holidays with a positive memory after so many negative ones throughout this season.

We had to score the thing first though... and Chris Wood had hold of the ball again. Mirco Antenucci was trying to prize it from his grasp and was probably explaining that it was his last game for Leeds; rumours were rife he was on his way this summer. Wood, on the other hand still had three years of his contract to see out. Just as it was starting to get embarrassing, Sol Bamba stepped in and pulled Mirco to one side leaving Wood to set himself for the kick. Fortunately, Chris Wood made no mistake as he smashed the ball just to the right of centre while Kirkland dived the other way. Immediately after the penalty, while the mad celebrations (with Antenucci refusing to partake and still looking stony faced) were going on in the Bill Shankly Kop, Grayson made another substitution. On came Jordan Hugill and off went Joe Garner. Have I mentioned before how Leeds are always susceptible to an opposition substitute?

There were ten minutes to go plus around three more likely to be added on; all I could think off was how terrible it would be if we now gave away a goal to destroy this feeling of elation. It just felt right that we'd be able to properly celebrate with Big Steve at the end and we didn't need any negative vibes in these last few minutes. But the one thing that has been constant with Leeds for many years now is that our moments of joy are usually very short lived. Right from the first day of the season when we took an 83rd minute lead against Burnley only to concede to a Sam Vokes goal just three minutes later, it has been a trait that has blighted us throughout this campaign. Bristol away saw us concede two in injury time to wipe away a 2 – 0 lead; Bobby Zamora hit an 89th minute winner for Brighton at Elland Road; Tom Ince snatched an equaliser for Derby just seven minutes after Wood got us ahead, and just 12 minutes from time. Ipswich scored in added time to grab all three points at Portman Road when we thought we'd got a point. Rotherham beat us at their place with a 90th minute penalty and we gifted QPR another penalty in the 87th minute that cost us two points at Elland Road. And so on and so on, all season. It was accepted practice for Leeds to gift points away at every opportunity. Daft as it sounds, had we seen those seven games out without conceding those late goals we'd have finished 7th this season, just 4 points off the play-offs. Looked at like that, this side of ours really isn't that far off what's needed. So, as we moved into the last few seconds of this game you'd have thought we would be on our guard…

Young Ronaldo Vieira got his debut with a minute or so of normal time to go. He replaced Stuart Dallas and it was presumably a move designed to waste time more than anything else. He'd been on the pitch three minutes when a long ball was pumped down the left side of the Leeds defence and Scott Wootton was in pole position to deal with it; it needed launching into row z near the corner flag but Wootton seemed to think it would roll over the by-line. We could tell from 100 yards away that it wasn't going to reach and substitute, Jordan Hugill knew it too. As soon as Hugill realised Wootton was dallying, he was on him. Wootton got in a tangle and fell over while trying to shepherd the ball and Hugill was free; he spotted Eoin Doyle in the middle. Doyle's shot was blocked but the rebound went straight back to Hugill and this time he fired it into the net. Wootton collapsed with his head in his hands, not for the first time this season and all around me there was no sympathy for the former Man U defender. I will be surprised if we ever see him in a Leeds shirt again. It was shocking and yet it was so typical of what we have been served up by Leeds in the closing minutes of games all season that there was a strange acceptance that it was just, the norm, to be expected. The whistle went seconds after the restart and the game was drawn and 2 more points had been peed away.

Steve Evans led all the players over towards us and up went the, *"There's only one Steve Evans"* chant. He was clearly in bits, making a heart sign with his hands and pointing at us all before tapping out a Leeds salute. Inevitably the Leeds fans then began the familiar crescendo roar expecting Evans to do his party piece fist pump and he didn't let us down. Three times in all we did that as had become the custom. Evans had won over the Leeds fans since his arrival and I guessed that most now wanted him to be given the chance to take us into next season. I was equally sure that most of the 5,000 odd fans in the Bill Shankly Kop knew he wouldn't get that chance.

Leeds would end the season in 13th spot with 59 points and so Kev lost his sizeable bet on a top half finish. I wondered if he'd be writing to Scott Wootton for a refund. Elsewhere in the Championship today, Burnley secured the title with a win at Charlton while Middlesbrough also won promotion with a home draw against Brighton, the Boro pipping Brighton on goal difference. In the play-offs, the Seagulls would face Sheffield Wednesday and Hull City would battle out the second semi with Derby. At the top of League One, Wigan and Burton Albion won automatic promotion to the Championship next season while Walsall, Millwall, Bradford and Barnsley would slug it out for the final place. Coming down from the Premier league we still did not know who would join Aston Villa although Sunderland did their chances of survival a power of good with a 3 – 2 win over Chelsea. If the Black Cats could beat Everton the following week then Newcastle and Norwich would be down[1].

The first player seemingly leaving the club this summer was Mirco Antenucci. He posted a message of thanks to the Leeds fans on his Instagram page which seemed to be a farewell note. Meanwhile, Steve Evans was being dignified in the extreme as he maintained he was waiting for Mr President to make a decision on his future. He told the BBC:

"I hope it's not the end, I really hope it's not. But if the decision is made for the benefit of the football club then I will endorse it.

"If they've got (Jose) Mourinho parked in the corner then I'd be the first to applaud him onto the pitch.

"I'm going to go home and wait to see what the president decides. I would've loved to have been in on Monday planning pre-season and maybe that will still happen, but who knows?"

In the week following the Preston game news leaked out of the club that Scott Wootton was being released after a bizarre cock-up was discovered whereby the contract extension he believed he had was never apparently ratified.

Someone else leaving the club was Ercole Cellino, Massimo's son and Eduardo's brother. He resigned as a director of the club.

Preston North End 1 **Leeds United 1 (Wood, (78 pen)**, Hugill (90+2)) 18,473 **(Leeds 5,464)**

---

[1] *Sunderland went on to beat Everton 3 – 2 so Newcastle and Norwich City were relegated.*

Pos	Team	Played	GD	Points
1	Burnley	46	37	93
2	Middlesbrough	46	32	89
3	Brighton	46	30	89
4	Hull City	46	34	83
5	Derby	46	23	78
6	Sheff Wed	46	21	74
7	Ipswich	46	2	69
8	Cardiff	46	5	68
9	Brentford	46	5	65
10	Birmingham	46	4	63
11	Preston	46	0	62
12	QPR	46	0	60
13	Leeds United	46	-8	59
14	Wolves	46	5	58
15	Blackburn	46	0	55
16	Forest	46	-8	55
17	Reading	46	-7	52
18	Bristol C	46	-17	52
19	Huddersfield	46	-11	51
20	Fulham	46	-13	51
21	Rotherham	46	-18	49
22	Charlton	46	-40	40
23	M K Dons	46	-30	39
24	Bolton	46	-40	30

The final Championship table looked like this; Leeds in 13th spot, little different to any of the last four seasons.

Mission: Impossible

This was ultimately another season of failure, the fifth season in a row we'd finished between 13th and 15th in the Championship. Not since Simon Grayson's side ended the 2010/2011 season just outside the play-offs have we seen any glimpse of a promotion attempt. As we waited to learn the fate of Steve Evans, things seemed very little different to the last two end of season scenarios. Both Brian McDermott and Neil Redfearn ended their Leeds careers in limbo, with Cellino refusing to speak with them, not involving them in pre-season plans and ultimately replacing them with a new head coach. It seems highly likely to me, as I write this final chapter, that exactly the same fate awaits Big Steve. It is hard to see how next season will be any different either, if another new coach comes in; they will face the same impossible situation. Cellino seems to be a difficult man to work for, falling out with all in his employ sooner or later.

There is some doubt over the future plans of Cellino though. On the one hand, it was announced in Italy that he had now been acquitted of any criminal charges in respect of the Range Rover case and indeed the vehicle was returned and he was no longer required to pay the 40,000 euro fine. That in turn meant that, subject to seeing the paperwork, the FL would rescind his 223 day ban; at least until any future criminal charges were proven. It seemed we had now found the Tom Cruise figure to play in our Mission: Impossible movie... Giovanni Cocco, Cellino's lawyer, seemed well capable of pulling off the odd miracle!

However, Cellino was also reported in the Times as saying he'd had enough of the club and was ready to sell his share if anyone was prepared to offer what he wanted. He'd said this many times before of course

The club is said to still be losing around £10m a year, making the temptation to cash in on the best talent in the current squad very tempting for Cellino. Yet we know that even the current squad is still four or five quality players short of a promotion challenging outfit. We've been in this situation for years of course, not just under Cellino but when we add in the erratic and combustible nature of the Italian it truly does suggest that any new coach coming in will be taking up another Mission: Impossible. It reminds me of an old joke that we can easily mould to fit the current situation. A Leeds fan, finding a magic lantern and given just a single wish, might well ask the genie to bring about world peace. *"That would take a miracle"*, the genie would answer. *"Do you have a second wish?"* *"Well, how about getting Leeds United back into the Premier League then?"* the Leeds fan asks. After a brief pause and a scratch of his head, the genie responds. *"Let's just have another think about that world peace idea then…"*

The only solution I can see is if there is out there somewhere an organisation or an individual with limitless resources that can buy out all of the current stakeholders in the club. That would include all of Cellino's interests, GFH and Ken Bates if he's still involved as some people continue to believe. We'd then need to see significant investment in the playing squad to bring in those four or five quality players to complete the current squad; the piano players Yorath is always talking about. The re-purchase of Elland Road and Thorp Arch would then reduce day to day running costs but would involve yet more major capital outlay. The owner would then have to gamble on the side getting into the Premier League within a couple of seasons, whereupon the new TV deal ought to more than cover the up-front investment during our first year in the top flight. With a successful team on the pitch and no rental to pay on Elland Road and Thorp Arch, the day to day finances would surely also correct themselves as Elland Road would be full to capacity week in week out. Is such a buyer out there somewhere? I'm not sure. If they are, I can't understand why they've not come forward before now. If they're not, then we are still in serious trouble; we cannot continue to lose money day to day as eventually the Cellino family will call a halt completely and without that super rich buyer the inevitable result will be another administration. If that happens we'd be sure to attract all and sundry as we did in the past, none of whom had the necessary wealth to take us forward. If ever there was a mission that looks impossible, Leeds United is it.

Lightning Source UK Ltd.
Milton Keynes UK
UKOW05f0322011216
288968UK00016B/323/P